Britain's Railways

1997–2005

Britain's Railways

1997–2005

Labour's Strategic Experiment

Terry Gourvish

OXFORD
UNIVERSITY PRESS

Great Clarendon Street, Oxford OX2 6DP

Oxford University Press is a department of the University of Oxford.
It furthers the University's objective of excellence in research, scholarship,
and education by publishing worldwide in

Oxford New York

Auckland Cape Town Dar es Salaam Hong Kong Karachi
Kuala Lumpur Madrid Melbourne Mexico City Nairobi
New Delhi Shanghai Taipei Toronto

With offices in

Argentina Austria Brazil Chile Czech Republic France Greece
Guatemala Hungary Italy Japan Poland Portugal Singapore
South Korea Switzerland Thailand Turkey Ukraine Vietnam

Oxford is a registered trade mark of Oxford University Press
in the UK and in certain other countries

Published in the United States
by Oxford University Press Inc., New York

British Library Cataloguing in Publication Data
Data available

Library of Congress Cataloging in Publication Data
Gourvish, T. R. (Terence Richard)
  Britain's railways 1997–2005 : Labour's strategic experiment / Terry Gourvish.
    p. cm.
  Includes bibliographical references and index.
  ISBN 978–0–19–923660–2
  1. Railroads and state—Great Britain. 2. Railroads—Privatization—Great Britain.
3. Railroads—Great Britain—Management. I. Title.
  HE3017.G68 2008
385.0941'09049—dc22   2008021578

Typeset by SPI Publisher Services, Pondicherry, India
Printed in Great Britain
on acid-free paper by
Biddles Ltd., King's Lynn, Norfolk

ISBN 978–0–19–923660–2

10 9 8 7 6 5 4 3 2 1

For S., more...

Contents

List of Illustrations

List of Figures

List of Tables

List of Interviewees

Strategic Rail Authority

Steve Atkins
Alan Bennett
Stephen Bennett
Richard Bowker
Julia Clarke
Richard Davies
Iain Dewar
Ceri Evans
John Gilbert

Mike Grant
David Grayson
Peter Hawthorne
Paul Mackie
Jeremy Mayhew
Nick Newton
David Norgrove
Philip O'Donnell
John O'Neill

Stephen Packham
Robert Plampin
David Quarmby
Jonathan Riley
Nicola Shaw
Jim Steer
Doug Sutherland
David Waboso
James Watson

Others

John Armitt (Network Rail)
Lewis Atter (DETR, Treasury)
Martin Ballinger (Go-Ahead Group)
Chris Bolt (ORR)
Richard Brown (Eurostar)
Bob Chauhan (Treasury, ORR)
Dan Corry (Adviser, DTLR, Treasury)
Alistair Darling (SoS, DfT)
Martin Deutz (KPMG)

Chris Green (Network Rail)
David Harding (Railtrack)
Mark Lambirth (DfT)
Moir Lockhead (FirstGroup)
Jeremy Long (GB Railways, MTR Corp)
Sir Richard Mottram (DETR, DTLR)
John Nelson (First Class Partnerships)
John O'Brien (OPRAF, Railtrack, Connex)

Simon Osborne (Railtrack)
Paul Plummer (ORR, Network Rail)
John Prescott (DPM)
Sir David Rowlands (DETR, DTLR, DfT)
Adrian Shooter (Chiltern Railways)
Anthony Smith (Passenger Focus)
John Swift (ORR)
Shriti Vadera (Treasury)
Anton Valk (NedRailways)
Tom Winsor (ORR)

Abbreviations and Acronyms

APEX	Advance Purchase Excursion
ASLEF	Associated Society of Locomotive Engineers and Firemen
ATOC	Association of Train Operating Companies
ATP	Automatic Train Protection
AWS	Automatic Warning System
BR	British Rail
BRB	British Railways Board
BRB(R)	British Railways Board (Residuary)
BTA	British Tourist Authority
CIT	Chartered Institute of Transport
CLG	Company Limited by Guarantee
CNRS	Company Neutral Revenue Support (freight grant)
CO	Cabinet Office
COO	Chief Operating Officer
COSOP	Cabinet Office Statement of Policy
CP	Control Period
CRUCC	Central Rail Users' Consultative Committee
CSFB	Credit Suisse First Boston
CTRL	Channel Tunnel Rail Link
DDA	Disability Discrimination Act
DEFRA	Department for Environment, Food and Rural Affairs
Dep Sec	Deputy Secretary
DETR	Department of the Environment, Transport and the Regions
DfT	Department for Transport
DG	Director General
DIP	Debt Issuance Programme
DLR	Docklands Light Railway
DOE	Department of the Environment
DOO	Driver-Only Operation
DPM	Deputy Prime Minister
DRS	Direct Rail Services
DTLR	Department for Transport, Local Government and the Regions
ECML	East Coast Main Line

Abbreviations and Acronyms

ECMT	European Conference of Ministers of Transport
ED	Executive Director
EIB	European Investment Bank
ELL	East London Line
ERTMS	European Rail Traffic Management System
EWS	English, Welsh & Scottish Railway
FFG	Freight Facilities Grant
FIAP	Fares Incentive Adjustment Payment
FOC	Freight Train Operating Company
FOI	Freedom of Information (Act, 2000)
GDP	Gross Domestic Product
GE	Great Eastern
GNER	Great North Eastern Railway
GSM-R	Global System for Mobile Communication—Railways
GW	Great Western
HLOS	High Level Output Specification
HR	Human Resources
HSC	Health and Safety Commission
HSE	Health and Safety Executive
HST	High Speed Train
IC	Intercity
IKF	Integrated Kent Franchise
IOS	Incremental Output Statements
IPPR	Institute for Public Policy Research
IT	Information Technology
ITT	Invitation to Tender
KfW	Kreditanstalt für Wiederaufbau
LSE	London and South-East
LT	London Transport
LTS	London Tilbury & Southend
MBO	Management Buy Out
MC	Management Contract
MD	Managing Director
MML	Midland Main Line
MOD	Ministry of Defence
MSCR	Minimum Support for the Current Railway
NAO	National Audit Office
NDC	National Disability Council
NDPB	Non-Departmental Public Body
NGCL	Network Grant Company Ltd.
NMGD	Non-Ministerial Government Department
NMS	Network Management Statement

NOS	Network Output Specification
NPV	Net Present Value
NWR	Network Rail
ODPM	Office of the Deputy Prime Minister
OFT	Office of Fair Trading
OIG	Objectives, Instructions, and Guidance
OMR	Operations, Maintenance, and Renewals
ONS	Office for National Statistics
OPRAF	Office of Passenger Rail Franchising
ORCATS	Operational Research Computerised Allocation of Tickets to Services
ORR	Office of the Rail Regulator, from 2004 Office of Rail Regulation
P&L	Profit & Loss
PFI	Private Finance Initiative
PIP	Punctuality Incentive Payment
PIXC	Passengers in Excess of Capacity
PPM	Public Performance Measure
PPS	Principal Private Secretary
PS	Private Secretary
PSR	Passenger Service Requirement
PTA	Passenger Transport Authority
PTE	Passenger Transport Executive
PUG	Passenger UpGrade (West Coast Main Line)
PUSS	Parliamentary Under-Secretary of State
R&A	Report and Accounts
RAB	Regulatory Asset Base (Railtrack, Network Rail)
RALMS	Rail, Aviation, Logistics, Maritime and Security (DfT)
RIDDOR	Reporting of Injuries, Diseases, and Dangerous Occurrences Regulations
RMT	National Union of Rail, Maritime and Transport Workers
ROSCO	Rolling Stock Leasing Company
RPC	Rail Passengers' Council
RPF	Rail Performance Fund
RPI	Retail Price Index
RPP	Rail Passenger Partnership
RSSB	Rail Safety and Standards Board
RSU	Rail Strategy Unit
RT	Railtrack
RUCC	Rail Users' Consultative Committee
RUS	Route Utilisation Strategy
ScE	Scottish Executive
SDO	Selective Door Opening (at short station platforms)

Abbreviations and Acronyms

SFIP	Short Formations Incentive Payment
SI	Statutory Instrument
SoFA	Statement of Funds Available
SoS	Secretary of State
SPAD	Signal Passed at Danger
SPV	Special Purpose Vehicle
SR	Spending Review
SRA	Strategic Rail Authority
SRNTP	Southern Region New Trains Programme
SRRO	Strategic Rail Regulatory Office
SSRA	Shadow Strategic Rail Authority
SWT	South West Trains
TAC	Track Access Charges
TAG	Track Access Grant (freight)
TCIP	Timetable Change Incentive Payment
TfL	Transport for London
TNA	The National Archives
TOC	Train Operating Company
TPE	TransPennine Express
TPFA	Transitional Projects Funding and Implementation Arrangements
TPWS	Train Protection and Warning System
TSGB	Transport Statistics Great Britain
TUPE	Transfer of Undertakings (Protection of Employment)
VfM	Value for Money
WA	West Anglia
WAGN	West Anglia Great Northern
WCML	West Coast Main Line

Preface

When I began the project for this book, Roger Ford asked me: 'Can it be true that you're going to write a third volume—putting you on a par with Tolkien?!' In fact, this is not quite the case, so I feel I should set the record straight. This book should not be seen as a companion to the two volumes on nationalized railways I wrote in 1986 and 2002. Rather it is an exercise in railway polity. It examines the way in which rail privatization has operated through the experience of the Strategic Rail Authority, which operated in shadow form in 1999, was established as a statutory body in 2001, and was then wound up some four to five years later.

I make no claim to have produced a definitive account of the period. The time allowed for the research and writing was fairly short—two years, and no research staff were employed. In November 2005, the SRA and Department for Transport agreed to support the research for a business history of the railways covering the period 1997–2005. After completion of the work in October 2007, the book was progressed as a straightforward commercial contract with Oxford University Press. I am greatly indebted to David Quarmby, Chairman of the SRA from 2004 to 2006, for initiating and sponsoring the project. I was fortunate to be given access to a fair amount of the surviving archival record of the period. My main source was the SRA's own archive, embracing the archives of its predecessors, the British Railways Board, and the Office for Passenger Rail Franchising. Although most of this voluminous collection was buried in deep store and hard to retrieve, I enjoyed unrestricted access to the SRA's Board and Board Committee minutes and papers, its Executive minutes and papers, and the files of the Chairman. In addition, the Department for Transport generously allowed me to consult its extensive collection of rail files. Access to the Treasury's papers was made more problematic by its earlier decision to move to electronic record-keeping. However, I was allowed to consult a selected group of electronic files, which were redacted and gathered together for my personal use. I was also able to see the Cabinet Office rail files, and the Prime Minister's files on rail and rail policy. Without such access, it would have been extremely difficulty to make sense of a complex period in railway history. There were of course distinct limits to my coverage. I did not consult the archives of either Network Rail or the Office of Rail Regulation, and

Preface

in due course other histories will doubtless follow to assess the contribution of these important railway institutions.

I should like to thank the members of an Independent Editorial Advisory Board which was constituted to oversee the project: Professor Stephen Glaister of Imperial College, the Chairman; Pen Kent and Terence Jenner, representing the SRA; Peter McCarthy and Philip Wood, representing the Department for Transport; and Professor Paul Johnson (succeeded in 2007 by Professor Janet Hartley), representing the LSE. The Board, which was administered most efficiently by Sonia Copeland, made numerous valuable suggestions for the enhancement of the manuscript. Peter Trewin, Secretary of the SRA, and subsequently Director, Legal and Secretarial of BRB (Residuary), supplied invaluable archival material of BRB/SSRA/SRA, first at 55 Victoria Street, SW1, then at Whittles House, N1, and provided a supportive environment in which to work. He also smoothed the path to many contacts within the railway industry. Richard Davies read the draft text and made a number of helpful suggestions for its improvement. Mike Anson, the researcher on my two previous books, gave me access to his private rail archive. He also read the draft text and steered me away from infelicities. Jo Anson once again provided a rigorous copy-editing of the manuscript. As always, Susan Gourvish encouraged me to make the writing more user-friendly. I also enjoyed valuable briefing meetings with David Quarmby, and useful exchanges, mostly by e-mail, with others well versed in the events of the period and especially Richard Davies, Roger Ford, and Tom Winsor. I owe a considerable debt to the interviewees, listed elsewhere, who were so generous with their time. Margaret Ritchie, PA to the SRA Chairman, was extremely helpful in guiding me through the Chairman's archives, and Joan Davies was, as ever, an excellent transcriber of interviews. At the Cabinet Office, Sally Falk arranged access to Cabinet Office papers and the Prime Minister's rail papers, while Ola Solaja fulfilled the same function at the Treasury. David Musson and Matthew Derbyshire of Oxford University Press were once again supportive publishers. Dr. Nick Hiley, Head of the Centre for the Study of Cartoons and Caricature at the University of Kent, helped me with cartoon images, and permissions were obtained from Steve Bell, the *Times, Daily Mail, Daily Express*, and *Private Eye*. I should also like to thank Steve Atkins (SRA), Joyce Bent (DfT), Pete Biggs (Passenger Focus), Colin Divall (York University), Colette Dollin (SRA), Paul Gardner (DfT), Keith Gray (Freightliner), Michael Lee (ORR), Vicki Martins (BRB [Residuary]), Sue MacSwan (ORR), Maria Moseley (SRA), Chris Nash (Leeds University), Nick Pidgeon (Cardiff University), Andrew Regan (Passenger Focus), Irene Ripley (Treasury), Nigel Salmon (Network Rail), Janet Sinclair (SRA), Paul Sizer (RSSB), Andrew Smith (Leeds University), Rob Stebbings (BRB [Residuary]), and Maurice Tomsett (BRB [Residuary]). In conclusion, I should state that I travelled fairly extensively on the railways during the period of writing. I made journeys to Bath, Birmingham, Cambridge, Charlton,

Exeter, Gatwick, Glasgow, Leicester, Norwich, Oxford, Paris, Reading, Stansted, Stourbridge, Wolverhampton, and York, on services provided by no fewer than 15 franchisees. I have greatly enjoyed my foray into contemporary railway history, and of course should make it clear that responsibility for what follows is mine alone.

T. G.

London E3
November 2007

1

Labour's Response to the Privatized Railway, 1993–8

1.1 Introduction: Rail policy, 1993–7

Few people have had kind words for the privatized railway structure constructed so hastily, yet laboriously, by John Major's Conservative Government from 1992. Undertaken in the name of competition, the reforms were inevitably compromised by economic and political realities. Britain's railways have always tended towards infrastructure monopoly, service concentration, and functional integration. Equally, public service considerations have influenced the industry since 1839, and these continue to demand the retention of substantial areas of government responsibility.[1] Nevertheless, over the period 1993–7 the industry was broken into around 100 separate institutional pieces. The main elements were Railtrack, owner of the rail infrastructure and the main railway stations; 25 passenger franchise or train operating companies (TOCs); 3 freight operating companies (English Welsh & Scottish, Freightliner, DRS); 3 rolling stock leasing companies (ROSCOs); and 19 companies—6 for track renewal, 7 for

---

[1] Cf. Terry Gourvish, 'The Regulation of Britain's Railways: Past, Present and Future', in Lena Andersson-Skog and Olle Krantz (eds.), *Institutions in the Transport and Communications Industries: State and Private Actors in the Making of Institutional Patterns, 1850–1990* (Canton, MA, 1999), pp. 117–32; Robert Millward, *Private and Public Enterprise in Europe. Energy, Telecommunications and Transport 1830–1990* (Cambridge, 2005), pp. 26–7.

Labour's Response to the Privatized Railway, 1993–8

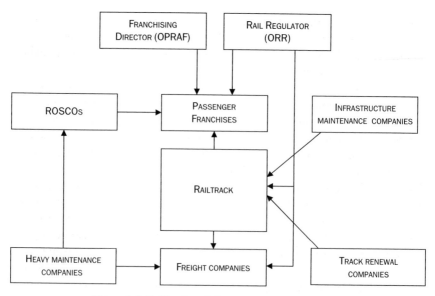

Figure 1.1 Railtrack and the privatized railway, 1997

track maintenance, and 6 for rolling stock maintenance—carved out of British Rail's civil and mechanical engineering departments (Figure 1.1).[2] This was uncharted territory for Britain's railways. Aspects of the policy were also unique over a broader canvas, conceived to inject private sector regimes into a loss-making industry. Railtrack, established as a government-owned company, was expected to become a private sector concern at a later, unspecified, stage. Shorn of engineering expertise in senior management—there was a lone engineer on the Board Executive at the time of flotation[3]—the company was designed to operate as a landlord, outsourcing services to maintain and develop its property base. The TOCs were also rather curious entities. Set up without substantial assets in order to facilitate ease of entry, they leased rolling stock from its new owners, the ROSCOs, and provided rail passenger services under a defined contract with the passenger regulator, the Franchising Director. Heavy maintenance of the stock was outsourced. Substantial amounts of government subsidy were required to maintain the network of defined services, and the bulk of this money was paid to the TOCs from Central Government via the Office of Passenger Rail Franchising (OPRAF). The TOCs had then to pay track access charges to Railtrack.[4] An

[2] See OPRAF, *Passenger Rail Industry Overview* (June 1996). In addition, there was a safety regulator, the Railway Inspectorate, now part of the HSE; local authority interests, mainly the PTEs; and unregulated and open access operators such as Eurostar and Heathrow Express.

[3] The engineer was Brian Mellitt, who had been Director of Engineering, London Underground, 1988–95. One of the non-executive directors, Sir Derek Roberts, was a distinguished engineer. SBC Warburg, *Railtrack Share Offer Prospectus*, 1 May 1996, pp. 58–9.

[4] Metropolitan public passenger transport was the responsibility of seven Passenger Transport Authorities (PTAs) operating through Passenger Transport Executives (PTEs).

economic regulator, the Rail Regulator, was appointed to grant licences to passenger and freight train operators and Railtrack. His prime responsibility was to monitor Railtrack's access charging in order to ensure that the company did not abuse its monopoly position.[5]

In the period to 1997 the Labour Party was faced with a search for an alternative to this complex apparatus. In the Commons and in party conferences, its gut reaction, after nearly a decade and a half of opposition, was to defend a nationalized industry. Thus, transport spokesman John Prescott, introducing a Commons debate on 12 January 1993, shortly before the publication of the Railways Bill, expressed his firm belief in public ownership, though his claim that a publicly owned railway could be modernized and adequately financed in the public sector was less easy to accept at face value. Prescott received strong support from MPs with railway trade union connections such as Gwyneth Dunwoody and Peter Snape. Dunwoody argued that 'destroying the present integrated system will not produce a better result for the passenger or the economy'; she condemned the Government's privatization proposals, contained in the White Paper *New Opportunities for the Railways* of 1992, as ill thought out and 'an unalloyed disaster'.[6] These opponents of the policy were accompanied, and even led, by other backbench critics committed to the preservation of an integrated, public sector railway, or else sceptical of the wisdom of proceeding with the existing policy of separating track, train service and maintenance, and introducing passenger franchising. The most influential was Robert Adley, Tory MP for Christchurch and Chairman of the all-party Commons Transport Committee. Having coined the phrase 'poll tax on wheels' to describe the risks in his party's railway policy, he repeated the view that 'party politics and public transport policy are very uneasy bedfellows', and made it clear that his solution to the difficulties facing the rail industry lay in the direction of increased investment rather than in a change of ownership. However, the impact of these arguments was soon blunted with Adley's untimely death in May 1993.[7]

After the successful passage of the Railways Bill in November 1993, and the long march towards implementation, the self-congratulatory tone of privatizing enthusiasts, captured in works such as *All Change*, edited by Roger Freeman,

---

[5] There are numerous accounts of the new railway framework, among them Ian Bartle, 'Britain's Railway Crisis—A Review of the Arguments in Comparative Perspective', *CRI Occasional Paper* 20 (2004), and Stephen Glaister, 'British Rail Privatisation—Competition Destroyed by Politics', *CRI Occasional Paper* 23 (2004). On the details of policymaking in the period 1992–4 see Terry Gourvish, *British Rail 1974–97: From Integration to Privatisation* (Oxford, 2002), pp. 392–435. For the period to 1997 see, *inter alia*, Christian Wolmar, *The Great British Railway Disaster* (Shepperton, 1996), and *Broken Rails: How Privatisation Wrecked Britain's Railways* (2001), updated as *On the Wrong Line: How Ideology and Incompetence Wrecked Britain's Railways* (2005); Jon Shaw, *Competition, Regulation and the Privatisation of British Rail* (Aldershot, 2000); and Roger Freeman and Jon Shaw (eds.), *All Change: British Railway Privatisation* (Maidenhead, 2000).

[6] *Parl. Deb. (Commons)*, 6th ser. (Session 1992–3), Vol. 216, 12 January 1993, John Prescott, c. 771–2, 782; Gwyneth Dunwoody, c. 797–9; Peter Snape, c. 811 ff. The Railways Bill was published on 22 January.

[7] Ibid. c. 805 ff.

Labour's Response to the Privatized Railway, 1993–8

Public Transport Minister, 1990–4, and the academic Jon Shaw, quickly evaporated in favour of outright condemnations of the policy, notably from Roger Ford of *Modern Railways,* and the freelance journalist Christian Wolmar.[8] But as the Conservatives' privatizing policy pursued its relentless course, with the clear aim of making its actions irreversible, threats of overturning the policy gradually gave way to a more pragmatic approach on the part of 'New Labour', particularly once Tony Blair had been elected party leader in July 1994. Thus, while John Prescott and Frank Dobson were able to promise successive party conferences (in 1993 and 1994) that Labour would bring the railways back into public ownership and control, their new, reforming leader was more cautious. His 1995 agenda included a promise to try to stop rail privatization, but he could give no commitment to taking the industry back into public ownership.[9] Opportunities to formulate a policy to reassert control, if not ownership, of the industry were provided by the emerging policy for Railtrack, which was established as a government-owned corporation in April 1994, and subsequently identified, in November, as a candidate for privatization.[10] Flotation duly took place on 20 May 1996. Labour's reaction was again mixed, though most voices were hostile. Clare Short, the shadow transport secretary, had opened a Commons debate on Railtrack a month earlier. In opposing the move, she denounced the 'fattening up' and 'sweeteners to get the company sold at any price'.[11]

It was difficult, however, to offer radical alternatives to a policy so advanced, particularly when large sums of government money would be required, and Gordon Brown was contemplating office as a prudent chancellor. Transport Secretary Sir George Young was able to tell the House that on an aggregate turnover basis nearly half of the industry had been transferred to the private sector, and he discomforted Short when he pointed out the Opposition's ambiguity on the issue: 'It is now in the absurd position of claiming to be opposed to the flotation of Railtrack, while at the same time refusing to say whether it would

[8] Freeman and Shaw's *All Change* included contributions from privatizers such as John Edmonds (ex-Railtrack), John Prideaux (ex-Angel Trains), and Julia Clarke (ex-Rail Freight Group). Criticism of the policy strengthened with contributions from Roger Ford, in his 'Informed Sources' column in *Modern Railways,* and Wolmar's *Great British Railway Disaster* and *Broken Rails.* Shaw provided a more measured assessment of passenger franchising in *Competition, Regulation and the Privatisation of British Rail.*

[9] *Evening Standard,* 9 January 1995, p. 2; *Independent,* 10 January 1995, p. 5; *Daily Mail,* 10 January 1995, pp. 1, 4; *Times,* 14 September 1995, p. 12. An internal argument within the Labour Party was avoided by setting up a working party to look into ways of ensuring a 'publicly owned, publicly accountable railway': *Times,* 16 January 1995, p. 1. Apparently, the working party never met: see *Independent on Sunday,* 24 March 1996, p. 7.

[10] *Parl. Deb. (Commons),* 6th ser. (Session 1994–5), Vol. 250, 24 November 1994, Brian Mawhinney (SoS for Transport), c. 729. On the background to the change of policy for Railtrack, which had been expected to remain in the public sector 'for the foreseeable future', see Gourvish, *British Rail 1974–97,* pp. 440–1; Philip Bagwell, 'The Sad State of British Railways: The Rise and Fall of Railtrack, 1992–2002', *The Journal of Transport History,* 3rd ser. 25:2 (September 2004), 112–13; Wolmar, *On the Wrong Line,* p. 79 ff.

[11] *Parl. Deb. (Commons),* 6th ser. (Session 1995–6), Vol. 275, 17 April 1996, Clare Short, c. 720–2.

buy it back.'[12] In fact, the New Labour leadership had tried to steer a course between Scylla (renationalization) and Charybdis (acceptance of a fait accompli). This had not been an easy task, since the Party's intentions were required to be made explicit in the Railtrack prospectus. Short, supported by Brown, favoured a plan to pay the £2 billion in annual government subsidy direct to Railtrack, using this relationship to acquire a controlling stake in the company over time. Brian Wilson, Short's deputy, backed by Prescott, now Deputy Leader, wanted a more radical policy, involving an exchange of Railtrack equity for preference shares, with voting rights transferred to the Government.[13] When Short made a lengthy speech on the issue on 29 March, the text of which was reproduced in the Railtrack prospectus on 1 May, a retreat from radicalism was evident. The language may have been bullish, but there was much hedging of bets. Thus, Labour promised to (*a*) achieve railway integration through regulation, making the Rail Regulator, who was responsible for overseeing access charges, more accountable to the Transport Secretary; (*b*) 'reconstitute British Rail as a fully publicly owned, publicly accountable company holding the public's interest in the rail network'; and (*c*) '*dependent on the availability of resources and as priorities allow* [my italics], seek . . . to extend public ownership and control over Railtrack'. The emphasis was firmly on ways of ensuring that the infrastructure company invested adequately in the rail network and that more of the proceeds from the sale of surplus assets were reinvested and did not leak away in profits.[14] All this was confirmed when Short addressed the Commons on 17 April. Labour, she declared, would 'use all the levers' at its disposal, with the intention of controlling Railtrack's economic behaviour. But a speedy return to the public sector was clearly ruled out.[15] In spite of the Opposition's hostility, and the information asymmetries produced by launching a company with such a limited track record, the flotation proved a great success. Short's interventions played into the hands of speculators by helping to keep the offer price low. Railtrack's equity was valued at £1.9 billion, apparently well below British Rail's asset valuation in 1993.[16] The issue was oversubscribed by a large margin, and the premium over the offer price

---

[12] Ibid. (Session 1995–6), Vol. 269, 15 January 1996, Sir George Young (SoS for Transport), in reply to Clare Short, c. 401, and Vol. 275, 17 April 1996, c. 722, 736–7; *Times*, 29 January 1996, p. 38.

[13] Interviews with John Prescott, 2 May 2006, and Tom Winsor (adviser to Short), 31 July 2006. See also *Financial Times*, 27 January 1996, p. 5; *Guardian*, 13 March 1996, p. 1; *Sunday Times*, 24 March 1996, p. 9; *Independent*, 7 April 1996, p. 3. The clash between Short and Wilson was public knowledge: *Independent*, 12 May 1996, p. 4; *Times*, 16 May 1996, p. 10, 27 May 1996, p. 2.

[14] Short, speech, 29 March 1996, reproduced with covering letter to SBC Warburg, in SoS for Transport and SBC Warburg, *Railtrack Share Offer Prospectus*, 1 May 1996, pp. 101–4.

[15] *Parl. Deb. (Commons)*, 6th ser. (Session 1995–6), Vol. 275, 17 April 1996, Clare Short, c. 724–5; Clare Short, 'A Better Route for Railtrack', *Financial Times*, 12 April 1996, p. 16.

[16] Bagwell asserts that the valuation was £6.5 bn: *Rise and Fall of Railtrack*, 113. Total proceeds were £2.5 bn, since the company repaid £586 m. in debt, with the Government cancelling a further £869 m. NAO, *The Flotation of Railtrack. Report by the Comptroller and Auditor General*, 16 December 1998, P.P. 1998–9, xiv, HC25, p. 1. Short's opposition had also served to discourage bidders for the ROSCOs in 1995, helping the MBOs to acquire the assets cheaply. Both she and Wilson lost the transport portfolio in the summer of 1996.

to private investors was a respectable 16 per cent on the first day of trading.[17] In subsequent reports by the Comptroller and Auditor General and the Committee of Public Accounts the flotation was criticized, the former suggesting that a further £1.5 billion might have been realized if the sale had been conducted in stages.[18]

After the flotation, the prospect that Labour could untangle the complex contractual web which now embraced the industry became more remote. A final debate on rail privatization in November 1996 revealed that the game was up. With the claim that over 70 per cent of the industry was now in private hands, the Minister for Railways and Roads, John Watts, and a bullish former transport minister, Steve Norris, rehearsed some of the pros and cons of the emerging structure with Labour's Keith Bradley, Gwyneth Dunwoody, and Glenda Jackson, their debate enlivened by numerous anecdotes. Labour clung to its pledge to re-establish a more integrated system, 'with stronger protection for the public interest', and 'a systematic framework' to encourage 'strategic decisions with wider Government policy on transport'. To achieve this Bradley referred to the intention to reconstitute British Rail as a strategic planning body, a 'fully publicly owned and publicly accountable company holding the public interest in the rail network'. Power to direct the Rail Regulator would be returned to the Secretary of State.[19] Tony Blair entered the lists at Prime Minister's question time on 18 February 1997. Seizing upon the resale of two of the ROSCOs for a substantial profit, he attacked Major for having facilitated 'profiteering' at the expense of the public purse. However, there was no reference to future policymaking.[20] Thus, in the general election of May 1997, voters seeking pointers as to the future political economy of Britain's railways had little to go on beyond the realization that the Conservatives favoured the process they had started, while Labour did not. In the latter's manifesto, it was clear that the railways were scarcely a central concern for a campaign which took as its rallying-cry 'education, education, education'. A short paragraph on the railways revealed Labour's realism in seeking 'to improve the situation as we find it, not as we wish it to be'. Reference was made to the creation of a new body, instead of a reconstituted British Railways Board (BRB). Labour's hopes were now pinned on 'more effective and accountable regulation by the rail regulator', and the establishment of 'a new rail authority, combining functions currently carried out by the rail franchiser and the Department of Transport'. Exactly how the changes would provide 'a clear coherent and strategic programme for the development of the railways' was not, of course, spelled out.

---

[17] *Financial Times*, 21 May 1996, pp. 9, 21, 46; *Times*, 21 May 1996, p. 25. The initial premium for international investors was 10%. The issue was oversubscribed 7 times, Wolmar, *On the Wrong Line*, p. 92, the international portion 10 times, NAO, *The Flotation of Railtrack*, p. 15.

[18] NAO, *The Flotation of Railtrack*, pp. 8–9; HC Public Accounts Committee, Report on *The Flotation of Railtrack*, 14 July 1999, P.P. 1998–9, xliv, HC256, para. 4.

[19] *Parl. Deb.* (Commons), 6th ser. (Session 1996–7), Vol. 285, 15 November 1996, c. 598–668, and specifically Keith Bradley, c. 614.

[20] Ibid. Vol. 290, 18 February 1997, Tony Blair and John Major, c. 740–1.

The promise of an 'integrated transport policy', on the one hand, and more public–private partnership in addressing transport needs, on the other, left much to be developed if, as expected, Labour were victorious.[21]

1.2 Rail performance, 1993–7

At the end of the financial year 1996/7 it was difficult to assess the impact of the new railway structure. The two regulators, John Swift, QC (Rail Regulator), and Roger Salmon (Franchising Director), had served for substantial portions of their five-year terms, and indeed had been acting as regulators designate since January 1993. However, for much of this time their work had been subject to the 'guidance' of the Secretary of State and there was more than a whiff of the 1947 Transport Act, with its conflict between financial and public service objectives. The Franchising Director was expected to act in accordance with the Minister's objectives for passenger rail services in negotiating, awarding, and monitoring the passenger franchises, and in making subsidy payments to the train operating companies. The Rail Regulator, whose first task was to approve agreements for access to the track, stations, and depots, was intended to function with more independence, but he too was subject to departmental guidance until the end of 1996. By April 1997 it was evident that both regulators had found their briefs challenging. Salmon, an ebullient merchant banker unacquainted with the ways of Whitehall and Marsham Street, became disenchanted with the job and decided to leave early, handing on the baton to the more emollient John O'Brien in November 1996.[22] Swift's remit was disconcerting. He was expected to protect the interests of users, promote use of the network, promote 'efficiency, economy, and competition' in the provision of rail services, and to 'have regard to' the financial position of the Franchising Director and the financial requirements of operators—elements which invited 'guidance' from government. From an early stage he voiced concerns about the extent of his independence.[23] And since he was expected to promote competition, while Salmon and O'Brien were required to sell franchises, there were evident risks of conflict in the relationship between them. The expectation that network benefits—through-ticketing, train information, etc.—would be preserved under the new, decentralized structure produced early problems which highlighted the blurring of responsibilities between the two regulators. Given the fluidity of the emerging situation it was difficult to assess their impact in this formative period.[24]

---

[21] Labour Party, 'New Labour Because Britain Deserves Better', Election Manifesto, 1997, p. 24.

[22] Interview with John O'Brien, 6 April 2006, and cf. press speculation in the *Independent*, 11 April 1996, p. 1, and *Financial Times*, 4 November 1996, p. 10.

[23] Interview with John Swift, 8 August 2006.   [24] Cf. Gourvish, *British Rail 1974–97*, pp. 423–7.

Labour's Response to the Privatized Railway, 1993–8

How well was the emerging structure working? Some contemporary critics, and notably Christian Wolmar, suggested that all was not well. Teething troubles with the new set of relationships were only to be expected. There was a fair amount of anecdotal evidence about service failures and ticketing restrictions, and early signs that the multiplication of transaction costs would create its own problems. Many of these difficulties were reported in Wolmar's 'mad' column in the *Independent*.[25] However, some of the criticisms were unduly harsh, since the privatized railway was very much a fledgling, and there had scarcely been time for the new owners to show their mettle. For example, the passenger franchising process had proved to be a protracted affair. Only 2 of the intended 25 franchises had been let before the start of the 1996/7 financial year (in February 1996), and the last 7 franchises were only let in the last four weeks of that year (2–31 March 1997).[26] Consequently, it was difficult for rail watchers to measure the changes made by April 1997.[27] The TOCs' unpublished profit and loss data for the year 1996/7 are necessarily limited, and care should be taken in their interpretation. They reveal that for 23 of the 25 franchises operating profits totalled £60 million (average: £2.6 million), and before tax profits were £32 million (average: £1.4 million), with 8 franchises experiencing losses.[28]

In considering the published statistical data, one would have expected *a priori* that performance would slip as the numerous parts of the integrated business were sold off, and thus assessment of the data would be more a critique of the dog days of the old guard than a verdict on the new. Passengers, or customers as they were now increasingly called, certainly experienced mixed fortunes. They evidently suffered from the initial, heavy-handed approach of those TOCs which assumed that it would be a relatively straightforward process to slim down the fat in British Rail operating, having failed to grasp that British Rail had already taken steps to improve its operating productivity in the time of Bob Reid I (1983–90). Thus, the actions of the bus company Stagecoach, operators of South West Trains, produced the threat of a £1 million fine from the Franchising Director when a 'driver restructuring initiative' led to a large number of train cancellations.[29] Similar difficulties were experienced by the Merseyrail operator, local bus company MTL Trust Holdings.[30] There was also a steady rise in the

---

[25] Wolmar, *Independent*, 5 March 1995, p. 10, 22 December 1996, p. 13. A compilation was subsequently published as *The Great British Railway Disaster*.

[26] Gourvish, *British Rail 1974–97*, p. 517.

[27] Note that a recent comparison of public and private sector operation omitted the transitional years, 1993/4, 1994/5, and 1995/6, from the analysis: Michael G. Pollitt and Andrew S. J. Smith, 'The Restructuring and Privatisation of British Rail: Was It Really That Bad?', *Fiscal Studies*, 23:4 (2002), 473.

[28] SRA/DfT database (data for WAGN and Scotrail not available).

[29] OPRAF, *R&A 1996/7*, pp. 5, 17–18; CCRUC, *Annual Report 1996/7*, p. 13; *Independent*, 12 February 1997, p. 16; *Times*, 18 February 1997, p. 2, 10 March 1997, p. 48, 9 May 1997, p. 25. An enforcement order was proposed in March but the action was withdrawn in May. See Nicholas Montagu (Dep Sec, DTp)–Young, 19 February 1997, DTp file R73/2/1 Pt. 2, John O'Brien (Franchising Director)–John Prescott (DPM and SoS for Environment, Transport and the Regions), 6 May 1997, Pt. 3.

[30] *Financial Times*, 22 March 1997, p. 4. No breach of franchise was reported in this instance, however: see OPRAF, *Annual Report 1996/7*, pp. 16–17.

number of passenger complaints to the users' committees as the national network was broken up into smaller managerial units (Table 1.1).[31] On the other hand, the number of complaints fell in the year 1996/7, for the first time in over 15 years,[32] and there were signs that a more imaginative, entrepreneurial approach was being applied to service provision, for example, with the introduction of family carriages on Great Western, and Sea Containers' promise of a revamp of the service on the East Coast Main Line.[33]

It is difficult to quantify the *overall* impact of the changes. The statistics on punctuality and reliability, imperfect as they may be in aggregate terms, suggest that train performance was fairly stable in the first half of the 1990s, and actually showed an improvement in 1996/7 (Table 1.1).[34] And if there were hiccups with some transitional arrangements, the more recent operational problems experienced by British Rail were still fresh in the public consciousness, not least those instantly recalled by the phrases 'leaves on the line' and 'the wrong kind of snow', or by the serious accidents at Clapham (1988), Purley (1989), and Cowden (1994).[35] Nor did the train accident data suggest that the initial impact of privatization had been deleterious. It is true that the total number of train accidents rose sharply in 1996/7, mainly as a result of a change in the system of reporting, but also through an increase in cases of vandalism.[36] But the number of 'significant' train accidents continued to fall steadily, expressed as a rate per million train-kilometres run (Table 1.1). Other indications were less optimistic. While the figures published by the Transport Department indicated that investment in the national rail infrastructure was holding up, investment in rolling stock fell sharply, from £524 million per annum in 1991/2–1993/4 to only £212 million per annum in 1994/5–1996/7 (Table 1.2). A check to the latter might have been expected as British Rail handed over responsibility to the TOCs—indeed, Roger Ford made much of the fact that there was a 1,064-day hiatus in orders to September 1996—but no one should have been sanguine about the state of network infrastructure investment, when spending on the Channel Tunnel services accounted for some 30 per cent of total rail investment in the period 1990/1–1993/4.[37]

---

[31] Cf. also *Evening Standard*, 15 August 1996, p. 2.

[32] CRUCC, *Annual Report 1996/7*, p. 40; *Independent*, 22 December 1996, p. 13.

[33] *Times*, 14 September 1996, p. 21, 25 September 1996, p. 17.

[34] The Passenger Charter statistics of punctuality and reliability should not be taken as a comprehensive measure of train performance: see note to Table 1.1.

[35] Gourvish, *British Rail 1974–97*, pp. 270–5, 341 ff.

[36] The number of train accidents on the national network increased from 897 in 1995/6 to 1,585 in 1996/7. The introduction of RIDDOR 1995 (SI 3163) accounted for much of the increase, with 465 cases of damage to drivers' cab windows being reported for the first time. But other cases of vandalism increased by 25%. HSE, *Railway Safety 1996/7*, pp. 23, 25, 39.

[37] From Mike Anson, 'Appendices', in Gourvish, *British Rail 1974–97*, p. 461, and see also p. 444; *Financial Times*, 7 September 1996, p. 5; *Guardian*, 12 September 1996, p. 17; *Modern Railways*, October 1996, p. 616.

Table 1.1 Rail performance, 1988/9–1996/7: traffic, passenger quality, and safety indicators

Year	Traffic		Passenger			Accidents	
	Passenger national rail (bn km)	Freight (bn tonne-km)	Punctuality indicator % trains on time (within 5 min, Inter-City 10 min)[a]	Reliability indicator (% trains run)[a]	Complaints to rail users' committees (no.)	Passengers killed in train incidents (national rail) (no.)	Signif. train incidents national rail (no. per m. train-km)
1988/9	34.3	18.1	—	—	4,997	34[b]	0.45[b]
1989/90	33.6	16.7	—	—	5,228	6[b]	0.35[b]
1990/1	33.2	16.0	—	—	8,053	0[b]	0.36[b]
1991/2	32.0	15.3	—	—	8,371	4[c]	0.26
1992/3	31.7	15.5	89.7	98.7	9,471	0	0.24
1993/4	30.4	13.8	90.3	98.8	9,928	0	0.27
1994/5	28.6	13.0	89.6	98.7	10,166	3	0.26
1995/6	29.9	13.3	89.5	98.8	11,640	1	0.19
1996/7	32.1	15.1	92.5	99.1	9,753	1	0.17

Source: cols. 1 and 2: *TSGB 2004*, revised by BRB/SRA material; cols. 3 and 4: *TSGB 1998*; col. 5: CCRUC, *Annual Report 1993/4*, p. 14, *1996/7*, p. 43; cols. 6 and 7: HSE, *Railway Safety 1996/7*, pp. 22, 28, 40, 118.

[a] The Passenger Charter punctuality and reliability data, constructed essentially to drive compensation payments to season ticket holders, provide only a limited assessment of train performance. For example, Sunday trains are excluded (except for Gatwick Express and Isle of Wight), exceptionally poor days could be voided, and the London commuting train data on punctuality cover only the Monday–Friday morning and evening peaks. On 6 June 2000 the Shadow SRA replaced the Charter information with the more comprehensive Public Performance Measure, a single measure combining punctuality and reliability, with all trains, all days, and no voiding. The new measure was used to generate data from 1997/8. See Anson, 'Appendix J', in Gourvish, *British Rail 1974–97*, pp. 504–6; OPRAF, *R&A 1996/7*, Appendix I; SSRA, *R&A 1999–2000* (July 2000), Appendix 3. My thanks also to John O'Neill (SRA).
[b] Accidents in calendar year.
[c] 1 January 1991–31 March 1992.

Table 1.2 Rail performance, 1988/9–1996/7: investment and government subsidy (£m., in constant 1996/7 prices)

Year	Investment			Passenger revenue support			Total support after other elements[b]
	Infrastructure	Rolling stock	Total	Central govt.[a]	Local govt.	Total	
1988/9	684	292	976	774	98	872	628
1989/90	858	306	1,159	627	110	738	1,041
1990/1	842	400	1,242	774	140	914	1,451
1991/2	962	519	1,480	1,033	137	1,170	1,813
1992/3	1,041	596	1,637	1,324	119	1,443	2,408
1993/4	824	456	1,280	1,001	179	1,180	1,763
1994/5	948	383	1,331	1,933	368	2,301	1,809
1995/6	931	207	1,137	1,770	374	2,145	450
1996/7	1,178	47	1,225	1,809	291	2,100	1,071

Source: SRA, *National Rail Trends Yearbook 2004/5*, pp. 47, 51, expressed in constant 1996/7 prices using GDP deflator (market prices).

Note: Cols. may not sum due to rounding.

[a] Includes level crossing grants.

[b] Changes in indebtedness, sale of ROSCOs, freight grants, etc.

Labour's Response to the Privatized Railway, 1993–8

During the planning of privatization, Treasury thinking had focused on three assumptions: that competition would be introduced; that the subsidy would fall progressively; and that rail transport was in terminal decline.[38] None showed signs of appearing immediately. Competition took a blow when after the decision was taken to divide British Rail's trainload freight business into three parts prior to sale, all three were acquired by one purchaser, a consortium led by Wisconsin Central, subsequently trading as English Welsh & Scottish Railway (EWS).[39] In the passenger market no fewer than 19 of the 25 franchises were being operated by bus companies which had emerged after the denationalization of the British bus industry in 1985. Diversifying into rail, they were unwilling to sign short-length agreements in circumstances where competition remained a possibility. Consequently, the initial opportunities for on-rail competition were severely constrained by the restriction on 'open access' provided by the Rail Regulator in 1994, and by the terms of the franchise agreements.[40] The reported revenue grant data made gloomy reading for those who expected government support to the industry to fall. Payments by OPRAF and local government bodies in support of passenger services averaged £2.18 billion per annum (in 1996/7 prices) in the three years to 1996/7, a level 73 per cent higher than in the previous three years, and 160 per cent higher than the average subsidy paid in the three years to 1990/1. However, the numbers were bound to rise with the building-in of operator margins of around 5–6 per cent of cost,[41] and the move to current cost depreciation.[42] Furthermore, optimists could point to the fact that after taking into account other elements (mainly changes in debt levels), which produced a credit of £2.6 billion in the two years to 1996/7, government support in 1994/5–1996/7 was in fact 44 per cent lower than in the previous three years (Table 1.2). One thing is clear: the rail business did not decline. As Table 1.1 shows, traffic was beginning to recover from the trough induced by the long recession of 1989–93, and after a slide of 17 per cent from 1988/9 to 1994/5, the number of passenger-kilometres travelled rose from 28.6 billion in 1994/5 to 32.1 billion in 1996/7, an improvement of 12 per cent, although at this level it was still short of the peak in 1988–9. Freight traffic, which appeared to be in terminal decline, and had fallen by 28 per cent between 1988/9 and 1994/5, increased by 16 per cent to 1996–7. Thus, the early verdict on privatization was equivocal. In the early months of 1997 both enthusiasts and critics could appeal to the evidence. Letters published in the *Times* on 17 January 1997 from the Secretary of State, George Young,

---

[38] Here cf. Treasury, *Implementing Privatisation: The UK Experience* (1997 edn.).

[39] Gourvish, *British Rail 1974–97*, p. 419.

[40] Bob Linnard (Railways Sponsorship, DETR)–Prescott, 16 September 1997 and 17 June 1998, DETR file R73/1/10 Pt. 1; ORR, *New Service Opportunities for Passengers* (September 1997), pp. 1–2, 11; Interview with John Gilbert (SRA), 24 November 2005.

[41] Interview with Stephen Packham (SRA), 15 November 2005. Insiders put the switch to private operation as costing an additional £1 bn in subsidy: Interview with Stephen Bennett (SRA), 15 November 2005.

[42] Gourvish, *British Rail 1974–97*, p. 441.

and a transport consultant, Barry Doe, indicated diametrically opposed positions, though an earlier leader had come down in favour of the process. 'Privatization,' declared the newspaper on the 13th, 'damned before the first detail had been worked out ..., has proved a modest but real success.'[43] Thus, when Major went to the country in May 1997, it was difficult to argue that Britain's railways had collapsed or were facing disaster. Only one British Rail business remained to be sold—Railfreight Distribution. And as Railtrack shareholders approached the date for payment of the second instalment on their shares, they could take comfort in the fact that the price stood at £4.65 on 30 April, a healthy premium over the £3.20 offer price.[44]

1.3 A new Government, another White Paper

The general election on 1 May 1997 produced a landslide for 'New' Labour, which took office for the first time since 1979. Its 419 seats, the highest number it had ever gained, produced an overall majority of 179.[45] The transport portfolio went to the Deputy Prime Minister, John Prescott, the son of a railwayman and with some 'shadow' experience of transport in the 1980s. He was supported initially by Dr Gavin Strang as Transport Minister, with Cabinet rank. However, there was little evidence that this representation in Cabinet would produce immediate reform of the existing railway structure. After all, most energy went into implementing Prescott's plans for a major structural change in Whitehall, with transport being subsumed in a monolithic Department of the Environment, Transport and the Regions.[46] In the Commons, there was no hint of change when the Queen's Speech was debated. Prescott confined himself to a brief tilt at the existing structure, and specifically, train cancellations by South West Trains.[47] In the weeks that followed, questions about infrastructure maintenance (following criticism of Railtrack by the Rail Regulator) and the future regulatory framework were raised by those seeking reform, notably by Gwyneth Dunwoody. Outside the Commons, Prescott, having criticized Railtrack for underinvesting, encouraged Swift to increase his control over the company's investment programme by altering the terms of its licence. The policy gathered pace after Railtrack announced pre-tax profits of £346 million in its first year in the private sector. The Regulator, overcoming some resistance from Railtrack

---

[43] Letters to the *Times*, 17 January 1997, p. 19; *Times*, leader, 13 January 1997, p. 19.
[44] *Times*, 1 May 1997, p. 35.
[45] David Butler and Dennis Kavanagh, *The British General Election of 1997* (Basingstoke, 1997), p. 252.
[46] Anthony Seldon, *Blair* (New York, 2004), pp. 409–15.
[47] *Parl. Deb. (Commons)*, 6th ser. (Session 1997–8), Vol. 294, 20 May 1997, John Prescott, c. 606.

and its Chairman, Sir Robert Horton, published proposals to achieve a closer monitoring of infrastructure investment in July, and the new licence condition—Condition 7—came into effect in September.[48]

However, only four months later the temperature rose with the Southall train crash. On 19 September a Swansea–Paddington train operated by Great Western Trains hit a freight train operated by EWS, killing 7 passengers, and injuring 139. Although criminal proceedings meant that it was 2½ years before it was possible to publish Professor John Uff's report on the accident in February 2000, the main cause quickly became common knowledge—the passing of a signal at danger (known as a SPAD). While human error was clearly to blame, commentators were disturbed by the revelation that neither of the available train control systems, AWS and ATP, had been functioning at the time of the crash.[49] This immediately raised doubts about the effectiveness of the current safety procedures, and in particular those of Railtrack and the franchisee.[50] In addition, at least one expert expressed concerns about the visibility of the signals, where gantries had been raised to accommodate the electrification of the Heathrow Express service.[51] Not for the first time in British railway history (cf. Armagh, 1889, Harrow, 1952, and Clapham, 1988), a major accident pushed the industry to the forefront of media attention, forcing the spotlight onto the organizational structure and its perceived weaknesses. Eventually, the complex chain of events was uncovered in Uff's report, revealing an ambiguity in the rules for operating with AWS and inadequate maintenance procedures in Great Western Trains (the company was fined £1.5 million in July 1999 for breaches under the Health & Safety at Work Act 1974). The report also suggested that some of the problems had resulted from the existence of divided responsibility for operating.[52] Did the Southall accident influence Labour's plans for the industry? The answer is yes and no. Prescott was anxious to avoid the mauling he had given Paul Channon over a series of transport accidents in 1987–8. Like Cecil Parkinson a decade earlier, he made a hasty undertaking to support a substantial investment in ATP, the

[48] Dunwoody, answered by Glenda Jackson (PUSS for Environment, Transport & the Regions), ibid. 22 May 1997, c. w158–9, Vol. 295, 2 June 1997, c. w59–60; *Financial Times*, 6 June 1997, pp. 23, 25, and 27 June 1997, p. 10; ORR, *Railtrack's Investment Programme: Implementation of New Licence Condition* (September 1997); *Independent*, 27 September 1997, p. 27; Interview with Swift, 2006.

[49] HSC, *The Southall Rail Accident Inquiry Report. Professor John Uff QC FREng* (2000), pp. i–iii. In the press revelations about the failure to operate with either ATP or AWS appeared at an early stage. Cf. *Scotsman*, 20 September 1997, p. 1; *Sunday Times*, 21 September 1997, p. 1; *Times*, 22 September 1997, p. 1; *Guardian*, 23 September 1997, p. 7.

[50] Concerns had already been expressed in an HSE report in 1996: HSE, *Maintaining a Safer Railway Infrastructure: Report on Railtrack's Management Systems for Contractors* (March 1996), and Wolmar, *On the Wrong Line*, p. 99.

[51] Stanley Hall, *Hidden Dangers: Railway Safety in the Era of Privatisation* (Shepperton, 1999), p. 106 and cf. also *Observer*, 21 September 1997, p. 8. Hall's concerns were given more force with the Ladbroke Grove accident in October 1999.

[52] *Evening Standard*, 17 July 1999, pp. 1–2; Uff, *Southall Rail Accident*, pp. 185–8, 201–6; and see also Wolmar, *On the Wrong Line*, p. 101 ff.

fail-safe system of train protection.[53] Public expectations about change, and, in particular, the need for reassurance about safety standards, may have been raised, but the Deputy Prime Minister had already embarked on the development of an integrated transport policy, in line with Labour's manifesto. Wishing to take a 'wider, more strategic view' of UK's transport requirements, from the standpoint of his enlarged Department, he was in the middle of a major consultation exercise when the accident occurred. The invitation to contribute had been issued in August 1997, with 14 November fixed as the closing date for submissions. A White Paper entitled *A New Deal for Transport: Better for Everyone* followed in July 1998.[54] Prescott's agenda was an extensive one, of course, with railways only part of the equation. The prospect of speedy and substantial reform was therefore remote. The Southall accident may have put the railways back on the front page of political awareness, but it did not really affect the timetable in the DETR.

While the White Paper was being prepared, the House of Commons Select Committee on Environment, Transport and Regional Affairs decided that its first enquiry should be concerned with the Government's plan for a Strategic Rail Authority, and the associated question of rail regulation. Evidence was taken by the Transport Sub-Committee over the period October 1997 to January 1998, with a lengthy report published in March.[55] But by this time the Department had already taken the first steps to implement Labour's plans by tackling the relationship between the Government and the two regulators. In November 1997 the Secretary of State issued a new 'Objectives, Instructions and Guidance' document to O'Brien, the Franchising Director, in place of that issued a year earlier by Young. The interests of the passenger were now recognized to be paramount in the regulator's work. He was asked 'to increase the number of passengers travelling by rail', manage existing franchise agreements in the interests of the passenger, and 'promote high levels of cost-effective investment in the network'. Consultation with the Minister was required before steps were taken to re-tender any franchise.[56] At the same time, a 'Concordat' document was agreed with Swift, the Rail Regulator, setting out the Government's objectives for the railways and seeking to influence his future actions. While the Regulator's

[53] Prescott, reported in *Daily Mail*, 20 September 1997, p. 2. After Clapham British Rail found the financial case for a national system of ATP to be weak: Gourvish, *British Rail 1974–97*, p. 351 ff. In May 1998 the HSC called for more limited spending of £250 m. on safety improvements, and in the following year new safety regulations required the introduction of TPWS.

[54] DETR, *Developing an Integrated Transport Policy* (August 1997), and *A New Deal for Transport: Better for Everyone*, P.P. 1997–8, cxliv, Cm. 3950 (July 1998).

[55] HC Select Committee on Environment, Transport and Regional Affairs, 3rd Report on *The Proposed Strategic Rail Authority and Railway Regulation*, March 1998, P.P. 1997–8, xxxviii, HC286-I, p. v and para. 1.

[56] Strang (for SoS for DETR), 6 November 1997, and Young, 28 November 1996, in OPRAF, *Annual Report 1996/7*, pp. 38–45. Earlier objectives, to secure improvement in the quality of passenger and station services, protect network benefits, and to encourage efficiency and economy in service provision, were retained.

independence was to be preserved, the Government's desire to see more passenger and freight traffic carried by rail was seen as a cornerstone of its developing integrated transport policy, and was therefore highlighted in the document, along with expectations that subsidies would be used to 'enhance services and maximize value for money', and that regulation would be 'more effective and accountable'. But a hint of difficulties to come was provided by the statement that full realization of the Government's objectives would require legislation, particularly to establish a new rail authority, leaving the precise relationship between the new body and the Regulator to be determined.[57]

Notwithstanding the clarifications of November 1997, the tensions inherent in the system of dual regulation continued to worry the regulators, as was clear from the evidence they gave to the Transport Select Committee. Thus, Swift admitted that the existence of shared functions had resulted in 'obscure boundaries' between the two offices, and O'Brien said that he fully expected his job to disappear, suggesting that it would make sense if one body were charged with the task of overseeing the passengers' interest.[58] A table provided by the DETR and reproduced in the Committee's report revealed that there were no fewer than 14 subjects in which the two regulators each had an interest.[59] There were other concerns too, not least the opinion of the Rail Regulator that Railtrack's spending on infrastructure renewals and maintenance had not been adequate, which, as we have seen, had led to a redrafting of the Network Licence Agreement in September 1997. On the other hand, the Regulator was frustrated that the ROSCOs lay outside his regulatory scope, and he also complained about his inability to include pricing and service quality conditions in the passenger operator licences, functions which were discharged by OPRAF.[60] In these circumstances, the Committee found that the concept of a strategic rail authority was universally welcomed within the industry as a way of introducing a strategic focus at the centre, something lacking since the British Railways Board had been effectively dismantled.[61]

In fact, the BRB was still in existence, though in a severely truncated form. The staff of this old bastion of the British public sector had been cut from 130,000 in March 1993 to under 2,400 in March 1998, and aside from residuary obligations, the only functions remaining with the Board were a responsibility

[57] Concordat between the Secretary of State for the Department of the Environment, Transport and the Regions and the Rail Regulator, 6 November 1997, reproduced in ORR, *Annual Report 1997/8*, Appendix 1.

[58] HC Transport Committee Report on *Strategic Rail Authority*, paras. 18–19, and Transport Sub-Committee, *Minutes of Evidence*, HC-286-II, O'Brien, QQ.549–51 and John Swift, Memo. October 1997, SRA02.

[59] HC Transport Committee Report on *Strategic Rail Authority*, para. 17, and DETR, Memo. on 'Strategic Rail Authority and Railway Regulation', October 1997, SRA01, para. 14, in *MOE*, HC286-II.

[60] Ibid. para. 21; Swift, Memo. October 1997, cit. paras. 14–20; Swift–Welsby, 2 October 1997, AN18/1787, TNA.

[61] Ibid. para. 121.

for the British Transport Police (staff: 2,159) and about £125 million of non-operational property.[62] Nevertheless, the Board remained active, and as early as February 1997 it had rehearsed the advice it might offer to an incoming Secretary of State after the general election.[63] The Chairman, John Welsby, drafted a paper anticipating a Labour victory, and when it was sent to Prescott it received a positive response. In July the new Secretary of State informed Welsby formally that he wished British Rail 'to maintain a cadre of expertise to provide advice on railway matters and, in particular, to bring forward proposals designed to help to achieve the Government's objectives for an integrated transport policy for inclusion in the White Paper which I intend to publish next year'.[64] After a joint DETR/BRB seminar in October new government objectives were formulated, emphasizing the pursuance of 'integration rather than competition', the restoration of public accountability, the promotion of strategic investment, and rates of return 'more closely related to the cost of provision'. The intention was not to change the structure of ownership arising from the 1993 Act, but rather to devise a more effective control mechanism for the industry's principal funding body, the Government.[65] By this time, the Board was well below strength, being four short of its statutory minimum. Consequently, four new non-executive members were hastily recruited in December to help with the task: Professor David Begg, Chairman of Edinburgh Council's transport committee; John Hughes, former Principal of Ruskin College Oxford; Ron Kennedy, former ASLEF activist and Chairman of Essex County Council; and Nicholas Wakefield, former Executive Director of SBC Warburg and deputy chief executive of London and Continental Railways, promoters of the Channel Tunnel Rail Link (CTRL). In the same month the Secretary of State set the Board revised objectives for its remaining activities.[66] The detailed policy work, which began in the autumn, was led by Welsby, Terence Jenner, the deputy solicitor, and Alan Nichols, with help from Tom Winsor, a young competition lawyer from Denton Hall, and Dr Paul King, an ex-British Rail manager now with KPMG. Much of the emphasis was on redefining industry leadership. Somewhat curiously in view of later events, Winsor recommended a curb on the Rail Regulator's powers, making him much more accountable to the Secretary of State. Other areas to be examined included the implications of a return to public sector operation,

---

[62] BRB, *R&A 1996/7*, p. 51, *1997/8*, p. 21; HC Transport Sub-Committee, *MOE*, HC-286-II, DETR, Memo. on 'British Railways Board: Current Functions and Responsibilities', October 1997, SRA01A.

[63] Presentation by John Palmer, BRB Minutes, 6 February 1997, AN167/63, The National Archives (TNA).

[64] Ibid. 10 April, 3 July 1997; Prescott–Welsby, 25 July 1997, DETR file R7/1/37 Pt. 1, reproduced in BRB, *R&A 1996/7*, p. 22; Peter Thomas–Charles Godfrey, 1 July 1998, DETR file R7/2/48 Pt. 1.

[65] Welsby–Prescott, 10 September 1997, Richard Threlfall (Prescott's PS)–Roy Griffins (Director (Railways), DETR), 13 October 1997, DETR file R78/1/15 Pt. 1; BRB Minutes, 16 October 1997, AN167/63, TNA.

[66] Ibid. 3 July, 16 October, and 4 December 1997; BRB, *R&A 1997/8*, p. 2.

regulatory options for the ROSCOs, assisted by KPMG, and a strategy for refranchising.[67]

From December 1997 consideration was given to the functions of a Strategic Rail Authority (SRA) in a paper destined for Prescott. By February 1998 this had taken the stance that such a body should have a 'central advisory and executive role', rather than serving merely as a 'more minimalist vehicle for promoting high level debate on the strategic direction of the industry'. To achieve this goal the Secretary of State would have to take back responsibility for defining the public interest from the Rail Regulator.[68] As the timetable for the White Paper slipped, and the prospects for early legislation faded, BRB members expressed some alarm at the prospect that an SRA might be merely bolted onto the existing structure, 'leaving the Regulator with many powers which in exercising he would have to have regard to policy criteria set down by the SRA'. If the latter were not 'sufficiently empowered' then the scope for radical reform would be inhibited.[69] Here was a major element of concern. The BRB thought that train service competition and track allocation capacity matters should be matters for the SRA, and was worried by the Regulator's response to the track access agreement submitted by Railtrack and Virgin Trains in relation to the upgrading of the West Coast Main Line (WCML). The Board felt that the Regulator's insistence that Railtrack provide improvements for other operators was not only loosely specified but also appeared to encroach on OPRAF's domain. There was also concern that if the SRA assumed responsibility for consumer protection it would create a conflict of interest when value-for-money issues were raised.[70]

At the same time the Commons Select Committee threw its weight behind the proposed reform. The DETR had supplied it with initial thinking about the SRA's shape and scope, notably that it would assume some departmental and OPRAF responsibilities, and combine planning and administrative functions. Thus, it would develop a 'strategic vision' for rail investment, progress worthwhile projects and encourage modal integration, as well as managing existing franchise contracts, and awarding freight grants. In supporting the policy, the Committee set down its own expectations for the new body. It noted that one of the Authority's key roles would be to deal with the related questions of reletting franchises falling due from 2003, considering requests for franchise extensions, and dealing with franchises which had failed. But it went further in suggesting that the

---

[67] Tom Winsor (Denton Hall), 'Railway Industry Review. Report to BRB', 17 December 1997, esp. paras. 4.20–3, 4.31–41, AN18/1792; BRB Minutes, 4 December 1997, cit., 12 March 1998, AN167/64; Alan Nichols, Memo. to BRB, 7 May 1998, AN167/180, TNA. Nichols was Director of Policy, BRB; King was the former Group MD, North & West, BRB.

[68] BRB Minutes, 12 February 1998, AN167/64, TNA; Welsby, 'The Role of a Strategic Rail Authority', March 1998, DETR file R78/12/15 Pt. 1. Winsor's suggestion that the Regulator should be responsible for enforcing the franchise contracts was rejected: Winsor, 'Railway Industry Review. Report to BRB', December 1997, cit. and Nichols, Memo. to BRB, 12 March 1998, AN167/179, TNA.

[69] BRB Minutes, 9 April 1998, AN167/64, TNA.

[70] Ibid. 12 February, 9 April, and 7 May 1998; Welsby–Prescott, 25 February 1998, Griffins–Linnard, 2 March 1998, DETR file R78/1/22 Pt. 1.

Authority should monitor Railtrack's performance in maintaining and invest-ing in the infrastructure, and encourage investment in rolling stock to prevent another hiatus in orders. It also advocated a moratorium on surplus property sales by BRB, argued that the Rail Regulator should be given greater powers over the ROSCOs, and continued to fly the kite of a government stake in Railtrack.[71]

Prescott had introduced his ideas to the Chancellor, Gordon Brown, in Decem-ber 1997.[72] Then in the following May he met Blair for a detailed discussion of his proposals, which promised an investment of £1.8 billion in transport. The discussion centred on elements of the policy concerned with *roads* (plans for congestion charging and a levy on private non-residential parking), where the Prime Minister was anxious not to antagonize the business community. There was little or no debate about the railways, other than that usage would be affected by the intention to reduce dependency on the motor car.[73] The assumption must be that while scarcely a number one priority, the proposals for adjusting the railways' regulatory regime enjoyed a broad consensus of support. The Deputy Prime Minister's *New Deal for Transport* in July, though less specific on details, was very much in line with the view taken by the Select Committee. A new SRA, a 'statutory body with board members appointed by Ministers', would have 'appropriate powers to influence the behaviour of key industry players'. In a supporting press release Prescott promised an end to the lack of strategic planning, the fragmentation of services, and passengers 'very much in second place to profits'. Britain's railways would now 'be more effective and accountable', with a 'clear, coherent and strategic programme for future development of the network'.[74] Emphasis was placed on SRA's activities within an integrated transport system and new devolutionary structures for Scotland and Wales. There would be close liaison with the local authorities and PTEs, and with local and national planning organizations to ensure compatibility with land use planning policies and social and environmental objectives. The SRA would ensure integration with other modes of transport and take over the powers of the Franchising Director, together with the DETR's task of making freight grants in England. It would set more demanding performance standards for train operators in all new or renegotiated franchises, and the option of returning a franchise to public sector operation as a last resort was reaffirmed. The SRA would also set the 'longer term policy framework' for competition between train operators, where the Rail Regulator was committed to more liberalization from September 1999.[75] The new body would also assume prime responsibility for consumer protection, in place of the Rail Regulator, and sponsorship of the existing CRUCC

---

[71] HC Transport Committee Report on *Strategic Rail Authority*, paras. 120, 129–132, 136–7, 141, 144, and cf. DETR, Memo. October 1997, cit. para. 28.
[72] Prescott–Brown, 5 December 1997, DETR file R78/1/22 Pt. 1.
[73] Prescott–Blair, 20 May 1998, Prime Minister [Blair]'s papers on meetings with the DPM, Pt. 1.
[74] DETR, *New Deal for Transport*, paras. 4.12, 4.14; DETR News Release no. 601, 20 July 1998.
[75] *Financial Times*, 8 October 1997, p. 9, 1 April 1998, p. 20.

and RUCCs would pass from the Regulator to the SRA.[76] The White Paper made it clear that the Government would look to the SRA to encourage a 'clear, understandable national fare structure', although there was little that could be done immediately given the existing framework, since regulated fares (season tickets, savers) were subject to an RPI minus 1 per cent directive from the Franchising Director until 2003, while discretionary fares (unrestricted walk-on fares, APEX tickets, etc.) were unregulated and protected in the franchise agreements.[77]

Prescott was more cautious than the Select Committee in addressing the position of the Rail Regulator and, in fact, he followed advice from BRB.[78] The *New Deal for Transport* argued that the SRA should not be responsible for the government subsidy and at the same time set the access charges which consumed such a large part of it. Consequently, the Regulator would be reconstituted as an economic regulator whose primary responsibility was to set track and station access charges and oversee the investment required by the SRA. The Regulator would also continue to monitor Railtrack's delivery of investment and maintenance. In this context it was noted that the Regulator's powers had been strengthened by the licence modification of 1997, where the new Condition 7 created specific obligations to maintain, renew, and develop the network, and both regulators were examining the company's Network Management Statement of March 1998. Nevertheless, the Government accepted the Select Committee's view that the Regulator's forthcoming review of access charges, affecting charging from 2001, would be a critical one, agreed that a concordat between the Regulator and the ROSCOs was required to protect the public interest, and promised that the Regulator would be given a new duty to take account of the Government's broad policy objectives for the passenger and freight railway, embracing integrated transport and sustainable development. In order to promote additional rail investment the Franchising Director was to be provided with two new funds. The first, controlled by the SRA, would support strategic investment to help tackle network bottlenecks or 'pinch points'. The second would provide a Rail Passenger Partnership to encourage local and regional initiatives. Finally, Prescott accepted, albeit rather reluctantly, the Select Committee's suggestion that there should be a halt to the sale of British Rail land pending an audit, and promised to boost the take-up of freight grants.[79] Elsewhere in the document, supportive noises were made about the need to maintain safety standards, and decisions by the Health and Safety Commission, to ensure that Mark I (slam-door) carriages were withdrawn by 1 January 2003, and to accelerate its review of Railtrack's role in safety, were welcomed.[80]

---

[76] This was in accordance with a recommendation of the Select Committee.
[77] DETR, *New Deal for Transport*, paras. 2.38, 4.13–21.
[78] BRB Minutes, 7 May 1998, AN167/64, TNA.
[79] Ibid. paras. 4.22–37; DETR News Release, 20 July 1998.
[80] DETR, *New Deal for Transport*, paras. 3.241–6.

What did this package of reforms amount to? Wolmar has noted that the *New Deal for Transport* was strong on ideas, but 'short on firm commitments'.[81] As we have suggested, the support for public transport and the restraint of private motoring were not priorities in Number Ten. In relation to railways the Government, forced to work within the existing framework, wished to achieve a tightening up of control at all levels—Railtrack, TOCs, and ROSCOs. But the prospects for a rail authority, operating as a quasi-autonomous, executive non-departmental public body (NDPB), were more difficult to gauge. The SRA was being heralded at a time when there was concern about the efficiency of NDPBs, which had been fuelled in many ways by the shift in emphasis towards the establishment of executive 'next steps' agencies within Whitehall departments. Contemporaneous reports by the Cabinet Office in 1997–8 drew on the practice of reviewing next steps agencies to seek a much sharper focus on performance measurement for the NDPBs. Despite the latter's 'arm's-length' status, they were expected to become more 'efficient, transparent, and accountable', and there was clearly scope for improvement in both target-setting and performance against target.[82] But whatever the chosen organizational form, to inject a new body into an already crowded railway industry was challenging, to say the least, given the evidence provided by both the Select Committee and the White Paper that it would not be possible to resolve all the overlapping responsibilities inherent in the system of dual regulation. The aims and objectives of the new body had been specified, but exactly how it would operate in relation to its sponsoring department and the Rail Regulator had not been worked out. It was difficult to see how, for example, the subsidy and investment funding functions could be handled without intervention from the DETR, and it was also far from clear whether the SRA would be able to live up to its name and impose its authority over established institutions such as Railtrack. In this situation, much would depend on the players involved: at Eland House in Victoria, Prescott and a succession of junior ministers, Strang giving way to John Reid, then Helen Liddell, then Lord [Gus] Macdonald in the period July 1997 to July 1999; Sir Andrew Turnbull, Permanent Secretary, then shortly after, on Turnbull's departure for the Treasury, Sir Richard Mottram, formerly Permanent Secretary of the MOD. Within the expanded Department, railways stayed at Great Minster House in Marsham Street, with David Rowlands as Director General for Railways, Aviation & Shipping, and Roy Griffins as Director (Railways). Following a further reorganization there were four railway divisions: International and General, led by Peter Thomas; Railways Sponsorship (Bob Linnard); Railway Economics & Finance (Philip Cox); and Channel Tunnel & Rail Link (Mike Fuhr).[83] Prescott's personal

---

[81] Wolmar, *On the Wrong Line*, p. 124.
[82] Cabinet Office, *Executive Non-Departmental Public Bodies 1998 Report*, December 1998, P.P. 1998–9, xcviii, Cm. 4157, and cf. earlier reports, CO, *NDPB Policy: Developing a New Approach* (April 1990), and CO and Treasury, 'Non-Departmental Public Bodies: A Guide for Departments', 1992.
[83] *Civil Service Yearbook 1998/99.*

standing presented another area of doubt. He certainly provided continuity in office at transport, something that was in itself rare,[84] but was often portrayed as a rather comic figure by the media. The roads lobby attacked him for mounting proposals for road pricing and car parking taxation while retaining the use of two Jaguar cars, and the 'two jags' jibe was in wide currency by the time the White Paper was published.[85]

Finally, the decision to shape a new authority by building on OPRAF and what was left of British Rail begged the question as to whether OPRAF in particular had developed in a satisfactory manner. A commissioned study of the developing organization and culture in OPRAF over the period 1993–6 provided pointers to the tensions that might lie ahead. Established as an NDPB rather than as an executive agency, the new Office made much of the fact that it had been set 'an impossible task to an impossible timetable' in 1993, and that its performance in letting franchises, while behind schedule, had, in the circumstances, been commendable. However, for our purposes, we should note that the creation of OPRAF as a rather fluid organization with a 'somewhat flat hierarchy' under Roger Salmon had received a mixed reception from the industry. Dismissed by some as 'a bit of a shambles', its developing ethos, while espousing the notion of public service, differed from the more disciplined approach of British Rail and much of Whitehall. Salmon himself had had no experience of railways, and little of management; his contacts with Ministers and senior civil servants were often grudging and brusque. The move from Marsham Street to Old Queen Street, near St. James's Park, symbolized this arm's-length stance. Relationships improved in 1995 after a report from Christopher Clarke of Samuel Montague, jointly commissioned by Salmon and Patrick Brown, Permanent Secretary at Transport, recommended organizational changes and sought to establish effective boundaries between the Department and its NDPB. Key roles were given to ex-railwayman Chris Stokes, who became Deputy Franchising Director, and O'Brien, a deal-making accountant from Granada Group, who became Operations Director (and subsequently Chief Operating Officer). After Salmon was replaced by O'Brien, and franchise sales were completed, there was a new emphasis on monitoring and regulation, instead of merchant banking functions. Nevertheless, it did seem likely that the legacy of OPRAF's developing experience as a semi-independent organization would perpetuate difficulties with its parent, the DETR, in the successor body.[86]

However, in the summer of 1998, this seemed some distance away. Legislation was required to create a new statutory body, along with the promised changes in

[84] Prescott held the transport brief until June 2001, his four-year stint being the longest since that of Ernest Marples (1959–64).

[85] Cf. *Daily Mail*, 5 February 1998, p. 15; *Financial Times*, 21 July 1998, p. 19, *Economist*, 25 July 1998, p. 54.

[86] Susan Hoyle, 'Organising OPRAF: Organisation and Culture in the Early Years of the Office of Passenger Rail Franchising 1993–96', 30 September 1996, pp. 1–4, 6–7, 9–14; Gourvish, *British Rail 1974–97*, pp. 423, 440; Interviews with O'Brien, 2006, and Nick Newton, 14 September 2006.

road pricing, and it quickly emerged that Prescott would not be able to include a transport bill in the crowded 1998–9 parliamentary session.[87] In December the Government's Comprehensive Spending Review had produced a public service agreement for the DETR which *inter alia* set it a target of increasing passenger-miles travelled by rail by 15 per cent by 2001/2 (over 1997/8), and of establishing a strategic rail authority by 2000–1, with a shadow body in place by spring 1999.[88] Clearly, some ingenuity was required if the institutional arrangements were to be brought forward.

[87] *Times*, 31 August 1998, p. 4, 9 September 1998, p. 2.
[88] Treasury, *Public Services for the Future: Modernisation, Reform, Accountability. Comprehensive Spending Review: Public Service Agreements, 1999–2002*, December 1998, P.P. 1998–9, ci, Cm. 4181, p. 28.

Labour's Vision

The Strategic Rail Authority and a 10 Year Plan, 1998–2000

2.1 Creating the Shadow Strategic Rail Authority, 1998–9

As thoughts turned to the means by which a shadow SRA could be constructed, it was soon evident that the change of direction was to be accompanied by a change in strategic personnel. Swift, O'Brien, and Welsby were, in the words of a No. 10 adviser, to be 'culled'. On 14 September 1998 Prescott informed Blair that he proposed to announce that he was ready: (*a*) to renegotiate franchises where this would offer real benefits to passengers as well as value for money; (*b*) to create a shadow SRA; and (*c*) to take the opportunity presented by the expiry of the contracts of the Rail Regulator, Franchising Director, and Chairman, British Railways Board, to 'put new people in these key jobs, emphasizing my determination to change the way the railway operates and to mesh OPRAF and BR together'.[1] There had been some dissatisfaction in Whitehall with all of the incumbents, although the Treasury had been happiest with O'Brien and OPRAF, and was keen to see the SRA built round OPRAF rather than round the rump of the British Railways Board.[2] Nevertheless, Prescott called in all three in September to

[1] Prescott–Blair, 14 September 1998, Prime Minister [Blair]'s papers on Rail Policy, Pt. 3. Blair expressed doubts about 'sacking people who are doing a good job': annotation, ibid.
[2] Jeremy Heywood (Blair's PPS), Note on file, undated, ibid.; BRB Minutes, 5 November 1998, AN167/64, TNA.

1. John Prescott announces purge of the Rail Regulators and expectations of the
Shadow Strategic Rail Authority, at the Labour party conference in Blackpool,
September 1998: Steve Bell, *Guardian*, 1 October 1998.

inform them that their appointments would cease.[3] This action was not as drastic
as it might appear. Welsby's contract was terminable on six months' notice, while
the appointments of Swift and O'Brien were due to end in November 1998 and
November 1999, respectively. The intention was that a new, part-time, Chairman
of British Rail would become Chairman of the SRA, and that a new Franchising
Director would become its Chief Executive. A reconstituted BRB would in time
become the SRA Board. Prescott hoped to have the new recruits in place by
April 1999, which would require the appointment of an interim Rail Regulator.[4]
Prescott announced his intentions at the Labour Party conference in Blackpool
on 30 September, an event marked by serious interruptions to the West Coast
rail service provided by Richard Branson's Virgin Trains, coming on top of an
observed deterioration in overall operating performance in 1997/8. Heading off
a motion from the RMT union to renationalize the railways, the Secretary of
State promised that he was 'switching the points . . . away from poor punctuality
and reliability, overcrowding and inadequate rolling stock towards a modern,

---

[3] Meetings, 21 September 1998, reported in DETR file R78/1/22 Pt. 2.

[4] Prescott–Blair, 14 September 1998, cit.; Morton, File Note, 23 September 1998, Sir Alastair Morton's
papers, SRA; OPRAF, statement from John O'Brien, 30 September 1998, www.sra.gov.uk/news/1998/9.

efficient, top-class service for the 21st century'.[5] However, by this time Swift had already tendered his resignation, being succeeded as Regulator by his chief economist, Chris Bolt, with effect from 1 December.[6] The removal of Swift, who had wished to stay on for a further two years to complete the first periodic review of Railtrack's access charges, had been a more public affair. Prescott's exasperation with the Rail Regulator had been rehearsed in the press on a number of occasions. He had been criticized for not flexing his muscles enough, the Department having been apparently unhappy when in November 1997 he bowed to pressure from the Association of Train Operating Companies (ATOC) and abandoned plans to name the operators who were giving inadequate information to passengers. More importantly, he had advocated a softer line in relation to the ROSCOs in his May 1998 report, where his preference for a code of conduct had met with a lukewarm response from Eland House.[7] The emergence of Tom Winsor as a front runner to replace him was also public knowledge several months before the appointment was made.[8] But the Franchising Director did not escape rebuke either, having been criticized for failing to impose sufficiently punitive fines on poor operators. Then, in March 1998, when FirstGroup announced its intention to take over Great Western (in which it already had a 24.5% stake), Prescott made it very clear that he expected O'Brien to extract passenger benefits in approving the change of franchise control.[9] In fact, the initiative for the move came from O'Brien.[10]

Prescott's frustrations, exacerbated by the difficulties he was experiencing in getting a slot for a railway bill in the new session,[11] spilled over in a theatrically acrimonious three-hour meeting with industry leaders on 26 November 1998. Prescott, accompanied by Reid, had called in representatives to respond to evidence of deteriorating operating performance, and in particular, a decline in punctuality, exacerbated by the autumnal leaf fall and flooding.[12] By this time there

---

[5] ORR, review of the rolling stock market: report to the Deputy Prime Minister (15 May 1998), ORR, *Annual Report 1997/8*, paras. 1.9–13, 6.6–7; *Independent*, 1 October 1998, p. 7; *Daily Mirror*, 1 October 1999, p. 2; *Times*, 1 October 1998, p. 14.

[6] Interview with Chris Bolt, 25 January 2007.

[7] *Times*, 6 November 1997, p. 2, 22 January 1998, p. 25, 26 May 1998, p. 45; *Guardian*, 7 November 1997, p. 23.

[8] *Sunday Times*, 20 September 1998, business p. 1, 27 September 1998, p. 9 and business p. 2; *Times*, 21 September 1998, p. 6. Other candidates for the post of Rail Regulator were reported to be James Jerram (BRB), Prof. David Begg (Robert Gordon Univ. Aberdeen, and BRB), and Philip Wood (DETR).

[9] Cf. *Times*, 6 March 1998, p. 35. O'Brien reported that c. £75 m. in passenger benefits had been secured over the three FirstGroup franchises: OPRAF, *Annual Report 1997/8*, pp. 5, 21–2. Passenger benefits were also enhanced when Go-Ahead acquired the management's shares in Victory Railways, operator of the Thames Trains franchise: ibid. and see also DETR file R73/2/2 Pts. 1–2.

[10] Interview with O'Brien, 2006.

[11] In December 1998 Prescott had obtained a promise that time might be found for a railway bill if agreement on handling House of Lords reform were reached. Ultimately, however, he was disappointed. Cf. Prescott–Margaret Beckett (Leader of Commons), 25 March 1999, Beckett–Prescott, 1 July 1999, Prime Minister's Rail Policy papers, Pts. 3–4.

[12] Cf. Gerald Corbett (Chief Executive, Railtrack)–Linnard, 9 December 1998, DETR file R73/1/22 Pt. 1.

was a widespread belief that standards were slipping. The media drew attention to the juxtaposition of escalating fines for franchise breaches and increases in TOC profits. Earlier in the year the *Times*, reporting that Go-Ahead's Thames Trains had been fined for short-length trains and punctuality breaches, had noted that the company's pre-tax profits for the half-year had more than doubled. In the summer FirstGroup's North Western franchise, inherited from Great Western, had attracted negative publicity for the shortcomings of its Greater Manchester services, which culminated in a five-day suspension of its Oldham Loop trains. [13] However, the immediate context for the meeting was the publication of the CRUCC's annual report for 1997/8. Using the Passenger Charter data published by OPRAF, the passenger watchdog asserted that service quality had 'plummeted' in comparison with the previous year. The standpoint of the Committee's Chairman, David Bertram, was more critical than that adopted by O'Brien, the Franchising Director. For example, there was a strong suggestion that punctuality, which had fallen on 35 of 53 service routes, had been affected by an overzealous pruning of drivers, and much was made of the fact that passenger complaints had doubled since the previous year. Some of the increase was clearly socially constructed in that it was now much easier for passengers to register complaints. But the watchdog found a strong correlation between declining quality and the number of complaints. [14] The operators replied with the claim that public expectations were rising, and suggested that some of their problems stemmed from an increase in patronage, with passenger mileage up by 7 per cent in 1997/8, and an increase in the number of services—indeed, in the case of Thames Trains additional services had been negotiated by the Franchising Director when approving Go-Ahead's takeover. [15] However, these arguments fell on deaf ministerial ears at the meeting. Prescott and Reid expressed their dissatisfaction with the emergence of a 'blame culture', where the TOCs and Railtrack were apparently attacking each other for service delivery problems. They threatened to introduce a tougher monitoring regime, which would be broadened to include general standards, such as the level of overcrowding, train cleanliness, and catering. On the other hand, the carrot of longer franchises was also dangled in front of operators, especially for the seven-year franchises due to expire in 2003/4. Longer agreements might be offered in return for improved service specifications and a greater investment in trains, an idea which owed its origin to a paper prepared by Paul King of BRB in 1998. [16] Industry representatives responded by undertaking to deliver a 10-point programme of measures over the next 12 months, and specifically to: recruit 800 new drivers; introduce 500 new vehicles; create a national punctuality task force

[13] *Times*, 28 February 1998, p. 29, 30 July 1998, p. 25, 29 September 1998, p. 29; OPRAF, *Annual Report 1998/9*, pp. 29, 85.
[14] CRUCC, *Annual Report 1997/8*, pp. 36–43, 47–8; OPRAF, *Annual Report 1997/8*, pp. 4, 7 and Appendix 2. The CRUCC, which conceded that 'much useful progress' had been made, was more measured in tone than the media reporting. Cf. *Times*, 27 August 1998, pp. 11, 19.
[15] OPRAF, *Annual Report 1997/8*, p. 71.   [16] BRB Minutes, 12 February 1998, AN167/64, TNA.

to look at 50 of the worst network bottlenecks; and raise standards year-on-year. A national rail summit was to be convened in February 1999 to elicit evidence of improvement and expose the industry to critical public comment. Some of the promises were scarcely earthshattering, and were due to happen anyway. But they could be taken as evidence of a new resolve to tackle problems in a more cooperative fashion.[17] Further evidence was provided by the regulators, who anticipated the transfer of responsibility for consumer benefits to the SRA by setting up a consumer benefits group to iron out areas of duplication and ease the process of transition.[18]

In the meantime there was some debate about how the promised SRA should be set up. In December 1998 Blair's PPS, Jeremy Heywood, suggested to Geoffrey Norris, transport specialist in the No. 10 Policy Unit, that Blair be briefed on Prescott's proposals for the SRA. At this stage there was still a possibility that a Bill might be squeezed into the current parliamentary session, though the idea was eventually dropped. There were evidently critics of the Prescott plan to build the new body around BRB and OPRAF, while retaining the essentials of the existing regulatory regime. Heywood had been advised informally by an 'industry expert' that the 'key flaw' in the existing arrangements was that neither Railtrack nor the TOCs had any real incentive to expand the business, since the government subsidy did not carry with it a traffic-related element. Instead of giving the SRA power to direct Railtrack investment, the Government should alter the subsidy regime to give both Railtrack and the TOCs a 'clear incentive' to increase rail traffic, whether by improving capacity, increasing train lengths, or enhancing reliability. The additional sums paid out would be offset by post-2001 savings derived from the Rail Regulator's revision of the access charges levied by Railtrack.[19] The idea, which was reminiscent of Michael Posner's notion of passenger-miles maximization in 1980,[20] was passed on to the DETR, but its response was negative. Chris Wood, PS to Richard Caborn, Minister for the Regions, pointed out that the anticipated Bill could not reopen the contractual framework underpinning the industry. The TOCs' operational commitments were specified in their franchise agreements, and the Bill could not impose a more onerous regime. But Railtrack had argued that the existing 'economic architecture' had established perverse incentives and was affecting operating performance, the TOCs being encouraged to increase usage rather than improve standards, and Railtrack not having sufficient incentive to invest because

[17] Prescott–Blair, 18 March 1999, Prime Minister's Rail Policy papers, Pt. 3; DETR News Releases, 24 and 26 November 1998; OPRAF, *Annual Report 1997/8*, p. 12; *Times*, 26 November 1998, p. 2, 27 November 1998, p. 2; *Financial Times*, 26 November 1998, p. 11, 27 November 1998, p. 10; *Daily Mail*, 27 November 1998, p. 19.

[18] ORR, *Annual Report 1998/9*, pp. 4–5, 15.

[19] Heywood–Norris, 14 December 1998, Prime Minister's Rail Policy papers, Pt. 3. The industry expert was not identified, but on the incentives established by the 'initial architecture' see Dieter Helm, 'A Critique of Rail Regulation', in Colin Robinson (ed.), *Utility Regulation and Competition Policy* (Cheltenham, 2002), p. 21.

[20] Gourvish, *British Rail 1974–97*, pp. 173, 510. Posner was a part-time member of BRB, 1977–84.

much of its income was fixed.[21] Here, the Rail Regulator and Franchising Director were currently reviewing the procedures to see if this could be addressed, for example in the forthcoming revision of access charges, but any action would have to lie outside the confines of the Bill.[22] The exchange was important because it indicated the limited parameters within which reform could be mounted. There was evidently frustration with both Railtrack's investment and the TOCs' operating performance. But neither could be tackled easily, and managers struggling with the day-to-day challenges of railway operating were only irritated when government frustration spilled over into the kind of crude condemnation which Prescott often exhibited.

The first national rail summit was held at the QE2 Centre in Westminster on 25 February 1999. In addition to receiving a progress report on the package of practical measures agreed in November, the intention was to allow the Government a platform to announce its longer term vision for the railways, highlight any positive steps it was contemplating to improve train operating performance, and introduce its appointed SRA messiah. Consequently, the Prime Minister, who wished to focus on service delivery in transport in addition to education and health, was asked to open the proceedings.[23] Of course, the event was carefully orchestrated, and consequently the media at first dismissed it as a 'stage-managed slap on the wrists' for the industry, to be attended by 'Whitehall sherpas, nominated industry scapegoats, carefully selected representatives of the public and regulators with an uncertain future'.[24] The outcome was more positive than this implied, however. The audience of about 150 people was addressed by clear heavyweights. The Government was represented by Blair, Prescott, Reid, and Glenda Jackson, Minister for Transport in London, while the railway representatives included Gerald Corbett, Railtrack's Chief Executive, Richard Brown of National Express, Christopher Garnett of GNER, and Ian Braybrook of EWS. Blair opened the proceedings by conceding that the railways' deteriorating performance had been affected by the rise in passenger numbers and more services. However, he also blamed 'mistakes and poor management', and in particular 'getting rid of too many drivers and other staff', unreliable rolling stock and infrastructural defects. The 'curse of a fragmented and incoherent industry' would be addressed by the SRA, he announced, a body to be established in shadow form pending legislation. However, more was needed. The industry had to improve its performance and act in a more customer-focused way.[25] Prescott

[21] Railtrack, 'Improving Train Performance—The Required Changes', 5 November 1998, Morton's papers, SRA.

[22] Chris Wood (Richard Caborn's PS)–Rob Read (Blair's PS, Parliamentary Affairs), December 1998, Prime Minister's Rail Policy papers, Pt. 3. One idea was to distinguish between RT's minimum investment, and additional investment, the latter to be rewarded by a risk premium.

[23] Kirstin Clark (Prescott's PS)–Read, 28 January 1999, Prime Minister's Rail Policy papers, Pt. 3, Milton–Rowlands et al., 1 February 1999, DETR file R73/1/22 Pt. 2 and see also R78/1/14 Pt. 2.

[24] *Times*, 22 February 1999, p. 44 (quoting a 'city analyst'), and 23 February 1999, p. 29.

[25] Blair, speech to rail summit, 25 February 1999, DETR file R73/1/22 Pt. 3, and see also Roger Ford, *Modern Railways*, April 1999, p. 227.

2. Government ministers castigate the railway industry for poor performance at the first national rail summit, February 1999: Paul Thomas, *Express*, 26 February 1999.

and Reid announced that the Government was prepared to renegotiate some of the existing franchises, set out the passenger benefit criteria to be satisfied, and undertook to issue OPRAF with new instructions on how to take the process forward. They also launched a National Passenger Survey, and two consultation exercises: the first to assist OPRAF in finding an operating performance measure superior to the existing Passenger's Charter, and the second intended to contribute to the SRA's first strategic plan. Finally, they continued to press the ROSCOs to 'restrict their market power', though they were soon persuaded to accept that a code of conduct would be sufficient regulation.[26] For its part the industry undertook to improve punctuality; secure a reduction in real fare levels; invest in 2,300 new vehicles so that by 2002 half of the fleet would be either new or refurbished; provide information systems at all stations by April 2000; and spend an additional £39 million on passenger security.[27] There was plenty to improve, of course, and the public part of the summit was not exactly cordial.[28] In fact, a TOC performance table for the calendar year 1998,

[26] Both OPRAF and the ORR favoured a code of conduct: DETR-SSRA/OPRAF officials meetings, 29 April, 13 and 27 May 1999, DETR file R73/1/7 Pt. 1. The summit speeches are in R73/1/22 Pt. 3.

[27] Prescott–Blair, 18 March 1999, ibid.; DETR News Releases, Nos. 171, 174, 25 February 1999; OPRAF, *Annual Report 1998/9*, pp. 12–13; *Parl. Deb. (Commons)*, 6th ser. (Session 1998–9), Vol. 326, Reid, written answer to Bernard Jenkin, 3 March 1999, c. w739–40.

[28] Cf. Nigel Harris, *Rail*, 10–23 March 1999, p. 71.

Table 2.1 TOCs' performance ranking table, 1998

Train operator	Franchisee	Punctuality (%)	Grade	Reliability	Grade	Chartered trains per 4-week period
Category A						
Island Line	Stagecoach	95.0	A	99.6	A	1,711
Category B						
ScotRail	National Express	95.9	A	99.4	B	44,203
Merseyrail	MTL	95.3	A	99.2	B	13,274
Central	National Express	93.1	B	99.5	A	11,036
Anglia	Railways	92.0	B	99.5	A	5,626
WAGN	Prism	91.2	B	99.1	B	18,691
Great Eastern	FirstGroup	90.8	B	99.6	A	14,746
Gatwick Express	National Express	90.1	B	99.6	A	4,415
Category C (10 franchises, not listed)						
Category D						
North Western	FirstGroup	90.9	B	98.2	D	35,426
Cardiff	Prism	86.3	C	98.1	D	7,050
Great Western	FirstGroup	84.5	D	99.0	B	3,311
Connex SE	Connex (Vivendi)	83.8	D	98.7	C	32,407
Thames	Go-Ahead	83.7	D	98.6	C	15,459
Cross Country	Virgin	82.3	D	99.3	B	2,233
Category E						
Silverlink	National Express	91.2	B	97.9	E	10,966

Source: Table of data provided at First National Rail Summit, 25 February 1999.

Note: Grades:
	Punctuality	Reliability
A:	95.0–100%	99.5–100%
B:	90.0–94.9%	99.0–99.4%
C:	85.0–89.9%	98.5–98.9%
D:	80.0–84.9%	98.0–98.4%
E:	79.9% and less	97.9% and less

produced by OPRAF a fortnight before the summit and ranking punctuality and reliability on a scale A–E, revealed that only one franchise had managed an A grade in both categories: the small-scale, uncomplicated Island Line (Isle of Wight), let to Stagecoach in October 1996 for only five years. Seven franchises were ranked in category B, but at the bottom disappointing results were evident in two of FirstGroup's three franchises and Virgin Rail's Cross Country (B + D), Prism's Cardiff franchise, Connex SouthEastern, and Go-Ahead's Thames Trains (C + D), and Silverlink (B + E) (Table 2.1). Commenting, Prescott said: 'In the final analysis I am prepared for the SRA to act as operator of last resort...I am not about to lift pressure to perform...there must be value for money for the public and substantial benefits for passengers in any extended franchise.'[29]

Prescott also took the opportunity to introduce Sir Alastair Morton to the industry as the new half-time Chairman of the British Railways Board, with a salary of £130,000, and prospective Chairman of the Strategic Rail Authority. The appointment, which had been announced on the day before the summit, had not been without its difficulties. The DETR had pointed out that there was a potential conflict of interest given Morton's holding of some 100,000 Eurotunnel shares, but understandably, and for emotional rather than financial reasons, he was unwilling to sell his holding, and he made the valid point that until his appointment as Chairman of the SRA had been confirmed by legislation, it was premature for him to do so. The only credible alternative to Morton seems to have been John Prideaux, but the substantial capital gain he had made on the sale of the Angel Trains ROSCO to the Royal Bank of Scotland in December 1997 would have made it difficult to defend the appointment, to say the least. Consequently, the Government decided to go ahead with Morton and leave the issue of his shareholding until the SRA was formally constituted.[30] His appointment, for three years from 1 April 1999, was slightly puzzling. Aged 61, Sir Alastair was essentially a corporate strategist and rationalizer (particularly evident when he was Chief Executive of Guinness Peat in the 1980s), but he had gained a reputation as a project-driver when Co-Chairman of Eurotunnel, 1987–96 (and Chief Executive, 1990–4). There was clearly a need for an authority figure, or as the DETR News Release put it, a 'high-profile champion' for rail users. Morton had certainly been a business rottweiler—at Eurotunnel he had exhibited enthusiasm, persistence, aggression, and volatility in equal amounts—but by 1999 he was a somewhat wounded one, having suffered health problems. In his own words, he was in his 'creaky sixties, rather than supple early forties'. More significantly, at Eurotunnel he had been no respecter of governments or the ways of Whitehall, and his numerous claims for compensation had not endeared him either to ministers or to civil servants. Nor had old hands at BRB forgotten the intense battles they had had with him when negotiating the Usage Contract for Channel Tunnel trains in 1986–7. Here, then, there was an element of risk, though it was mitigated by the knowledge that Morton had performed valuable service for the Government in heading a group to advance the Private Finance Initiative, and had also advised Prescott on matters relating

[29] DETR News Release, No. 174, 25 February 1999.

[30] DETR News Release, 24 February 1999; HC Public Accounts Committee, MOE, 3 June 1998, Prideaux, Q. 136 ff.; Peter Unwin (Prescott's PPS)–Heywood, 24 February 1999, Prime Minister's Rail Policy papers, Pt. 3. On Morton's potential conflict of interest see also Sonia Phippard (Deputy Director, Machinery of Govt Divn, CO)–Anita Bharucha, 18 February 1999, Prescott–Blair, 22 February 1999, Read–Unwin, 24 February 1999, ibid.; David Rowlands (DG Railways, Aviation & Shipping, DETR)–Prescott, 19 February 1999, Morton–Prescott, 22 February 1999, DETR file R78/1/30 Pt. 1.

to the Channel Tunnel Rail Link when the project was bailed out in June 1998. Also regarded as 'city friendly', he was expected to push as hard for a 'substantial and coherent investment' in railways as he had for Tunnel investment.[31] Morton thought the SRA should be 'a small team...existing on the boundary of the interface between the public and private sector'.[32] He wanted it staffed by 'highly competent people rather than [being] cobbled together from grudgingly-seconded civil servants and padded out with a large number of lower-level functionaries'.[33]

Press reaction both to the summit and to the news of Morton's appointment was generally favourable. It was followed by the announcement in March of the appointment of Tom Winsor as the new Rail Regulator. Winsor, who was relatively young (41), had begun his career in Scotland before joining Norton Rose in 1984. He then became a partner at Denton Hall in 1991, where he worked on the privatization of the Northern Ireland electricity industry. In 1993–5 he had been seconded to the Office of the Rail Regulator (ORR) as chief legal adviser. He had advised Short at the time of Railtrack's flotation, and Prescott after the 1997 election. Advice had also been given to the TOCs, including Virgin Rail, and to BRB.[34] Said to be 'railway mad', he enjoyed Prescott and Morton's vote over the incumbent, Chris Bolt, because he promised to deliver 'dynamism' and a 'tough-minded approach'. His appointment from 5 July at a salary of £165,000 meant that he had agreed to take a significant reduction in his earnings. Something of an unknown quantity, he was to prove every bit as tenacious as Morton, and certainly no accommodating agent of the Government, although whether this was anticipated in March 1999 is not clear.[35] The *Times* asserted that the railway industry now had two heavy hitters in Morton and Winsor,[36] but as the examples of Richard Beeching (BRB) and Christopher Hinton (CEGB) had demonstrated in the past, there was always a degree of risk in recruiting outsiders to carry out high-profile political tasks.[37] The new recruits were undoubtedly talented people with a broader experience in commerce and the law, but it remained to

[31] DETR News Release, cit.; Morton, draft article, 13 August 2001 (subsequently published as 'Fortress Whitehall Comes Off the Rails', *Spectator*, 6 October 2001), Morton's papers, SRA; Terry Gourvish, *The Official History of Britain and the Channel Tunnel* (Abington, 2006), p. 292 ff.; *Times*, 22 February 1999, p. 44, 25 February 1999, p. 30; *Guardian*, 3 September 2004, p. 31; *Observer*, 28 November 2004, business, p. 11.

[32] Dr John Reid (Minister for Transport)–Prescott, 15 February 1999, DETR file R78/1/30 Pt. 1.

[33] Sir Alastair Morton–Sir Richard Mottram (Permanent Secretary, DETR), 5 January 1999, ibid.

[34] Interviews with Winsor, Prescott, and Swift, 2006. On advice to BRB see Winsor, 'Railway Industry Review. Report to BRB', December 1997, cit. Winsor also sent a copy of his report to the DETR: DETR file R78/1/15 Pt. 1.

[35] DETR News Release, 23 March 1999; Prescott–Blair, 23 March 1999, Prime Minister's Rail Policy papers, Pt. 3; Morton–Rowlands, 9 March 1999, DETR file R78/1/30 Pt. 1; *Times*, 24 March 1999, p. 25.

[36] *Times*, 27 March 1999, p. 31.

[37] Terry Gourvish, *British Railways 1948–73: A Business History* (Cambridge, 1986), pp. 322–6; Leslie Hannah, *Engineers, Managers and Politicians. The First Fifteen Years of Nationalised Electricity Supply in Britain* (1982), pp. 186–90. Some DETR officials expressed concerns about the choice of Morton and Winsor: Interview with Sir Richard Mottram, 21 June 2007.

be seen how they would cope with the exigencies of the political landscape, its timescales and parliamentary accountability, which of course make it difficult for responsible ministers to give someone a job and merely let them get on with it. The third appointee was less well known. In April the DETR announced that Mike Grant would become Franchising Director on 1 May, with the same salary as Winsor's. Briefly Deputy Director of Property at Railtrack, he had been Director of Corporate Finance and Group Treasurer of Eurotunnel, 1987–98, where he had worked closely with Morton. A down-to-earth Liverpudlian with a railway civil engineering background, he had had experience of both the DOE and the BRB before retraining as a finance man.[38] Nevertheless his past relationship with Morton caused the *Financial Times* to ask, rather impishly, whether the stewardship of the railways would be safe in the hands of men who had run up a corporate debt of £9 billion at Eurotunnel.[39]

2.2 Morton's Shadow Strategic Rail Authority: strategy and structure, 1999–2000

The Shadow Strategic Rail Authority (SSRA)—dubbed 'sSRA' in its first annual report—began operating in the summer of 1999. It had a rather schizophrenic existence at first, with 10 or so of the 168 remaining staff at BRB moving to Old Queen Street, St. James's Park, while most of the 140-strong OPRAF staff remained across the river at Golding's House, Hay's Lane, near London Bridge. Coordination, if not comfort, improved when the two came together at 55 Victoria Street in April 2000, by which time staff numbers had increased to 250 (28 BRB, 222 OPRAF).[40] At Board level, the Authority began life with only two executive members—Morton, and James Jerram, the Vice-Chairman of BRB, who stayed on until the end of the 'shadow' period. The position of Mike Grant was initially somewhat imprecise. Appointed for five years as the Franchising Director of OPRAF and Chief Executive designate of the SRA, he could only have a non-executive status on the BRB/SSRA Board, although he clearly discharged executive functions, and was referred to as 'Chief Executive of the SSRA' (Table 2.2). At non-executive level some of the BRB members who had been advising the DETR moved over to the SSRA, but only one—Professor David Begg, whom Prescott had appointed to lead the Commission on Integrated Transport, stayed for any length of time. And with the early disappearance of

---

[38] Prescott–Blair, 1 April 1999, Prime Minister's Rail Policy papers, Pt. 4; DETR News Release, 7 April 1999; *Times*, 7 April 1999, p. 23; Interview with Mike Grant, 9 August 2006.

[39] *Financial Times*, 8 April 1999, p. 27.

[40] Staffing as at 31 March 2000: SSRA, *Annual Report 1999/2000*, p. 15. Increased numbers required the additional use of 25 Victoria St.

Table 2.2 The British Railways Board and Shadow Strategic Rail Authority, August 1998–August 1999

BRB	Age[a]	Salary[b] (£'000)	Appointed	Resigned	BRB/SSRA	Age[a]	Salary[b] (£'000)	Appointed	Resigned
Executive members									
John Welsby (Chairman, part-time)	59	96	October 1996	March 1999	Sir Alastair Morton (Chairman, half-time)	61	130	April 1999	January 2001[c]
James Jerram (Vice-Chairman)	59	102	October 1996	—	James Jerram (Vice-Chairman)	59	106	—	December 2000
Tony Roche	55	147	April 1996	August 1998					
Paul Watkinson	58	137	October 1994	January 1999					
Part-time (non-executive) members									
Prof. David Begg	42	9	December 1997	—	Prof. David Begg	42	9	—	January 2001[c]
Kazia Kantor	49	9	June 1987	—	Kazia Kantor	49	9	—	June 1999
John Hughes	72	9	December 1997	—	John Hughes	72	9	—	May 1999
Ron Kennedy	63	9	December 1997	—	Ron Kennedy	63	9	—	May 1999

(cont.)

35

Table 2.2 (continued)

BRB	Age[a]	Salary[b] (£'000)	Appointed	Resigned
Nicholas Wakefield	n.a.	9	December 1997	November 1998

BRB/SSRA	Age[a]	Salary[b] (£'000)	Appointed	Resigned
Lew Adams	59	9	July 1999	January 2001[c]
Lord (Bill) Bradshaw	62	9	July 1999	January 2001[c]
Michael Grant (FD, OPRAF, Chief Executive, SSRA)	45	165	May 1999	January 2001[c]
David Jefferies	65	9	August 1999	January 2001[c]
Pen Kent	61	9	August 1999	January 2001[c]
David Quarmby	57	9	July 1999	January 2001[c]

Board officers

Peter Trewin (Secretary)
Terence Jenner (Solicitor)

Source: BRB and SSRA, R&A.
[a] At 1 April 1999.
[b] BRB: last annual recorded (excluding bonuses); SSRA: annual on appointment.
[c] SRA established 1 February 2001.

3. Morton's SSRA Board, on the visit of Lord 'Gus' Macdonald, Minister for Transport, to Old Queen Street, 9 September 1999 (SRA). Left to right: Mike Grant, James Jerram (standing), David Begg (sitting), Pen Kent, David Jefferies, Lord Macdonald, Lord 'Bill' Bradshaw (standing), Lew Adams, David Quarmby, Sir Alastair Morton.

Kazia Kantor, John Hughes, and Ron Kennedy, there was an urgent need for new blood. Consequently, five members were appointed in July and August 1999 (Table 2.2), and a further seven in May 2000 (Table 2.3). The first group were Morton nominees, bringing the authority much-needed expertise in the fields of transport, utility, and financial management: Lew Adams, former General Secretary of ASLEF; Bill Bradshaw, a career railwayman and former General Manager of British Rail's Western Region in the early 1980s; David Jefferies, former Chairman of London Electricity and National Grid; Pen Kent, a former Director of the Bank of England; and David Quarmby, Chairman of the British Tourist Authority and the Docklands Light Railway and a member of Transport for London.[41]

The second group were less well-known, but reflected the Department's determination to achieve more representative appointments to public office (under the Nolan rules), as well as satisfying commitments in the Transport Bill to include

[41] Griffins–Prescott, 29 April 1999, Griffins–Peter Thomas (Divn Manager, Railways Int. & General, DETR), 5 May 1999, DETR file R78/1/30 Pt. 2. Lew Adams was not a direct nominee but was welcomed by Morton: Morton–Prescott, 19 April 1999, R81/1/2 Pt. 2. For reservations expressed by Helen Liddell, briefly the Transport Minister, about Jefferies and Kent see Liddell–Prescott, 29 June and 28 July 1999, ibid.

Table 2.3 Non-executive membership of the SSRA, 1999–2000

Name	Appointed	Age on appointment	Background
Lew Adams	July 1999	59	General Secretary, ASLEF, 1994–9
Prof. David Begg	December 1997 and June 1999	42[a]	Director, Centre for Transport Policy, Robt Gordon Univ., 1997–; Chairman, Transport Ctee., Edinburgh City Council, 1994–9
Lord (Bill) Bradshaw	July 1999	62	GM, Western Region (BRB), 1983–5; Research Fellow, Wolfson College Oxford, 1985–2000; transport spokesman, Liberal Democrats
Michael Grant	May 1999	45	Franchising Director, OPRAF, 1999–; Railtrack, 1998–9; Eurotunnel, 1987–98
David Jefferies	August 1999	65	Chairman, 24/7 Utility Services, 1999–; London Electricity, 1981–8; National Grid, 1990–9; Viridian, 1994–8
Pen Kent	August 1999	61	Director, Bank of England, 1988–97; PFI Panel, 1993–7; Member, Commonwealth Development Corp., 1995–
David Quarmby	July 1999	57	Chairman, BTA, 1996–; DLR, 1999–; Member, Transport for London, 2000–
Willie Gallagher	May 2000	41	Director of Customer Services, Scottish Power Group
David Grayson	May 2000	44	Director, Business in the Community, 1995–; Chairman, National Disability Council, 1996–2000
Ann Hemingway	May 2000	52	Head of Sales, British Gas Trading
Jeremy Mayhew	May 2000	41	Director, BBC Worldwide, 1995–2001
Adrian Montague	May 2000	52	Director, Kleinwort Benson, 1994–7; Chief Executive, PFI task force, 1997–2000; Dep. Chairman, Partnerships UK, 2000–
Janet Rubin	May 2000	51	Freelance HR Director; HR Director, B&Q, 1987–90, WH Smith, 1990–3, Littlewoods, 1993–7
Kevin Small	May 2000	34	Chairman, RUCC Western England; Councillor, Swindon BC

Source: SRA.

[a] Age at June 1999.

members for Scotland and Wales.[42] Morton was nervous about the move, fearing that the resultant composition might weaken the SRA's authority. 'I refuse to be in a position', he told Macdonald, the Transport Minister, 'where a Treasury whippersnapper can claim more refined judgement than the SRA because it is full of anoraks and single-issue campaigners.'[43] Certainly, the new recruits helped to broaden the constituency by providing specialists in consumer relations (Willie Gallagher, Ann Hemingway, and Kevin Small), PFI (Adrian Montague), disability (David Grayson), the media (Jeremy Mayhew), and human resources (Janet Rubin) (Table 2.3). Of course, a commitment of only two days a month for a period of two years meant that there were distinct limits to the amount of help that non-executive members could offer. In any case, the Board had been assembled with little regard to how individuals might be blended into an effective policymaking and monitoring team, and its impact was further constrained by the 'hands-on' approach of Morton. Essentially he wanted to act as both Chairman and Chief Executive, and with little evidence of a strong independent element within the shadow board, this intention was at odds with the code of best practice established by the Cadbury Committee in 1992.[44] Furthermore, his vision of the independent role of the Board did not dovetail well with traditional Whitehall lines of accountability which ran from the Permanent Secretary of the sponsoring department as the Principal Accounting Officer to the Chief Executive of the NDPB. The relationship necessarily produced elements of tension, but these could usually be resolved with give and take on both sides. However, there was little evidence that Morton was the man to work within these constraints, and arguments about the command structure were to become an enduring source of friction between the SRA and the Department. Finally, his physical separation from the managers at OPRAF strengthened the sense of organizational disjunction, and the latter were often somewhat disconcerted by spontaneous interventions made by the Chairman on subjects where prior consultation with colleagues was desirable.[45]

Below Board level, executive management was built around existing OPRAF managers operating from Hay's Lane: Nick Newton, handling franchise replacement and management; David Revolta, finance and administration; and Chris Stokes, responsible for railway development, freight, and rolling stock. Terence Jenner, BRB's solicitor, operated the legal function from Old Queen St., where the secretariat was led by Peter Trewin. Paul McKie discharged the public affairs function until Chris Austin's appointment as Director, External Relations in October (Figure 2.1). From the end of May 1999 Morton led a

[42] Transport Act 2000, c. 202.
[43] Morton–Lord Macdonald of Tradeston (Minister for Transport), 10 September 1999, DETR file R81/1/2 Pt. 4.
[44] Interview with Jeremy Mayhew, 7 December 2006; *Report of the Committee on the Financial Aspects of Corporate Governance* (1992).
[45] DETR–SSRA/OPRAF officials meeting, 30 March 1999, DETR file R73/1/7 Pt. 1.

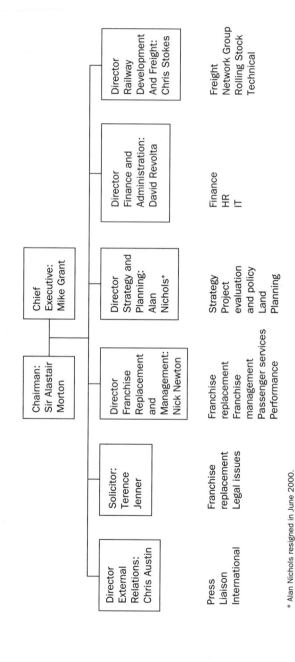

Figure 2.1 Shadow Strategic Rail Authority organization chart, June 2000

Source: SSRA, *R&A 1999/2000*, p. 15.

* Alan Nichols resigned in June 2000.

chairman's committee, consisting of himself, Grant, Jenner, Newton, Revolta, and Stokes, which was intended to focus on 'strategic tasks'. Other aspects of the Authority's work were left to an executive group chaired by Mike Grant, which held its first meeting in late June.[46] An early emphasis on refranchising was reflected in the establishment of a Renegotiation (later Replacement) Steering Group and a Replacement Policy Issues Group (subsequently Replacement Executive).[47]

The Government's expectations for the new authority were included in a new set of instructions and guidance for the Franchising Director, issued on 29 September 1999, and in new objectives for BRB, issued, rather belatedly, on 15 February 2000. The new instructions and guidance were based on a document drawn up by the outgoing Franchise Director, O'Brien, in March 1999. The Secretary of State expressed the desire that there should be 'close and effective working relations' between OPRAF, the ORR, and DETR, including 'appropriate consultation and cooperation' with the Rail Regulator over consumer protection and freight grants. On investment the Franchising Director was instructed to continue to provide an annual assessment of the 'type and level' of passenger services the industry should provide, and an evaluation of the adequacy of Railtrack's investment plans to provide for these. Extensive prior consultation was requested. In relation to new schemes, the Franchising Director was to administer the two new funds announced in the White Paper—the Rail Passenger Partnership and Infrastructure Investment Fund, offer 'clear and well-publicized guidance and assistance' to local authorities, and consult with the Secretary of State before entering into significant commitments in connexion with new investment. On franchise management the Secretary of State instructed the Franchising Director to notify him of any issue, including breaches, where a significantly adverse effect on either passengers or the Exchequer was likely. On franchise renegotiation, the Franchising Director was asked to pursue best value for money objectives, taking into account the commitment of the operator to 'performance, customer service, innovation, investment, and efficiency', and the extent to which extra or earlier investment, better performance, integrated transport measures, and a stronger consumer voice were likely; similar factors were to be taken into account when considering changes of franchise control. Again, ministerial consent was required before entering into any new commitments.[48] The British Railways Board was required to achieve a 'seamless transition' from Board to SRA. The main task was to work closely with the Franchising Director in preparing an assessment of the network's capability. This work was to form the

---

[46] SSRA Executive Minutes, 25 June and 28 October 1999, SRA file 57/01/01 Pt. 1.

[47] Ibid., 28 October 1999; SSRA Executive Replacement Issues [henceforth Replacement Executive] Minutes, 29 October 1999 and ff., SRA file 57/01/06 Pt. 1.

[48] Secretary of State for Transport, Instructions and Guidance for the Franchising Director, 29 September 1999, www.sra.gov.uk, and cf. O'Brien–Morton, 1 April 1999, Chairman's Committee papers, SRA file 02/20/01 Pt. 1. The OIG also contained instructions on network benefits (through-ticketing), performance (publication of a quarterly bulletin), and protection of minimum service levels.

basis of a first strategic plan, to be prepared within six months of the passenger service assessment, which would also have to respond to Railtrack's Network Management Statement for 1999/2000 and provide inputs into the Rail Regulator's current review of access charging. On franchise renegotiation, Morton was expected to support Grant in ensuring that 'best value for money' was achieved. The Secretary of State also expected the Board to offer advice on rail freight, and to 'bring forward from time to time...specific proposals for increasing capital invested in the railway industry'.[49]

What was the new body able to do? After a short time it became clear that the SSRA, while charged with considerable responsibility, enjoyed little power. With Morton at the helm, there were lots of fancy words but little action. 'We act, therefore we are', declared Morton in his first annual report, but although on its foundation the SSRA was expected to 'start work as soon as possible on producing a strategic plan for the industry including rail freight',[50] progress was to prove frustratingly slow. This is not to say that the new body was short of ideas. At meetings with Prescott and Blair in July 1999 and in numerous speeches thereafter, Morton appealed for 'investment, investment, investment'. He threw his full weight behind the idea of building upon the White Paper's reference to an infrastructure fund to establish a Public–Private Partnership to be led by the SRA and Railtrack.[51] However, it was difficult to deliver anything before firm expenditure plans were in place and the critical relationships with Railtrack, the Rail Regulator, and the TOCs had bedded down. Morton, it must be assumed, was well aware of this. In his early public pronouncements he was careful to make realistic forecasts. 'Neither oil tankers nor capital-intensive rail industries are turned around quickly', he said in May. 'For decades the network has not been allowed to plan for growth...delivering the rail service the public wants and needs may take ten years.'[52]

On refranchising, where the SSRA and OPRAF could use existing powers, the general lead, as we have seen, had come from Prescott, advised by BRB, before Morton had been appointed. The intention that the 18 passenger service franchises due to expire in 2003/4 be renegotiated in return for customer benefits was, of course, entirely laudable. However, the policy taken forward by Morton and Grant extended far beyond existing powers and was ultimately to prove rather fruitless. At first the policy was rather uncertain, with a 'bottom-up' approach to franchise mapping. Grant, in particular, was not sure whether to

[49] Macdonald–Morton, 15 February 2000, reproduced in BRB, *R&A 1999/2000*, pp. 6–8. The letter also set out objectives for BRB itself, encompassing the Channel Tunnel Usage Agreement, Property Sales (priority to be given to transport use), British Transport Police, and residual obligations. The BRB had started the process of drafting objectives as early as October 1998: BRB Minutes, 1 October and 5 November 1998, AN167/64, TNA; Welsby–Prescott, 2 October 1998, Peter Trewin's papers.

[50] DETR News Release, 1 April 1999, and see also SSRA News Release, 7 July 1999.

[51] Morton, speech to Chartered Institute of Transport Conference on Priorities for the SRA, 30 June 1999, RAM disks; Griffins–Prescott, 24 June 1999, Mike Grant, Memo. 9 July 1999, SSRA Chairman's Committee Minutes, 5 and 12 July 1999, SRA files 02/20/01 Pt. 1, 02/20/02 Pt. 1.

[52] SSRA News Release, 19 May 1999.

pursue renegotiations with incumbents or to organize outright competitions, and officials from the DETR reported that the SSRA had been 'all over the place' at a meeting in September 1999.[53] In addition, the preparation of a new template franchise agreement ruffled feathers elsewhere, particularly at the ORR, where Winsor complained about a number of potential encroachments on his responsibilities for track access agreements.[54] The enduring problem, however, was that the SSRA's emphasis upon franchise *replacement* and *output* maximization was accompanied not only by an optimistic assessment of the funding possibilities but also by a rather simplistic appreciation of the nature of the major players, and especially Railtrack and the TOCs. Morton tended to the view that Railtrack would and could act as an efficient provider of capital in the public interest, that the inter-city and London-serving TOCs would provide both capital and cost-effective efficiency if given the right incentives, and that a £3 billion rail infrastructure fund managed by the SRA could be used to 'lever in' large sums from the private sector. These were very large assumptions and were ultimately to prove misplaced.[55] The difficulties were evident from an early stage. At a meeting with Prescott, Alan Milburn, the Treasury Chief Secretary, and Lord Macdonald, the Transport Minister, in September 1999, Morton expressed his desire to get on with the renegotiations. He argued that in order to deliver Government's objectives, the TOCs needed to achieve a greater level of investment in railway capacity and services in partnership with Railtrack. Longer franchises of 10–20 years would require higher levels of investment and a better service, and the TOCs might need revised subsidy profiles and premium payments. Morton explained that the TOCs would first approach the SSRA with plans for their existing networks, together with any ideas they might have about neighbouring franchises. Refranchising would then begin with GNER, operators of the East Coast Main Line (ECML) franchise, where there had already been discussions about investing in new tilting trains in return for a longer term, and with some of the London-commuter franchises. The SSRA intended to have four or five contracts negotiated by June 2000. That this approach would be politically as well as administratively difficult to execute was evident from the initial reactions of the Treasury. The Chief Secretary expressed concerns that the process would distract the TOCs from the primary purpose of improving current performance, that there would be no effective competition to provide better value for money in the deals, and, most importantly, that there would be an impact on the spending review. Here lay the essential problem. Aside from the dependence for success

---

[53] Linnard–Peter Loosely (DETR), 7 September 1999, DETR file R78/1/22 Pt. 4.

[54] SSRA Chairman's Committee Minutes, 17 January, 14 and 21 March 2000, SRA file 02/20/02 Pt. 2; SSRA Replacement Executive Minutes, 9 March and 14 July 2000, 57/01/06 Pt. 1; DETR–SSRA/OPRAF officials meeting, 16 and 29 November 2000, DETR file R73/1/7 Pt. 2; Stephen Fidler (DETR)–Mark Coulshed (Head of Railways Sponsorship Divn, DETR), 25 July 2000, R73/1/26 Pt. 5.

[55] Morton, speech, 30 June 1999, cit.; SSRA, 'Briefing for DPM's Seminar, July 1999', 1 July 1999, SSRA Chairman's Committee papers, SRA file 02/20/01 Pt. 1, Chairman's Committee Minutes, 5 July 1999, 02/20/02 Pt. 1; David Grayson, Note on 'SRA Board', 2 November 2005.

on the TOCs, who we have noted were not asset owners (so to expect them to transform themselves into capital investors required an imaginative step change), an 'output-driven' strategy required investment and, in many cases, a modified subsidy profile, and both required resources. Thus, whatever the flexibilities offered by a Public–Private Partnership, the Government would have to find more for rail transport. As Sir Alastair reminded Ministers, 'he did not know how the improvements wanted by Ministers could be achieved without investment, and . . . where that investment was considerable, a public contribution would be required'.[56] The SSRA was given the go-ahead to start the renegotiation process, but Milburn warned him that it would have to be aligned with work on the spending review. The SSRA should work jointly with the DETR and Treasury on the issues, and the latter should not be 'merely consulted once a deal had been renegotiated'.[57] The prospect of imaginative responses by the TOCs was also something of a Holy Grail. After all, their major concern was to manage franchises with relatively tight specifications and a declining subsidy regime. The bus companies had underestimated the learning curve they faced in running more complex rail services, and had overestimated the savings expected from operating, particularly in depots. Creative ideas were not high on their list of priorities, and there were also some concerns that Railtrack's investment programme, contained in the Network Management Statements, lacked credibility in some areas and did not reflect the need to respond to the rise in passenger volumes.[58]

In spite of the attendant difficulties, the SSRA invested a considerable managerial effort in attempting to reshape the existing structure. The refranchising process began in August 1999 with an invitation to the TOCs to respond to the prospect of expiry. In November the first batch of franchises to be replaced was identified: GNER, Chiltern, and Connex South Central. In March 2000, six companies were shortlisted for the three franchises, and then heads of terms were reached with 'preferred counterparties' for two of them: Chiltern, with the incumbent, M40 Trains (owned by John Laing), in August; and South Central, with Govia (Go-Ahead and the French operator, Via GTI), in October. Both promised substantial investment: Chiltern £371 million, South Central, up to £1.5 billion.[59] The GNER franchise proved more difficult to progress, however. Plans for the ECML had been stimulated by clear evidence of overcrowding on the route, and in October 1997, GNER, owned by Sea Containers, had offered to invest in tilting trains in return for an infrastructure upgrade and an extension

---

[56] Nigel Milton (Prescott's PS)–Jeremy Pocklington [PS to Alan Milburn (Chief Secretary, Treasury)], 17 September 1999, Prime Minister's Rail Policy papers, Pt. 5.

[57] Ibid.; Morton, 'Request to and Briefing for Ministers', 1 September 1999, Morton's papers, SRA. The message was repeated by Milburn's successor, Andrew Smith, and by Macdonald: Smith–Prescott, 22 November 1999, DETR file R73/1/26 Pt. 1; Macdonald–Morton, 10 March 2000, Morton's papers, SRA.

[58] Cf. Richard Brown (Chief Executive, Trains Divn, National Express), presentation, BRB Minutes, 9 April 1998, AN167/64, TNA.

[59] SRA, *Annual Report 2000/1*, pp. 25–6.

Table 2.4 Submissions to the SSRA for an upgrade of the ECML, February 2000 (£m.)

Sponsor	Investment	Sources				
		Railtrack	ROSCOs	TOC	SPV	Other
GNER/Sea Containers	3,284	2,007	60	159	1,008	50
Virgin East Coast	5,811	1,124	46	—	4,641	—
Hull Trains	295	65	220	10	—	—

Source: Chamberlain, Memo. 25 February 2000, SRA file 57/01/07 Pt. 3.

from 7 to 15 years. With the encouragement of the Government, O'Brien, then the Franchising Director, had embarked upon negotiations with GNER, the ROSCOs, and Railtrack.[60] By the beginning of 2000 this had become a £3.3 billion investment package for a 20-year term. However, the project became more difficult to assess when it was challenged by Virgin East Coast, a Virgin–Stagecoach joint venture supported by Bechtel, which submitted its own proposals in February. The latter promised something quite different, viz. a new high-speed line to be built from south of Peterborough to north of Doncaster, to the west of the existing route. To add to the complexity, Hull Trains also entered the fray. An open access operator owned by GB Railways, the Anglia franchisee (80%) and Mike Jones and John Nelson of Renaissance Trains (20%), it had obtained the support of both the SSRA and the Rail Regulator to operate a Hull–London service, and submitted a proposal for a more modest £295 million investment. With these very different bids, and a variety of investment partners and funding mechanisms (see Table 2.4), the SSRA found the assessment process a headache.[61]

Bids for a second tranche of franchises were invited in December 1999. These involved six strategic areas: Thameslink 2000; London commuting; Birmingham and Manchester bottlenecks; services around London; Wales and Northwest; and TransPennine. By March 2000 three replacement franchises had emerged: South West, where shortlisting was completed in August; Central; and TransPennine Express (the inter-urban elements of the North East franchise, Northern Spirit). Work was also carried out on others in varying states of development: an

[60] O'Brien–Prescott, 17 September 1998, Linnard–Reid and Prescott, 14 October 1998, DETR file R78/1/14 Pt. 1. On Railtrack work in scoping the upgrade with and without tilting trains see SRA 11/20/06 Pt. 1.
[61] ORR, *Annual Report 1999/2000*, pp. 15–16; Jason Chamberlain (SSRA), Memo., SSRA Replacement Executive Minutes, 25 February 2000, SRA files 57/01/06 Pt. 1, 57/01/07 Pt. 3; Interview with John Nelson, 24 October 2007. Renaissance Trains had had an earlier proposal for a Sheffield–London service blocked by MML. Hull Trains' services began on 25 September 2000, three weeks before the Hatfield accident on 17 October.

expanded Thameslink (Thameslink 2000), where proposals were invited in June; Wales and Borders, and Wessex, which emerged after consultation exercises; Anglia/Humber; and 'Orbirail' (round-London services building on Silverlink). By the summer of 2000 a new franchise map had been produced for 22 franchises, divided, as British Rail had done in the 1980s, into three sectors, Intercity, London/South-east commuting, and Regional. The aim was to create fewer but more substantial TOCs, reduce the number of operators working into each of the main London termini, and keep inter-city and commuting businesses distinct.[62]

However, the practical outcome of over a year of effort by SSRA/OPRAF was disappointing, and the SRA was forced to admit, in its annual report for 2000/1, that the process was taking longer than 'originally planned or hoped'.[63] Several factors were responsible for the limited progress. First, the path dependency of the original British Rail schema of 25 franchises imposed itself on the process and it was soon clear that, whatever Morton's ambitions, there was more 'refranchising' than 'replacement'. Second, there were the distractions caused by tinkering at the edges, especially in the subsidized sector, where, for example, a proposal to transfer Merseyrail to the local PTE was under consideration. Third, broader ambitions sometimes carried with them political consequences, as was seen in the expectations raised by the prospect of a Welsh franchise. In contrast with the position in Scotland, the idea not only flew in the face of network realities but was also weakened by the absence of devolved powers for railways in Cardiff.[64] Fourth, radical changes to the choice of operator ran the risk of raising matters of competition law, particularly since the passage of the Competition Act of 1998, as was seen with Virgin's bid for the ECML franchise (see below). Fifth, policymaking was complicated by the instability exhibited by some of the weaker franchises, where operators, having signed up to tough subsidy reductions, had overestimated the impact they would have on costs. In December 1999 it emerged that the Northern Spirit franchise was not viable with the existing subsidy profile, and the operator, MTL, was facing an immediate cash crisis. The company was predicting a loss on the franchise of £14 million for 1999/2000, and a group loss of £8.5 million. In breach of its banking covenants, it clearly had to be bailed out; and in February 2000 Arriva, a bus company, agreed to buy the company for £34.7 million and take over its franchises (MTL also operated Merseyrail) on a one-year basis.[65] Prism was also experiencing difficulties. Having been rather

[62] A secondary aim was to counter criticism that a piecemeal approach was deterring potential bidders. Coulshed–Macdonald, 12 May 2000, DETR file R73/1/26 Pt. 3; SSRA, 'Building a Better Railway' (June 2000) and Press Release, 20 June 2000 and see also Chairman's Committee Minutes, 21 March 2000, SRA file 02/20/02 Pt. 2; Memo. 2 March 2000, SSRA Replacement Executive Minutes, 6 April 2000, 57/01/06 Pt. 1, 57/01/07 Pt. 6. The Island Line was excluded from the list of 22.

[63] SRA, *Annual Report 2000/1*, p. 25.

[64] Macdonald–Grant, 8 March 2000, DETR file R78/1/14 Pt. 2.

[65] SSRA Chairman's Committee Minutes, 5 and 24 January 2000, SRA file 02/20/02 Pt. 2, Executive Minutes, 16 December 1999–17 February 2000, 57/01/01 Pts. 1–2. The Northern franchise made pre-tax losses of £19.0 m. in 1999/2000.

rash in bidding for franchises, it found that burgeoning losses on its Cardiff and
Wales & West franchises could no longer be offset by profits from c2c (formerly
LTS) and WAGN, and in an agreement hastily reached with the SSRA in June
2000 its four franchises were transferred to National Express, which bought the
company for £166 million and now held 9 of the 25 agreements.[66] At the same
time, concerns were also being expressed about the financial health of the Anglia
franchise, though there was no immediate risk of termination given the strength
of GB Railways' balance sheet.[67] But distractions such as these inevitably complicated the process of franchise redesign.

Last and certainly not least, the attempt to grant 20-year franchises for
improvements to be achieved via Special Purpose Vehicles or SPVs was not only
challenging in itself but failed to receive the backing of either the Treasury or
Railtrack. Despite the Government's publication of an ambitious *10 Year Plan*
in July 2000 promising substantial sums for investment (see below), Treasury
officials were more inclined to challenge the assumption that the growth in
demand for rail services would be sustained, and felt that additional investment
should either be squeezed out of Railtrack or captured through the fare-box.[68]
While the new 20-year Chiltern franchise agreement was eventually signed in
February 2002, with substantial funding from John Laing and the Royal Bank
of Scotland, the others were to prove more problematic, and were dealt with on
an entirely different basis, affected by the aftermath of the Hatfield accident in
October 2000 (see Chapter 3). The Heads of Agreement with Govia for South
Central were not converted into a new agreement and the franchise was relet on
a shorter, and much revised, basis in 2003. Negotiations for the ECML proved
to be both protracted and complex. Here, there was a plain demonstration of the
barriers to the speedy resolution of ambitious refranchising. GNER's proposal for
tilting trains was a rather puzzling solution for a route that was much straighter
than, for example, the West Coast route, Virgin's plans for a new, high-speed line
raised broader questions of project specification, timescale and cost. The SSRA
quickly expressed doubts, not only about Virgin's cost estimates but also about
Railtrack's ability to fund and project manage the scheme, especially given its
difficulties with the escalating cost of the West Coast upgrade (see below). It also
considered a more proactive approach to the investment process by examining the
possibility of itself negotiating a track access agreement for the high-speed paths.
But, at the same time, it nursed fears of a challenge under competition law if

---

[66] SSRA Chairman's Committee Minutes, 17 and 24 January and 13 June 2000, SRA file 02/20/02
Pt. 2, Executive Committee Minutes, 20 April, 11 May, 2 August and 12 October 2000, 57/01/01 Pt.
2. The franchise accounts for 2000/1 revealed pre-tax profits of £13.0 m. for c2c + WAGN, and pre-tax
losses of £30.3 m. for Cardiff + Wales & West. The latter's subsidy per passenger-mile was only 12.4p in
1999/2000, one of the lowest for regional rail franchises: SSRA, *Annual Report 1999/2000*, p. 48.

[67] John Allen, Memos. 11 November 1999, 2 February 2000, SSRA Executive Minutes, 12 November
1999, 3 February 2000, SRA files 57/01/01 Pts. 1–2, 57/01/02 Pts. 4, 7. Anglia's pre-tax losses in
1999/2000 were £1.7 m.

[68] Milburn–Prescott, 12 August 1999, DETR file R78/1/14 Pt. 2.

Virgin were to end up operating both the East and West Coast routes. These fears proved well-founded when the OFT decided to examine the issue in the autumn of 2000.[69] Such complex considerations were far from being resolved when the Hatfield accident threw the industry into turmoil. In any case, the emergence of a 'quick fix' alternative to long-term franchises was evident as early as August 2000, when National Express, operators of the Midland Main Line, were given a two-year extension, a period allowed for in existing agreements, in return for passenger benefits (chiefly investment in infrastructure and rolling stock) put at £238 million.[70] Others were to follow.

On investment, progress was necessarily limited during the 'shadow' period. Morton's intention was to capitalize on opportunities offered by the Rail Regulator's forthcoming review of Railtrack's track access charges for passenger services. He had expectations of a 'regulatory windfall' from the process, to be used either directly by Railtrack in increased investment or returned to the SRA for it to undertake the same. Funds for the SRA 'lever' were also to come from: premiums paid by TOCs which operated profitably; fines and penalties imposed by the Rail Regulator and SRA on Railtrack and the TOCs for operating shortcomings; British Rail's cash reserves of c.£800 million; and the bid for a share in the Government's Capital Modernisation Fund.[71] Aside from the availability of finance for projects where the gestation period might be long and the rate of return uncertain, the stumbling block here was that parts of the industry were being asked for their strategic ideas before the SSRA had itself provided a vision for the future enhancement of the network. The preparation of a first strategic plan, originally expected to appear in the autumn of 2000, took much longer than expected, and, in the event, the plan was not published until January 2002, by which time Morton had been succeeded by Richard Bowker. The SSRA did produce the required assessment of service needs, in April 2000. Over a hundred ideas for network enhancements, provided by numerous interested parties, were assembled by the SSRA as 'incremental output statements' and submitted to the Regulator to be used as part of the charges review process. However, the activity did not amount to a plan, and such 'vision' as there was emerged from the DETR, which produced a *10 Year Plan* in July 2000. This promised spending of £63 billion on the railways, £29 billion of it to be provided by the public sector. In addition to capital investments of £4 billion on renewal schemes such as the WCML, £5 billion would be provided for the CTRL, and a £7 billion SRA-managed Rail Modernisation Fund was promised to lever in private sector capital.

---

[69] Chris Stokes, Memo. 28 February 2000, SSRA Replacement Executive Minutes, 30 March, 6 September and 23 November 2000, SRA files 57/01/06 Pt. 1, 57/01/07 Pt. 3; Richard Bowker, in *Rail*, 1–14 February 2006, pp. 36–7.

[70] National Express obtained premium reductions totalling £27 m. NPV while consenting to a 2% improvement in operating performance. James Vickers, Memos. 14 and 20 July 2000, SSRA Replacement Executive Minutes, 6–20 July 2000, SRA files 57/01/06 Pt. 1, 57/01/07 Pts. 8–9.

[71] Griffins–Prescott, 12 July 1999, DETR file R78/1/14 Pt. 2; SSRA Chairman's Committee Minutes, 14 June 1999, SRA file 02/20/02 Pt. 1.

The intention was to facilitate an increase of 50 per cent in passenger traffic and 80 per cent in freight over the decade.[72] However, Morton was dismayed by a switch in emphasis from revenue to capital investment, which by reducing the sums potentially available to support the TOCs would, he felt, compromise the plans for longer franchises.[73] In addition, the status of the Plan, or rather the prospect of converting aspiration into firm and speedy commitment, was another matter, and here attainment was threatened by first, the interventions of the Rail Regulator in the access charges review, and second, the aftermath of the Hatfield accident (see below).[74]

Of course, there were 'mega-projects' inherited from OPRAF days: the badly needed and much-delayed refurbishment of the WCML, where Railtrack had committed itself to a major upgrade in October 1997 via the controversial 'PUG2' contract with Virgin; the CTRL; and improvements and extensions to the north–south London services under the banner 'Thameslink 2000'. None was exactly raising the banner of successful project management and private–public funding. The WCML upgrade gave Railtrack considerable problems, especially through its reliance upon 'moving block signalling', an innovative but untried technology, and it soon emerged that the PUG2 contract left much of the risk with Railtrack. Indeed, as early as July 1999 Corbett had admitted to Morton that PUG2 would be 'perfectly horrendous in ultimate cost and difficulty'.[75] The cost of the project had been put at £2.2 billion when it was endorsed by the Rail Regulator in June 1998, but when it was re-evaluated in November 1999 a switch to conventional signalling had been made and costs were now estimated to be £5.85 billion. By this time Winsor, supported by the SSRA, had expressed concerns that Railtrack had not established robust plans to meet its contractual and regulatory commitments, and the disclosure of cost escalation was quickly followed by a draft enforcement order requiring Railtrack to provide assurances about the project timetable and undertakings to users of the line on capacity.[76] The £5.2 billion CTRL scheme had proved difficult to promote given early Channel Tunnel revenues, and by 1998 there had been a very real likelihood that the project would collapse. Railtrack had stepped in as a 'white knight', and

---

[72] References to £60 bn [total] and £26 bn [public sector] in the published plan exclude £3 bn of revenue support for privately funded infrastructure enhancements. DETR, *Transport 2010: The 10 Year Plan* (July 2000), pp. 44–5, Note by DETR officials, in Rowlands–Stephen Byers (SoS for Transport), 24 July 2001, DETR file R78/1/54 Pt. 1. On the SSRA's strategic plan see Philip O'Donnell (SSRA), Memo. 5 July 1999, Chairman's Committee Minutes, 21 June and 12 July 1999, SRA file 02/20/02 Pt. 1 and 02/20/01 Pt. 1; John Larkinson (SRA), Memo. May 2000, 57/01/02 Pt. 10.

[73] Of the £29 bn in promised public sector expenditure, £14.7 bn was to be capital support and £14.4 bn revenue support. Prescott–Morton, 17 July 2000, DETR file R78/1/19 Pt. 1.

[74] Cf. Morton–Rowlands, 19 December 2000, DETR file R78/1/43 Pt. 1.

[75] Morton, file note, 8 July 1999, Morton's papers, SRA.

[76] The order was confirmed in May 2000. Winsor–Morton, 25 August 1999, SSRA Chairman's Committee papers, SRA file 02/20/01 Pt. 2; O'Donnell, Memos. 26 November and 9 December 1999, SSRA Executive Committee Minutes, 28 October and 16 December 1999, 57/01/01 Pt. 1; Railtrack plc, *R&A 1999/2000*, p. 4; ORR, *Annual Report 1999/2000*, pp. 14–15.

Prescott had agreed to provide additional government support.[77] The Thameslink 2000 project was complicated by the requirements of the CTRL at St. Pancras, and by its impact on interchanges elsewhere in central London, for example at Farringdon and Moorgate. The SSRA confirmed enhanced plans for the £830 million scheme in September 1999, but continued to express concerns about cost escalation, and its fears were scarcely assuaged when a lengthy public enquiry began in June 2000. This was not completed until May 2001, a report was not published until July 2002, and further problems lay ahead.[78] The concept of the SPV, a consortium of investors and engineering companies which would execute and then sell on a major project, was worked up with the help of Lazards and Linklaters, and some progress was made in introducing it into the plans for the new South Central and ECML franchises. But by this time it was becoming clear that the idea did not appeal either to Corbett and Richard Middleton (the Commercial Director) at Railtrack, or to Mottram at the DETR, or to officials in Number Ten, where Blair had asked for independent work on rail strategy. In these circumstances nothing was firmed up.[79] Limited progress was made elsewhere. The Rail Partnership scheme was launched in May 1999, and the first successful bids were announced in December. Seven schemes had been approved by the end of 1999/2000, with a total funding of £11.3 million: the (short-lived) Anglia Crossrail service (Chelmsford–Basingstoke), and improvements in Edinburgh, Leeds, Sheffield–Hull, Middlesborough–Whitby, Durham and Bath–Bristol.[80] On the freight side, it was difficult for the SSRA to make headway with limited powers, and no franchises to manage. Nevertheless, work began on a grant-based freight strategy to promote growth, following Julia Clarke's appointment as Director, Freight in June 1999, and there was some encouragement with the appearance of new entrants such as Mendip Rail and GB Railfreight.[81] In December the SSRA launched a competition for a prize of up to £5 million for 'innovative solutions in rail-based logistics'. By June 2000 three schemes, led by Blue Circle, Excel, and Minimodal, had been awarded a total of £6 million.[82] However, in comparison with the needs of an overstretched network all this really amounted to bailing with teaspoons.

[77] Gourvish, *Britain and the Channel Tunnel* (2006), pp. 380–2.

[78] SSRA Executive Committee Minutes, 29 June 1999, SRA file 57/01/01 Pt. 1; Paul McKie (SSRA), Memo. 16 September 1999, 57/01/02 Pt. 2; OPRAF, *Annual Report 1998/9*, p. 36; SRA, *Annual Report 2001/2*, p. 38, 2002/3, p. 26.

[79] Corbett–Morton, 16 February and 9 March 2000, Morton's papers, SRA; Brian Hackland (Policy Unit, No. 10)–Blair, 16 May 2000, Prime Minster's Rail Policy papers, Pt. 8; Morton–Macdonald, 17 May 2000, Morton's papers, SRA; Coulshed–Macdonald, 23 May 2000, DETR file R78/1/14 Pt. 2; SSRA Chairman's Committee Minutes, 21 March 2000, SRA file 02/20/02 Pt. 2; Replacement Executive Committee Minutes, 9 and 16 March, 17 August 2000, 57/01/06 Pt. 1. At Number Ten work was commissioned from Richard Dobbs and Matthew Elson (using McKinsey's work) and from Tim James (Sheffield University) and David Nissan.

[80] SSRA, *Annual Report 1999/2000*, pp. 8, 34.

[81] ORR, *Annual Report 1999/2000*, p. 19. GB Railfreight was launched by Jeremy Long's GB Railways.

[82] Ibid. p. 40.

If progress was limited, we must have some sympathy with the new Authority. The legislation necessary to empower the SSRA was slow to emerge and the delay did little to give political backing to the new NDPB. While a Railway Bill received its second reading in July 1999, it was later subsumed in a larger Transport Bill which was not given a first reading until December, in the next session. Progress remained leisurely, and the royal assent was not obtained until 30 November 2000, the last day of the 1999–2000 Session. Consequently, the body's shadow status continued until 1 February 2001, with a general election only four months away. On top of this, the waters were muddied by the emerging tensions between Railtrack and the new Rail Regulator, which began to have an impact upon Railtrack's attitude to investment planning. Relations between the infrastructure provider and its economic regulator began to deteriorate soon after Winsor's arrival in July 1999. He pursued his responsibility for reviewing track access charges with a zeal that was quickly seen to be customary, and he sometimes infuriated those who wished to see a more flexible grey in railway relationships rather than a simple black and white. In approaching the monitoring of Railtrack's performance, he certainly took a tougher line. Winsor's predecessor, Bolt, had already started the process, commissioning a report from Booz Allen Hamilton which revealed a number of shortcomings.[83] The company had promised to reduce passenger train delay minutes by 7.5 per cent in each of the years 1998/9 and 1999/2000. When the improvement emerged as only 2 per cent for 1998/9, Winsor encouraged Bolt to insist on a one-year catch-up for 1999/2000, giving Railtrack the extremely demanding target of reducing delays by 12.7 per cent. He also proposed a penalty of £4 million per percentage point shortfall.[84] The Regulator's draft track access review for 2001–6, published in draft form in July 2000 and in final form in October, was of course a critical intervention. Analysed in more detail in Chapter 3, here we should note that Winsor sought to minimize the impact on the SSRA's financial commitments to the industry while fulfilling a statutory responsibility to safeguard Railtrack's ability to finance infrastructure renewals and investment. The latter appeared to take precedence. He was thus relatively sympathetic to Railtrack's requirements in raising the Regulatory Asset Base (RAB) by a substantial amount and increasing the pre-tax real cost of capital from a suggested 5–6 per cent to 8 per cent. Consequently, access revenues were to rise by about 35 per cent in the first year, and by 5 per cent per annum in real terms thereafter. On the other hand, his approach to performance and possessions was to maintain tougher targets, with a penalty of £3.6 million per percentage point missed.[85] From the SSRA's

---

[83] Bolt–Prescott, 12 April 1999, Morton's papers, SRA.

[84] Bolt–Corbett, 23 April and 2 June 1999, Winsor–Corbett, 29 July and 18 August 1999, Morton's papers, SRA; Stokes, Memo. 24 May 1999, SRA file 02/20/01 Pt. 1; ORR, *Annual Report 1999/2000*, pp. 12–13.

[85] ORR, *The Periodic Review of Railtrack's Access Charges: Final Conclusions*, Vol. I (October 2000), esp. pp. 8–13; DETR–SSRA/OPRAF officials meeting, 15 December 1999, DETR file R73/1/7 Pt. 2; ORR, *Annual Report 2000/1*, p. 15; Helm, 'A Critique of Rail Regulation', p. 30.

perspective, Winsor's review had been more supportive of the infrastructure company than of the SRA's budget and the public purse. Initial calculations were that there would be an adverse impact of £1.5 billion, causing the DETR to add £2.3 billion to the railway allocation under the *10 Year Plan*.[86]

Railtrack, for its part, was scarcely presenting itself as a sophisticated and sensitive corporation. The company exhibited a rather simplistic attitude to its commercial operations, preferring to deal at arm's length with its contractors rather than building strategic alliances with them to produce incremental improvements in efficiency and productivity. The emerging culture tended towards the arrogant, especially in dealings with its TOC customers, some of whom found its approach unnecessarily high-handed. One example was provided by Railtrack's contention that it would benefit from a 'volume incentive' in the access charges review. But, as the SSRA pointed out, the impact of such a device would be to further weaken the influence of TOCs on the development of the network.[87] There were also frictions between the Regulator and the SSRA, the latter being regarded by the former as something of a cuckoo in the nest. When legislation was being drafted in 1999 Winsor opposed the idea that the SRA should have the power to refer licence modifications to the Competition Commission, which he felt would serve to diminish his independence. Morton had made his general stance clear at an early stage, in a letter to Prescott.

Whilst having an independent Regulator is an effective safety valve for arbitrating over conflicting private sector interests a publicly accountable railway still funded by significant taxpayer funds requires that the overall strategic direction and vision for the industry is set by the SRA. This argues for a statutory duty on the Regulator to 'give effect' to the plans and policies of the SRA.[88]

Winsor did not agree, of course, as was evident from Denton Hall's criticisms of the draft Railways Bill.[89] The SSRA, for its part, was worried that the Regulator's more adversarial stance vis-à-vis Railtrack was focusing the company's attention on responding to incentives at the expense of outputs.[90] There was also much argument over the precise responsibilities of the two bodies when major projects were being advanced. Thus, with the WCML upgrade, Winsor felt that the SRA should pay for the renewals element unconditionally, while the SSRA

[86] Morton–Macdonald, 16 October 2000, Morton's papers, SRA; Chairman's Committee Minutes, 24 October 2000, SRA file 02/20/02 Pt. 2; Note by DETR officials, 24 July 2001, cit.

[87] O'Donnell, Memos. 18 November and 20 December 1999, SRA files 57/01/02 Pt. 4, 02/20/01 Pt. 3, and cf. Richard Bowker, in *Rail*, 6–19 July 2005, pp. 40–3, 28 September–11 October 2005, p. 42, 21 December 2005–3 January 2006, p. 36.

[88] Morton–Prescott (draft), 24 May 1999, SRA file 02/20/01 Pt. 1.

[89] Cf. Terence Jenner, Memos. 19 and 23 August, 4 October 1999, SRA files 02/20/01 Pts. 1–2, 02/20/02 Pt. 1; SSRA Executive Committee Minutes, 29 June and 19 August 1999, 57/01/01 Pt. 1, Chairman's Committee Minutes, 23 August and 4 October 1999, 02/20/02 Pt. 1.

[90] DETR–SSRA/OPRAF officials meeting, 20 October 1999, DETR file R73/1/7 Pt. 1, and see also SSRA Executive Committee Minutes, 23 September 1999, SRA file 57/01/01 Pt. 1.

thought that its Value for Money duty required that completed work be certified before payment would be made.[91] The SSRA was also doubtful about Railtrack's financial health. Morton made many sniping remarks about the adequacy of its balance sheet to support the necessary infrastructural investment, which grew shriller as successive Network Management Statements promised more and more decadal investment: £17 billion in 1998, £27 billion in 1999, and £52 billion in 2000.[92] His executives noticed that the company's experience with the WCML upgrade was making it extremely risk averse on cost estimation and project management, while it was also arguing with the new authority about the sharing of development costs for the ambitious schemes connected with refranchising.[93] Relationships between Railtrack, on one side, and the Regulator and SSRA, on the other, deteriorated when it emerged, in early 2000, that the costing of the WCML upgrade was 'opaque and confusing' and lacked a 'robust audit trail'. There followed an acerbic debate about the apportionment of costs between 'enhancement' and 'renewals', a calculation with implications for the SRA's financial liability in the charges review.[94] But one must appreciate Railtrack's predicament. Struggling to assemble knowledge about its core activity, it had some grounds for complaint in being asked to respond to SSRA- and TOC-led schemes for enhancement. These produced a great deal of project assessment and costing work where progress was hindered by the rudimentary nature of some of the information provided.[95] Finally, the regulators were also disturbed by merger and acquisition activity which had the effect of reintegrating sections of the railway, and worked against concurrent aspirations to facilitate more competition in service provision. In addition to the assemblage of nine franchises by National Express, there was Stagecoach, which had bought the Porterbrook ROSCO in 1996 and was operating two franchises. It then acquired an interest in two more when it bought a 49 per cent stake in Virgin Rail in June 1998. The SSRA's policy was to pursue competition 'for the market' rather than 'in the market', but this was being threatened by reductions in the number of corporate players.[96] By the time the Hatfield accident threw the counters into the air, the major railway institutions were finding it difficult to maintain a consistent approach

[91] Cf. Stokes, Memo. 18 July 2000, SSRA Chairman's Committee Minutes, 25 July 2000, SRA file 02/20/01 Pt. 8, 02/20/02 Pt. 2.

[92] Railtrack, *Network Management Statements, 1998–2000*.

[93] Cf. Stokes, Memo. 24 May 1999, SRA file 02/20/01 Pt. 1, Memo. 28 February 2000, 57/01/07 Pt. 3; Corbett–Grant, 30 March 2000, O'Donnell, Memo. 13 April 2000, 57/01/02 Pt. 9.

[94] Chris Stokes, Memo. 3 February 2000, O'Donnell–Stokes, 2 March 2000, SRA file 57/01/02 Pts. 7, 8. Railtrack's cost submission was 'audited' for the ORR by Booz Allen Hamilton: Stokes, Memo. 9 June 2000, 57/01/02 Pt. 10.

[95] Cf. Stephen Fidler (Macdonald's PS)–Linnard, 9 March 2000, DETR file R73/1/22 Pt. 8.

[96] Cf. Richard Davies (SSRA), Memo. 4 May 2000, SRA file 57/01/02 Pt. 9. On concerns about Stagecoach's anti-competitive behaviour see Swift–John Bridgeman (DG, OFT), 7 September 1998, DETR file R73/2/1 Pt. 5, Grant–Graham Eccles (MD, South West Trains), 17 December 1999, and Grant–Macdonald, 22 December 1999, Pt. 6. Stagecoach sold Porterbrook to Abbey National in 2000: *Financial Times*, 4 April 2000, pp. 25, 52.

to the major factors of management and control affecting the industry, and the insertion of the SSRA had yet to make its mark in an industry struggling to align investment with increased business, and respond to the higher transactions costs associated with a more adversarial corporate environment.

2.3 Equilibrium disturbed: Ladbroke Grove and after

If the SSRA's broader strategic activity got off to a slow start, it was also busy continuing OPRAF's monitoring of existing franchises, and thereby contributing in some respects to the day-to-day management of the industry. This involved, *inter alia*, presiding over the mix of negotiations, incentives and penalties in relation to train performance (i.e. PIP, SFIP, and TCIP), passenger service requirements, the adjustment of fares, and overcrowding (via the PIXC regime).[97] In addition, Prescott asked the new Authority to undertake a number of studies to review capacity problems in London (north–south, east–west) and the West Midlands, and work also began on the concept of a south London Metro, and on a high-speed line for the East Coast. The Deputy Prime Minister also asked the Authority to examine the causes of the slow rate of rolling stock procurement. As a result the SSRA set up action teams to address the issue, and took special action on the old slam-door BRB Mark I stock, mounting a procurement strategy by inviting manufacturers to submit expressions of interest in a programme to replace 1,500 vehicles by 1 January 2003 or 1 January 2005, if the existing stock were modified.[98] On fares, the Authority applied the mechanism of price capping regulated fares, by RPI to 1999, and by RPI −1 per cent from 2000. OPRAF's performance-related regulation of London commuter fares (FIAP) was also retained.[99] The overall effect of fares modifications was to keep the average level just below the level of inflation for the period 1995–8, but there were real increases in 1998–9 and 1999–2000.[100] And consumer attention inevitably began to focus upon the 60 per cent of fares which were unregulated, and in particular the rising price

[97] There were incentive payments for punctuality (PIP), short formations (SFIP), and timetable changes (TCIP), plus specific incentives for some inter-city services. Net payment to the SSRA in 1999/2000 was £3.3 m.: SSRA, *Annual Report 1999/2000*, p. 31. For overcrowding the PIXC measure was developed, viz. Passengers in Excess of Capacity.

[98] SSRA, *Annual Report 1999/2000*, pp. 10, 22–4, 41–2. Some of the difficulties in procurement were caused by the absence within Railtrack of an accurate codification of structure gauges. Cf. BRB Minutes, 11 October 1999, AN18/578, TNA.

[99] FIAP: Fares Incentive Adjustment Payment. Fare levels for a basket of fares were able to move between RPI + 2% and RPI − 2%.

[100] SRA, *National Rail Trends Yearbook 2004–2005*, p. 43. We should note that real increases in the average fare paid may be affected by factors other than TOC pricing decisions, e.g. by consumers 'trading up', and by the fare regulation mechanism (since regulated fares are tied to historic rises in RPI, there may be real increases when the RPI is falling). Cf. Dodd and Sexton, Memo. 21 July 1999, Mark Smith, Memo. 3 October 2000, SRA file 57/01/02 Pt. 1 and 14.

and reduced availability of cheap walk-on fares.[101] This monitoring work continued against a background of continuing operational difficulties, attributable to both Railtrack and the TOCs. In accordance with the policy thrust provided by Number Ten, attention was given to this by the SSRA, and a National Passenger Survey was launched, together with a new, more comprehensive performance measure, the PPM, which was introduced in June 2000, after the Second Rail Summit, and at Prescott's request, included calculations for earlier years (from 1997/8). The SSRA also identified an aspirational punctuality target to guide it in refranchising decisions. This was that 15 of every 16 trains (93.75%) should arrive on time.[102] A fuller analysis of operational performance is given in Chapter 3, but suffice it to say that at the time of the second summit in May 2000, where the industry was at pains to demonstrate that the promises made in the previous year had been fulfilled, the figures remained disappointing.[103]

But safety was also a concern after the Southall accident, and it was not long before the industry's equilibrium was disturbed again with another serious accident on the Great Western main line out of Paddington, this time at Ladbroke Grove, on 5 October 1999. A Thames Trains' Paddington–Bedwyn Turbo passed a red signal and crashed into a First Great Western Cheltenham–Paddington HST. Much has already been written on the accident, which provoked considerable public disquiet and resulted in a lengthy public enquiry (undertaken by Lord Cullen), a mountain of evidence, the mobilization of passengers affected by the accident, and a notable piece of agitprop theatre.[104] For our purposes we should observe that the prime cause was human error, a SPAD (Signal Passed at Danger). Nevertheless, the accident, in which 31 people lost their lives, led to a forensic examination of corporate and institutional relationships within the rail industry and raised general issues relating to the governance of the privatized railway: the failure of Railtrack, described by Cullen as 'lamentable', to respond to the recommendations made by enquiries into incidents in the same area in 1995 and 1998; the decision of Thames Trains not to install the ATP system, which would have prevented the SPAD; the introduction of electric wiring for the Heathrow Express service into crowded signalling gantries for an already complex operating environment, with bidirectional running; deficiencies in the performance of the Railway Inspectorate, part of the Health and Safety Executive;

[101] Cf. CRUCC, *Rail Passenger Franchise Replacement. A Fare Price?* (March 2000), pp. 1, 5, and Barry Doe, *Rail*, 1–14 February 2006, pp. 50–1.
[102] Morton, speech to Second Rail Summit, 25 May 2000; SSRA, *Annual Report 1999/2000*, pp. 20, 28.
[103] SSRA Chairman's Committee Minutes, 11 July and 11 September 2000, SRA file 20/02/02 Pt. 2, Gavin Bostock, Memo. n.d. (September 2000), 57/01/02 Pt. 13. On the Second Rail Summit see DETR file 73/1/22 Pts. 5–8.
[104] HSC, *The Ladbroke Grove Rail Inquiry. The Rt Hon Lord Cullen PC*, Pt. 1, 2 (2001); Sir David Hare, play, *The Permanent Way* (2003). Wolmar devotes a chapter to the accident in *On the Wrong Line*, pp. 137–54. The accident also affected the SSRA. David Revolta was on the Great Western train and never fully recovered from the experience. His deputy Martin McGann stood in for him from February 2000 and succeeded him as finance director in September.

a complacent attitude to SPADs within the signalling control centre at Slough; and shortcomings, similar to those noted during the Southall enquiry, relating to Railtrack's zonal management, and the TOCs' driver recruitment and training. All were put under the microscope.[105] What impact did the accident have on the industry? The analyses of accident rates have encouraged the view that this was a period when railways were 'safer' than they had ever been.[106] But in terms of lives lost this was a major catastrophe, and there is no doubt that the renewed and lengthy spotlight which was shone on railway safety disturbed already fragile relationships. A further round of Railtrack-bashing followed on from revelations about its 'culture of apathy and lack of will to follow up promised actions'.[107] The company's failure to respond to concerns expressed by First Great Western about the number of SPADs in the Paddington area was a particularly damaging revelation.[108] This provided fuel for those who were beginning to question its capability. Its concurrent announcement of higher profits, for example, gave impetus to campaigns, such as that mounted by Piers Morgan and *The Mirror*, for the introduction of Automatic Train Protection.[109] The company's share price had already fallen from its peak of £17.68 in November 1998, but in the aftermath of Ladbroke Grove, the price fell below £12, and in late November, below £10.[110] But criticisms of the industry emanating from government also served to alienate some parts of the industry from the Blair administration and the process of reform. Railtrack, in particular, had some cause for complaint. In the immediate aftermath of the accident the Number Ten press office was worried that the Government's procrastination over the adoption of TPWS, an alternative to ATP, might attract adverse criticism. It therefore let it be known that an imminent report from the Health and Safety Executive would recommend that Railtrack's safety responsibilities should be removed. In fact, the report was much more cautious, merely stating that the idea should be examined. This rather sly attack

[105] HSE, First Interim Report, 8 October 1999, Internal Inquiry Report, 5 April 2000, *The Management of Safety in Railtrack* (February 2000), *The Train Collision at Ladbroke Grove 5 October 1999* (December 2000); Cullen, *Ladbroke Grove Rail Inquiry*, Pt. 1, pp. 2–5, 52–62, 79–80, 94–9, 105–6, 109–19, 127–39, 143–4, 157–9, 173–5. Wolmar contends that Cullen was rather tough on the signallers, but 'lame' about the design of the track layout: *On the Wrong Line*, pp. 146–8. The decision of Thames Trains not to fit ATP was made in the knowledge that a more reliable system—TPWS—would be introduced, a decision which Cullen found to be entirely reasonable: Cullen, *Ladbroke Grove Rail Inquiry*, Pt. I, p. 155. The company argued that the use of operating practices such as bidirectional working rested on the premise that Great Western would be operating with ATP: Interview with Martin Ballinger (ex-Group Chief Executive, Go-Ahead Group), 31 May 2006.
[106] Cf. statistics of significant and fatal train accidents per train-km and passenger-km: Gourvish, *British Rail 1974–97*, pp. 360–2; John Curley (Railtrack), presentation to Second Rail Summit, 25 May 2000, DETR file R73/1/22 Pt. 7; Andrew W. Evans, in *Modern Railways*, March 2001, pp. 23–7.
[107] Cullen, *Ladbroke Grove Inquiry*, Pt. 1, p. 113, cit. in Wolmar, *On the Wrong Line*, p. 3.
[108] Cullen, *Ladbroke Grove Inquiry*, Pt. 1, p. 259, Wolmar, *On the Wrong Line*, pp. 145–6.
[109] Piers Morgan (Editor, The Mirror)–Blair, 5 November 1999, and reply, 22 November 1999, Prime Minister's Rail Policy papers, Pts. 5–6. Morton thought that Morgan was being encouraged by Corbett: Morton–Grant, 12 October 1999, Morton's papers, SRA.
[110] The share price fell from £13.31 on 4 October to £11.55 on 12 October, and after fluctuating fell to £9.92 on 22 November and £9.54 on 26 November: *Financial Times*, 5 October–30 November 1999.

on Railtrack impressed upon its executives that it could look for no support from politicians.[111] When Corbett had breakfast with Blair at Number Ten a few weeks later the exchanges were blunt. A pacifying letter sent to the Prime Minister after the event could not disguise Corbett's anger. 'I believe', he wrote, 'that the public's reluctance to give us credit for [the railway industry's] achievements is largely due to criticisms from politicians and the Rail Regulator who too often choose to highlight the negatives, instead of the positives.'[112] However, more negatives were on the way. Another serious accident at Hatfield occurred on 17 October 2000, just after the Ladbroke Grove enquiry sittings had ended. This was to have an even more profound effect on the strategy and structure of the industry.

By the time of Hatfield doubts were emerging about the effect of Labour's tinkering with the Tories' privatization framework. It was of course difficult for Morton, Grant, and Winsor to achieve instant improvements in an activity that resembled a juggernaut. The headlong rush to privatize Railtrack and let the passenger franchises had left the industry with a set of loosely specified and, in some areas, unsatisfactory, contractual relationships in which delivery and monitoring required attention. Winsor had made it clear that Railtrack had to improve its performance as a business, but was equally certain that further revenue from the public purse would be required to fund infrastructural improvement. Morton and Grant had embarked on an adventurous policy of long franchises, but this appeared to be unravelling just as it was being made explicit. Furthermore, some of the SSRA's more rhetorical statements—for example the promise of 'rapid investment in rail, on a scale not seen since the mid-1950s'[113]—invited comparisons, not only with the British Transport Commission's ill-fated Modernisation Plan of 1955–65 but with Railtrack's more extravagant promises. This not exactly happy start for the new strategic body was accompanied by suggestions that its early interventions were not being welcomed by the infrastructure company and its regulator. In a speech in 2001, Winsor likened himself to a referee presiding over two important team captains in Railtrack and the SRA.[114] Morton took a quite different view; borrowing the analogy, he saw himself as the manager, with Railtrack in midfield and Winsor in goal. The difference of view was striking and important. At the same time public perceptions of the railways were of an industry which may have produced incremental gains in services, but at the expense of punctuality, and after Ladbroke Grove there were strong suspicions

---

[111] HSE, *Review of Arrangements for Standard Setting and Application on the Main Railway Network: Interim Report*, 5 October 1999, Morton–Mottram and Morton–SSRA Chairman's Committee, both 11 October 1999, Morton–Grant, 12 October 1999, Morton's papers, SRA; Wolmar, *On the Wrong Line*, p. 153. Ministers pressed on with their intention to remove the Safety and Standards Directorate from Railtrack: cf. *Parl. Deb. (Lords)*, 5th ser. (Session 1998–9), Vol. 605, Macdonald, statement, 11 October 1999, c. 14.

[112] Corbett–Blair, 9 November 1999, Prime Minister's Rail Policy papers, Pt. 5.

[113] SSRA, *Annual Report 1999/2000*, p. 18.

[114] Winsor, speech to IPPR Conference, 21 February 2001, in DETR file R73/1/3 Pt. 2.

that fragmentation had not helped safety control. The target-setting mentality of Number Ten, in focusing on operating performance, suited the politicians seeking quick fixes in advance of a general election, and such an approach was more attractive than the burden of long-term financial commitments. The *10 Year Plan* represented an advance in identifying the need to put infrastructure improvements in place that had a long gestation period, but how far the Treasury would be able to give the plan unequivocal support was another matter. It had already expressed the concern that some of the deals for longer franchises would take too large a slice of the available cake.[115] Nevertheless, before Hatfield, the numbers had been produced, and there were expectations of delivery. However, there was a vulnerability in the political economy of the railways, which was demonstrated by Morton's resentment of Macdonald, the Transport Minister, who, he felt, had been placed there to act as a Blairite trimmer and curb upon Prescott's transport ambitions.[116] Relations between the two, once fairly cordial, deteriorated as the financial implications of Winsor's charges review became clearer. By May 2000 Macdonald was also insisting on a Memorandum of Understanding between the DETR and the SRA to restrain Morton's tendency to press ahead with policy without giving the Department adequate notice.[117] Morton, on the other hand, told the Minister: 'I did not build a Channel Tunnel to qualify me to work for Mr Coulshed [Head of DETR Railways Sponsorship Division] or any other Grade 7 civil servant. I've created an SRA to contain the expertise; if you filter it through officials, you don't need it.'[118] A potential conflict about the role of Mottram and Grant as 'accounting officers' for the SRA was also surfacing.[119] One may speculate on what might have happened had there been no Hatfield crash. Action would have centred on the introduction of the new charges regime and the attempt to square this with the SRA's long franchise policy and the parameters of the *10 Year Plan*. But Hatfield put paid to all that.

[115] Cf. Smith–Macdonald, 19 October 2000, DETR file R73/1/26 Pt. 6.

[116] Prescott certainly did not share this view: Interview with Prescott, 2006.

[117] Cf. Morton–Grant, 24 February 2000, Morton–Macdonald, 30 March and 9 May 2000, Macdonald–Morton, 22 May and 1 June 2000, Morton's papers, SRA.

[118] Morton, file note on meeting with Macdonald, 15 June 2000, ibid.

[119] Morton–Macdonald, 14 September 2000, ibid.

3

The Hatfield
Watershed, 2000–1

3.1 Introduction

The Hatfield accident on 17 October 2000 threw the industry into something resembling organized chaos. The cause of the accident was promptly established: a broken rail, which derailed a GNER King's Cross–Leeds train. In the event, it was decided not to hold a public enquiry into the accident, in which four passengers were killed and 70 were injured. But if the causes were less complex than those identified at Southall and Ladbroke Grove in 1997 and 1999, the impact of this incident was to prove more catastrophic. It threw the infrastructure provider, Railtrack, into a corporate panic from which it never recovered, challenged the funding for railways negotiated in the *10 Year Plan* and the Government's Spending Review of 2000, and therefore limited the ambitions of the Strategic Rail Authority. It also affected the performance of the railway as seen through the operating benchmarks for Railtrack and the TOCs. In this chapter, we begin by examining the performance of the privatized railway in the period up to the accident, examine the 'political economy' of Hatfield, and then assess its impact in more detail.

3.2 Performance *ex ante*: operating costs, profits, and subsidy, 1997–2000

By the time of Hatfield it was possible to make a more informed assessment of the performance of the privatized railway. Annual data were available to the end of the financial year 1999/2000, while monthly and quarterly data were available for the first half of 2000/1. Commentators also had the benefit of a report by the National Audit Office on passenger rail service improvement.[1] Turning first to operating performance, the unveiling of the superior Public Performance Measure (PPM) in June 2000 heralded a more intrusive examination of the train operators' performance in relation to punctuality and reliability. This combined measure of the two variables, which was backdated at Prescott's request,[2] provided data from 1997/8 and indicated that Railtrack and the TOCs were struggling to cope with the consequences of catering for a continuation of rising demand. The number of passenger-kilometres travelled increased by 20 per cent from 1996/7 to 1999/2000, while freight tonne-kilometres increased by 21 per cent over the same period. At 38.5 and 18.2 billion respectively, both traffics were now at a higher level than at the peak of 1988/9 (Tables 3.1 and 1.1). Indeed, the passenger figures were at their highest since petrol was rationed, first in the immediate post-war period, and then in 1957.[3] With Railtrack's initial business planning, access charges regime, and performance mechanisms predicated upon a steady or declining state, it is no surprise to find that performance was slipping. The PPM, that is, percentage of trains arriving on time, which was calculated as 89.7 in 1997/8, fell to 87.9 and 87.8 over the next two years, with an evident deterioration in the second quarter of 2000/1, that is, July–September 2000, in the months immediately prior to Hatfield (Table 3.1), a phenomenon drawn to Macdonald's attention by Grant in October. A number of factors were at work, but Grant highlighted rolling stock faults, exacerbated by the 'sweating' of existing assets, Railtrack equipment and infrastructure failures, congestion problems arising from more intensive network usage, and an insufficient number of drivers.[4] The problem was serious enough for ATOC and Railtrack to suggest to the SSRA that it would take 3–5 years before a substantial improvement could be made.[5] Overcrowding was another area of concern, and where measured was on the increase, though the data being collected were far from complete.[6] The level of passenger complaints measured by the rail users' committees reflected

---

[1] NAO, *Action to Improve Passenger Rail Services*, 3 August 2000, P.P. 1999–2000, xciii, HC842.

[2] Linnard–Grant, 14 September 1999, DETR file R80/1/11 Pt. 2.

[3] 1946: 47.0bn; 1947: 37.0bn; 1957: 36.4bn DfT, *TSGB 2005*, pp. 104–5.

[4] Grant–Macdonald, 5 October 2000, Morton's papers, SRA, and see also Iryna Terlecky (SSRA), Memo. 3 October 2000, SRA file 02/20/01 Pt. 10; NAO, *Passenger Rail Services*, p. 31.

[5] George Muir (ATOC) and Richard Middleton (Railtrack)–Grant, 5 September 2000, SRA file 02/20/01 Pt. 10.

[6] NAO, *Passenger Rail Services*, pp. 4, 38–47.

Table 3.1 Rail performance, 1996/7–2000/1: traffic, passenger quality, and safety indicators

Year	Traffic		Passenger performance			Passenger complaints		Total passenger delay minutes (million)	Responsibility for delay: Railtrack's share (%)—passenger only	Accidents	
	Passenger national rail (bn km)	Freight (bn tonne-km)	Charter (%)	Punctuality and reliability (%)	PPM (%)	To rail users' committees (no.)	To TOCs (no.) per 100,000 journeys			Passengers killed in train incidents (national rail) (no.)	Significant train incidents national rail (no. per million train-km)
1996/7	32.1	15.1	92.5	99.1	n.a.	7,376	n.a.	11.9	56	1	0.17
1997/8	34.7	16.9	92.5	98.9	89.7	14,735	n.a.	12.7	53	7	0.12
1998/9	36.3	17.3	91.5	98.8	87.9	18,777	120	14.5	47	0	0.15
1999/0	38.5	18.2	91.9	98.8	87.8	14,635	109	14.0	45	29	0.13
2000/1	38.2	18.1	n.a.	n.a.	79.1	14,129	131	23.8	60	10	0.14
2000/1 Q1	9.9	4.6			88.3		95	3.1	46		
2000/1 Q2	10.6	4.6			86.6		119	3.7	42		
2000/1 Q3	8.8	4.2			64.3		160	8.2	68		
2000/1 Q4	8.8	4.7			76.3		152	8.8[a]	64[a]		

[a] Periods 10–13.

Note: CRUCC/RPC complaints data differ from those given in Table 1.1 in that London data were calculated on a different basis from 1998/9 (recording only 'appeal complaints' as complaints) and were therefore excluded. In 1996/7, complaints including London amounted to 9,753, and without London, 7,376; the figures for 1997/8 were 19,792 and 14,735, respectively. See RPC, Annual Report 2001/2, p. 39, and my thanks to Andrew Regan for explaining the change.

Source: SRA, National Rail Trends Yearbook 2004–5, pp. 3, 14–15, 20, 28–9; rail network delay minutes data, Network Rail and DfT; TSGB 2005, pp. 64, 105, 108–9; RPC, Annual Report 2004/5, p. 50; HSE, Railway Safety 2000/1, pp. 32, 42, 132; Railtrack, delay minutes graphs, 15 April 1999, Morton's papers, SRA.

the fluctuations in punctuality, reliability, and overcrowding. Thus, the number of complaints (excluding London), 7,000 in 1996/7, doubled in 1997/8, then increased by a further 27 per cent in 1998/9. In the next two years there were over 14,000 complaints, more than 20 per cent higher than the previous peak in 1995/6 (Tables 3.1, 1.1). New data provided by the TOCs and reported to the SSRA, which related complaints to the number of passenger journeys, again reflected the deterioration in performance in the months prior to Hatfield, with a 25 per cent increase in the complaints level in the second quarter of 2000/1 (Table 3.1). The incentive and penalty regimes operated by OPRAF/SSRA and Railtrack, in relation to the TOCs, also indicate the difficulties in maintaining performance benchmarked to historic British Rail 'standards' with higher traffic volumes. Thus, OPRAF made a net payment of £13.0 million to the TOCs in 1997/8, but in the following year received a net payment of £4.0 million, and the SSRA collected £3.3 million in 1999/2000.[7] The 'delay minutes' data calculated by Railtrack for use in its dealings with the TOCs and the ORR also reveal a decline in performance. The total minutes of delay experienced in passenger operations, which amounted to 11.9 million in 1996/7, rose to 14.5 million in 1998/9, though there was a modest improvement in 1999/2000 (14.0 m.).[8] Under pressure from the Rail Regulator, Railtrack produced an improvement in its performance, its share of the responsibility for delays falling from 56 per cent in 1996/7 to 45 per cent in 1999/2000 (Table 3.1). At the same time the delays caused by maintenance and renewal problems also fell, by 26 per cent from 1995/6 to 1999/2000. However, whether Railtrack's actions carried with them the risk of prejudicing safety was another matter.[9] The NAO, while observing in August 2000 that punctuality and reliability had been slightly better than with British Rail, observed significant variations in performance from TOC to TOC, and made the point that the existing incentive mechanisms were relatively weak, and where they encouraged a response, often worked in a perverse way. Thus, operators with trains running very late tended to persist with them in order to avoid making cancellations, even though the overall effect of the action was to add to timetable disruption.[10]

The overall safety record is also more difficult to assess. The accident at Ladbroke Grove produced a sharp rise in the number of passengers killed in train accidents in 1999/2000, but the number of train accidents on the national network remained stationary at around 1,600 incidents per annum in the period 1996/7–2000/1,[11] and the key measure, significant train accidents per train-kilometre, continued to exhibit an improvement. At only 0.13–0.14

[7] OPRAF/SSRA, *Annual Report 1997/8–1999/2000.*

[8] Delay minutes data from Network Rail, ATOC, and DfT.

[9] NAO, *Ensuring that Railtrack maintain and renew the railway network*, 12 April 2000, P.P. 1999–2000, lx, HC397, pp. 3, 29–30.

[10] NAO, *Passenger Rail Services*, pp. 2–3, 25–9.

[11] Total accidents: 1,585, 1996/7; 1,652, 1997/8; 1,623, 1998/9; 1,638, 1999/2000; 1,546, 2000/1. HSE, *Railway Safety 1996/7–2000/1*, corrected figure for 1999/2000 from Paul Wilkinson (ORR).

in 1999/2000–2000/1, the accident rate was much lower than in the late 1980s and early 1990s (Tables 3.1, 1.1). The difficulty of assessment applies also to the overall economic health of the industry, in relation to investment, cost control, and profitability. The DETR's investment data indicate that total investment rose by 121 per cent from 1996/7 to 2000/1. Infrastructure investment increased by 87 per cent over the same period, and there was a notable improvement in the disappointing rolling stock procurement record since privatization, with investment in 2000/1 up 10-fold on the low base in 1996/7 (Table 3.2). The cost-effectiveness of the new regime is quite another matter, and here the published statistics had little to offer. Far from easy to unravel given the disintegration of functions, it was left to social scientists to attempt an assessment from the available financial information.[12] Nevertheless, data from Railtrack and the TOCs provide important indications, and in the sense that some costs were passed through to the Government in the form of increased subsidy, the data of government support to the industry is indicative of general trends.

A priori one would expect the level of government support to have fallen, as the downward subsidy taper built into franchise agreements began to bite. In fact, central government revenue support to the TOCs in constant 2000/1 prices fell from £1.9 billion in 1996/7 to only £0.8 billion in 2000/1, a reduction of 57 per cent, and total support (by central and local governments) fell by 51 per cent. However, after taking into account other elements, overall support actually rose in 1997/8 (by 69 per cent), and did not return to the 1996/7 level until 2000/1 (Table 3.2). Pressure on the main players is evident. For example, Railtrack's net debt (borrowing less cash in bank) was rising steadily before Hatfield: standing at £499 million on 31 March 1997, the debt rose steadily to £1,271 million in March 1999, and £2,186 million on 30 September 2000, a more than threefold increase in $3\frac{1}{2}$ years.[13] For the TOCs, the pressure on profitability arising from reduced subsidy profiles was alleviated by increases in revenue from higher patronage, but the additional traffic put pressure on operating costs.[14] The subsidy paid per passenger-kilometre fell steadily from 5.2p in 1997/8 to 3.5p

---

[12] See, for example, Gerald Crompton and Robert Jupe, 'Delivering Better Transport? An Evaluation of the Ten-Year Plan for the Railway Industry', *Public Money and Management*, 22:3 (September 2002), 41–7; Jean Shaoul, '*Railpolitik*: The Financial Realities of Operating Britain's National Railways', *ibid.* 24:1 (January 2004), 27–36, and 'The Performance of the Privatised Train Operators', *Catalyst Working Paper*, September 2005; Andrew J. S. Smith, 'Are Britain's Railways Costing Too Much? Perspectives Based on TFP Comparisons with British Rail 1963–2002', *Journal of Transport Economics and Policy*, 40:1 (January 2006), 1–44; Robert Jupe and Gerald Crompton, ' "A Deficient Performance": The Regulation of the Train Operating Companies in Britain's Privatised Railway System', *Critical Perspectives on Accounting*, 17:8 (2006), 1035–65.

[13] Railtrack plc, *R&A 1996/7* et seq.; information from Stephen Bennett (SRA). There was a proportionate increase in the debt of Railtrack Group plc. Cf. Shaoul, '*Railpolitik*', 34.

[14] For alternative analyses of the TOC accounts, see KPMG Transaction Services, 'Report to SRA on Analysis of Historic TOC Financial Performance', 9 October 2002, SRA; Edward Thomas (KPMG Transaction Services), 'Overview of TOC Financial Performance', 11 July 2003, DfT file R73/1/26 Pt. 13; Shaoul, 'The Performance of the Privatised Train Operators'; Jupe and Crompton, 'A Deficient Performance'.

Table 3.2 Rail performance, 1996/7–2000/1: investment and government subsidy (£m., in constant 2000/1 prices)

Year	Investment			Passenger revenue support			Total support after other elements[a]
	Infrastructure	Rolling stock	Total	Central government	Local government	Total	
1996/7	1,286	51	1,338	1,975	318	2,293	1,169
1997/8	1,517	121	1,638	1,516	398	1,914	1,971
1998/9	1,886	182	2,068	1,237	349	1,586	1,671
1999/0	2,041	239	2,280	1,046	316	1,362	1,461
2000/1	2,404	554	2,958	847	283	1,130	1,250

[a] Changes in indebtedness, sale of ROSCOs, freight grants, etc.

Source: SRA, National Rail Trends Yearbook 2004/5, pp. 47, 51, expressed in constant 2000/1 prices using Treasury, GDP deflator (market prices), 2007.

in 1999/2000 and 3.4p in 2000/1. For 'commercial' franchises such as Gatwick Express and GNER, the reduction exceeded 50 per cent to 1999/2000 (Table 3.3). The TOCs' operating accounts for 1997/8 to 1999/2000 (pre-Hatfield) indicate that profitability, averaging £5.89 million per operator in 1997/8 and £5.67 million in 1999/2000 (Table 3.3), was largely a function of increased traffic, which produced 31 per cent more in revenue in 1999/2000 compared with 1996/7 (21% in constant prices).[15] Thus, although the share of revenue made up by subsidy fell from about 37 per cent in 1997/8 to 27 per cent in 1999/2000,[16] total income (the fare-box plus subsidy) was maintained. While a substantial proportion of expenditure was fixed in the form of access charges, there were some upward cost pressures, particularly with labour,[17] such that total operating costs did not fall as anticipated, but instead were 0.9 per cent up on the 1997/8 baseline in 1999/2000. For franchises such as Chiltern and Cardiff, the increase in costs was more substantial (Table 3.3). So on the eve of Hatfield the indications were that while the rail industry was serving a greater number of customers, the cost of doing so with a network which had barely been enhanced since privatization and where rolling stock procurement had been both leisurely and focused upon replacement rather than net additions was being passed onto consumers in the form of operational difficulties. And while the more visible element of government support—the subsidy paid to TOCs—had fallen, the total amount of support in constant 2000/1 prices, £1.97, £1.67, and £1.46 billion in the three years 1997/8–1999/2000, was substantially above the £1.17 billion provided in 1996/7 (Table 3.2).

3.3 The Hatfield accident

Responsibility for the broken rail that caused the accident at Hatfield was quickly attributed to Railtrack and its contractors, Balfour Beatty Maintenance Ltd., although the legal process took five years to complete. It was not until October 2005 that fines of £13.5 million were imposed, the greater part of the penalty falling upon the contractor.[18] Immediately after the accident, the Government asked the HSE to produce a preliminary report. But from the outset the condition of the track was identified as a significant factor, and Macdonald pointed this

[15] Passenger revenue data from DfT, *TSGB 2005*, p. 118.

[16] Taken from Jupe and Crompton, 'A Deficient Performance', 1053; Shaoul's calculations are 38% and 28%, 'Performance of Privatised Train Operators', 27.

[17] There are several calculations showing rising unit labour costs, for example, for 1997/8 to 1999/2000: 13.7% ('average wage costs per employee', Shaoul, 25), 9.5% ('cost per employee', Jupe and Crompton, 1053), and 8.2% ('staff costs per head', KPMG).

[18] Railtrack's successor, Network Rail, was fined £3.5m. and Balfour Beatty £10m. (reduced to £7.5m. on appeal): *Times*, 8 October 2005, p. 4, 6 July 2006, p. 47. The accident has been examined at some length in Ian Jack, *The Crash that Stopped Britain* (2001), and Wolmar, *On the Wrong Line*, pp. 155–88.

Table 3.3 TOCs' operating costs, pre-tax profits, and government subsidy received per passenger-km, 1997/8–2000/1

	1997/8	1998/9	1999/2000	2000/1	% change 1997/8–1999/2000	% change 1997/8–2000/1
Income (£m.) average	199.3	202.5	203.6	196.8	+2.2	−1.2
Operating costs (£m.) average	192.2	195.3	194.0	191.7	+0.9	−0.3
Pre-tax profits (£m.) average	5.89	6.21	5.67	3.68	−3.7	−37.5
Subsidy per passenger-km (pence)	5.2	4.3	3.5	3.4	−32.7	−34.6
Individual franchises:						
Income (£m.):						
Chiltern	50.3	55.8	59.5	63.1	+18.3	+25.4
South West	393.4	421.4	449.6	463.1	+14.3	+17.7
North Western	257.4	246.2	236.6	222.8	−8.1	−13.4
Merseyrail	80.8	78.4	73.0	69.7	−9.6	−13.7
Operating costs (£m.):						
Chiltern	48.0	54.1	57.6	63.9	+20.0	+33.0
Cardiff	29.2	31.0	32.3	32.4	+10.6	+11.0
Great Eastern	163.1	164.7	169.0	131.1	+3.6	−19.6
Silverlink	118.2	115.6	116.9	104.9	−1.1	−11.2
Pre-tax profits (£m.):						
Great Western	28.77	26.08	41.54	41.95	+44.4	+45.8
South West	15.91	37.77	39.23	56.59	+146.6	+255.7
North Western	0.39	−10.08	−14.57	−63.27	–	–
Cross Country (Virgin)	2.33	−7.06	−20.80	−35.24	–	–
Subsidy per passenger-km[a] (pence)						
Gatwick Express	−3.3	−4.2	−5.2	−6.0	+57.6	+81.8
GNER	1.5	1.1	0.4	0.2	+73.3	+86.7
Wales & West	9.4	8.3	7.7	7.0	−18.1	−25.5
Island Line	40.1	37.1	32.9	33.7	−18.0	−16.0

[a] Subsidy paid by OPRAF/SRA + PTEs (excludes incentive payments). For individual TOCs, a rise in subsidy, or a fall in 'negative subsidy', that is, premium, is regarded as a negative result. A reduction in subsidy, or an increase in negative subsidy, is regarded as positive.

Source: SRA.

out to the Lords on 19 October 2000, two days after the accident.[19] By this time Railtrack had conceded publicly that a broken rail was the likely cause and Corbett, the Chief Executive, had offered to resign.[20] On the 20th the HSE, in its first interim report, stated that 'early indications suggest that the likely cause was a broken rail and that this, in turn, was the result of a track defect'.[21] This was confirmed in a second interim report in January 2001: 'All the evidence points to the derailment having been caused by fracture and subsequent fragmentation of a rail…There were multiple pre-existing "rolling contact fatigue" cracks and "extensive spalling".'[22] Inspection by Railtrack of the damage at the site of the crash suggested that the track should have been renewed at an earlier stage, especially for high-speed running: the ill-fated train was travelling at 115/17 mph (185–8 kph), close to the section's maximum permitted speed, when it came off the track. It subsequently emerged that cracked rails had been found at the site 21 months before the accident, and the defective section of the track had been identified for replacement 10 months earlier.[23] Renewal work had been started, and then stopped. An agglomeration of shortcomings in relation to the monitoring of track quality, the procurement of renewals and maintenance work from contractors, and the management of the contractor–client relationship had built up in Railtrack's infrastructure work, and this undoubtedly contributed to the neglect at Hatfield. Corbett told Blair that 'the problems stemmed in part from significant under investment in the network over many years'.[24] However, a more plausible explanation was that Railtrack's more commercial approach to the engineering function, with a tendency to choose maintenance over renewal, and the introduction of a strategy of replacing assets when necessary rather than at set intervals—given the unfortunate name 'Project Destiny'—exposed the company to risk, and the problem was exacerbated by the lack of a comprehensive asset condition register. Here, the transfer of the maintenance and renewal functions from British Rail had produced a knowledge gap as well as a cultural and organizational hiatus, but Railtrack had made no concerted effort to remedy the deficiencies prior to Hatfield.[25] This broad diagnosis was confirmed

---

[19] Grant, Note of 'Telephone Conversation with Vic Coleman (Chief Inspector of Railways, HSE)', 18 October 2000, SRA; *Parl. Deb. (Lords)*, 5th ser. (Session 1999–2000), vol. 617, Macdonald, statement, 19 October 2000, c. 1196–8. Macdonald was encouraged to make a statement by Lord Strathclyde, ibid. 18 October 2000, c. 1030–1. The Commons was not sitting, and Prescott was visiting China.

[20] *Evening Standard*, 18 October 2000, pp. 1–2, 13; Railtrack, News Release, 19 October 2000.

[21] HSE, 1st interim report on train derailment at Hatfield, 20 October 2000, SRA.

[22] HSE, 2nd interim report on train derailment at Hatfield, 23 January 2001, SRA. Rolling contact fatigue was the HSE's preferred description of the phenomenon known as 'gauge corner cracking', where the head of the rail cracks; spalling = flaking or splintering of the metal.

[23] *Times*, 19 October 2000, p. 1, 8 October 2005, p. 4; *R. v Railtrack plc, Balfour Beatty and others*, 6 September 2005.

[24] Simon Virley (Blair's PS)–Peter Unwin (Prescott's PS), 20 November 2000, Cabinet Office file on 'Rail Transport', R14/6 Pt. 2. Corbett had expressed this view on earlier occasions, for example, at a meeting with Blair on 18 May: Virley–Fidler, 18 May 2000, ibid.

[25] Wolmar, *On the Wrong Line*, pp. 157–68; Francis Terry, 'The Nemesis of Privatization: Railway Policy in Retrospect', *Public Money and Management* (Jan–Mar 2001), 5; Glaister, *British Rail Privatisation*, pp. 33–4.

by the reports that followed: in October 2001, from a panel of experts appointed by Railtrack's Safety and Standards Directorate (from January 2001 a separate subsidiary known as Railway Safety); and in August 2002, from a special HSE investigation board.[26]

The immediate response to the Hatfield accident contrasted sharply with British Rail's handling of major accidents in the past.[27] Not only did the British Transport Police and HSE retain occupancy of the line for a considerable time— the line remained closed for 24 days,[28] but Railtrack gave every indication of an organization in panic, one which did not have either the necessary information or the confidence to assess the condition of the infrastructure elsewhere. Thus, at 22.00 hours on the day of the accident, emergency speed restrictions were introduced across the network at 81 locations where similar problems were suspected, and where track was due to be renewed; a 20 mph limit was applied where signs of spalling were evident.[29] This action, the prelude to a National Recovery Programme, erred on the side of extreme caution. Within a week 272 speed restrictions were in force, and 1,850 sites with cracked rails had been found; by late November over 850 restrictions had been introduced, and 3,400 sites had been discovered.[30] Among the more controversial aspects of the activity was a decision by local Railtrack managers to close the West Coast Main Line north of Gretna on 25 October.[31] Similar actions were taken when the accident was followed by serious flooding, which affected the Southern and Great Western Zones in particular.[32] The climate in which all this was done must be appreciated. First, several parties—the HSE's Chief Inspector of Railways, the Rail Regulator, the National Audit Office, and the Public Accounts Committee—had already expressed concerns about Railtrack's safety management, and these had been articulated in reports published earlier in 2000.[33] There was a particular interest in the incidence of broken rails. Winsor had already asked the company, in

[26] Railway Safety, 'Derailed Passenger Train ID38…17 October 2000', October 2001; HSE, 'Hatfield Derailment Investigation. Interim Recommendations of the Investigation Board', August 2002.

[27] A point made by Bill Bradshaw, Bradshaw-Morton, 7 November 2000, SRA. It was also made with characteristic force by Roger Ford: 'Informed Sources', *Modern Railways*, December 2000, pp. 20–2.

[28] Brian Hackland (Blair's PS)–Blair, 8 November 2000, Prime Minister's Rail Policy papers, Pt. 9; *Birmingham Evening Mail*, 10 November 2000, p. 6.

[29] *Times*, 20 October 2000, p. 1.

[30] Hackland–Blair, 26 October 2000, Railtrack, Report to Ministers on 'National Recovery Programme', 24 November 2000 and 'Meeting with the Prime Minister…27 November 2000', Prime Minister's Rail Policy papers, Pts. 8–10; Virley–Unwin, 10 and 30 November 2000, Cabinet Office file R14/6 Pt. 2; Railtrack News Release, 2 April 2001.

[31] Sleeper services were also cancelled on the 24th. Hackland–Blair, 25 October 2000, Prime Minister's Rail Policy papers, Pt. 8; *Glasgow Evening Times*, 25 and 28 October 2000, p. 2; *Independent*, 26 October 2000, pp. 1, 4; *Financial Times*, 28 October 2000, p. 1.

[32] Cf. *Evening Standard*, 30 October 2000, pp. 2–3; *Plymouth Evening Herald*, 30 October 2000, p. 2; *Times*, 31 October 2000, p. 2; *Guardian*, 13 November 2000, p. 12.

[33] HSE, *The Management of Safety in Railtrack* (2000), report commissioned by Prescott after the Ladbroke Grove accident; NAO, *Ensuring that Railtrack…* (2000), cit.; HC Public Accounts Committee, Report on *The Office of the Rail Regulator: Ensuring that Railtrack Maintain and Renew the Railway Network*, 23 August 2000, P.P. 1999–2000, lxx, HC536.

4. Gerald Corbett and Railtrack receive heavy criticism for the response to the Hatfield accident, October 2000: *Private Eye*, 3 November 2000.

August 1999, to reduce the numbers, and in June 2000 he had requested detailed plans, since there had been an increase from 752 breaks in 1995/6 to 952 in 1998/9 and 917 in 1999/2000.[34] Only two months before the accident, having failed to receive in his view a satisfactory answer, he had commissioned, together with the HSE, an independent report from American consultants on the matter. Submitted eight days after the accident, this recommended an extensive reassessment of Railtrack's rail defect management. The authors found weaknesses in rail testing, rail replacement, and the response to the growing problem of rolling contact fatigue, where the practice of rail grinding was not being pursued systematically.[35] Winsor's somewhat relentless pursuance of the company continued with the demand for eight modifications to Railtrack's network licence as part of his access charges review, including the transfer of the company's Safety and Standards Directorate to a new subsidiary, an insistence on the establishment of a comprehensive asset register, and independent evaluation of the sufficiency of its maintenance and renewals activity.[36]

Second, the media, while expressing serious concern—the *Times* referring to 'shockwaves of disbelief', were quick to point the finger at Railtrack, though the majority view was that Corbett should stay on as Chief Executive (the Board turned down his offer to resign). Matters became worse with the news of another derailment on the 19th, at Stafford.[37] Finally, Labour and Conservative politicians, engaged in an uneasy truce to avoid feeding the 'adversarial blame culture' surrounding the industry, also put pressure on the infrastructure provider. Thus, Bernard Jenkin, the Shadow Transport Secretary, replying to Prescott's Commons statement on 24 October, referred to the evident trade-off between train performance and safety, and suggested that Railtrack's failure to introduce a speed restriction at Hatfield prior to the accident had been influenced by the existence of the penalty regime for delays.[38] Labour backbencher George Galloway tabled an early day motion, which was highly critical of Railtrack and referred to 'corporate manslaughter'.[39] The Transport Committee announced that it was also investigating the matter and took evidence from Corbett and two other directors, Richard Middleton (Commercial) and Chris Leah (Safety and Environment), on 1 November. Here Corbett conceded that there was a conflict between

[34] Winsor–Corbett, 12 August and 12 November 1999, 30 June and 4 August 2000, www.rail-reg.gov.uk; HSE, *Railway Safety 2000/1*, p. 99.

[35] Kevin Sawley and Richard Reiff (Transportation Technology Center Inc.), *Rail Failure Assessment for the Office of the Rail Regulator* (October 2000), and see also ORR, *Annual Report 2000/1*, pp. 6, 28; Wolmar, *On the Wrong Line*, pp. 171–6.

[36] ORR, *Annual Report 2000/1*, pp. 3–4, 6.

[37] *Times*, 18 October 2000, p. 23; Wolmar, in *Evening Standard*, 18 and 19 October 2000, p. 13; *Independent*, 19 October 2000, pp. 1, 5; *Financial Times*, 20 October 2000, p. 1. Support for Corbett was somewhat puzzling, since prior to the accident he had been throwing his weight around the industry like a latter-day Philip Shirley, Beeching's famous 'outsider'.

[38] *Parl. Deb. (Commons)*, 6th ser. (Session 1999–2000), vol. 355, Prescott, statement, 24 October 2000, c. 136–8, Jenkin, reply, c. 138–9.

[39] *Rail Politic*, 27 October 2000.

5. Gwyneth Dunwoody, campaigning Chair of the House of Commons Transport Committee, is removed from the Committee, then quickly reinstated after backbench opposition, July 2001: Steve Bell, *Guardian*, 12 July 2001.

performance incentives and safety, and the Committee concluded that Railtrack's management of the contractors had been 'totally inadequate', pointing to 'systematic, often-repeated failings in the company's management systems and leadership'.[40] On 26 October Prescott convened a mini-rail summit to review the action taken. Morton was asked to review ways of optimizing network management, and subsequently cross-industry working groups were created, presided over by a Steering Committee (subsequently reconstituted as a Rail Industry Group). In late November a Rail Recovery Action Group, headed by Macdonald, was established to oversee the industry's efforts to return the railway network to normal.[41] After very little involvement in railways over the past three years, the Prime Minister took a direct interest in the crisis. He condemned Railtrack's initial efforts as 'simply not good enough'[42] and called in rail industry leaders to

[40] HC Select Committee on Environment, Transport and Regional Affairs, 1st Report on *Recent Events on the Railway*, December 2000, P.P. 2000–1, ix, HC17, paras. 10 and 22, and MOE, 1 November 2000, Corbett, QQ. 41, 57. See also Wolmar, pp. 177–8.

[41] SSRA Chairman's Committee Minutes, 24 October 2000, SRA file 02/20/02 Pt. 2; DETR News Release, 26 October 2000; Virley–Unwin, 10 and 20 November 2000, cit.; David Hill (ODPM)–Linnard, 6 December 2000, DETR file R10/5/73 Pt. 1; Morton-Prescott, 23 November and 21 December 2000, Morton's papers, SRA; BRB Minutes, 11 January 2001, SRA.

[42] Blair, annotation on Hackland–Blair, 25 October 2000, Prime Minister's Rail Policy papers, Pt. 8.

brief him on no fewer than three occasions in November.[43] However, in January 2001 Ministers decided not to hold a public enquiry into the accident. Lord Cullen, who was already investigating the Southall and Ladbroke Grove accidents, was asked to add Hatfield to his general safety brief. The Government was content for criminal prosecutions to be brought against managers in Railtrack and Balfour Beatty. The process was a protracted one. Cullen's report did not appear until September 2001, the HSE investigation board's report was published in August 2002, and criminal charges were not brought until July 2003.[44]

The impact of Hatfield on an already beleaguered company was predictably severe. Both the non-executive Chairman, Sir Philip Beck (who had succeeded Sir Robert Horton in July 1999), and the Chief Executive, Corbett, came under considerable pressure, but it is important to understand that this had been building up for some time. Morton's files for 1999 reveal growing criticisms (from both the SSRA and the Regulator) of aspects of Railtrack's asset management, ranging from gauging policy and train acceptance to general track condition, highlighted by problems with rail corrosion in the Severn Tunnel. And Corbett had conceded that the company had failed to take account of the impact of increased traffic volumes on the network.[45] Attacks on the company intensified after the Ladbroke Grove accident. At that time Morton had thought that there was a considerable risk that Railtrack's management would 'implode'. He was certainly not impressed by the rather anonymous Beck, and feared that Corbett might resign at that time.[46] A month after Hatfield Corbett *did* resign. More than anyone in the company he had seen the need for reform of maintenance and renewal management and had introduced some much-needed controls, although he had also presided over 'Project Destiny'. But having stayed on to start the Recovery Programme, he was showing signs of increasing strain, and was succeeded by Steven Marshall, the finance director.[47] Aged 43, Marshall had an accounting background, and his direct experience of railways was limited. He had been chief executive of Thorn before joining Railtrack, and like Corbett had also worked at GrandMet. He took up his high-profile appointment after less than a year with the company. The new Chief Operating Officer, Jonson Cox, had even less experience, having been appointed as the company's Director of Operations only 11 weeks previously. At the same time Beck announced that he would be leaving soon. He had asked the Board to commence the search for a successor, and had had private talks with the DETR about possible candidates.[48]

[43] On the 9th, 16th, and 27th: Cabinet Office file R14/6 Pt. 2.

[44] Cullen, *The Ladbroke Grove Inquiry. Pt. 2 Report* (September 2001), esp. pp. 170–1; HSE, 'Hatfield Derailment Investigation', 2002, cit. Manslaughter charges were dropped during the Old Bailey trial in July 2005.

[45] HSE News Release, 29 April 1999; Bolt–Corbett, 29 April 1999, Corbett–Bolt, 14 June 1999, Grant–Corbett, 30 September and 29 October 1999, Corbett–Grant, 1 October 1999, Morton's papers, SRA.

[46] Morton–Grant, 12 October 1999, ibid.

[47] Blair was told that Railtrack's non-executive directors had initiated Corbett's departure: Hackland–Blair, 17 November 2000, Prime Minister's Rail Policy papers, Pt. 9.

[48] Hackland–Blair, 19 January 2000 (sic: in fact 2001), ibid. Pt. 6.

He was eventually replaced in June 2001 by John Robinson, an engineer (FREng, FIChemE), who was chairman of George Wimpey and RJB Mining and had been chief executive and then chairman of Smith & Nephew.[49] Although some managerial strengthening took place, with Richard Middleton's move from the commercial to the technical function, and the appointments of David Harding as Finance Director and Andrew McNaughton as Chief Engineer, Railtrack entered the most critical phase in its short history with relatively inexperienced senior executives in key positions. However, changes at the top had little impact on the fundamental problems exposed by Hatfield. Railtrack had propelled itself into a headlong and expensive maintenance binge, the operational and financial consequences of which were bound to be extensive. The company cut a sorry figure as it complained bitterly about its plight, and its standing with the Rail Regulator and the Government deteriorated as it sought financial assistance in the form of further adjustments to the access charges review, the final conclusions of which had been published just after the accident, on 23 October.[50]

As we have seen, questions had been raised about the effectiveness of the company as an infrastructure provider ever since the time of Swift. The company had itself admitted that the incentives it faced could have perverse consequences, and Winsor had racked up the regulatory admonitions, pressing the company to establish a reliable and complete asset register in September 2000. The conspicuous absence of such a register had handicapped effective management of the infrastructure in several ways, for example, in adding considerably to the delays in the acceptance of new rolling stock for service, a factor which caused manufacturers to complain to both Winsor and Morton.[51] Winsor, under pressure himself from the TOCs and the major freight operator, EWS, also pressed Railtrack to produce operator-specific recovery plans, and another enforcement order was issued, on 2 January 2001, before the plans were finally presented on the 18th.[52] The company's credibility was undoubtedly damaged by its rash promises to return the network to normal. The failure to do so was evident to Blair, who was becoming increasingly frustrated by Railtrack, and at a meeting with company executives on 27 November 2000, told them that the current situation was

---

[49] Railtrack News Releases, 17 November 2000 and 17 May 2001; Railtrack, *R&A 1999–2001*; *Railnews*, December 2000, pp. 1–2; David A. Harding, 'Railtrack: The Administration Order of October 2001 in the Context of Government's Regulation of Railways', University of Nottingham MPhil thesis, 2005, pp. 136–8. The search for a new chairman was reported to have been tough, and a number of candidates were approached without success, including John Parker (Babcock, GKN, Brambles and Lattice): Hackland–Blair, 23 March 2001, Prime Minister's Rail Policy papers, Pt. 13; *Financial Times*, 18 May 2001, p. 2.

[50] ORR, *Periodic Review: Final Conclusions* (2000), cit.

[51] See Per Staehr (COO, ADtranz) and Martyn Vaughan (MD, Alstom)–Winsor, Morton, and Grant, 5 July 1999, DETR file R73/1/5 Pt. 1; David Humphrey (SSRA), Memo. 3 October 2000, SRA file 57/01/02 Pt. 14, James Jerram (Vice Chairman, BRB)–Morton, 20 November 2000, SRA; ORR *Annual Report 2000/1*, pp. 3, 17; ORR, *Notice of Proposed Modification to Railtrack's Network Licence: Asset Register* (March 2001), p. 5.

[52] Winsor–Marshall, 30 November 2000, in Hackland–Blair, 1 December 2000, Prime Minister's Rail Policy papers, Pt. 10; Order, 2 January 2001, in ORR, *Annual Report 2000/1*, pp. 24–5.

'totally unacceptable' and that 'the promises made at earlier meetings simply had not been met'.[53] But Railtrack persisted with further promises, undertaking to return 85 per cent of the network to normal by the end of January 2001, and the remainder by Easter. Most insiders were well aware that the timescales for rail procurement and engineering work made this unrealistic, and the serious overrunning of work at Willesden and Leeds provided proof of this.[54] After further slippage was evident, Winsor produced another enforcement order, on 20 March, requiring Railtrack to restore normal operations to most of the network by 21 May.[55] At this point only 153 of the total of 1,342 speed restrictions imposed as a result of concerns about gauge corner cracking were still in force, though these took some time to remove, and when the Rail Recovery Action Group held its final meeting on 18 June, concern was expressed about the extent of 'ordinary' speed restrictions.[56]

Railtrack, for its part, sought to challenge the adequacy of Winsor's review, which envisaged access charges of £8.836 billion and network grants of £5.067 billion in the second control period (CP2, 2001/2–2005/6).[57] Of course, by seeking more financial assistance from the regulatory process, this in practice meant imposing an additional financial burden on the SRA, and behind the Authority, the Government, which, as we noted earlier (pp. 51–2), had just responded to the review by finding an additional £2.3 billion to support the enhancements to be delivered by Railtrack and the SRA. In November 2000, when the half-year results were announced, the company stated that it was making an exceptional charge of *c.*£250 million (soon expected to be double that) in the second half of the financial year to cover penalty payments and the re-railing programme. At the same time it declared that the charges review, where much of the revenue took the form of income deferred until the third financial control period (CP3, 2006/7–2010/11) would strain its financial capability to invest in the £8 billion of enhancements which the Regulator had concluded could be financed in control period 2, the first five years of the 10 Year Plan (2001/2–2005/6). Railtrack was also critical of Winsor's tougher performance benchmarks and penalty rates, and felt that his new efficiency targets were 'unattainable' after Hatfield.[58] Pressure was applied by the company in the knowledge that with the Transport Act 2000 having received the royal assent, on 30 November, it was empowered

[53] Virley–Unwin, 20 and 30 November 2000, Cabinet Office file R14/6 Pt. 2.

[54] Virley–Blair, 5 January 2001, Prime Minister's Rail Policy papers, Pt. 11; SSRA Chairman's Committee Minutes, 2 and 16 January 2001, SRA files 02/20/02 Pt. 2; BRB Minutes, 11 January 2001, Grant, report to SRA Board, 26 January 2001, SRA.

[55] Virley–Unwin, 27 February 2001, Prime Minister's file on Bilaterals with DPM, Hackland-Blair, 2 May 2001, Rail Policy papers, Pt. 14; ORR, *Annual Report 2000/1*, p. 7.

[56] Railtrack, Presentation to the National Task Force, 9 May 2001, Railway Recovery Report No. 32, 23 May 2001, Richard Spoors, Report to DTLR, 11 June 2001, Richard Morris (SSRA)–SSRA Chairman's Committee, 20 June 2000, Morton's papers, SRA.

[57] ORR, *Periodic Review: Final Conclusions* (2000), I, Appendices D and E.

[58] Stuart Connolly (Head of Railways Economics and Finance Divn, DETR)–Malcolm Macdonald (DETR), 10 November 2000, DETR file R10/5/77 Pt. 1; Railtrack News Release, 13 November 2000.

to take an appeal against the charges review to the Competition Commission.[59] Time was short, however, since Winsor had given the company a deadline of 15 January 2001 for doing so.[60] On 12 December Railtrack's advisers, Rothschilds, briefed the Treasury on the company's difficulties, in a presentation with the subtitle 'On the Brink'. The merchant bankers rehearsed the elements in dispute between the company and the Regulator, and argued that the determination for CP2 had left a financing gap of some £1.5 billion. They suggested that by bringing forward £1 billion in cash from CP3 into CP2 the prospect of the company making a matching rights issue would be strengthened.[61] A departmental meeting with ministers, also attended by Morton, Grant, and Prescott's special adviser, Joe Irvin, was held on the 22nd to discuss Railtrack's concerns, together with the prospects for the second section of the Channel Tunnel Rail Link, which Railtrack had an option to purchase. Mottram advised Prescott and Macdonald that it was legitimate for the company to raise the cash flow issue with the Government, but the Ministers were reluctant to agree to bring forward the £1 billion requested, and Prescott was by no means unhappy with the prospect of a reference to the independent Competition Commission. He and Macdonald agreed that Rowlands should write to Railtrack stating it was for Railtrack to resolve its differences with the Regulator. However, Rowlands made the point that such a reference would inevitably delay the work on enhancement and refranchising.[62]

Shortly before the 15 January 2001 deadline, Railtrack and its advisers Rothschilds repeated the view that the deferral of payments under Winsor's access charges review had left the company in a 'precarious' position. Now Hatfield compounded this, such that it was unable to raise the finance to fund even its existing contractual investment commitments, let alone the £8 billion in enhancements for 2001-6.[63] The SSRA Board minuted that 'Railtrack was not fit for purpose as an organisation capable of delivering an efficient, well maintained infrastructure'.[64] However, no one was very anxious to push matters to an irreconcilable crisis point. Winsor rejected the idea of altering his conclusions, or of relaxing his deadline, despite pressure exerted by Prescott at Dorneywood, but he acknowledged via a 'comfort letter' that the post-Hatfield position of the company might represent a 'material change of circumstances', opening

[59] The origins of this lay in Winsor's concerns about shortcomings in the existing review process relating to pricing, and interim reviews: Prescott–Macdonald, 12 April 2000, Cabinet Office file R14/6 Pt. 2.

[60] The statutory 42-day notice was given: ORR, *Review Notice*, 4 December 2000, ORR.

[61] N. M. Rothschild & Sons, 'Railtrack and the Regulatory Review: On the Brink', December 2000, DETR file R10/5/77 Pt. 1.

[62] Hill–Rowlands, 9 January 2001, ibid.

[63] Connolly–Malcolm Macdonald, 8 January 2001, Connolly–Peter McCarthy (DETR), 10 January 2001, ibid.; Rothschild, 'Railtrack and the Regulatory Review: On the Brink—Toppling Over?', 9 January 2001, Prime Minister's Rail Policy papers, Pt. 11 (annex). Morton complained that while Railtrack was pressing the Government about the precariousness of its position it was allowing financial markets to believe that Winsor's review had been generous, thereby creating a false market in its shares: Morton–Marshall, 4 January 2001, Morton–Prescott, 10 January 2001, Morton's papers, SRA.

[64] BRB Minutes, 11 January 2001, SRA.

the way to a further, 'interim' review which would address, in particular, the timing of the revenue streams.[65] On the 15th Railtrack accepted the terms of the review, but at the same time made it clear that it expected the Government and the SRA to give ground on the deferred funding, which would make an early interim review unnecessary. By this time the company put the direct costs arising out of Hatfield at £600 million and was expecting a 'significant loss' for the financial year.[66] The Government was anxious to reach an agreement with an election imminent. When Blair met Brown and Prescott on the 23rd, he said that he was attracted to the idea of a relaunch package for Railtrack, though there were evident complications, not least the difficulties with the East Coast Main Line franchise (see below) and Railtrack's involvement in the Channel Tunnel Rail Link.[67] After weighing up the options, including renationalizing or taking a stake in Railtrack, the Government preferred at this stage to embark on a package of financial support.[68] A settlement with the SRA and Railtrack was made, on 1 April, the starting date of the new charges regime. Under the agreement, given the codename 'Project Endeavour' and set out in a letter from Grant to Marshall, revenue payments under the October 2000 review were to be accelerated, giving the company approximately £1.5 billion earlier than envisaged (in CP2) in additional network grants: £1.3 billion for the core business, £0.2 billion for project development support. The company was also given support (later put at £462 million) to make up the anticipated shortfall in expected income from freight operators (a separate review of access charges for freight was still proceeding).[69] In return, Railtrack undertook not to apply to the Regulator for an early interim review, and agreed a statement of principles with the Government, which emphasized the company's obligations to customers and stakeholders. Railtrack promised to effect an improvement in its organization by separating the core operations business from enhancements, conceding the leading role in the latter to the SRA. It also undertook to appoint a non-executive director to represent the consumer voice[70]; refrain from paying exceptional or special dividends to shareholders for five years; peg dividend growth to earnings

[65] Hackland–Blair, 12 January 2000 (sic: 2001), Prime Minister's Rail Policy papers, Pt. 6; Winsor–Rowlands, 13 January 2001, enclosing 'Periodic Review: Draft Statement on the Implications of Hatfield', DETR file R10/5/77 Pt. 1; ORR, *Annual Report 2000/1*, pp. 15–16.

[66] The £600m. = £400m. in penalty payments, £180m. for re-railing, and £20m. for flooding damage. Steve Marshall (Chief Executive, Railtrack)–Winsor, and Railtrack News Release, both 15 January 2001, DETR file R10/5/77 Pt. 1; Hackland–Blair, 16 January 2000 (sic: 2001), Prime Minister's Rail Policy papers, Pt. 6.

[67] Virley–Unwin, 24 January 2001, Prescott–Blair, 14 February 2001, Prime Minister's Rail Policy papers, Pt. 12. On the background to 'Project Endeavour' see Morton's papers, SRA and Harding, thesis, 2005, p. 119 ff. Harding was Finance Director of Railtrack in 2001.

[68] Hackland–Blair, 16 and 23 March 2001, Prime Minister's Rail Policy papers, Pts. 12–13.

[69] Grant–Marshall, 1 April 2001 (the 'Letter agreement'), SRA. The complex formulae for paying grants were set out in Appendix II. On the background to 'Project Endeavour' see Harding, thesis, 2005, p. 119 ff.

[70] Harding asserts that this stipulation was contrary to company law, thesis, 2005, p. 121. Certainly, Railtrack protested about it, and although in the agreement it proposed to appoint such a director, nothing was done. See Marshall–Grant, 28 March 2001, SRA file 11/13/27 Pt. 4.

growth; and raise £250 million in preferred equity by 31 March 2002. At the same time the company reached agreement with the SRA on the framework and timetable for its network enhancement partnership with the Authority. This would take the form of a securitization, off-balance sheet vehicle known as 'Renewco', to be finalized by 30 June 2001, and to include a joint venture for the East Coast Main Line (see below). Railtrack's obligations to Thameslink 2000, a project acknowledged to be 'subject to a number of uncertainties', were capped at a further £150 million, and the company agreed to use 'reasonable endeavours' to enter into SPV agreements for the South Central franchise, provided that these were 'reasonably commercially acceptable'. Existing projects such as the West Coast Main Line upgrade and the Channel Tunnel Rail Link (Phase I) were to proceed, while others, including the Chiltern upgrade, were to continue under new arrangements. Feasibility studies of new enhancement projects were to be supported to the extent of £100 million for at least six months, with 75 per cent paid by the SRA. The latter was to receive an additional £155 million from the Government over two years to fund its project development work.[71]

The April agreement did not put an end to Railtrack's lobbying for financial relief. When its full-year results were announced in the following month, it declared a pre-tax loss of £534 million, but drew critical responses from the media by maintaining its dividend and paying Corbett a substantial (£1.4m.) severance payment. The company had been forced to set aside £733 million as a post-Hatfield exceptional charge, £561 million of which had been paid to the train operators. Notwithstanding the benefits it had derived from the April agreement, it calculated that a £1 billion gap would need to be bridged by efficiency gains, while a further £2 billion was needed to meet the 'on-going implications' of Hatfield. It would therefore seek an interim review by the Regulator.[72] Yet it was clear that the company had failed to meet Winsor's requirement to return the network to normal by 21 May, and at the time of the April agreement it had admitted that the cost of upgrading the West Coast Main Line had risen to £7.2 billion.[73] With further revisions not ruled out, there were media reports that the costs of the upgrade were 'spiralling out of control'. Estimates of upgrading the East Coast line were also revised upwards, and further damaging publicity resulted from the resignation of the director responsible for major projects, Simon Murray. Railtrack's share price fell to £4.77 when its results were announced; by early June, transactions were taking place at below the flotation price of £3.80,

---

[71] Grant–Marshall, 1 April 2001, cit.; 'Statement of Principles Agreed between HMG and Railtrack', 2 April 2001, DETR News Release, 2 April 2001, Macdonald–Smith, 3 April 2001, DETR file R78/1/43 Pt. 4; Railtrack News Release, 2 April 2001, R73/1/5 Pt. 1; SRA Board Minutes, 5 April 2001; SRA, *Annual Report 2000/1*, pp. 4–5. At the same time, Prescott gave the go-ahead to Phase II of the CTRL, from Southfleet to St. Pancras. Railtrack secured a release from its option to purchase the line, and construction was entrusted to a new PPP led by London & Continental Rlys and Bechtel.

[72] Railtrack Group plc, *R&A 2000/1*, pp. 1, 38–41; Harding, thesis, 2005, pp. 127–9; *Evening Standard*, 24 May 2001, p. 41; *Guardian*, 29 May 2001, p. 24; *Independent*, 22 June 2001, p. 1.

[73] £7.174bn in Railtrack, draft working capital review, 1 April 2001, p. 15, and see Railtrack plc, Business Plan, 2001, p. 3, Endeavour Agreement documentation, SRA.

and financial commentators were beginning to question the company's viability, armed with a report from the brokers ABN-Amro which valued the shares at only 58p and warned investors that the equity was 'in danger of being wiped out'.[74] With the approach of a general election, held on 7 June, the continuing crisis not only strained relations between Railtrack and the Government but also affected the relationship between the emergent SRA, the Department, and the Treasury (see below). The latter was unsurprisingly displeased at having to make the additional provision in April, which strengthened the view in Whitehall that Railtrack had not got a grip on its assets, and that its rising level of debt was 'unsustainable in the long term'.[75] At the end of June, John Kay, writing in the *Financial Times*, argued that the 'financial case for renationalising Railtrack is compelling...Giving back to the shareholders the £3.80p they paid at flotation would end their misery.'[76] By this time departmental officials felt that Railtrack was unlikely to be able to finance much more than £3 billion of the £13 billion in enhancements earmarked for private sector funding under the 10 Year Plan.[77]

The immediate impact of Railtrack's response to the Hatfield accident on operators, both passenger and freight, was quite simply catastrophic. There was particular disruption to Anglo-Scottish services, Thameslink, and London–Ipswich/Norwich services.[78] From the start ATOC made it clear that it would expect compensation for the damage to its members' businesses, and put pressure on Railtrack, and even threatened legal action.[79] When on 22 November a generous compensation package for season ticket holders was introduced by ATOC and Railtrack, following promptings from the SSRA and the Department, the SSRA offered the TOCs temporary support by deferring until the end of the financial year the (Schedule 7) penalty payments due under the incentive scheme for Period 8 (15 October–11 November 2000). The Authority also offered Intercity operators, who were not covered by the scheme, comparable support.[80] But there was a distinct limit to its generosity. The SRA pressed for the

[74] ABN-Amro, circular, 4 June 2001, DfT, disclosure documentation for *Weir and Others v. the Secretary of State for Transport and Department for Transport* (2005), vol. K3. The valuation was very close to an earlier Railtrack assessment of 60p a share which was shared with the Department in March: John W. Smith (Director, Regulation & Government, Railtrack)–Lewis Atter (Railway Economics & Finance Divn, DETR), 16 March 2001, ibid. vol. K2. See also Justice Lindsay, Approved Judgment in *Weir and Others*, 14 October 2005, paras. 38, 48–9; *Evening Standard*, 5 June 2001, p. 1; *Independent*, 3 April 2001, p. 10, 15 June 2001, p. 2.

[75] Macdonald–Smith, 3 April 2001 and reply, 4 April 2001, DETR file R78/1/43 Pt. 4; Linnard, brief for incoming SoS for Transport, Stephen Byers, 11 June 2001, R78/1/62 Pt. 1. See also Rowlands–Byers, 8 June 2001, and Coulshed–Byers, 12 June 2001, DfT, Weir doc. vol. K4.

[76] *Financial Times*, 27 June 2001, p. 15.

[77] DTLR railway economics and finance division paper, 24 July 2001, DTLR file R78/1/54 Pt. 1.

[78] Hackland–Blair, 25 October and 8 November 2000, annex B, Cabinet Office file R14/6 Pt. 2 and Prime Minister's Rail Policy papers, Pt. 8.

[79] Hackland–Blair, 1 December 2000, ibid. Pt. 10; Richard Brown (Chairman, ATOC)–Winsor, 11 April 2001, fax copy in DETR file R73/1/3 Pt. 2.

[80] Virley–Unwin, 20 November 2000. cit.; Grant–Macdonald, 16 November 2000, Grant–Brown, 16 and 22 November 2000, SRA; Connolly–Macdonald, 20 November 2000, Connolly–Grant, 18 January 2000, DETR file R10/5/73 Pt. 1. More limited compensation was also offered for Period 9.

repayment of sums not spent in making compensation, and was initially unwilling to provide financial support to ATOC when the latter suggested a national rail marketing campaign and a 25 per cent cut in leisure fares promotion to attract passengers back to rail, arguing that in the circumstances the promotion was premature.[81] The TOCs squealed at this in a characteristically risk-averse way, and the Government was drawn into the argument. Macdonald intervened, declaring that some operators were 'facing genuine and serious financial difficulties' and pointing out that the SRA should not be 'seen to profit from the consequences of Hatfield'. This prompted another Morton blast: 'Are we to understand that the Minister for Transport is contemplating an instruction to the SRA to transfer to the public purse risks that were assumed by and belong to the private sector?'[82] However, after arguments about its 2001/2 budget were resolved, the SRA was persuaded to climb down, and the TOCs were afforded some relief. The SRA agreed only to recover the proportion of deferred payments not used to compensate passengers in Period 8, that is, £4.1 million of the £13.3 million due, and the Authority also undertook to invest £3 million of the net payment on a rail advertising campaign in June.[83] Nevertheless, the sums flowing back into the public sector from the private sector were still large. Passenger operators were required to make net payments of £92.5 million for the year 2000/1, compared with only £3.3 million in the previous year.[84]

There was no doubt that punctuality and reliability deteriorated badly after Hatfield. However, precise and meaningful measures are rather elusive since the operators quickly worked to emergency timetables, which made it difficult to benchmark the results with earlier periods. At the SSRA Grant took the decision not to publish four-weekly performance data for Period 8, but instead to provide quarterly data later on.[85] These results certainly revealed the scale of the decline. In the third quarter of 2000/1, that is, October–December 2000, only 64 per cent of trains were on time compared with 87 per cent in the previous quarter (Table 3.1), and although performance in the autumn quarter always fell off with leaf-fall, and in 2000 was exacerbated by serious flooding, the decline was much worse than 'normal' (i.e. 26%, cf. only 9% in 1999/2000). Poor performance was most marked with the long-distance operators such as Virgin (West Coast and Cross Country) and GNER, and the London peak commuting services. The third-quarter results showed a fall from 80 to 48 per cent for long-distance and

[81] Grant–Brown, 16 February 2001; SRA Executive Committee Minutes, 2 and 8 March 2001, SRA file 57/01/01 Pt. 3.

[82] Jane Blackmore (DETR)–Macdonald, 19 February 2001, DETR file, R10/5/73 Pt. 1; Grant–Macdonald, 6 February 2001, reply 20 February 2001, and Morton–Macdonald, 23 February 2001, SRA.

[83] SRA Executive Committee Minutes, 8 March 2001, SRA file 57/01/01 Pt. 3; Grant–Macdonald, 19 April 2001, and Grant-Byers, 15 June 2001, SRA; Mottram–Jeremy Long (Chief Executive, GB Railways), 17 May 2001, DETR file R10/5/73 Pt. 1.

[84] SRA, *Annual Report 2000/1*, p. 113.   [85] Grant–Macdonald, 2 November 2000, SRA.

Table 3.4 Effect of Hatfield accident on TOC income and P&L, September 2000–March 2001 (£m.)

	Period 7: 17 Sep. 2000–14 Oct.	Period 8: 15 Oct.–11 Nov.	Period 9: 12 Nov.–9 Dec.	Period 10: 10 Dec.–6 Jan. 2001[a]	Period 11: 7 Jan.–3 Feb.[a]	Period 12: 4 Feb.–3 Mar.	Period 13: 4–31 Mar.	% change cf. 1999/2000						
								7	8	9	10	11	12	13
All franchises														
Fare-box income	294.315	231.911	226.476	157.833	241.989	252.760	251.259	+12.4	−15.4	−15.9	−19.8	−5.8	−4.9	−5.2
Pre-tax P/L	30.722	18.724	14.887	−11.040	−27.544	17.254	18.066	/	−43	−54	+61	−412	−26	−24
GNER franchise														
Fare-box income	32.209	18.738	16.755	8.462	18.145	20.472	22.336	+13.2	−35.9	−40.1	−53.1	−30.1	−25.0	−19.1
Subsidy	0.453	0.454	0.453	0.453	0.453	0.453	0.453							
Railtrack performance payments	0.211	9.383	10.329	9.693	0.339	0.300	0.270							
Operating costs	−16.518	−16.977	−15.981	−10.070	−15.571	−15.325	−16.536	/	−145	−161	+293	−446	−410	+278
Pre-tax P/L	3.796	−1.644	−1.888	13.307	−1.490	−2.229	10.858							

[a] Four TOCs reported for 22 days in Period 10 and for 34 days in Period 11, instead of the standard 28 days.

Source: Reports to SSRA/SRA Executive Committee, 2000–1, SRA file 57/01/02 Pts. 16–22.

from 86 to 50 per cent for London commuting.[86] Recovery was evident in the first quarter of 2001/2, though punctuality was well below pre-Hatfield standards, and indeed remained so over the next four years.[87] The delay minutes data support these findings. In periods 8–13 of 2000/1, the total was 15.5 million, more than double the 7.1 million in the previous year; Railtrack's responsibility for the delays rose from 3.1 million or 44 per cent of the total in 1999/2000 to 10.6 million or 68 per cent (and see also the quarterly data in Table 3.1).[88]

The financial impact of the Hatfield accident on the TOCs was closely mon-itored by the SSRA/SRA and the four-weekly analyses are summarized in Table 3.4. Here, fare-box income and pre-tax profits are compared with the data for the previous year, though the results for Periods 10 and 11 (10 December 2000–3 February 2001) were affected by the fact that four of the TOCs reported for non-standard lengths (see note to Table 3.4). However, in the eight weeks after the accident, broadly Periods 8 and 9, fare-box income was 15–16 per cent down on the previous year, and for the directly affected operator, GNER, income was 36 and 40 per cent down on 1999 for Periods 8 and 9. Profit trends are tricky to interpret, with the lumpiness of performance payments and other factors, but overall pre-tax profits were 43 and 54 per cent lower in Periods 8 and 9 compared with those in the previous year, and GNER profits were 145 and 161 per cent lower (Table 3.4), while its SSRA rating slipped from 'Green' to 'Amber'. By the end of the financial year some recovery was evident, though TOC fare-box income was still 5–6 per cent down on the previous year, and for GNER income was 19–25 per cent lower.[89] In March 2001 the SRA Board was told that while only one franchise had been driven into a loss at group level, the post-Hatfield slump had exacerbated deep-seated financial problems with the Anglia and Central franchises, where much of the demand was 'dis-cretionary'. Indeed, in December 2000, Grant, faced with the possibility that GB Railways would withdraw financial support from Anglia Railways, had offered the company a £1 million support package to enable the franchise to continue.[90] Clearly, the difficulties experienced by the TOCs in the aftermath of Hatfield, compounded by the disarray of Railtrack, provided a major headache for the fledgling SRA.

---

[86] SRA, *National Rail Trends Yearbook 2004–5*, pp. 15–16. Wolmar contends that for several TOCs punctuality fell from 90% to under 25% in the month after Hatfield: *On the Wrong Line*, p. 185.

[87] SRA, *Yearbook 2004–5*, p. 15.   [88] Delay minutes data, DfT/ATOC.

[89] Data for Periods 12 and 13: S. Hatch (SRA), Memos. To SRA Executive Committee, 12 April and 23 May 2001, SRA file 57/01/02 Pts. 21–2.

[90] Grant–Macdonald, 6 and 8 December 2000, Grant–Long, 8 December 2000, SRA Board Minutes, 1 March 2001, SRA; Interview with Jeremy Long, 25 May 2007.

4

The Strategic Rail Authority and Railtrack After Hatfield

4.1 SRA ambitions frustrated: strategy and franchising

The impact of the Hatfield accident on the SRA and its plans was extremely unfortunate. The resultant hiatus upset the Authority's preparations for functioning in full statutory form, assembling a strategic plan, and conducting the complex negotiations with Railtrack to produce a public–private vehicle for enhancement investment. At the same time, Morton's relationship with the Government, which had begun to deteriorate in the wake of Winsor's track access review, was stretched to breaking point by the further pressures on financing. Railtrack's post-Hatfield crisis promised to change what were already regarded in Whitehall as high numbers for maintenance and renewal, challenging Morton's longer-franchise policy and making his tendency to operate outside the Treasury box unacceptable. Morton, for his part, was frustrated by the implied brake on an investment strategy which in part had been devised by, and had certainly been encouraged by, the Government.

There was an evident exasperation in government with the failure of the SRA to produce a strategic plan. Officials felt that that had been the primary purpose for the creation of the Authority, and those in the Treasury in particular were unable to see how investment projects could be presented and signed off without seeing how they fitted into the strategic whole. Morton, however, argued that the Department's 10 Year Plan had de facto set the broad parameters, but that detailed planning, for which he had no personal enthusiasm, had been jeopardized, first by Railtrack's difficulties, then by the generosity of the access charges review, and finally by Hatfield, which had knocked the industry sideways.[1] Within the SSRA, staff, led by Richard Davies, had been busy preparing a substantial document which offered a full range of investment priorities.[2] However, Morton insisted that this long and rather complex piece of work be replaced by a more flexible 'agenda'. When just before Christmas (2000) he sent Rowlands an 'incomplete first draft' of the plan, he told the Permanent Secretary that the draft would be shortened to emerge as a 'strategic agenda' in January (2001).[3] The product of the Chairman's own efforts, this finally materialized in March.[4] There is no doubt that the delay, and the debates which accompanied it, damaged the SRA's credibility in some circles, and fed an emerging belief in government that the new body did not have an adequate grip on either priorities or funding mechanisms. This was made worse by the delay in progressing the ECML franchise, though to be fair, progress here was affected by Railtrack's announcement in February that costs would be much higher than suggested earlier.[5] Nevertheless, whoever was to blame, doubts began to surface about Morton's capacity to provide strategic leadership, which were compounded by his illness, and Blair was briefed to this effect by his advisers, along with the worries about the structure of Railtrack.[6] Morton, on the other hand, felt that planning had been prejudiced in the heat of the post-Hatfield maelstrom, and argued that it was self-evidently difficult to produce detailed information on projects with any confidence. When Railtrack's advisers, Rothschilds, had presented their 'On the Brink' briefing for the Treasury in December 2000, he told Rowlands that this was 'the straw that breaks the camel's back'. As we have seen, Rothschilds had indicated that Railtrack would not be able to finance the work which its stakeholders expected without a review of income in CP2. Morton's response, sent to Rowlands at the Department, was to criticize the 'increasingly chaotic

---

[1] Cf. Morton–SSRA Board, 18 October 2000, Morton–Rowlands, 19 December 2000, Grant, 'File Note of Meeting with Treasury On Thursday 4th January 2001', and BRB Minutes, 11 January 2001, SRA.

[2] Richard Davies (SSRA), Memo. to SSRA Executive Committee, 5 December 2000, SRA files 57/01/02 Pt. 16.

[3] SSRA Chairman's Committee Minutes, 19 December 2000, SRA file 02/20/02 Pt. 2; Morton–Rowlands, 22 December 2000, DETR file R78/1/43 Pt. 1

[4] SSRA Chairman's Committee Minutes, 30 January 2001, SRA file 02/20/02 Pt. 2; SRA, *A strategic agenda* (March 2001).

[5] Morton–Macdonald, 27 February 2001, DETR file R78/1/43 Pt. 1; Grant, 'File note of meeting with Sir Alastair Morton, Sir Philip Beck and Steve Marshall on Tuesday 13th February 2001', SRA.

[6] David Miliband (No. 10 Policy Unit)-Blair, 14 February 2001, Prime Minister's Rail Policy papers, Pt. 12. Morton suffered a long bout of thyrotoxicosis in 2000–1: Morton–SRA staff, 25 October 2001, SRA.

rush towards a new regime for Railtrack'. He made a plea for a moratorium to sort out the 'increasingly chaotic array of "understandings" masquerading as a 10-year funding plan for the SRA'. 'Taxpayers' monies', he announced, 'should not be hurled in hasty bucketloads at Railtrack without gaining appropriate influence over their priorities and programmes for investment in enhancement and major renewals.' He was particularly sore at the switch in emphasis from front-end revenue funding to back-end capital investment in the plan, which he felt was bound to compromise his refranchising policy.[7] Later on, he made it clear that he much preferred a Regulator's review of Railtrack to the Endeavour agreement of April 2001.[8]

The relationship between the Department and its NDPB was also affected by re-opened arguments about the responsibilities, status, and rewards of the Chairman and the Chief Executive. With the Transport Act 2000 operational from the end of November, the date for the formal constitution of the SRA was approaching. As the appointment letters to SRA-designate members were being drawn up, Morton pressed the Department for extended contracts and more money. He had done so informally in September 2000. Then in December he wrote formally to Prescott to seek a ten-month contract extension for himself (i.e. to 31 January 2003) and a two-year extension for Grant (to 31 January 2004). He also felt his existing salary of £130,000 for 130 days a year or 2.5 days a week should be increased to £195,000 to match the time he was really putting in, namely, at least 195 days or 3.75 days a week. At the same time he argued that Grant's salary should also be increased to £195,000, and wanted Board members to be paid for the committee work they were doing.[9] While officials had some sympathy for the position of Grant (after all, Winsor had a five-year appointment) and that of the Board members, there was less support for Morton and for the suggested salary hikes. Morton was already being paid substantially more than any other NDPB chair, and Grant was one of the better paid chief executives.[10] The Department made some attempt to find a compromise, and it was suggested, for example, that Grant might be offered an additional two years at his existing salary, with 156 days (3 days a week) for Morton.[11] After some negotiation, Grant was offered the post of Chief Executive until 30 April 2004. However, a decision on Morton was deferred until new directions and guidance were finalized and a strategic agenda and plan had been published.[12] However, there was another bone of contention, this time about corporate governance

---

[7] Rothschild, 'On the Brink', December 2000, Morton–Rowlands, 19 December 2000, cit. and see also Morton–Byers, 19 October 2001, DTLR file R78/1/43 Pt. 3.

[8] Morton–Byers, 12 June 2001, SRA.

[9] Morton–Prescott, 13 December 2000, DETR file R78/1/30 Pt. 3.

[10] Coulshed–Macdonald, 8 September 2000, Fidler–Roy Phillips, 5 January 2001, ibid.

[11] Linnard–Macdonald and Prescott, 24 January 2001, ibid.

[12] Grant–Linnard, 16 January 2001, SRA; Linnard–Grant, 31 January 2001, Coulshed–Macdonald and Prescott, 23 February 2001, DETR file R78/1/30 Pt. 3. Grant's salary was eventually raised to £174,879: Coulshed–Grant, 21 August 2001, Morton's papers, SRA.

responsibilities. In accordance with general policy for the NDPBs, there were to be two accounting officers: an internal executive (Grant); and a departmental official (Mottram, the permanent secretary of DETR). Morton and Grant, supported by Pen Kent, challenged this, arguing that the SRA Board, with an executive chairman, chief executive, and active non-executive members, should have the responsibility for corporate governance. This was firmly resisted by the Department. Mottram emphasized that Grant's responsibilities as the SRA's accounting officer flowed from his own, which were to 'ensure that public funds are used for the purposes for which they are intended by Parliament'.[13] Thus, when the SRA was established as a body corporate on 15 January 2001, with full operational status from 1 February, there was plenty of concern about the new body and its capabilities.

The contents of the March *strategic agenda* did little to dispel this. Of course, the agenda was not intended to be a firm plan; that was promised in the autumn. However, there was not a great deal of meat in the document, the text being as retrospective as forward-looking. Bearing the marks of the Chairman's personal intervention, the agenda was also irritatingly slick with its nine listed challenges presented in a 3 × 3 matrix: 'SPG'—safety, performance, growth; 'PFI'—passengers, freight, infrastructure; and 'PPP'—public–private partnership.[14] The 88-page main volume contained 14 pages of introductory and historical background, 12 pages of 'challenges', and a list of schemes running to 36 pages. That left a core of only 26 pages dealing with passenger franchising, providing a 'tour d'horizon' of the possibilities; freight regeneration, where hopes were pinned on increased government support; and infrastructure enhancement, where PPP was held to be fundamental to the SRA's 'investment-led strategy'. There was also a second volume summarizing key documents such as the 10 Year Plan and the Regulator's review. The long list of schemes, both large and small, provided brief descriptions under the headings 'scope' (size), 'criteria' (goals), and 'immediacy' (when needed), but a prioritization of the investments was not attempted. Rather the list was intended to 'serve as a menu and as a consultative document'.[15] Disappointing many in Whitehall, Morton's agenda encouraged a consensus to emerge within the Department to the effect that the SRA's work lacked both precision and focus. When the incoming Secretary of State, Stephen Byers, was briefed in June 2001, he was told that the SRA's 'present ambitions are unfocussed and unaffordable ... they must have their card marked to be more realistic in planning and get a grip on the refranchising process'.[16]

---

[13] Grant–Mottram, 9 January and 9 February 2001, Mottram–Grant, 1 and 22 February 2001, and see also Morton–Prescott, 9 January 2001, Trewin–Bowker, 23 November 2001, SRA; Fidler–Mottram, 16 January 2001, DETR file R78/1/30 Pt. 1; Hill–Rowlands, 26 September 2000, Hill–Lord Macdonald's PS, 29 January 2001, DETR file R7/1/42 Pt. 2; Interview with Mottram, 2007.

[14] SRA, *Strategic Agenda*, I, p. 16.   [15] Ibid. I, p. 51.

[16] Linnard–Byers, 11 June 2001, DTLR file R78/1/62 Pt. 1.

The Strategic Rail Authority and Railtrack After Hatfield

Of course, behind the disagreements between the Department and the NDPB lay a fundamental battle about money, brought to a head by the post-Hatfield difficulties of Railtrack. The company had quickly come to the realization that Winsor's access charges determination was, in fact, far from generous. On a standardized accounting basis the required revenue for the core business had been set at £1 billion less than the company had claimed, and the assumption of a 17 per cent improvement in efficiency over the control period was regarded as unrealistic. On top of this, there was now an acceptance that the contract with Virgin for the WCML upgrade had been drawn up so as to leave the infrastructure provider very much exposed to risk, while post-Hatfield pressures left little or no room for manoeuvre.[17] These problems lay outside the control of the SRA, of course, but they clearly threatened Morton's strategy for improvement. At an early stage (January 2001) Morton made it clear that the 10 Year Plan was being challenged by the funding realities, and according to Morton, by a new emphasis in the Plan on capital grants for the WCML. He indicated that the first tranche of franchise commitments would leave nothing until CP3 for the dozen or so other franchises, and that if Railtrack were to get £1 billion more cash in CP2, the SRA would be unable to disburse funds for enhancement of the network before April 2007, unable to help freight, and unable to continue the policy of replacing the seven-year franchises with longer ones. The characteristically trenchant conclusion was that 'Taken together those three "unables" spell termination of the Government's rail strategy and eliminate any need for an SRA in place of OPRAF.'[18] In the first half of 2001 there were intense negotiations between the SRA and the Department in relation to the Authority's budget for 2001/2, and the 'affordability' of its existing investment plans. In February a budgetary overspend of £351 million on top of Spending Review calculations of £1.3 billion was identified, most of which, including the safety requirements of the Uff/Cullen Report, lay outside the SRA's control; in the following month the 'variance' was put at £404 million. After the April agreement with Railtrack the gap had been reduced to £140 million, but attention then turned to the affordability of the 10-year investment programme. Numerous 'iterations' of an affordability model were produced, with number 26 showing that estimated costs had risen from £29 billion in the summer of 2000 to £38 billion a year later. A 'do minimum' alternative also revealed a substantial increase in costs, from £29 to £32 billion.[19]

The Treasury, for its part, was unsympathetic to the Authority's initial financial management in this period of flux. Officials believed that the way in which

[17] On Railtrack's perceptions, see Lew Adams (SSRA Board Member)–Morton, 27 October 1999, SRA, and Harding, thesis, 2005, pp. 86–90, 111–18.

[18] Morton–Macdonald, 25 January 2001, SRA. Cf. also BRB Minutes, 11 January 2001: 'Absent the Solution of Both Railtrack's and the SRA's funding problems, the Ten Year Plan could not be delivered.'

[19] SRA Executive Committee Minutes, 8 June 2001, SRA file 57/01/01 Pt. 3; Grant–Linnard, 6 June 2001, and SRA Board Minutes, 1 February–7 June 2001, SRA.

the budget issue had been handled, together with the late explanation of the initial 'Renewco' concept, were 'symptomatic of the SRA's highly unsatisfactory approach to public expenditure issues'.[20] The pressure had been stoked up by Martin Wheatley, head of housing and urban transport at the Treasury, who wrote formally to John Ballard, the DETR's principal finance officer in March 2001 to express 'growing concerns' about the SRA's approach to financial management. There were, he said, 'serious shortcomings'. Commitments had been 'entered into beyond what was prudent', the level of spending on staff and consultancy was excessive, and the 2001/2 budget had been prepared in a way that assumed more resources than in the Comprehensive Spending Review of 2000.[21] Morton and Grant strongly denied these allegations. The SRA's position was that the 2001/2 budget of £1.3 billion had been assembled from departmental figures, not its own, and that the former had been 'no more than guesstimates'. As we have seen, the Authority's own 'bottom up' analysis indicated a budget some £400 million higher. Grant explained to Linnard that elements in the franchise replacement process could not be costed with accuracy at such an early stage and it was therefore essential to retain a measure of flexibility in funding.[22] But by this time it was clear that relationships were showing signs of strain. Paranoid about leaks, Morton went so far as to send his Board a 'provocative' note on 'SRA finances' to see if it would be passed to the Department; it arrived there on the following afternoon.[23] The atmosphere was scarcely helped by incorrect statements in the press. For example, the *Guardian*'s transport editor contributed a piece on 19 February 2001 reporting Railtrack's request for £2 billion in funding. He cited senior SRA executives as the source of the observations that Railtrack was facing bankruptcy, that it was incapable of managing its business, and that Morton had ordered a halt to any further funding for rail maintenance. This latter, clearly mistaken, idea was condemned by Morton as a 'farrago of nonsense', but articles such as these did nothing to help the SRA to exert its influence within the industry.[24]

Difficult as it was for the Authority to function in a calm environment, it proceeded to set itself up as a statutory body. The Transport Act 2000 set out its purposes: to promote the use of the railway network; secure the development of the network; and contribute to the development of an integrated system of transport of passengers and goods.[25] Organizational changes were made incrementally over the course of 2000, and by February 2001 the SRA was organized around

---

[20] Smith–Macdonald, 4 April 2001, cit.

[21] Mottram–Grant, 14 March 2001, enclosing Martin Wheatley (Head of Housing and Urban Transport, Treasury)–John Ballard (PFO, DETR), 12 March 2001, SRA.

[22] Grant–Mottram, 15 March 2001, Grant–Linnard, 23 March 2001, SRA.

[23] Morton–SRA Board, 20 and 22 March 2001, SRA.

[24] Keith Harper, *Guardian*, 19 February 2001, p. 2; Morton–Editor, *Guardian*, 19 February 2001, SRA Board Minutes, 1 March 2001, SRA.

[25] Transport Act 2000, c. 38, s. 205.

The Strategic Rail Authority and Railtrack After Hatfield

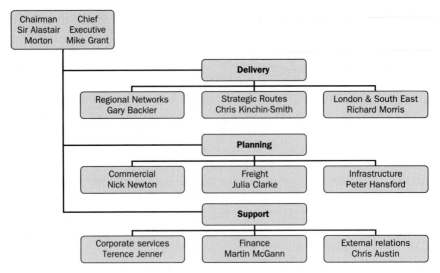

Figure 4.1 SRA organization chart, February 2001

Source: SRA.

nine departments, providing in Morton's familiar 3 × 3 matrix, delivery, planning, and support (Figure 4.1).

In comparison with the early shadow organization the main changes were in the directorate, which was strengthened and more sharply focused. Earlier there had been only three directors for franchise replacement, strategy/planning, and railway development. Now there were six. Delivery was entrusted to directors for strategic routes, regional networks, and London & South East, echoing British Rail's sector management. Planning was divided into commercial, freight, and infrastructure. In these areas only Nick Newton (Director, Commercial) provided executive continuity (cf. Figure 2.1). Executive management, as before, was built around the Executive Committee, and the Chairman's Committee (the Executive plus Morton).

The Authority pressed on with the basic tasks of performance monitoring and franchise management, inherited from OPRAF, and added new functions: consumer protection functions, including sponsorship of the Rail Passengers Council and the passenger committees, transferred from the ORR; support for PTE-specified services (budget in 2000/1 *c.*£200m.), inherited from the DETR; and responsibility for the British Transport Police, transferred from the BRB. But its main thrust was to continue with the process of strategic planning, refranchising, and the financing of network enhancement, in which, as we have seen, there was much to do. In the 'shadow' period, refranchising work had identified three for potential longer franchises and investment, namely, Chiltern, GNER (ECML), and South Central, and in addition, work had been carried out to develop further tranches, and six franchises were listed in the Annual Report for

2000/1: tranche 2—South West Trains, TransPennine Express, Central, and Thameslink; and tranche 3—Wales & Borders and Wessex.[26] The SRA attempted to make as much progress as possible with its franchising activity, but these efforts were blunted by financing concerns, such that all three of the first tranche remained in a state of uncertainty. For Chiltern, the most developed and technically simplest of the three, Railtrack's difficulty in providing rigorous estimates of the upgrade cost of 'Project Evergreen' delayed the signature of an agreement. An escalation in the costs was first revealed in January 2001, then in July Railtrack and M40 submitted a tender price of £204 million, 16 per cent higher than the cap of £176 million included in the heads of terms. A further complication was caused by the recommendation of the Uff/Cullen enquiry that the line be used to operate a pilot scheme for the European Train Control System. And the much-heralded blockbusters—ECML and South Central—were constrained not only by funding anxieties but also by political involvement.[27] In essence the SRA's ambitions were hindered by the risk aversion of both Railtrack and the Treasury. After Hatfield, Newton observed that 'It remains difficult to achieve any meaningful productive engagement with Railtrack. Their overriding propensity for risk avoidance has predictably been reinforced by the current charges review issue.'[28] Thus, the ECML negotiations with GNER and Virgin were hit by Railtrack's revelation in February 2001 that the estimated cost of the upgrade had risen from £1.89 billion to £3.95 billion, and, to a lesser extent, by the company's unwillingness to negotiate in detail with the parties until a preferred bidder had been selected. A cost review was initiated and some hard looks were directed at the proposal, including the expenditure of £1 billion on the Newcastle–Edinburgh section to save only five minutes in journey time.[29] In April the competing parties for the franchise were invited to respond to the opportunity to participate in a joint venture, and the increase in cost was pointed out.[30] The delay in reaching a decision frustrated all parties, and the negotiations were not always conducted in an entirely confidential manner, much to Morton's annoyance.[31] The SRA explored the idea of halting the competition, giving GNER a two-year extension, and reopening the matter when Virgin's performance on WCML and Cross Country was clearer. But at its meeting on 7 June 2001 the Board elected to go ahead with the refranchising. Like all

---

[26] SRA, *Annual Report 2000/1*, pp. 27–8.

[27] This had been evident when the Department delayed an announcement of a preferred bidder in October 2000 after Treasury concerns about affordability. See Morton–Macdonald, 16 October 2000, Andrew Smith–Macdonald, 19 October 2000, and for later involvement, SRA Franchise Replacement Executive Minutes, 24 May 2001, and Franchise Replacement and Renegotiation Progress Reports, nos. 31–41, 15 March–1 August 2001, SRA files 57/01/06 Pt. 1, 57/01/07 Pts. 14–16.

[28] Nick Newton, Report to SRA Board, 26 January 2001, SRA.

[29] SRA Board Minutes, 1 March 2001, SRA.

[30] Grant–Richard Bowker (Group Commercial Dr, Virgin Management) and Christopher Garnett (Chief Executive, GNER), 3 April 2001.

[31] See Tim Reardon (SRA), letter to SRA Board members, 15 May 2001, Morton–Board Members, 30 May 2001, SRA.

such competitions, the paperwork was enormous, and a series of financial and economic complexities, including differences in pricing strategies, made decision-making difficult. The Virgin–Stagecoach proposal offered a lower bid for subsidy, but there were doubts about the business model, and the downside risk therefore appeared greater; the GNER's tilting train was found to offer a better overall technical solution, and its performance and customer satisfaction records were better. While question marks could be raised about the enduring profitability of both parties over the projected life of the new franchise, GNER held only one franchise, while Virgin was exposed to considerable risks associated with the WCML and Cross Country. Finally, competition issues would be raised if Virgin were to operate all three of these strategically important routes. After weighing up all these considerations, the Board chose GNER as the preferred counterparty.[32] As to South Central, where GoVia had already been selected, negotiations were continuing to facilitate an early handover of the franchise by Connex. The change was eventually effected in August 2001. The prospects were scarcely any better with the other tranches. In March 2001 heads of terms were agreed with Stagecoach for a 20-year replacement franchise for South West Trains, specifying £1.7 billion in investment (including provision for the replacement of the Mark I stock, agreed in April). Elsewhere, for example, with Central, TransPennine, and Thameslink 2000, only limited progress was made before the general election, after which the franchising policy was completely revised (see below).

At the same time, a considerable effort was made to turn 'Project Endeavour' into 'Renewco' by the deadline of 21 July 2001 (after the three-week consultation period if Renewco was not achieved by 30 June). In April, as we have seen, Railtrack had agreed to proceed on its own with WCML and CTRL, projects which were too far developed to transfer, but was happy to pass the developmental and project management responsibilities for other enhancements to the SRA. New enhancements were to be taken through project development groups, who were to 'define, prepare, price and prioritise projects', and then onto competitive tendering by SPVs.[33] The process was of course affected by concurrent refranchising negotiations and discussions with the Department and Treasury over the SRA's budget. SRA managers conducted feasibility studies, and an affordability model was developed for the various options; a project manager, Kevin McGreal, was also appointed, in April.[34] Work on the establishment of an appropriate vehicle for investment was undertaken with the help of consultancy advice from

[32] Morton, Memos. 5 and 7 June 2001, SRA Board Minutes, 3 May and 7 June 2001, SRA. The idea of using tilting trains was dropped shortly afterwards: cf. James B. Sherwood (Sea Containers)–Morton, 20 August 2001, SRA. Morton's strategy of using Virgin as a stalking horse for GNER was a rather dangerous one.

[33] Development work on the enhancement structure had been carried out over the course of 2000: Philip O'Donnell, Memo. to SSRA Executive Committee, 8 March 2000, O'Donnell and Peter Hansford, Memo. to BRB, 5 October 2000, SRA; Interview with Philip O'Donnell, 23 June 2006.

[34] SRA Executive Committee Minutes, 19 April 2001, SRA file 57/01/01 Pt. 3.

Lazards, Linklaters, and PricewaterhouseCoopers, and there were numerous discussions with Railtrack at a detailed level, including a joint awayday (14 May). Railtrack also took the decision to separate enhancement, under Marshall, from operations, under Jonson Cox. However, this organizational change, specified in the Endeavour agreement, worried the SRA because it was felt that the restructuring would be made according to the 'Plump Porcupine Model', whereby operations would be made profitable, leaving the support for enhancements exposed. There was a distinct lack of enthusiasm for the latter in Railtrack House, and this was made clear by the revelation in May that it did not think it would be able to fund enhancements without further financial support.[35] Grant and Morton were clearly frustrated by the lack of progress, and Grant went so far as to question the company's ability to proceed, asking, 'Is Railtrack holed below the waterline?'[36]

The Government expressed the view that the SRA's franchising replacement activity should be directed at a limited number of affordable projects—that is, Chiltern, South West Trains, South Central, Thameslink, and the ECML—in itself a fairly long list—but some distance short of the SRA's ambitions. It was difficult, however, for the SRA to receive full government support for its franchising initiatives when these had not been turned into fully costed projects and the general environment in the industry was uncertain. Thus, the Department, prompted by Treasury concerns, held back from sanctioning the selection of a preferred bidder for the ECML, both before and after the redrafting process in April 2001, arguing that it was necessary to consider the outcome of a concurrent review of affordability and phasing of the replacement programme. The Renewco initiative for enhancements remained in an ill-developed state, and here the fears of the Treasury that the joint venture would still count as being in the public sector provided a serious obstacle. Consequently, a breach of the Endeavour obligations seemed likely. The onset of a general election only served to further stifle decision-making, and little was achieved.[37] Morton had nailed his colours to the *10 Year Plan* objectives: a 50 per cent increase in passenger traffic; an 80 per cent increase in freight traffic; and reductions in overcrowding in London. In his annual report for the year he complained that 'events and lack of resources have slowed delivery and undermined confidence'.[38] This may have been true, but a critical report from the Public Accounts Committee in July 2001 expressed the view that the SRA needed to act with more urgency to improve passenger services, and both ministers and civil servants, whether rightly or wrongly, expected more of a body which, whatever its statutory position, had had two years at the coalface.[39]

---

[35] Ibid. 15 and 24 May, 8 June 2001.   [36] Grant, presentation to SRA Board, 7 June 2001, SRA.
[37] Grant–Macdonald, 23 May 2001, Grant–Linnard, 20 June 2001; SRA Chairman's Committee Minutes, 5 June 2001, SRA file 02/20/02 Pt. 2.
[38] Morton, statement, 5 July 2001, SRA, *Annual Report 2000/1*, p. 4.
[39] HC Public Accounts Committee, Report on *Strategic Rail Authority: Action to improve Passenger Rail Services*, 18 July 2001, P.P. 2000–1, l, HC392.

4.2 'Exit Morton, pursued by a Byers'[40]

The general election on 7 June 2001 resulted in a second victory for 'New Labour'. Dubbed an 'apathetic landslide',[41] the turnout was under 60 per cent, a record low. Nevertheless, Labour won 413 seats to the Conservatives' 166 and the Liberal Democrats' 52, and its overall majority (167) remained substantial. Railways had figured very little in the campaigning, though psephologists maintained that the post-Hatfield delays had hurt the Conservatives more than Labour.[42] The new Government promptly reorganized transport at departmental level. Prescott remained DPM, but the DETR was broken up. The Department for Environment, Food and Rural Affairs (DEFRA) was created by merging Agriculture and Environment, and a Department for Transport, Local Government and the Regions (DTLR) was established with Stephen Byers appointed Secretary of State for Transport, Local Government and the Regions, and John Spellar as Transport Minister. Byers, a former law lecturer at Newcastle Polytechnic, was MP for Tyneside (North), and a committed Blairite. But having served as Treasury Chief Secretary and Secretary of State for Trade and Industry, his move to transport was widely regarded as a downwards step. Spellar, MP for Warley, was a former trade union official and member of Labour's 'old right'.[43]

Morton, briefing Byers with a flurry of memoranda, made it clear that he 'was disinclined to continue' as SRA Chairman. He referred Byers to a meeting he had had with Prescott in April, where he had suggested that if the Secretary of State left after the election then he would also do so: 'It looked likely', he said, 'that I would leave between July and next March.'[44] Now, with Byers having barely had time to sit at his new desk, Morton sent him a letter of 'welcome'. Disenchanted by the turn of events, he had boldly advanced what he saw as the basic requirements for the industry, and had tried to encourage leadership at the top via the Rail Industry Group. But he felt that the central problem was 'a severely inadequate Railtrack'. 'The widening gulf between what it can pay for and what HMG must therefore give it is becoming absurd.' An accompanying enclosure set out the 'key issues'. Ministers, said Morton, had to decide by mid-July whether to persist with the existing strategy or revise it, and this had to be done before the SRA's strategic plan was sent out for consultation. He offered Byers two options: Option A, to persist with the commitment to the 10 Year Plan; and Option B, to revise the strategy around a set of realistic

---

[40] Morton, draft for *Spectator* article, 13 August 2001.

[41] Pippa Norris (ed.), *Britain Votes 2001* (Oxford, 2001), p. 1.

[42] David Butler and Dennis Kavanagh, *The British General Election of 2001* (Basingstoke, 2002), pp. 19, 250–1.

[43] *Rail Politic*, 8 June 2001. David Jamieson (Plymouth Devonport) became PUSS for transport. At the same time, three former Conservative transport secretaries joined the Lords—Sir Norman Fowler, Tom King, and John MacGregor.

[44] Morton, file note of meeting with Prescott on 10 April 2001, 17 April 2001, SRA.

'high-low-minimum' alternatives, and slow down the process of refranchising. Expressing his preference for Option B, Morton also argued that the existing industry structure should change. There were swipes at both Railtrack and the Rail Regulator. Any list of 'big structural questions', he said, would include the following:

(A) Should the present Railtrack be maintained in being, despite (1) the collapse of its competence and valuation; and (2) over £6 billion in capital grants (i.e. without return) being promised to it, and £2.5 billion demanded by it, when its market capitalisation is 25–30 per cent of the total? Should it be split geographically or by function? Have the problems grown beyond 'mere' remanaging of the company? If not, can the present team manage it? By when?

(B) When the public purse becomes the principal puppetmaster of a helpless Railtrack, why is the latter's funding and performance monitoring delegated to an independent regulator rather than to Railtrack's de facto parent company, the SRA. Imminent legislation on safety regulation could be used to permit the SRA to absorb ORR.

(C) Given this parent company situation, should the SRA pass funding through a 50/50 or 49/51 'Rail Partners UK' (or Rail Fund) associate in order to limit PSBR implications to only what the public purse actually pays into the industry?

As to process, Morton repeated a familiar complaint. Ministers had to decide whether the SRA was to be (A) 'a specialist sub-division under the Railways Directorate . . . with the Minister of State as de facto Chairman', or (B) a 'technically and financially specialised executive agency, to which authority and capital are delegated'. Morton naturally preferred (B). Option (A), the 'conventional answer in Whitehall', was, he thought, 'inappropriate for leading the rail industry out of the present morass. It places demands on civil servants they are not equipped to answer'. Option (B) should be taken forward by a new Chairman, 'someone at least eight years younger than him'.[45] Five days later, Morton provided Byers with a fuller memorandum on Railtrack. Contending that it was becoming 'steadily more and more absurd to pump more cash' into the existing structure, he offered seven alternatives: maintaining the status quo ('not credible'); renationalization ('not sensible'); national vertical integration ('unrealistic'); regional vertical integration; break-up (two options); and extraction of national network control. He favoured the first of the break-up options, based on geographical zones. Railtrack would remain a private sector company, but the SRA would take a 29 per cent shareholding and secure its leadership of Railtrack Group. The company's property assets would be sold to strengthen the balance sheet.[46] Morton's was not a lone voice. Some of his ideas were being advanced by respected analysts, such as Dieter Helm of OXERA,

[45] Morton–Byers, 7 June 2001, enclosing 'Key Issues for the New Secretary of State responsible for Transport', 6 June 2001, SRA.
[46] Morton–Byers, 12 June 2001, enclosing 'Railtrack (RT) and Industry Structure', same date, SRA. A third letter complained that Linnard, now Director, Railways, had told the SRA to confine itself to selected objectives under the 10 Year Plan: Morton–Byers, 14 June 2001, SRA.

who supported a radical reform of Railtrack and the merger of the SRA and the ORR.[47]

What did Byers make of all this? Briefed by his officials to accept the view that *both* Railtrack and the SRA were flawed organizations, there was little prospect of his standing in the way of a Morton exit.[48] And within weeks it became clear that the restructured Department's strategy for the industry was to be very different from that envisaged by the SRA Chairman. Morton later recalled that Byers decided to eliminate the SRA from its central role by issuing new draft directions and guidance, which subjugated its decision-making to Departmental requirements. Then he ordered a strategic plan (to be produced by November) which had to live within the funding currently available. Finally, without consulting officials, he abandoned the long-term franchising policy, under instructions direct from Number Ten.[49] It is difficult to substantiate the claim that Byers had acted without consultation on the orders of the Prime Minister's Office. Nevertheless, there is no doubt that after only five months of statutory existence, the Authority was instructed to change tack, and that Byers wanted 'quick wins' from franchise extensions, in preference to the uncertainties produced by a longer-term approach.[50] A new, more prescriptive draft of ministerial directions and guidance, sent to Morton on 27 June, and published as part of a consultation process on the following day, was intended to ensure that the SRA worked 'with the grain of Government policy'. The emphasis was squarely upon 'focus, realism and delivery'. The Authority was now expected to refocus on 'making the existing structures work and delivering improvements now'. Its primary objective was to 'deliver *relevant targets* [my italics] from [the] 10 Year Plan'. This required early franchise replacement 'only where it represents an affordable, and value for money, approach'.[51] A draft franchising policy statement followed. Published on 16 July, it emphasized flexibility of response and the use of existing franchise agreements, which provided for extensions of up to two years. The two-year extension awarded to Midland Main Line in August 2000 (above, p. 48) was heralded as an example of what was required.[52]

These requirements clearly stuck in Morton's craw. The SRA had been pressing the Department to provide a Section 26 Direction (confirming the choice of a preferred counterparty) for both the East Coast and TransPennine franchises, and was clearly disappointed by the prevarication, though the election provided

---

[47] Dieter Helm (New College Oxford, and Director, OXERA), 'Whither Railways?', OXERA rail conference, 19 June 2001, SRA.

[48] Rowlands–Byers, Linnard–Byers, both 12 June 2001, DfT, Weir doc. vol. K4.

[49] Morton, draft for *Spectator* article, 13 August 2001.

[50] David Hill (Byers's PS)–Rowlands, 26 June 2001, DTLR file R7/1/42 Pt. 2.

[51] Byers–Morton, 27 June 2001, SRA Board Minutes (special strategy meeting), 28 June 2001, 'Draft Directions and Guidance to the Strategic Rail Authority', enclosed in Jenner, Memo. to SRA Board, 5 July 2001, SRA; Directions and Guidance, interpreted in John Spellar (Minister for Transport)–Sarah Boyack (Minister for Transport, Scottish Executive), 29 June 2001, DTLR file R73/1/26 Pt. 9.

[52] DTLR News Release, 13 July 2001, and Draft Policy Statement on 'Passenger Rail Franchising', 16 July 2001. See also Hill–Coulshed, 28 June 2001, DTLR file R78/1/14 Pt. 3.

a convenient reason for delay.[53] From the Government's perspective, however, the news that there would be a funding gap of around £2 billion during CP2 for the franchise replacement programme was extremely disturbing and it is clear from the finance director's reports to the SRA Board in the summer of 2001 that a number of elements in the franchising replacement programme did not enjoy budget cover.[54] But the revised policy, a 'do-minimum' alternative held to be consistent with the funding available, was problematic for the SRA. Its Board believed that it 'overturned the broad objectives of the 10 year plan'. The new approach, which envisaged replacing franchises on a like-for-like basis when they fell due, and identifying those franchises which offered the best prospects of contributing to the key targets of the plan, was held to skew the objectives from outcomes to outputs, 'by re-imposing targets which were susceptible to simple measurement'.[55] Morton was dismissive of the draft statement, which had not been produced by the Railways Directorate. 'Had those preparing it consulted the SRA', he told Byers, 'they would have learned a lot from the work in this direction already in hand here.'[56] But the SRA had no alternative but to comply with governmental requirements. Byers refused to approve a 20-year franchise for ECML in July, and negotiations with GNER for a two-year extension began immediately.[57] When Morton met Byers on 24 July he conveyed the SRA's view that in some cases better value for money was likely to arise through alternative short- to medium-term measures, later called 'enhanceable franchises', instead of simple two-year extensions. Six franchises might be considered for the latter, but the problematic, 'cost-plus' franchises such as Merseyrail, Northern, and Cardiff required more radical redefinition, as did others 'where the geography was changing'.[58] There was some support for this position within the Department, and the SRA was encouraged to 'do whatever is best to obtain benefits, long or short term'.[59] On 23 August Grant sent the Secretary of State the Authority's 'considered views on an appropriate re-franchising/franchise extension programme'. The response was complex, requiring seven pages to explain. Franchises were grouped into no fewer than six categories (Table 4.1). The recommendation was to introduce the enhanceable franchise concept into negotiations for categories 2, 3, and 4, where expiry would occur in 2004. The SRA proposed to invite competitive proposals for each franchise comprising the 'base' (as existing) plus a series of progressive enhancement options. A franchise length of eight years was

[53] Morton, Memo. 5 June 2001, Chris Kinchin-Smith (SRA), Memo. 7 June 2001, enclosing Grant–Macdonald correspondence, 3 May–1 June 2001, SRA Board Minutes, 7 June 2001, SRA.

[54] Martin McGann (ED, Finance and Administration, SRA), Memos. to SRA Board, 7 June and 5 July 2001, SRA.

[55] SRA Board Minutes, 28 June and 5 July 2001, SRA. Cf. also Anthony Hilton, in *Evening Standard*, 16 July 2001, p. 35.

[56] Morton–Byers and Morton–SRA Board, 16 July 2001, SRA.

[57] DTLR News Release, 18 July 2001; Byers–Morton (drafted by Coulshed), 21 July 2001, DTLR file R73/1/26 Pt. 9.

[58] Morton–SRA Board and Chairman's Committee, 25 July 2001, SRA.

[59] Coulshed–Byers, 19 July 2001, DTLR file R73/1/26 Pt. 9; Byers–Morton, 21 July 2001, cit.

The Strategic Rail Authority and Railtrack After Hatfield

Table 4.1 SRA categorization of franchises, August 2001

Categories	Franchises	Comments
1. Future determined	Chiltern South Central South West Trains Midland Mainline TransPennine (Northern/North Western)	Proposal to continue with TransPennine
2. Opened up	Wales & Borders Wessex Merseyrail Northern	Proposal to replace now; expiry in 2004
3. Replace on expiry	Greater Anglia (GE, Anglia, WA) Island Line (extended in 2001 to 30 September 2003)	No urgency; expiry 2004
4. Heavy loss-makers	Central ScotRail	Negotiate with National Express; expiry 2004
5. Two-year extensions	East Coast Main Line Silverlink Connex South Eastern First Great Western Thames Thameslink/Great Northern	Potential to extend
6. No action	Gatwick Express c2c West Coast Cross Country	Long-term franchises

Source: Grant–Byers, 23 August 2001, SRA.

preferred. Grant asked the Secretary of State to agree to an announcement of the new approach in the first half of September.[60] Byers was not disposed to hurry. Morton had made it clear that he intended to be gone by the end of October, and would not be taking charge of the preparations for the SRA's strategic plan, required under the new directions and guidance to be published in November.[61] The Secretary of State was therefore minded to delay an announcement about franchising to allow Morton's successor to be involved. There were also financial implications of course. Grant had explained that while all existing franchises could be replaced on a 'do-minimum' basis within the funding available under the 10 Year Plan, delivery of a 50 per cent increase in passenger traffic and a

---

[60] Grant–Byers, 23 August 2001 (two letters), SRA.

[61] Morton–SRA Board &c., 25 July 2001, cit., Morton–SRA Strategic Plan Committee, 1 August 2001, SRA. Morton drafted a letter of resignation on 26 July, but in the event delayed giving the formal three months' notice until September: Morton–Byers, 13 September 2001, SRA.

40 per cent (i.e. scaled down) increase in freight traffic would require £900 million to be brought forward from CP3 to CP2.[62] Officials conceded that the Plan had been 'back loaded too far', and were sympathetic to the SRA's position. Byers eventually sanctioned the policy in a letter to Grant on 18 October, though he continued to express concern about the financial implications.[63] But by this time Railtrack was in administration, and the railway world had been turned upside down once more.

4.3 Exit Railtrack

Railtrack's difficulties had not disappeared, of course, and within months the Secretary of State, in a surprise move, placed the company in administration, on 7 October 2001. How did this come about? This is not the place to examine events in the forensic way inspired by the shareholders' action against the Government in *Weir and Others v. the Secretary of State for Transport and Department for Transport* (2005). A separate volume would be required to make a detailed evaluation of the mountains of memoranda, minutes, e-mails, and policy briefings in order to discover what was done when, and who said what to whom. The intention here is to pick a way through the numerous assessments of committed commentators, self-interested players, back protectors, apologists, and buriers of bad news. We can certainly state that the belief that Railtrack was, in Grant's words, 'holed below the waterline' enjoyed wide currency in the months after Hatfield. The SRA and Morton had said so, civil servants had briefed Byers to that effect, the TOCs had lobbied the Regulator hard with complaints about the company, and the respected analyst Roger Ford had argued that the railway infrastructure should be renationalized.[64] Winsor added to the clamour when, in a speech at the Institution of Electrical Engineers in June, he had advised Railtrack to put away the 'begging bowl', a remark which produced an adverse reaction in the City.[65] We have already seen that Morton had rehearsed a number of radical options for the reform of Railtrack when he wrote to Byers in the same month. But well before that some radical ideas had been circulating in Whitehall. For example, in December 2000 Prescott had responded to the Hatfield crisis by 'getting some quiet work done on options' for Railtrack.[66] And in February

---

[62] Grant–Byers, 23 August 2001, cit. In fact, the total to be brought forward was £883m. Coulshed–Byers, 17 September 2001, DTLR file R73/1/26 Pt. 9. With freight commitments and other demands, the total to be advanced was £1.2bn.
[63] Byers–Grant, 18 October 2001, ibid. Pt. 10.
[64] Roger Ford, *Modern Railways*, September 2001, p. 20.
[65] Winsor, 12 June 2001, www.rail-reg.gov.uk.
[66] Jeremy Heywood (Blair's PPS)–Unwin, 21 December 2000, Prime Minister's file on Bilaterals with DPM.

2001, when discussions which were to lead to the Endeavour agreement were in progress, an internal DETR paper had examined 'proposals for breaking the Railtrack monopoly'. The aim was to explore alternatives to the company in order to progress network enhancement, an exercise which was running in parallel with that mounted by the SRA. Splitting Railtrack into a core company and an enhancement company was considered, as were the prospects for an independent SPV. And in the process the idea of converting Railtrack into a 'not-for-profit trust' was raised.[67] The disclosure process for *Weir and Others* revealed that Byers had been provided with a preliminary memorandum outlining options for Railtrack as early as 12 June, and that departmental meetings had been held on 15 and 20 June, culminating in a decision to invite the Treasury to join the Department in examining options 'involving alternative owners and management'.[68]

It is clear that the SRA made genuine attempts to progress the 'Endeavour' agreement of April 2001. But although Railtrack had been required to produce a working capital statement confirming its financial health, and this had been verified by both Lazards and KPMG,[69] doubts persisted about the strength of the company as the negotiations proceeded. Publication of Railtrack's Network Management Statement for 2001 on 31 May also failed to inspire confidence. The SRA noted that the plans for maintenance and renewal during CP2 were £3 billion higher than the CP2 provision, and the document was 'stronger on good intentions than hard targets of improvement'.[70] Priorities had certainly been developed for an enhancement programme, including Southampton–WCML, Felixstowe–Nuneaton (freight route), Cherwell Valley, and London–Stansted, in addition to the ECML and Thameslink. These schemes were being progressed with the aid of additional funding of £28 million belatedly made available in July.[71] On 28 June the SRA Board, encouraged by Morton, debated options for Railtrack, whose share price had fallen sharply to £3.18, below the flotation value.[72] The possibilities, which included a public sector stake, a Competition Commission review, breaking up the monopoly, and vertical integration, were rehearsed, but no firm conclusions were reached.[73] Further work on Renewco, by early July rechristened 'NGCL', that is, Network Grant Company Ltd., continued.

[67] Phil Carey (DETR)–Linnard and Coulshed, 20 February 2001, DETR file R10/5/81 Pt. 1. Carey–Gareth Evans, 21 and 22 February 2001, formed part of the evidence taken in *Weir*. See DfT, Weir doc. vol. K2; Lindsay, Judgment, para. 36.

[68] Coulshed–Byers, 12 June 2001, cit. and subsequent meetings, referred to in ibid. paras. 57–65 and minuted in Hill–Rowlands, 25 June 2001 (two memos.), DfT, Weir doc. vol. K5. See also Carey-Byers, 12 June 2001, Shriti Vadera (adviser, Treasury)–Ed Balls (chief adviser, Treasury), 21 June 2001, ibid. vols. K4–5. As early as February, Blair had told Prescott that he wished to see joint work undertaken on options: Virley–Unwin, 27 February 2001, cit.

[69] SRA Board Minutes, 5 April 2001, SRA; Harding, thesis, 2005, pp. 122–4.

[70] O'Donnell, Memo. 6 June 2001, SRA Board Minutes, 7 June 2001, SRA.

[71] O'Donnell, Memo. 19 July 2001, Spellar–Grant, 9 July 2001 and reply, 11 July 2001, SRA file 57/01/02 Pt. 23; O'Donnell, Memo. to SRA Board, 2 August 2001, SRA.

[72] Price at 26 June 2001: *Financial Times*, 27 June 2001, p. 1.

[73] SRA Board Minutes, 28 June 2001, SRA.

The Strategic Rail Authority and Railtrack After Hatfield

The intention was that NGCL would arrange a £1.4 billion revolving credit facility with the banks, in order to bridge the financing gap between the profile of grants and the profile of regulatory revenue. But the Treasury's anxieties about the device remained, and its officials continued to nurse hopes of a 'purely private sector' approach to enhancement. The impasse raised the possibility that Railtrack would return to the Regulator and reopen the charges review.[74] As the 21 July deadline approached, Morton informed Byers that there was a serious danger of the SRA being in breach of the Endeavour agreement.[75] In fact, Railtrack did not press the matter, and negotiations between the two parties to resolve the 'classification' problem continued in August and September, with the help of their respective auditors.[76] The process was complex, and the financial risks were difficult to estimate, particularly because Railtrack made it clear that its ability to engage in enhancement activities would be severely constrained. SRA officials therefore moved to the proposition that a project management contractor should take the place of Railtrack in the management process.[77] When the SRA Board considered the establishment of the NGCL, non-executive members were moved to express anxieties about the payment of such a large sum to Railtrack and the absence of a guarantee that funds would be allocated to SRA to meet its obligations to NGCL.[78] In the event, the consent of ministers was not given and the plan for Railtrack took an entirely different direction. At the end of September it emerged that the Government was not proceeding with Renewco ahead of the 1 October deadline for a £500 million payment to Railtrack in grants under the Endeavour agreement. The reluctance of the Office of National Statistics to accept that the NGCL arrangements met the criteria for off-balance sheet accounting was given as a reason for the absence of ministerial approval, although it later emerged that the plans for taking Railtrack into administration were an equally potent reason for rejection.[79] Morton thought the Renewco failure underlined the need for the SRA to have satisfactory delegated authority, and be able to liaise directly with the Treasury on specialized financial matters.[80] There must have been some surprise in SRA circles at the treatment of Railtrack, since the Authority had accepted Byers's earlier view that there should be a period of stability in which to assess options, and that consequently nothing should be done to make Railtrack's position

[74] O'Donnell and David Thomas (SRA), Memos. to SRA Board, 2 July 2001, SRA.
[75] Morton–Byers, 18 July 2001, SRA.
[76] Thomas, Memo. to SRA Board, 3 September 2001, SRA.
[77] SRA Chairman's Committee Minutes, 14 August 2001, SRA file 02/20/02 Pt. 2.
[78] Minutes of an informal meeting of the SRA Board, 13 September 2001, Morton–Mottram, 13 September 2001, SRA.
[79] Under the agreement, a deferred grant of £336.59m was paid to Railtrack on 1 October, and a further £162m in revenue grant was paid at the end of the month. SRA Chairman's Committee Minutes, 25 September, and 2 October 2001, SRA file 02/20/02 Pt. 2, Grant–Mottram and McGann–David Harding (FD, Railtrack), both 28 September 2001, SRA Board Minutes, 4 and 16 October 2001, SRA–Railtrack, 30 October 2001, SRA.
[80] Morton–Mottram, 1 October 2001, SRA.

worse.[81] This period proved to be extremely short, and Morton's exasperation was revealed in his parting shot in the *Spectator*, published the day before the administration order. Here he asserted that it was not the first time he had been 'hugely depressed by the surreally poor quality of the dialogue between Treasury, Ministry and agency'.[82]

The SRA was not involved in Whitehall's deliberations about Railtrack's future.[83] When the administration order was revealed, the SRA board minuted that neither Morton nor Grant had been informed of the discussions between Railtrack and the Government prior to 6 October. 'For the Authority to be kept in ignorance of major issues pertaining to the strategic development of the industry prevented it from fulfilling its statutory obligations', the Board continued, a statement that was scarcely auspicious for an incoming chairman.[84] Morton had been obviously fishing for clues when he met Byers on 24 July:

I said we needed to know if he was coming to drop the other shoe soon—announce a new policy towards the structure around Railtrack. He said he was thinking hard about it, taking into account the alternatives I offered him in my note of 12 June and was not in a position to make any move yet. I repeated my caution we needed to be very careful as there is at most one reorganisation left in this very sick company.[85]

In fact, Byers would soon formulate a policy for the 'other shoe'. On the following day, 25 July, he met the newly installed Chairman of Railtrack, John Robinson, with Spellar, Mottram, David Rowlands, now Director General of RALM,[86] David Hill (Byers's PS), and Dan Corry (a DTLR adviser) also present.[87] Robinson told him that having appointed Credit Suisse First Boston (CSFB) as financial consultants to examine the state of the company, he had discovered that its position was precarious. He asked for a suspension of the existing regulatory regime, together with a 'soft letter of comfort' for Railtrack's bankers to facilitate a 'going concern' statement when the half-yearly results were published in November, in effect a government guarantee of its debt. No agreed record of the meeting was made, however, and indeed Robinson specifically asked that notes be not taken of his remarks about financing proposals. Consequently, recollections about exactly what was said have differed.[88] The two men clearly misread each

---

[81] Jenner, Memo. to SRA Board, 5 July 2001, SRA; Transport stocktake meeting with Blair, 5 July, reported in Virley–Unwin, 6 July 2001, DfT, Weir doc. Vol. K5.

[82] Morton, *Spectator*, 6 October 2001, p. 37.

[83] Morton, Breakfast with Frost, BBC1, 18 November 2001.

[84] SRA Board Minutes, 16 October 2001, SRA.

[85] Morton–SRA Board, 25 July 2001, cit. The DTLR's mss notes of this meeting are in DfT, Weir doc. vol. K6.

[86] RALM = Railways, Aviation, Logistics, and Maritime, DTLR.

[87] Record of minuted sections of Byers's meeting with Robinson, 25 July 2001, in Hill–Rowlands, 30 July 2001, published as Supplementary Note, 27 November 2001 in response to a request from the Transport Select Committee, www.dft.gov.uk.

[88] The DTLR's mss notes of this meeting are in DfT, Weir doc. vol. K6. See also Interview with Rowlands, 2007; Harding, thesis, 2005, p. 140 ff.; Wolmar, *On the Wrong Line*, pp. 190–1; Lindsay, Judgment, paras. 87–95; Robinson interview, *Financial Times*, 16 October 2001, www.ft.com.

other's intentions, as they had done at an earlier meeting on 27 June. Robinson thought he was offering the Government a solution to the Railtrack problem, and with CSFB was working up a financial plan, bypassing the Regulator, which was later given the codename 'Project Rainbow'.[89] Byers took the meeting to indicate that unless the Government ignored the principles enshrined in the 'Endeavour agreement' and provided the company with substantial support, the game was up. The Government could not agree to Robinson's demands, and 'Project Ariel' was initiated.[90]

After the meeting CSFB produced a pessimistic evaluation of Railtrack's prospects. This was shared with the Department on 27 July, as the prelude to what Railtrack intended would be a joint response to the funding problem. In retrospect the decision to disclose the information may have been unwise, particularly since the presentation included a reference to the three 'R's—renationalization, receivership, or restructuring—and it was suggested that insolvency would be a very real possibility in the absence of government support.[91] Further presentations were made on 1 and 7 August, where CSFB concluded that additional funding of £4.7 billion was required. The Department's manuscript record expressed it as 'lots of dosh please'.[92] Meanwhile within Whitehall, serious steps were being taken to examine the options for Railtrack independently, with the help of Treasury adviser, Shriti Vadera, and others. Vadera, an experienced investment banker from Warburg Dillon Read, had been advising the Chancellor on PPP and PFI issues, notably in relation to the London Underground. She had attended high-level transport meetings at Number Ten in 1999 and had been sent material on Railtrack's problems since the end of 2000.[93] Freed from the normal restraints of civil service etiquette, she was more trenchant than most in putting her point of view. Documents released to the Court in *Weir and Others* indicate that from the beginning she had been enthusiastic about replacing Railtrack and keen to pursue the insolvency route.[94] But while Justice Lindsay, in his judgment on the

[89] Harding has noted that CSFB had used the same codename in a similar evaluation of National Air Traffic Services: thesis, 2005, p. 143.

[90] The Government's recollections were presented by Byers in his Commons Statement on 15 October, *Parl. Deb. (Commons)*, 6th ser. (Session 2001–2), Vol. 372 Pt. 2, c. 954, and in evidence before the Transport Select Committee on 14 November 2001, HC Transport Local Government and Regions Committee Report on *Passenger Rail Franchising and the Future of the Railway Infrastructure*, 31 January 2002, P.P. 2001–2, xxxvi, HC239, QQ. 844–50.

[91] CSFB, 'Project Rainbow', presentation to DTLR, 27 July 2001, DfT, Weir doc. vol. D3; Lindsay, Judgment, para. 96; HC Transport Committee Report on *Passenger Rail Franchising*, January 2002, para. 35.

[92] DTLR mss notes of meetings on 1 and 7 August 2001, CSFB, 'Project Rainbow', 7 August 2001, DfT, Weir Doc. vols. K7 and D4; Lindsay, Judgment, paras. 105, 110; Harding, thesis, 2005, pp. 143–4.

[93] Virley–Unwin, 14 July 1999, Prime Minister's Rail Policy papers, Pt. 4; Morton–Rowlands, 19 December 2000, cit. (copied to Vadera). On Vadera, see www.red-star-research.org.uk and Tom Bower, *Gordon Brown* (2005), p. 312.

[94] Vadera, e-mail to Wheatley, 26 July 2001, reported in *Daily Telegraph*, 29 April 2005, collection of Tom Winsor (henceforth 'Winsor archive'); Vadera–Adonis et al., 31 July 2001, enclosing 'Project Ariel: whether and how to restructure the industry', DfT, Weir doc. vol. K7, and Lindsay, Judgment, paras. 102–3.

The Strategic Rail Authority and Railtrack After Hatfield

Weir case, was anxious to draw a distinction between the advising role and the formal responsibilities of civil servants and ministers, it is quite clear that the advisers were merely pushing at an open door.[95] The view that Railtrack needed a radical restructuring was widespread within Whitehall, and in the summer of 2001 the discussion was about means, not ends. After all, there had been little 'comfort' for the incoming Secretary of State when he was told by Robinson on 27 June that the company's financial situation was worse than he had first thought, and that relations with the Regulator were 'appalling'.[96] Officials knew that there was a wide gap between the access charges review and the company's projections, and that substantial risks were associated with the WCML upgrade and the CTRL. Indeed, anyone who cared to peruse the 'contingent liabilities' statement in Railtrack's accounts for 2000/1 would have been left in no doubt that the company's prospects were far from secure. The statement concluded that 'the scale of the contingent liabilities described above, if they were to materialise, could, in aggregate, seriously prejudice the Group's financial position'.[97] In any case, at the end of June, Marshall, Railtrack's Chief Executive, having received a preliminary report from CSFB which argued that 'Liquidity/Solvency [is] a real issue without Government support', warned Winsor, with copies to the DTLR and SRA, that the company was in a precarious state.[98] Inside the Treasury, Wheatley recirculated a paper which had been drafted at the time of the Endeavour agreement and rehearsed possible structural options for Railtrack: renationalization, a government equity stake, a not-for-profit trust, vertical integration, and a regional organization. Highlighting the fact that Railtrack had continued to experience problems of undercapitalization after the Endeavour agreement, he drew the conclusion that 'current arrangements' might have to be 're-engineered'.[99] Vadera was one of the recipients, and when she attended a 'transport stocktake' meeting with the Prime Minister on 5 July she spoke against Byers's contention that the industry needed a period of stability. Railtrack, she argued, could not be stabilized in the short term. 'The company was not correctly incentivized to carry out its core responsibility of getting the trains to run on time. It was not properly capitalized and had no capacity to bear risk. More radical changes to the structure of the company needed to be considered as a matter of urgency.' However at this stage ministers were more concerned with 'quick wins' for rail users, that is, making the existing system work more effectively.[100]

[95] Interview with Dan Corry, 15 February 2007.
[96] DTLR mss note of meeting on 27 June 2001, Hill–Spellar's PS, 4 July 2001, DfT, Weir doc. Vol. K5; Lindsay, Judgment, paras. 69–70.
[97] Railtrack plc, R&A 2000/1, note 36 to accounts, and see also Lindsay, Judgment, para. 47.
[98] CSFB, 'Project Rainbow: Steering Group Meeting 1', 28 June 2001, and Marshall–Winsor, 29 June 2001. My thanks to David Harding for these references. The letter was attributed to Harding in Lindsay, Judgment, paras. 74–5.
[99] Wheatley–Ed Balls, 20 June 2001, enclosing Ros Moss, 'Railways—Long Term Options', n.d., DfT, Weir doc. Vol. K5.
[100] Virley–Unwin, 6 July 2001, cit.

Robinson's leadership of the company may have played into the hands of hawks in the Treasury and DTLR, and he was often too candid for his own good. For example, in a private meeting with Morton in August he conceded that Railtrack was 'terribly fragile' and thought the company had no strategy.[101] Harding has asserted that both he and Marshall were less sanguine about the reliance on CSFB. The financial advisers may have exaggerated the gloomy nature of the company's position, and the prospects for going to the market may have been brighter than was suggested. Harding expressed the view that the company could continue trading with existing bank facilities until at least April 2002, or longer if spending were curtailed, the risks associated with the WCML upgrade constrained, and a comfort letter obtained, with a renegotiation of bank facilities. This possibility was dubbed 'Plan B' or the 'muddle through' option, and Harding raised it with the Department in September, though he quickly withdrew it when Robinson made it clear that 'Project Rainbow' was the only way forward.[102] Nevertheless, civil servants and advisers could scarcely be blamed for planning for the worst, and the basic premise of 'Project Rainbow', that the Government should provide finance on an 'emerging-cost basis' and receive equity on a sliding scale related to performance and the level of support given, was unlikely to succeed unless it produced the required escape from the public sector. There were also difficulties in the Government accepting the notion that both the dividend and the value of the equity should be propped up.[103] While 'Project Rainbow' was worked up in detail—the Department engaged Schroder Salomon Smith Barney as advisers and CSFB's final presentation was made on 18 September[104]—officials continued to work on an alternative. The direction of their efforts was soon clear. On 3 August Byers presented Blair with the narrowing options: Railtrack could be either restructured, taken over, or converted into a not-for-profit trust. In any event, wrote Byers, 'It may be advisable to take Railtrack into protective special railway administration and events could even mean it is inevitable, as a prelude to moving to the chosen option.'[105] On 23 August Ernst & Young were instructed to advise the Department on whether Railtrack was insolvent within the terms of the railway legislation.[106] A *de facto* renationalization of the company was examined, together with the not-for-profit alternative, which Byers, the Department, and Number Ten appeared to favour, though at this stage no firm decisions had been taken.[107] When Byers met Blair and Brown on 5 September, the choice seemed to have narrowed to a dormant equity solution vs. a no-equity company limited by guarantee (CLG). The Prime Minister expressed

---

[101] Morton, file note, 13 August 2001, Morton's papers, SRA.

[102] Linnard, 'Ariel: Discussions with Company', 10–11 September 2001, DfT, Weir doc. vol. K11.

[103] DTLR, 'Review of CSFB's presentation of 7th August', n.d., ibid. vol. K7; Harding, thesis, 2005, pp. 144–52; Lindsay, Judgment, paras. 110, 117–18, 129, 148–50.

[104] CSFB, 'Project Rainbow', draft proposal, 18 September 2001, DfT, Weir doc. vol. D7.

[105] Byers–Blair, 3 August 2001 (drafted by Rowlands, 2 August 2001), ibid. vol. K7; Lindsay, Judgment, para. 106.

[106] Ibid. para. 127.   [107] Ibid. paras. 120–5, 135–6.

the view that the option chosen should deliver the most effective management of the railway infrastructure, while the Chancellor was anxious to ensure that the preferred solution did not 'score' as public sector spending. However, the cost implications of an administration route were not discussed.[108] In the week leading up to CSFB's presentation of a revised version of 'Project Rainbow' on 18 September, Whitehall's policy crystallized around the rejection of 'muddling through', and the acceptance of administration, to be followed by the establishment of a CLG. A persuasive precedent with the advisers had been the acquisition of Welsh Water by Glas Cymru, under the chairmanship of the former Treasury Permanent Secretary, Terry Burns.[109]

On 19 September Byers met Blair and Brown to discuss the future of Railtrack. Also present were Rowlands, Andrew Campbell, now Byers's PS, and some of the burgeoning group of advisers clustered round Number Ten, the Treasury, and the DTLR: Blair's Senior Policy Adviser, Brian Hackland, Ed Balls, Chief Adviser to the Treasury, Andrew Adonis, Head of Policy at Number Ten, Vadera, the Treasury adviser, and Corry from DTLR. Byers rehearsed the options available to the Government. He dismissed Railtrack's latest 'Rainbow' proposal, which involved extra government support and guarantees for shareholders, and also rejected the idea of a 'muddle through' alternative. He clearly favoured the establishment of a not-for-profit CLG, which 'would ensure that the public interest was paramount'. Railway administration offered the best route to achieve this, but would require the company's cooperation.[110] Blair asked whether it would be difficult to proceed without the cooperation of Robinson, Railtrack's Chairman. Brown was concerned about costs. He said that the £33.6 billion provided for rail spending in the *10 Year Plan* could rise to £45 billion if rescue plans went wrong. He then referred to a list of 10 key issues which needed to be resolved before a decision were taken. They included arrangements for interim financing of the administrator; valuation; treatment of £4.5 billion of lender debt; and ensuring that future debt did not count as public expenditure. Blair was prepared to support the CLG concept provided it resolved two principal problems: Railtrack's poor quality management and the 'crippling impact of the current regulatory arrangements'. Vadera advised that a CLG could be financed off the balance sheet through the revenue stream arising from access charges plus debt financing.

---

[108] DTLR mss notes of meeting, 5 September 2001, Brian Hackland (Senior Policy Adviser, No. 10)–Andrew Campbell (Byers's PS), 7 September 2001, DfT, Weir doc. vols. K9–10, and cf. also Lindsay, Judgment, paras. 143–4, and Bower, *Brown*, pp. 356–7.

[109] Project Ariel Steering Committee Minutes, 12 September 2001; Linnard–Byers, Lewis Atter (now Head of Transport Team, Treasury)–Brown, and Adonis–Blair, all 14 September 2001, DfT, Weir doc. vol. K11; Lindsay, Judgment, paras. 159–65. Arthur Andersen was engaged on 13 September to consider whether the Government could petition successfully for an administration order: Andersen–DTLR, 14 September 2001, ibid. vol. K11. On precedents for a CLG see Tony Grayling, *Getting back on track: reforming the ownership and regulation of Britain's railways* (IPPR, 2001), pp. 19–22.

[110] Byers had informed Blair on the previous day that advisers had been unable to unearth any 'killer blow' to force Railtrack into administration. Byers–Hill, 18 September 2001, DfT, defendants' disclosure file 62, and see also *Daily Telegraph*, 30 April 2005, Winsor archive.

It would 'offer improved clarity and performance'. Rowlands was also enthusiastic, pointing out that a CLG would produce a better alignment of incentives for Railtrack and the TOCs. There was clearly anxiety about making a decision. Blair noted that if the company were forced into administration it would protest and the position of the 250,000 small shareholders required careful thought. Byers was asked to be ready to conduct negotiations with Robinson on 28 September. A regulatory overhaul was also clearly in mind, and the intention was to issue powers of direction to prevent Winsor's intervention.[111]

By the 28th the policy was becoming clear. Progress had been made in answering the Chancellor's 10 questions. The DETR's advice was that the cost of administration might require £1.5 billion of government funding, and that the 10 Year Plan might still be deliverable if major renewals were financed by debt and the new company were 'significantly more efficient' than its predecessor.[112] Railtrack was due to present its final proposals to the DTLR on 3 October, when the outcome of discussions with Virgin to constrain the cost of the WCML upgrade was expected. Byers would make a decision on the 5th, prior to a meeting with Robinson. Further discussions, conducted by officials and consultants, would take place over the weekend, with an announcement to the Stock Exchange on the 8th. The Government faced three difficulties. First, there was still uncertainty as to whether the CLG would count as public sector. Second, anticipated changes to the regulatory and performance regime would not be easy to establish. Within Number Ten the idea of establishing a single regulatory body to replace the SRA and the ORR was appealing, but this would complicate the search for a successor to Morton, and Winsor would need careful handling. The evidence suggests some nervousness about involving and confronting Winsor, who, like Morton, had been kept in the dark. Finally, policy towards the shareholders had not been determined. Advisers had calculated that the equity would be worth 'zero or less', but a deal with Robinson was held to depend upon sympathetic treatment of the shareholders.[113] Railtrack's final meeting with the Government on 3 October produced nothing substantial, other than further intimations that the company's financial predicament remained serious.[114]

Two days later, Winsor and Robinson were informed of the Government's decision to provide no further financial support for Railtrack plc, and of its intention to place the company in administration and replace it with a CLG. At 4.00 pm on

---

[111] Hackland–Campbell, 21 September 2001, Prime Minister's Rail papers, Pt. 3 and DfT, Weir doc. vol. K12; DTLR mss notes of the 19 September meeting, ibid.; Lindsay, Judgment, paras. 181–2. In July, Blair reportedly asked whether the Government had powers to replace the Rail Regulator before his contract expired: private information.

[112] Hill–Rowlands, 28 September 2001, DfT, Weir doc. vol. K15.

[113] Hackland–Blair, 28 September 2001, Andrew Adonis (Head of Policy, No. 10)–Blair, 4 October 2001, Prime Minister's Rail papers, Pt. 3; Lindsay, Judgment, paras. 185, 190.

[114] DTLR, Note of 'Meeting to discuss Project Rainbow…3 October 2001', DfT, Weir doc. vol. K15; Lindsay, Judgment, paras. 194–9.

5 October, with the markets closing, Winsor met Byers and Rowlands; Robinson's meeting followed at 4.45 pm. Once again, recollections of what was said differ. Hackland, briefing Blair, said that Robinson did not appear surprised by the decision, and that both he and the Board were prepared to see Railtrack go into administration, though he made much of their fiduciary duties to shareholders. Once Winsor had 'got over his initial surprise', said Hackland, he confirmed that Railtrack was in 'dire financial straits' and left the meeting 'apparently relatively happy', having agreed to Byers's request to work up ideas on the new regulatory arrangements that would be required.[115] This version of events appears unduly sanguine. Material provided for the *Weir* case indicates that Robinson expressed not only surprise but also some anger at the decision, and that Winsor was far from happy.[116] The Regulator had every reason to be indignant, perhaps more so than Morton. Dismissed by Vadera as a 'total wild card', he was in fact very much a known quantity. With a penchant for the contractual and the letter of the law, he would obviously seek to defend his position as an independent regulator. Indeed, Byers was more accurate in describing him as 'uncompromising and legalistic'.[117] The Government had been anxious to keep him out of a solution.[118] He, in turn, has asserted that the Government behaved reprehensibly in bypassing him. Winsor's file note of his meeting with Byers on 5 October records his surprise that Railtrack's finances should have deteriorated so suddenly. It also records that when Winsor suggested that Robinson might respond by making an immediate application to him for an early interim review, Byers made it clear that if a review were sought the Government would introduce emergency legislation to prevent it; indeed, a draft Bill was quickly prepared. Winsor replied by pointing out the adverse effect such an action would have on the position of independent utility regulators and on the financial markets. It would also damage the Government's PFI policy.[119]

How convincing is Winsor's later suggestion that he could have provided a lifeline for Railtrack, by conducting an emergency review of the charges structure?[120] There is some contemporary support for this view. Vadera, in an

---

[115] Hackland–Blair, 5 October 2001, Prime Minister's Rail papers, Pt. 3 and DfT, Weir doc. vol. K16.

[116] DTLR mss notes of meetings on 5 October 2001, Hill–Rowlands, 6 October 2001 (two memos.), ibid. vol. K16; Lindsay, Judgment, paras. 209–13. On surprise elsewhere in Railtrack, see Simon Osborne (Company Secretary & Solicitor, Railtrack), reported in *Legal Director*, December 2001, pp. 10–11. My thanks to Vicki Martins for this reference.

[117] Vadera–Corry et al., 2 October 2001 (19.59), Byers–Blair, 29 June 2001, DfT, Weir doc. vols. K15 and K5; Lindsay, Judgment, para. 78.

[118] Cf. DTLR mss note on 'PM Rail Trilateral—on Railtrack', 19 September 2001, DfT doc. vol. K12; Linnard–Chris Houston et al. (SSSB), 19 September 2001, cit. in *Daily Telegraph*, 30 April 2005, Winsor archive.

[119] ORR, File/Attendance Note on 'Railway Administration Order', 6 October 2001, and summary in *Daily Telegraph*, 31 March 2005, Winsor archive, and see also Railways Bill, 10 October 2001, enclosed in Winsor–Author, 10 May 2006. Winsor also drew the conclusion that both Byers and Rowlands felt that 'Project Rainbow' had never been regarded as a serious proposal by the Government. This assertion was rejected by Justice Lindsay, Judgment, para. 211.

[120] Winsor, in *Financial Times*, 1 August 2005, p. 2, Winsor archive.

infamous e-mail sent three days before the 5 October meetings, told Dan Corry: 'We cannot silence him over the weekend and if he stands up and says he has a grand plan which could keep the company solvent we're up the creek.'[121] And yet there was little likelihood of Railtrack turning to the Regulator for support. The company had already found Winsor's attitude to have been unhelpful, and even hostile. Harding has recalled that Winsor had been less comforting after the Endeavour Agreement, and in June he had told the company that 'the involuntary liquidation of Railtrack may be in the best interests of the UK Rail Industry'.[122] Robinson had always felt that a reference would not provide funds in time, and, in any case, its outcome would be too uncertain to serve as a viable rescue plan. Consequently, although Robinson and Marshall, the Chief Executive, went through the motions (in Winsor's words) in approaching Winsor at the eleventh hour to explore the possibilities of a review, it was scarcely possible to conduct one on Saturday evening with a court hearing due on the following day. Consequently, no application was made to the Regulator by the company.[123] On 7 October the Secretary of State successfully petitioned the High Court for a railway administration order. Four managers from Ernst & Young were then appointed as the administrators.[124] The Railtrack Board did not oppose the order.[125]

Robinson may have been rather naive in his dealings with the Government, but an enduring question was whether the latter had acted with probity, and in particular whether it had obtained sufficient information to establish beyond doubt that Railtrack was insolvent. The immediate reaction to the move was subdued. While Jo Moore, Byers's adviser, had been unwise to suggest that the '9/11' atrocity in the United States offered an ideal opportunity to bury bad news, the fact was that in the aftermath of 9/11 the air strikes on Afghanistan on 7 October served to deflect some of the media's attention from the administration order. And although there were many who applauded the decision to tackle the ailing infrastructure company, parliamentary debate, and the action taken by Railtrack shareholders to attempt to gain redress from the Secretary of State, ensured that broader questions relating to the decision did not go unanswered.

[121] Vadera–Corry et al., 2 October 2001, cit.

[122] Marshall–Winsor, 29 June 2001, DfT, Weir doc. vol. K5; Winsor in ORR, File/Attendance Note on 'Interim Review', 7 October 2001, Winsor archive; Harding, thesis, 2005, pp. 126, 130–1.

[123] Again, there are differences as to what was exactly discussed. See ORR, File Note, 7 October 2001, cit., Railtrack, News Release, 9 October 2001, Lindsay, Judgment, paras. 220–1; Harding, thesis, 2005, p. 157. Marshall tendered his resignation as Chief Executive on the 8th, though he agreed to serve his six-month notice period: Railtrack, News Release, 8 October 2001.

[124] Alan Bloom, Chris Hill, Scott Martin, and Mike Rollings. DTLR News Release, 7 October 2001; Railtrack, News Release, 7 October 2001.

[125] Harding, thesis, 2005, pp. 156–7.

'Oh, holy one. I bring terrible news about your Railtrack shares.'

6. Railtrack is placed in administration, October 2001: Mac, *Daily Mail*, 19 October 2001.

4.4 Conclusion

The decision to take Railtrack into administration and reject the alternative of another review of the company's requirements by the Regulator may have been Byers's and the Government's, though it is equally clear that the company itself played a part in its own demise. Not for nothing did Wolmar, with characteristic élan, ask whether Railtrack's demise was 'corporate lynching or assisted suicide'?[126] The answer, of course, was both. A universal view emerged that the company was not 'fit for purpose' and that a radical solution was required, notwithstanding the rights and interests of shareholders in a private sector company. Byers's pronouncements, and revelation of the Jo Moore e-mail, served to hinder public understanding of the move. Byers presented administration as a proactive step he had taken, rather than indicating that it was the inevitable consequence of the Government's refusal to write a blank cheque in circumstances where insolvency appeared to be imminent. The plight of Railtrack's shareholders, who had been referred to in somewhat intemperate language by the advisers as 'grannies', remained a problem to be resolved. Vadera and Corry had been determined that they should not be compensated,[127] but following administration, a deal was

---

[126] Wolmar, *On the Wrong Line*, p. 192.
[127] Vadera–Corry and Adonis e-mails, 28 and 29 August 2001, DfT, Weir doc. vol. K8.

struck, and in the end there was a distribution of £2.52 a share, 90 per cent of the value on suspension on 8 October 2001. While some distance short of the average value of the shares in the three years before administration (£9.90), the eventual settlement may be regarded as generous when compared with the experience of shareholders in Eurotunnel, or indeed, Marconi and Enron, where the situation had been equally disastrous. But with the benefit of hindsight we might ask whether administration was the optimal route for the Government to take, given both the cost of administration and the cost of establishing and maintaining the new company, Network Rail (see below, pp. 179–85). On the other hand, it is by no means clear that the other options—'muddling through', and an application to the Regulator—neither of which were explored in depth, would necessarily have produced a better result for stakeholders in the railways. Certainly, a reference to Winsor could not have been arranged very quickly.

An additional problem was that the hiatus of administration coincided with the demise of SRA franchising Mark I, the resignation of Morton and his replacement by Richard Bowker, with effect from 1 December. The intention was that a more pragmatic regime would emerge with a more realistic strategy for the railways, but equally some of the aspirations of the post-1997 regime were rather lost sight of in the furore over Railtrack, and areas such as freight, where access charges had been modified in October 2001, certainly suffered. Morton's period had not been comfortable, and we must ask whether he was the right man for the job. Mottram told him that he was a 'big picture person', concerned about the 'longer term', and was thus less congenial to ministerial requirements, which necessarily focused on early, visible improvements within the life of a parliament. But why should Morton have fallen back on a severely constrained approach when the Government itself had produced the 10 Year Plan? All sides in the industry had had to react to a fundamental change, from a steady state or declining railway system to a growing one. This required boldness and imagination, and Morton certainly had both. The SRA Chairman may have been guilty of failing to produce a comprehensive planning document in good time, but he was able to point out that neither the Department nor the Treasury had responded either quickly or enthusiastically to his SPV proposals in 1999, and that their nervousness about the financing implications of the developing refranchising proposals in 2001 had served to erode the SRA's credibility. Morton clearly felt his strategy had been undermined, and hoped that his successor would 'put Humpty Dumpty together again'. His Board supported this position, noting that over the previous year 'the Authority's resources had been diverted by the decisions or priorities of others'.[128]

---

[128] Pen Kent–Morton, 17 July 2001, and Kent, Notes, 2 August 2001, Morton–Mottram, 31 July 2001 (draft—not sent?), SRA. See also Morton-Sherwood, 21 August 2001, SRA: 'I use the image of three horses pulling a cart labelled strategy on wheels labelled money. The wheels have come off and all three horses have been shot in recent months. They are Railtrack, the SRA, and long-term franchises.'

The Strategic Rail Authority and Railtrack After Hatfield

The Morton period was an exciting, not to say exhausting, one for railway governance. Lots of good ideas were generated, but little hard progress appears to have been made. There was also evidence that the SRA 'animal' would not be easy to fit into the labyrinthine railway framework. The TOCs resented the Authority's micro-management of franchise contracts, but were nervous about engaging too forcefully in the public policy arena when the SRA held such sway over franchising decisions.[129] All too often Morton and Grant were forced to walk a tightrope as they tried to establish a coherent growth strategy for a fragmented industry.[130] The organizational structure and responsibilities of the Authority were defended staunchly by Morton, Kent, and others, but equally the Department defended its position on NDPBs. Mottram reminded Kent that while 'it may well be appropriate to adopt many of the approaches to corporate governance applied in the private sector . . . the SRA is not a private sector organisation'. Ultimately, the Department would set the SRA's budget, although of course the process would be 'iterative' and there would be close liaison. He felt impelled to point out that the Department's relationship with the SRA was 'the least satisfactory of all the relationships it has with its many executive NDPBs'.[131] And one might suggest that some of the doubts about how the SRA Board structure was operating were entirely legitimate. How much Whitehall understood about the way in which it operated is not clear, but the archives indicate that large piles of PowerPoint presentations did not provide an ideal method for enabling non-executive board members to get an adequate grip on the business.[132] When in May 2002 the SRA's Investment and Procurement Committees, which had reported to the Executive, were replaced by an Investment and Procurement Committee reporting to the Board, Jeremy Mayhew was astonished by the apparent lack of financial discipline and control mechanisms.[133] Nor were the Department impressed with what appeared to be the absence of a unified view at Board level. While the Authority was preparing its strategic plan, Morton insisted on producing, and circulating, a personal plan of his own.[134] By the summer of 2001 the DTLR was inclined to bypass the SRA in major policymaking. Mottram had told Kent that the Department did not trust the Authority, and he conceded that the relationship between the two was 'dysfunctional'. In the last months of Morton's period as Chairman, the SRA's non-executive members joined him in opposing Byers's new directions and guidance, which they regarded as too prescriptive, emphasizing 'control and containment'. Morton went further, finding them 'inappropriate in principle and

[129] Interview with Ballinger, 2006.
[130] Cf. Roger Ford, *Modern Railways*, December 2000, p. 31.
[131] Mottram–Kent, 16 May 2001, SRA.
[132] Cf. David Grayson (SRA Board Member), e-mail–Trewin, 14 May 2001, SRA.
[133] Interview with Mayhew, 2006, and see SRA Investment Committee Minutes, 2001–29 May 2002, SRA Investment and Procurement Committee Minutes, 12 June 2002 et seq., in SRA SP59 Box 4.
[134] His plan followed the prescriptions he had given Byers in June, but in addition poured cold water on a CLG formula for Railtrack: Morton–Byers, 19 October 2001, enclosing 'Statement of Strategy', SRA.

in detail'.[135] Their complaints went unheeded. There were other reasons for dissatisfaction. Morton was annoyed that Byers had decided to establish his own Rail Delivery Group, which he felt duplicated the Rail Industry Group he had set up after Hatfield.[136] And both he and Grant were furious at not being informed in advance of Bowker's appointment or his starting date, while the Department's tardiness in reappointing three SRA Board members whose terms had expired— Adams, Kent, and Quarmby—was taken to be evidence of 'incompetence or gross discourtesy'.[137] There may have been some truth in this, but the DTLR was clearly consumed by the Railtrack issue. Having told the SRA that the new ministerial team had 'little appetite for radical solutions to the problems of the railways',[138] the Department had embarked on one of the most radical solutions of all, the conversion of Railtrack into a not-for-profit company. The consequences of this policy would be significant and long-lasting.

[135] SRA Non-executive board members–Byers, 8 August 2001, enclosed in Morton–Byers, 15 August 2001, Morton–Byers, 13 September 2001, Morton-SRA Board, 14 September 2001, SRA.

[136] Byers–Morton, 3 July 2001 and reply, 10 July 2001, SRA. Byers felt that the two bodies had distinct roles, with *his* group, which first met on 27 July, focusing on 'delivering service improvements and on coherent presentation', Byers–Morton, 19 July 2001, SRA.

[137] Grant–Byers, 23 October 2001, Morton–SRA Board members, 26 November 2001, copied to Mottram, SRA.

[138] Kent, meeting with Mottram, 18 June 2001, reported in Kent–SRA Board and McGann, 20 June 2001, SRA.

The Strategic Rail Authority and the Railway, 2001–4

The Strategic Vision

5.1 The appointment of Richard Bowker

The search for a successor to Morton began in July 2001, once Sir Alastair had confirmed that he was ready to go early. The Department engaged headhunters, and also conducted some informal soundings of its own. Rowlands approached three serious candidates. He had lunch with John Armitt, an experienced civil engineer with Laing who had taken on two difficult briefs as chief executive of first Union Railways (Channel Tunnel Rail Link) and then Costain. He consulted Adrian Montague, an SRA Board member and deputy chairman of the former Treasury PFI vehicle Partnerships UK. And he also had dinner with Richard Bowker, the Group Commercial Director of Virgin Group, and Co-Chairman of its rail subsidiary, Virgin Trains. Armitt, considered a 'credible candidate', was reported to be keen on the job; Montague, however, was 'in two minds': 'He thinks the job is almost impossible to do.' Bowker also spoke frankly. He told Rowlands that at the age of 35 he was very much a 'doer' and therefore was not attracted to the Chairman's job alone. He made it clear that he *would* be interested in combining the posts of Chairman and Chief Executive. Rowlands thought Bowker 'able, sensible and, given that he started life with London Underground on their PFIs, understanding of the public–private sector interfaces and where people like the Treasury are coming from'.[1] Soon afterwards, Montague withdrew. Having stepped down from the SRA Board when his term of office expired on 31 July, he told Byers that 'the SRA is a largely discredited organization. It needs a fresh mandate and renewed authority.'[2] In August, the formal process of selection produced a first list which included Michael Grabiner, former chief executive of Energis, Sir Michael Lyons, Chief Executive of Birmingham City Council, David Quarmby, an SRA Board member, Mike Kinski, former chief executive of Stagecoach, and Ian McAllister, the MD of Ford UK.[3] By September, there was a shortlist of two, Bowker and McAllister.[4] The choice was finely balanced. Bowker was rather young, but McAllister, though more experienced and likely to prove a more effective public figure, was not so knowledgeable about the railway industry. McAllister was happy to act as a non-executive chairman, but was unable to start until February. Bowker was able to take up the post earlier, but he was only interested in a full-time executive appointment.[5]

Bowker was appointed in October and started work on 1 December 2001. Morton told Byers that his successor needed to be younger—'young, fit, wily and ambitious',[6] and certainly the appointee was most of this. Studiedly informal— he eschewed neckties—he was an economics/economic history graduate from Leicester University who had a passion for Blackburn Rovers FC, rock music, and canals (he owned a boat called *Pots and Pans*). He joined London Underground as a finance trainee, and subsequently qualified as a management accountant and, after work on the procurement of new trains for the Northern Line, he went to Babcock and Brown, the American infrastructure and project management company which had acquired a stake in the ROSCO, Angel Trains. In 1997, he was seconded to Virgin Rail to procure trains for its two franchises, Cross Country and West Coast, and he helped to negotiate the PUG2 upgrade contract for the WCML. Having helped to set up Quasar Associates, a project finance advisory business, in 1999, he advised Abbey National on the acquisition of the Porterbrook ROSCO in April 2000. As Commercial Director of Virgin from September 2000, he personally negotiated the company's post-Hatfield compensation settlement with Railtrack and was leading its bid for the ECML franchise. The decision to appoint him for five years at a salary of £250,000, plus a performance-related bonus of up to £50,000, certainly underlined expectations in Whitehall that he would be a 'big hitter'. Intended to have 'strategic vision, an understanding of big

---

[1] Rowlands–Linnard, 11 July 2001, DTLR file R78/1/30 Pt. 4. Bowker also told Rowlands that neither Chris Green (CE, Virgin Trains) nor Christopher Garnett (CE, GNER) were interested in the post.

[2] Adrian Montague–Byers, 10 August 2001, ibid.   [3] Mottram–Spellar, 14 August 2001, ibid.

[4] Three was reduced to two when Mike Grabiner withdrew.

[5] Coulshed–Hackland, 17 September 2001, Mottram–Byers, 26 September 2001, ibid.

[6] Morton–Byers, 7 June 2001, and speech to IEA, 26 June 2001, SRA.

projects, and a capacity to form a constructive relationship with government', he was expected to bring fresh ideas to the post.[7] But could a 'big hitter' prosper as Chairman of an NDPB? Evidence of the political complexities involved surfaced at a very early stage when Bowker examined his offer of appointment, together with the accompanying 'job description' he had requested. Doubts about including it were evident, with Departmental officials concerned that the statement opened up the potential for conflict between the statutory objectives of the SRA and the personal responsibilities of the Chairman. Coulshed warned Mottram that 'some of the difficulties experienced with Sir Alastair Morton were of this kind'.[8] Officials suggested the inclusion of a 'gloss' asserting that Bowker should 'provide effective leadership for the Strategic Rail Authority, ensuring that its staff and other resources are best deployed to meet the objectives above, its statutory remit, and the term [sic] of any directions and guidance issued to it by the Secretary of State'. Bowker protested, and in the final schedule, the offending words were removed, but the exchanges were surely a foretaste of the conflicts which might arise between the Chairman's perceived contractual requirements and his statutory responsibilities as defined by the Government.[9] We should also note that Bowker's insertion into the SRA came at a time when its Board and senior management had been somewhat bruised by events. The Board had not been taken into the Government's confidence over Railtrack's administration and was not given prior notification of Bowker's appointment, while the tardiness in reappointing non-executive board members whose contracts had already been extended by two to three months scarcely improved relations between the NDPB and its sponsoring department, and contributed to David Jefferies's decision to leave.[10] Thus, the appointments of Adams, Kent, and Quarmby, which had expired in June/July 2001, were first extended until 31 October, and then for a further month in November. Eventually, reappointments for a further three years were made.[11]

Bowker also faced other immediate challenges. First, his appointment came too late to affect the SRA's strategic plan, about which the Department had expressed anxieties. The document was well on its way to publication, and indeed was sent to the DTLR in draft form in Bowker's first week (it was eventually published

[7] Melanie Sturtevant (DTLR)–Mottram, 17 July 2001, DTLR file R78/1/30 Pt. 4; Hill–Rowlands, 25 June 2001, DfT, Weir doc. vol. K5; *Financial Times Weekend Magazine*, 29 June 2002, pp. 20–2.

[8] Fred Croft (DTLR)–Martin Capstick (Mottram's PS), 23 October 2001, Coulshed–Mottram, 23 October 2001, DTLR file R78/1/30 Pt. 4.

[9] Capstick–Croft, 23 October 2001, ibid.; Byers–Bowker, 24 October 2001, initialled by Bowker, 8 November 2001, DTLR file R81/1/7 Pt. 1; Interview with Richard Bowker, 9 August 2006.

[10] Morton–SRA Board, 26 November 2001, SRA.

[11] Fidler–Byers, 26 October 2001, DTLR file R81/1/7 Pt. 5; SRA, *Annual Report 2002/3*, p. 97. The delay in finding a new chairman for the SRA was given as an explanation for the short-term extensions. Neither Bradshaw nor Jefferies sought reappointment. Bradshaw favoured a centralized and integrated solution for the railways: Bradshaw–Morton, 5 February and 12 June 2001, SRA.

on 14 January 2002).[12] Second, the Chairman's former job as a Virgin employee raised a potential conflict of interest since the SRA was involved in issues surrounding the Railtrack–Virgin renegotiations about the WCML upgrade. Here, Bowker promised to be not so much a poacher-turned-gamekeeper, as a poacher continuing to poach. A key figure in negotiating the Virgin contract with Railtrack, he had told Rowlands that PUG2 had been ' "lethal" for Railtrack'.[13] The matter became more urgent when Bowker was spotted in a public house near the Sea Containers HQ talking to Jim Steer, of Steer Davies Gleave, advisers to Virgin Rail.[14] The meeting may have been an innocent one—the two were after all friends—but Mottram was sufficiently persuaded to brief the SRA. Following that advice, the SRA Board, at its meeting on 6 December, endorsed proposals which required Bowker to be excluded from all matters relating to the upgrade, which were to be handled by Grant until commercial heads of terms were agreed by the two parties.[15] The departure of the Chief Executive 11 days later upset this arrangement, and the matter was handled at Board level by Pen Kent as alternate Chairman, and at executive level by Chris Kinchin-Smith, the ED, Strategic Routes. This messy state of affairs was clearly unsatisfactory, and on 21 January Rowlands wrote to Bowker to inform him that in the Department's view the exclusion should no longer apply. The next day a special Board meeting endorsed this view. Circumstances, apparently, had changed. It was now argued that sufficient time had elapsed since Bowker's active involvement with Virgin, and that in the interim the options for the upgrade had 'narrowed down considerably', with all users forced to give up some existing or prospective capacity. Indeed, the SRA's prime interest in securing the optimal utilization of the route required Bowker's active involvement, though he would continue to be excluded from considering compensation issues. With the original scheme now somewhat emasculated, and a clear need for strong project management, it was important that Bowker be involved in the SRA's efforts to maximize network benefits.[16] The episode produced more than a few awkward moments at the beginning of the new chairman's term. On 16 January, Kent complained to Byers when the Department sought to impose a decision on capacity utilization for the WCML. The SRA had not been involved when officials reached an agreement in principle with Virgin for a 10 trains an hour timetable, causing Peter Trewin, acting as interim accounting officer, to point out to Mottram that the SRA had not been able to assess the value for money aspects of the deal. Julia Clarke, the Executive Director, Freight, had also expressed disquiet about the implications for freight traffic on the WCML. Byers and the Department subsequently climbed down,

---

[12] SRA Executive Committee Minutes, 7 December 2001, SRA file 57/01/01 Pt. 3. Bowker did attend an SRA Executive awayday at Hitchin Priory on 12/13 November 2001, prior to starting.

[13] Rowlands–Linnard, 11 July 2001, cit.

[14] Nick Wells (Mottram's APS)–Linnard, 14 November 2001, DTLR file R81/1/7 Pt. 1.

[15] Peter Trewin (Secretary, SRA), Memo. 6 December 2001, SRA Board Minutes, 6 December 2001.

[16] Rowlands–Bowker, 21 January 2002, SRA Special Board Meeting Minutes, 22 January 2002.

but Kent was also unhappy about the decision to withdraw the conflict of interest arrangement, the product of another rapid 'bounce' from the DTLR without prior consultation.[17]

5.2 Reshaping the SRA

Another complicating factor in the relationship between the new Chairman and his Board was Bowker's revelation that he intended to combine the roles of chairman and chief executive. This spelled the end for Grant, who left the organization almost immediately, on 17 December.[18] The decision seems to have been taken rather hastily, however, leaving some issues unresolved. It was not clear that the Nolan rules had been followed, and there was a need to appoint a new accounting officer, and to secure modifications of the Chairman's employment status, the SRA's management statement, and its financial framework. It was not until February that the Department provided a formal endorsement of the Board's proposals to combine the posts, and revised terms and conditions for the new Chief Executive were not approved until June.[19] Reorganization and new appointments followed. At Board level, there was clearly scope for change with the departure of six non-executives. Three somewhat disenchanted members had already left: Bradshaw, Montague, and Jefferies. They were joined by three more on the expiry of their contracts in April 2002: Hemingway, Rubin, and Small (Table 5.1). Their departures presented an opportunity to strengthen the Board, and Bowker suggested to Byers that he would like to establish high-level capability in commercial experience, experience of government and the civil service, and in engineering and operations.[20] However, the recruitment process

---

[17] Kent–Byers, 16 January, Trewin–Mottram, 17 January, and Pen Kent, Note for Record, 21 January 2002, Chris Kinchin-Smith, e-mail, 18 January 2002, and Memo. to SRA Board, 28–9 January 2002, SRA; Interview with Julia Clarke, 2 November 2006. Winsor had also expressed disquiet about the proposed statement on capacity allocation, which he felt was a clear intrusion into his jurisdiction: ORR, File Note, 6 February 2002, Winsor archive.

[18] Bisson–Blair, 17 December 2001, Prime Minister's Rail papers, Pt. 3. There was some anxiety about the combination of roles at board level. The matter was subsequently raised by Quarmby and Kent in January 2003, but the decision was taken to retain the status quo, but with additional checks and balances, including the appointment of a Senior Independent Director (Kent) in addition to that of Deputy Chairman (Quarmby). SRA Board Minutes, 16 January 2003; Quarmby, Memo. on 'SRA Corporate Governance: Combined role of Chairman and Chief Executive', February 2003, SRA, and interviews with Mayhew 2006, Jim Steer, 6 March 2007, and David Norgrove, 28 March 2007.

[19] Part of the delay was caused by the need to consult the Treasury, and to respond to Counsel's opinion that the remuneration for the two posts should be split. See Coulshed–Lewis Atter (Head of Transport Team, Treasury), 28 January 2002, Mottram–Kent, 13 February 2002, Fidler–Trewin, 13 June 2002, DTLR file R81/1/7 Pt. 1; Ashley Ibbett (Sir Richard Wilson (Cabinet Secretary)'s PS)–Capstick, 24 October 2001, R78/1/30 Pt. 5; Bowker, Memo. on 'Board Organisation', 20 December 2001, SRA Board Minutes, 20 December 2001, 10 January, 7 March and 13 June 2002.

[20] Bowker–Byers, 1 March 2002, SRA.

Table 5.1 The SRA Board, December 2001–September 2004

	Age[a]	Salary[b]	Appointed[c]	Resigned	Background
Richard Bowker, Chairman and Chief Executive	35	£250,000 + b	Dec. 2001	Sep. 2004	Transport: LT; Babcock & Brown; Virgin
Nick Newton, Chief Executive	58	£180,000 + b	Sep. 2004	Nov. 2006	Transport: LT
Part-time (non-exec) members[d]					
Lew Adams	62	£9,229	July 1999	Aug. 2005	Railways: ASLEF
Millie Banerjee	56	£14,190	Dec. 2002	Aug. 2005	Utilities: BT
David Begg	45	£9,229	Dec. 1997	Mar. 2005	Transport: Edinburgh City Council, CIT
Willie Gallagher	43	£9,229	May 2000	Oct. 2005	Utilities: Scottish Power
David Grayson	46	£9,229	May 2000	Aug. 2005	Business in the Community, NDC
Ann Hemingway	54	£9,229	May 2000	Apr. 2002	Utilities: British Gas
Pen Kent[e]	64	£9,229	Aug. 1999	Nov. 2006	Banking: Bank of England; PFI
Janet Lewis-Jones	52	£14,190	Dec. 2002	Aug. 2005	Law/Water: Glas Cymru, British Waterways
Jeremy Mayhew	43	£11,000	May 2000	Nov. 2006	Media: BBC, Spectrum
David Norgrove	55	£14,190	Dec.2002	Apr. 2005	Civil Service: Treasury; No.10; M&S
David Quarmby[f]	60	£9,229	July 1999	Mar. 2006	Transport: LT, BTA, Sainsbury
Janet Rubin	52	£9,229	May 2000	Apr. 2002	Human Resources: SHL
Kevin Small	35	£9,229	May 2000	Apr. 2002	Railways: RPC

b = bonus.

[a] At 1 Dec. 2001 or on appointment if later.

[b] At 1 Dec. 2001 or on appointment if later.

[c] Date of first appointment to either BRB, SSRA, or SRA.

[d] Left in 2001: Lord (Bill) Bradshaw (June), David Jefferies (Oct.), Michael Grant (Dec.).

[e] Became Senior Independent Board Member and paid £19,000 in 2002–3; Chairman Apr.–Nov. 2006.

[f] Became Deputy Chairman in June 2002 and was paid £18,000 in 2002–3; became Chairman Sep. 2004.

Source: SRA.

was not an easy one and the headhunters' efforts to entice a senior official from the Treasury proved a failure.[21] In any case, the Department was keener to satisfy the Government's broader aim to produce more diversity in board appointments, and, in particular, to find people to represent the railway passenger, the consumer, and Wales.[22] The new recruits of December 2002, Millie Banerjee, Janet Lewis-Jones, and David Norgrove, were chosen from a list of over 600 applicants.[23] They undoubtedly possessed skills and experience in utilities, financial management, and consumer affairs. Banerjee had had a successful career in BT, Lewis-Jones had worked in the water industry after a legal career, and Norgrove, from Marks & Spencer, had been Thatcher's private secretary when the bidder for the Channel Tunnel concession was decided in 1986 (Table 5.1).[24] But they also satisfied the Government's aspirations in relation to gender, ethnic diversity, and devolution.

The DTLR might have thought that Bowker would provide an effective break with the SRA's earlier leadership, but there was more than a hint of Morton in Bowker's radical prescriptions for the railway and in his presentational style. His recommendations for the industry were introduced at an early stage, being shared with the Prime Minister at a presentation on 22 November 2001, and presented to the SRA Board on 6 December. Like Morton, he believed that 'the ills of the industry stemmed from a fundamental failure of process and people', and like Morton he was critical of Railtrack's management failure, though he felt the problems had been compounded by the 'perceived lack of leadership and strategic direction from the SRA'. However, there were also differences in his approach. The new Chairman wanted to simplify the railway. He argued for 'fewer TOCs with fewer interfaces', and a single TOC for each of the complex locations and termini in the rail network. The approach to franchising should focus on operational and performance improvements as much as on investment. While Byers had redirected attention to short-term solutions, Bowker felt that the possibility of future integration and merger should not be ruled out. And in what was essentially a more TOC-related approach, he argued that the operators would thrive if supported by a coherent strategic planning framework, a simpler structure, and reformed performance and compensation regimes. To that end, a competent successor to Railtrack was clearly essential. In addition, the working relationship between the SRA and the ORR should be improved (later formalized as the Concordat, see below, p. 182). Finally, Bowker asserted that the railways would benefit from the establishment of a common purpose to be provided by a 'Rail Business Plan based on transparency of all the costs,

---

[21] John Kingman, Harry Bush, and Philip Wynn Owen were approached: Bowker–Kingman, 10 January 2002, Douglas Board (Dep.-Ch. Saxton Bampfylde Hever)–Bowker, 7 February 2002, SRA.

[22] Mark Lambirth–Bowker and Sheila Hewitt (Legal Services Commission), 9 September 2002, DTLR file R78/1/30 Pt. 5.

[23] Coulshed–Lambirth, 22 July 2002, ibid.   [24] Gourvish, *Britain and the Channel Tunnel*, p. 275.

benefits, risks, trade offs and strategic decisions, supported by rigorous and prioritised analysis'.[25]

First, it was essential to reform the institution within which Bowker operated. Below the Board, he was anxious to strengthen the Authority at executive level. With a Chairman/Chief Executive at the helm out went the Chairman's Committee, replaced by a Monday morning executive meeting known as 'Prayers', which first met in December 2001 and was then convened more formally from May 2002.[26] Bowker had inherited a cluster of incomplete schemes, notably the WCML, King's Cross/St. Pancras, South Central, Mark I stock replacement, Southern third-rail power supply upgrade, and enhancements such as the Felixstowe–Nuneaton freight route. A policy for Railtrack required the SRA's involvement, while Morton's franchise replacement policies, redefined by Byers, had left a number of existing franchises in varying stages of development. Operating performance and capacity allocation also required attention. The new Chairman, who was certainly not lacking in confidence, immediately requested that executive directors take direct action to champion identified priorities within their domain. By 20 December, at his first executive committee meeting, Bowker said that the existing organizational structure lacked coherence in certain directions—he referred specifically to the divided responsibility for franchise replacement, for example—and wanted a reorganization based on primary processes—operations, strategic planning, and transactions. Freight was to be left as a separate, 'cross-cutting' group, enabling freight considerations to figure in decisions taken elsewhere.[27] He felt that the existing organization, based on 'delivery', 'planning', and 'support' (Figure 4.1), was defective, in that the delivery groups were completely detached from the planning groups, encouraging 'silo thinking'. Early in the New Year, he told Byers about his plans for streamlining the executive management on this basis in order to make it 'much more effective and energised'. In essence, this meant introducing a project management model and the establishment of three new posts with salaries of c.£150,000: a chief operating officer, responsible for franchise management and performance; an MD for strategic planning; and an MD for 'transformation/commercial deals', who would act as a 'service provider' for planning and operations, turning 'the strategies and plans into reality'. The new appointees would replace the five EDs for commercial, infrastructure, regional networks, strategic routes, and London & South East. At the same time, Bowker proposed to

[25] Bowker, 'Delivering a Safe, Reliable and Better Railway', 22 November 2001, SRA; Nick Bisson (Policy Advisor, No. 10)–Campbell, 23 November 2001, Prime Minister's Rail papers, Pt. 3; SRA Board Minutes, 6 December 2001; O'Donnell–Bowker, 17 December 2001, SRA.

[26] Bowker–SRA Executive, 3 January 2002, and SRA Executive Prayers Minutes, 23 May 2003 and ff., SRA file 57/01/12A Pt. 1. The last Chairman's Committee meeting was on 30 October 2001. In addition to 'Prayers', there were informal executive meetings on Wednesdays and Fridays.

[27] SRA Executive Committee Minutes, 20 December 2001, SRA file 57/01/01 Pt. 3; Interview with Jonathan Riley, 20 November 2006. Bowker repeated his intentions at a special board meeting also held on 20 December 2001. He also showed a proactive approach to the 2002/3 budget: Bowker–EDs, 1 February 2002, SRA.

create a director of human resources and a director, media, with the existing Executive Director, External Relations, Chris Austin, becoming Executive Director, Corporate Affairs (Figure 5.1).[28]

Under Bowker, the SRA moved to a more centralized, executive structure, reminiscent of Parker's British Railways Board in the 1970s. The main changes were effected in April and May 2002. The Board's committee structure was rationalized, with the number of committees and panels reduced from 12 to 3. An Investment and Procurement Committee, chaired by David Quarmby, replaced the Executive's Investment and Procurement Committees,[29] and procedures were immediately tightened up.[30] The Board meetings were to be attended by the leading executives. And like Parker, Bowker wanted the non-executives to become more involved in management and to be paid more as a result. He also proposed to establish the post of deputy chairman, an option in the Transport Act 2000, and David Quarmby was appointed in June.[31] Executive management changes accompanied the restructuring at Board level. In April, Nick Newton, the existing Commercial Director, was appointed as Chief Operating Officer and Jim Steer joined the Authority as MD, Strategic Planning in May. Steer, well known to Bowker, as we have noted, was appointed on a three-year secondment from his consultancy firm, Steer Davies Gleave. There was the possibility of another conflict of interest problem here, but the Board was assured that 'robust arrangements' had been put in place to prevent such conflicts.[32] At the same time, replacements for the finance director, Martin McGann, who left to join Pillar Property, and the solicitor, Jenner, who retired, were needed. They were succeeded by Doug Sutherland, from Scottish Water, who replaced McGann on a part-time basis in May (full time from July), and by Tim Reardon, who took up the redefined post of General Legal Counsel in April. Other appointees were Sandra Jenner (no relation to Terence), from the Financial Services Authority, who became MD, Human Resources in December 2001 and played a leading role in managing the reorganization process, and Ceri Evans, from leading PR firm Golin/Harris, who became ED, Media (later ED, Communications) in July 2002, to improve the SRA's 'message development and media management'. In February 2003, a Technical Director was added. David Waboso joined the SRA

---

[28] Bowker–Byers, 8 January 2002, SRA; SRA Board Minutes, 10 January 2002; Interview with Bowker (2006).

[29] The Procurement Committee, which awarded contracts in the range £0.5–25.0m., reported via the Finance Director. See Jack Paine (Head of Procurement, SRA), Memo. 12 February 2001, SRA Executive Committee Minutes, 14 February 2001, SRA files 57/01/02 Pt. 18, 57/01/01 Pt. 2.

[30] Bowker, Memo. on 'Corporate Governance: Committee Structure', SRA Board Minutes, 2 May 2002 and see also 4 July 2002; Quarmby, Memo. on 'Investment & Procurement Committee—The First Six Months', SRA Board Minutes, 6 February 2003; SRA Investment and Procurement Committee Minutes, 12 June–24 July 2002, SRA SP59 Box 4; Interview with Mayhew (2006).

[31] SRA Board Minutes, 2 May and 6 June 2002; Bowker–SRA staff, 22 April 2002, SRA; Transport Act 2000, s. 203 (1). For Parker's Board, see Gourvish, *British Rail 1974–97*, p. 28 ff.

[32] SRA Board Minutes, 2 May 2002.

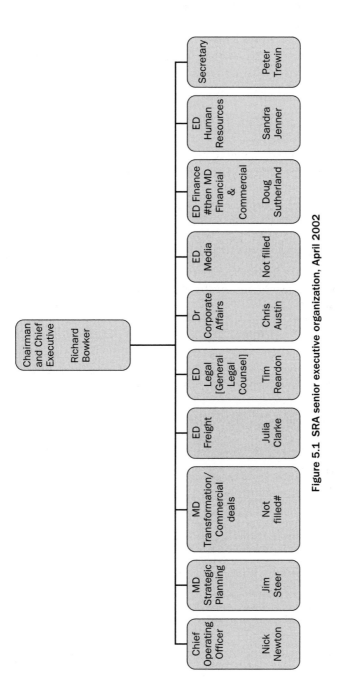

Figure 5.1 SRA senior executive organization, April 2002

after working on the DLR and Jubilee Line Extension projects in London.[33] It proved difficult to attract a suitable applicant to the transformations post, however, and in April 2002 Bowker asked Sutherland to combine the financial and commercial functions.[34] But although the received wisdom in Whitehall was that Bowker had been effective in strengthening the SRA management, a view articulated when the question of his annual bonus was considered,[35] the combination of the relatively laid-back Newton and the newcomer Sutherland was far from optimal. Their interaction with the Chairman & Chief Executive tended to overload the latter, and he soon elected to make changes. The departure of Sandra Jenner to Ofcom in January 2003 provided the opportunity to ask Nicola Shaw to act as Chief Operating Officer, taking in the human resources function; Newton then became MD, Operations (Figure 5.2). Shaw, granddaughter of the London Transport manager and railway historian Michael Robbins, was a young (33) manager who had left the ORR to join Bechtel. She had impressed Bowker, who initially arranged her secondment from Bechtel to lead the SRA team handling the CLG proposal for Railtrack (see below, pp. 171–2). As COO, she was given the responsibility for delivering the SRA's business plan and effecting internal change.[36] There was a need for both. The demands of attempting ambitious changes to the organization were considerable, and tensions were created when there was recruitment to and from other parts of the industry. For example, there were further anxieties about a conflict of interest when Kinchin-Smith went to FirstGroup in May 2002, and two executives left in unhappy circumstances: Mary Combs, from Risk and Assurance in September 2002, and Julia Clarke, the ED, Freight, early in 2003.[37] The rather volatile Evans may have worked hard to produce a better press for the rail industry, but he was soon to provide unwelcome as well as welcome publicity for the Authority when stoutly defending SRA policy.[38]

---

[33] SRA Board Minutes, 20 December 2001, 7 February, 11 April, 4 July, 5 December 2002; Bowker–Byers, 16 April 2002, SRA.

[34] Ibid. 2 May 2002; SRA Executive Committee Minutes, 13 May 2002, SRA 57/01/01 Pt. 3; Interview with Doug Sutherland, 21 June 2007.

[35] See correspondence in DTLR file R81/1/7 Pt. 1.

[36] SRA Board Minutes, 6 February 2003; Bowker–SRA Nominations and Remuneration Committee, 21 January 2003, Bowker–Alistair Darling (SoS for Transport), 24 January 2003; SRA Executive Minutes, 29 January, 13 February, and 27 March 2003, SRA file 57/01/01 Pt. 4; Interview with Bowker (2006). A proposal to transfer the secretarial function to Shaw was resisted: Bowker, e-mail–Kent, 25 January 2003, SRA.

[37] Bowker–Kinchin-Smith, 19 April 2002, SRA; SRA Minutes, 5 September 2002, 16 and 27 January 2003. Combs left after an investigation into the audit function, though there was no suggestion of impropriety, and Julia Clarke, who was married to Lord Berkeley, Chairman of the Rail Freight Group, vacated her post after an unproven allegation of a breach of confidentiality following the publication of an article by her husband in *Rail Professional*. A foyer copy of the SRA's *Freight Quarterly* (Winter 2002), which referred to Julia Clarke as Executive Director for Freight, was annotated 'until shot by the Gestapo'. SRA Board Minutes, 27 January and 6 February 2003; Interview with Clarke (2006), and see also *Rail Freight Group News*, Jan.–Feb. 2003 p. 19; *Private Eye*, 7 March 2003, p. 10, 13 June 2003, p. 10.

[38] On Evans's injudicious remarks about Lord Berkeley, FirstGroup and the Rail Regulator, the latter's role described as akin to a 'supermarket price-checker', see *Guardian*, 3 May 2003, p. 6; *Independent*, 6 May 2003, p. 5, 5 January 2004, p. 1; *Private Eye*, 7 March 2003, p. 10; Wolmar, *On the Wrong Line*, pp. 223–4.

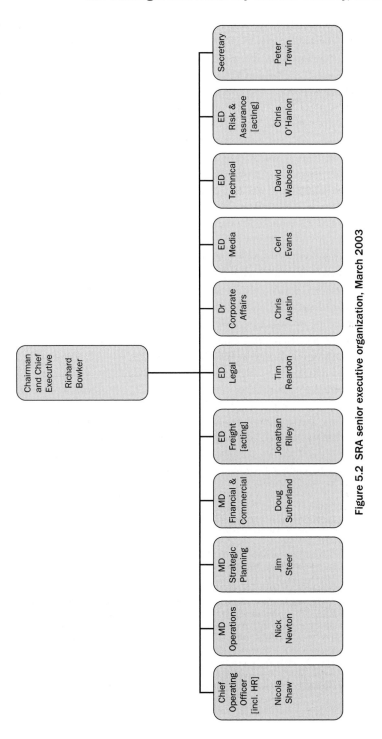

Figure 5.2 SRA senior executive organization, March 2003

The Bowker–Newton–Shaw nexus also required another adjustment, in September 2003. Essentially, Newton and Shaw swapped portfolios, with Shaw taking on the TOC management role as MD, Operations, and Newton the delivery and human resources functions as Deputy Chief Executive. The immediate impetus may have been the SRA's decision to take back the South Eastern franchise from Connex (see below, pp. 150–2), for which Newton became responsible. But it was also apparent that Newton was giving way to Shaw. The operations function was to be 're-engineered', with a greater degree of delegated responsibility in the directorate and a firmer grip on decision-making.[39] Accompanying these changes, there was a concerted effort to effect a cultural transformation of the organization, symbolized by executive salaries which were higher than civil service rates for equivalent posts.[40] Clarity about the responsibility for delivering the several elements of SRA objectives was the aim. By the spring of 2003, there was a mission statement, the anodyne tag 'Britain's Railway, properly delivered', and a corporate plan packed with exhortatory principles, which were also reproduced on unattractive SRA coffee mugs (Figure 5.3), in which the Authority undertook to be 'Clear and Consistent', 'Disciplined', 'Bold', 'Engage' internally and externally, and be 'Resilient'. All this certainly distinguished the SRA from its sponsoring department.[41] And it was also evident that the change of direction, with institutional simplicity the goal, involved a substantial increase in the planned establishment at the SRA, which was put at 549 in October 2002, more than double the number in April 2000.[42] It is true that actual staff numbers were lower than the planned establishment, and some attempts were made to constrain numbers after Bowker had told the Transport Select Committee in July 2003 that 'we have 499 people',[43] but the head count increased from 342 in October 2002 to 489 in March 2004.[44] On top of this, a substantial number of consultants and contractors were engaged, some covering unfilled posts, but most working on defined projects: the total was given as 181 in March 2004.[45] Of

---

[39] Cf. James Vickers, Memo. to SRA Executive, 11 December 2003, SRA file 57/01/02 Pt. 49; Interview with Nick Newton, 14 September 2006. At the same time Austin became ED, Community Rail Development. Bowker, e-mail to staff, 4 September 2003, SRA Board Minutes, 4 September 2003, SRA Executive Committee Minutes, 14 August and 11 December 2003, SRA file 57/01/01 Pt. 4.

[40] The senior executives were paid £130,000–156,000 in 2003/4: SRA, *Annual Report 2003/4*, p. 112.

[41] SRA, Corporate Plan 2003–4; Interview with Robert Plampin (SRA), 17 November 2005. The SRA's remodelled annual report for 2003/4 was designed by 'Spin of London'.

[42] SRA Organization Summary 16 October 2002, in Chris Hills (SRA), Memo. 20 December 2002, SRA Executive Committee Minutes, 13 February 2003, SRA file 57/01/01 Pt. 4, and see *Private Eye*, 28 November 2002, p. 10.

[43] HC Transport Committee Report on *The Future of the Railway: MOE*, P.P.2003–4, HC145-II, Bowker, response to Graham Stringer (MP for Manchester Blackley), 8 July 2003, Q352.

[44] *Parl. Deb. (Commons)*, 6th ser. (Session 2003–4), Vol. 422 Pt. 2, 17 June 2004, Tony McNulty (PUSS, DTLR), written answer to Damian Green (MP for Ashford), c. 1049w; SRA, *Corporate Plan 2004–5*, p. 33. The number for March 2004 was given as 454 by McNulty, and the 'average employed' during 2003/4 as 429 (with BRB(R) and RPC 523, but excluding BTP [2,242] and the acquired franchise South Eastern Trains [3,498]): SRA, *Annual Report 2003/4*, p. 112.

[45] *Parl. Deb. (Commons)*, 6th ser. (Session 2003–4), Vol. 422 Pt. 2, 21 June 2004, McNulty, written answer to Green, c. 1246w.

Figure 5.3 Exhortatory SRA mug, 2003

course, it could be argued that this was a major agency with a budget in 2003/4 of £3.35 billion. The SRA's administrative costs, including the Rail Passenger Council and BRB (Residuary), were, at £159 million, under 5 per cent of the total spend.[46] However, an alternative view, and one put to the Prime Minister, was that the Authority was rather bureaucratic and overstaffed, particularly when its actual powers were taken into consideration.[47]

5.3 The SRA's strategic plans, 2002–3

The Authority's long-awaited *strategic plan* was published in January 2002. Drafted by Richard Davies, director of strategic planning, it heralded a fertile period of planning under Bowker, Steer, and Davies. Shortly afterwards, the SRA set itself the task of preparing an appropriate case for rail in anticipation of Winsor's access charges review in 2003 and the Government's 2004 Spending Review. The intention was to exert more control of the industry's costs, and

[46] SRA, *Corporate Plan 2003–4*, p. 31.
[47] Bisson–Blair, 17 December 2001, Prime Minister's Rail papers, Pt. 3.

specify the outputs required from Network Rail by means of capacity utilization work and the formulation of route utilization strategies. The milestones were set out in a Route Map document published in October 2002.[48] A further strategic plan followed in January 2003, and there were other strategic documents too: corporate plans, in March 2003 and 2004; a fares review, a strategy document for the WCML (both June 2003); a rolling stock strategy (December 2003); a capacity utilization policy (December 2002) and network utilization strategy (June 2003); the specification of network outputs (i.e. maintenance and renewals strategy) (September 2003); a 'Sensitive Lorry Miles' analysis, recalculating the benefits of shifting freight from road to rail, in May 2003, which followed the earlier freight strategy of May 2001; a document making the 'wider case for rail', *Everyone's Railway*, in September 2003, and, finally, a strategy for branch lines (community railways), in November 2004. The publications were ample evidence that, in contrast with the Morton period, the SRA's planning function was fully functional during Bowker's chairmanship.[49]

The *Strategic Plan* of 2002 was more forward-looking than its predecessor, the *agenda* of 2001. There were some bold promises, the product of a change of thinking in the autumn of 2001, when during the plan's preparation stage the SRA Board had argued that the case for rail investment should be made, especially in the light of the Hatfield crisis.[50] Thus, Bowker provided a Panglossian foreword, the first of a series of statements he was to make over the next two years, in which he promised 'a clear direction and a clear set of priorities' to enable 'stakeholders to plan with more certainty than ever before'. He confirmed the Government's targets, enshrined in the *10 Year Plan*, to handle an appreciable rise in rail traffic (50% in passenger-km, 80% in freight tonne-km, 2000/1–2010/11), and to reduce overcrowding for London's commuters. The tone was clearly aspirational. Bowker's vision embraced an all-round improvement in rail services such that passenger and freight customers would use rail 'as their mode of choice'. He wanted to see 'fewer accountants, fewer lawyers, and fewer consultants' and more engineers, operators, and project managers. He also emphasized the need for the several parts of the industry to work together, and argued for a

---

[48] SRA, *The Value of Rail: Route Map to 2004* (October 2002); Steer, Memo. 2 September 2002, SRA Executive Committee Minutes, 11 and 26 September 2002, SRA files 57/01/02 Pt. 37, 57/01/01 Pts. 3 and 4. The approach involved 10 steps: major project reviews; capacity utilization; value of rail studies; cost reduction initiatives; route-based analysis of VfM options; fares policy; external opportunities and threats; scenario tests; funding and risk structure; and a holistic review of the value of Rail.

[49] SRA, *The Strategic Plan* (January 2002), *The Strategic Plan 2003: Platform for Progress* and *Route Descriptions* (January 2003), *Corporate Plan 2003–4* and *2004–5*; *Fares Review Conclusions 2003* (June 2003) [consultation paper July 2002]; *West Coast Main Line Strategy* (June 2003) [consultation October 2002]; *Rolling Stock Strategy* (December 2003) [consultation paper June 2003]; *The SRA's Strategy: Specification of Network Outputs* (September 2003) [consultation paper July 2003]; *Freight Strategy* (May 2001), *Sensitive Lorry Miles: Results of Analysis* (May 2003); *Capacity Utilisation Policy: Statement of Principles* (December 2002), *Network Utilisation Strategy* (June 2003); *Everyone's Railway: The Wider Case for Rail* (September 2003); *Community Rail Development Strategy* (November 2004) [consultation paper February 2004].

[50] Cf. Jefferies–SRA Board, SRA Board Minutes, 3 September 2001.

period of stability after the traumas of Hatfield.[51] Half of the 116-page document focused on key issues, the SRA's role in determining priorities, and the priorities themselves, in essence the short-, medium-, and long-term projects required to deliver the Government's *10 Year Plan* at a cost to the public sector of £33.5 billion.[52] There were two annexes, the first a brief analysis of the rail market for passengers and freight, the second containing detailed 'delivery plans', that is, developmental expectations for strategic routes (intercity and cross-country), London and the South-east, regional networks (which were not to be crowded out by priorities elsewhere), and freight. Six areas for action were identified: safety; stability and structure; performance; major infrastructure projects; the cost base; and skill shortages.[53] Detailed proposals and broadbrush strategies were combined in the document. Thus, the short-term priorities included plans for improvements to Bodmin Parkway station (a Rail Passenger Partnership scheme), down to a cycle shed and toilets, while 10 pages later the discussion of longer-term aspirations included the prospects for three favourites: a new high-speed line between London and Scotland, the London Crossrail scheme, and improved links between the Channel Tunnel and the regions.[54] It was not always easy to see the wood for the trees, but those who cared to persevere were able to locate a timetable with 'indicative timescales', though not costings, for the major projects in the period to 2010 (Table 5.2). By 2005, the SRA expected to complete the WCML, Cross Country, and Chiltern upgrades, replace the old Southern Region slam-door stock, and improve the third-rail power supply; by 2010 a whole series of infrastructure upgrades were to be completed, including the CTRL, ECML, Thameslink 2000, TransPennine, South Central, and key freight routes. A large programme of incremental improvements was promised, along with development work on more ambitious schemes such as London Crossrail and the EU-endorsed but undeveloped ERTMS safety system. The list was impressively long, and provided a contrast with what British Rail had been able to attempt in the years after the Modernisation Plan of 1955–65. And although optimism abounded—the 'prospects for Britain's railway have never been better', claimed Bowker—some important caveats were inserted into the plan. It was recognized that the Hatfield accident had created more uncertainty in the industry and that it was imperative to establish a sound successor to Railtrack. The SRA, when estimating the cost of implementing the *10 Year Plan*, had not attempted to second-guess the financing implications of creating the 'new Railtrack', and had assumed that the new body would be financed on the same model as the old,

---

[51] SRA, *Strategic Plan* (2002), pp. 1, 5–7. A 43-page summary document was also published.

[52] The figure of £33.5bn represented an increase of £4.5bn over the £29bn originally announced. This was produced by £2.5bn for charges review adjustments and year-end adjustments to the SRA's budget, and £2bn arising from the Endeavour agreement with Railtrack in April 2001. See Malcolm Macdonald–Dan Corry, 15 January 2002, DTLR file R78/12/43 Pt. 4.

[53] SRA, *Strategic Plan* (2002), pp. 14–22.   [54] Ibid. pp. 43, 53–4.

Table 5.2 SRA Strategic Plan 2002: 'indicative timescales', 2002–10

	Completion	Priority
By 2005		
Infrastructure		
WCML upgrade ('scaled back', i.e. 125 mph)	2005	s
CTRL Phase I	2003	s
Chiltern upgrade	2005	s
Cross Country upgrade	2005	s
Rolling stock		
Replacement of 1,700 Mark I (slam-door) vehicles + 3rd rail power supply upgrade	2004	s
New trains for MML, Connex South Eastern	2005	s
Safety		
TPWS (effective at up to 70 mph)	2003	s
Other performance enhancements		
Continue refranchising and redraw map		s
Increased (£430m.) rail partnership fund for small schemes		s
Freight facilities grants and small freight schemes		s
Improved benchmarking/monitoring of TOC performance		s
Review of TOC incentive and compensation schemes		s
Improving measures of customer satisfaction		s
Review of timetable and PSRs (minimum service levels)		s
Improved introduction of new rolling stock		s
Improved track possessions regime		s
Implementation of disability discrimination act		s
Addressing skill shortages, for example, via a national rail academy		s
By 2010		
Infrastructure		
CTRL Phase II to St Pancras	2007	m
Thameslink 2000	2008	m
East London Line extension	2006	m
West Anglia route modernization	2007	m
ECML upgrade	2010	m
South Central upgrade	2008	m
TransPennine upgrade	2006	m
Felixstowe–Nuneaton freight route	2010	m
Southampton–West Midlands freight route	2009	m
South West Trains upgrade	2010	m
Other		
Incremental Output Statements (track, signalling, stations)	2007	s/m
Work on development schemes via SPVs, etc.		
South London metro		
London Crossrail: East–West and Hackney–Merton		
Great Western upgrade		
Airport links: Heathrow–Waterloo ('Airtrack'), Glasgow, Edinburgh		
Safety: ERTMS schemes		
West Midlands and Manchester capacity studies		

Source: SRA, *The Strategic Plan* (January 2002), pp. 49, 53 and annex II, *Summary*, pp. 37–8.
s: short term; m: medium term.

a 'planet-sized assumption', according to Bowker. In addition, the Authority's plan did not take into account 'the implications of any increased operating costs that Railtrack may have experienced post-Hatfield'. Nor were any costs arising from the European Commission's interoperability directives of 1996 and 2001 and implementation of the Uff and Cullen safety recommendations[55] included in its calculations. The SRA also warned that if only the existing medium-term projects were completed, then it would not be possible to meet the *10 Year Plan*'s targets. Passenger traffic would increase by only a third, and freight traffic by only 10 per cent, and overcrowding targets would be exceeded in nearly all of the London TOCs.[56]

How was the plan received? There was clearly relief in Whitehall circles that the long-promised document had seen the light of day, but there was disappointment in the English regions at the apparent bias in favour of London and the South-east in the investment programme. The interests of Yorkshire, Birmingham, and the West Midlands appeared to some MPs to have been subordinated, and although the point was made that over 70 per cent of rail journeys were made in London and the South-east, ministers faced some uncomfortable meetings, and officials blamed Morton for having stirred up 'unrealistic expectations' of projects suggested by the SRA's earlier studies of Manchester and the West Midlands.[57] More importantly, however, the Treasury was disappointed that the SRA was still showing itself to be 'project-led' rather than 'outcomes-led'. As an official put it, 'Rather than focussing upon outcomes and first thinking about how fares, franchising and renewals could help make the most of existing capacity, and only then looking at the case for enhancements, the document still appears to be driven by a list of grand projects which would be nice to do.'[58] And lurking behind the document was the realization that delivery of the plan rested upon the hardy perennial of available funding, which in turn was influenced by the ability of Railtrack, its successor and the TOCs to contain railway costs. Indeed, doubts were expressed in *Modern Railways* in February and March 2002 as to whether funds were sufficient to support all the committed projects in the plan, and its leading journalist, Roger Ford, came up with a cost estimate of his own. This suggested that the public sector faced a bill of at least £25 billion, excluding the power supply upgrade for lines south of London, the safety enhancements recommended in the Uff/Cullen report, and routine rolling stock and infrastructure renewals. Since Ford was working with costings for the WCML (£6.4bn), ECML (£2.9bn) and Thameslink 2000 (£2.0bn) which

[55] *Report of Joint Inquiry into Train Protection Systems* (chaired by Professor Uff and Lord Cullen) (29 March 2001).

[56] SRA, *Strategic Plan* (2002), pp. 5–6, 9, 25–6; Interview with Bowker, 2006.

[57] Cf. Barrie Sheerman (MP for Huddersfield)–Byers, 21 January 2002, Ann Taylor (MP for Dewsbury)–Byers, 23 January 2002, Sir Albert Bore (leader, Birmingham City Council)–Byers, 30 January 2002, Fidler–Byers, 8 February 2002, DTLR file R78/1/43 Pt. 6.

[58] Note on SRA's Strategic Plan, draft 38, n.d. [c.30 October 2001], Treasury file TRA/B/3 Pt. 1 [redacted].

were much lower than current SRA and Railtrack estimates, the delivery of the package within the funding parameters must have been in doubt. Bowker was already expressing anxieties about the 'over-ambition' of projects such as the ECML upgrade (see below, pp. 131, 135), and the SRA's annual report for 2001/2, published in July, warned that 'recent cost increases in infrastructure mainte- nance, renewal and investment remain a serious concern'.[59] More realism was apparent when the plan was updated in January 2003, after further pressures on the industry. Railtrack had at last been taken out of an expensive period of admin- istration, and its successor, Network Rail, had been established in October 2002. But considerable problems remained. Rising rail costs were beginning to domi- nate the public debate. The Potters Bar accident on 10 May 2002 had raised fur- ther questions about safety and the maintenance function. Concerns were being expressed about the fragility of several franchises operating on a 'cost-plus' basis. Finally, the SRA's budget had suffered a cut of £312 million over a three-year period from 2003/4 (£242 million in 2003/4) at the hands of Alistair Darling, who had become Transport Secretary on 28 May following Byers's enforced departure, and was now presiding over the Department for Transport, after yet another reorganization.[60]

The revised plan, like its predecessor, was weighty. Volume 1, entitled *Platform for Progress*, ran to 115 pages, with chapters on railway reform, costs, the plan- ning approach, improvement by 2005, and the SRA's project portfolio. Volume 2, *Route Descriptions*, provided 50 pages of detail delineating the routes in the network: the main lines radiating from London; the Capital's commuter lines; the regional networks in England (Greater Anglia, Chiltern, West Midlands, North West, North East), Scotland and Wales; and the strategic freight routes. This time Bowker's foreword was more measured. Some progress was flagged up. Network Rail had been established; a more credible plan for the WCML upgrade had been put in place; the TPWS safety system had been introduced 'on time and on budget'; and a new franchising policy had been launched. But the SRA Chairman also conceded that there had been setbacks, the Potters Bar accident taking safety to the top of the public agenda once more. And now the message was that of addressing the very real difficulties which railway policymakers faced. The challenges posed by cost escalation and lagging performance and service quality had intensified, and the prospects for investment were being constrained by the rising cost of operating and maintaining the existing services and the infrastruc- ture. The costs of providing services (Network Rail + operators) had risen from £6.1 billion in 1999/2000 to a projected £9 billion in 2002/3, public sector support (including support from the PTEs) had risen from £1.4 to £2.5 billion, but these

[59] *Modern Railways*, February 2002, p. 4, and Ford in ibid. March 2002, pp. 18–20; SRA, *Annual Report 2001/2*, p. 31.

[60] SRA Board Minutes, 5 December 2002, Rowlands–Bowker, 20 December 2002, SRA. The Depart- ment for Transport (DfT) succeeded the DTLR on 1 June 2002 and was designed to focus solely on transport matters. Most of the DTLR's other functions passed to the Office of the Deputy Prime Minister.

7. Alistair Darling becomes Transport Secretary after the resignation of Stephen Byers, May 2002: Steve Bell, *Guardian*, 30 May 2002. Pictured: Gordon Brown, Tony Blair, John Prescott, and Alistair Darling.

increases had not been matched by the 9 per cent growth in revenues (Table 5.3). An estimated deficit of £1.5 billion for 2002/3 clearly endangered the prospects for investment, whether the source was public or private.[61] A table of 31 specific investment plans indicated the current state of play (Table 5.4). The WCML upgrade had been redefined in an SRA draft strategy, published for consultation purposes in October 2002, and some of the other key projects were identified for 'de-scoping' or deferral: the upgrades for the ECML, South Central, and South West Trains, the larger freight, and new RPP schemes. Thameslink 2000 and the East London Line were under negotiation. Planning problems had surfaced, but concerns about 'affordability' had also prompted reviews and revised timescales. Newer and more ambitious projects, such as a new North–South Line and airport links in Scotland were being 'developed' or 'consulted upon', with no firm promises made, there was no mention of a Great Western upgrade, and the knife was being wielded to the incremental output and Disability Act schemes. Franchisees were now required to examine the scope for economies, including 'sensible housekeeping measures such as a selected thinning of some franchised

[61] SRA, *The Strategic Plan 2003: Platform for Progress* (2003), pp. 4–5, 10, 36–7.

131

Table 5.3 Railway operating expenditure and revenue, 1999/2000–2002/3 (£bn)

	1999/2000	2002/3[a]	% change
Expenditure			
Infrastructure[b]	2.8	5.0	+79
Franchised passenger services[c]	2.8	3.6	+29
Freight services[d]	0.5	0.4	−20
Total	6.1	9.0	+48
Revenue			
Passenger and freight[e]	4.4	4.8	+9
Railtrack/Network Rail open access and rental income	0.1	0.2	+100
Public sector support[f]	1.4	2.5	+79
Total	5.9	7.5	+27
Industry-wide operating deficit	0.2	1.5	+650

[a] Estimates based on data to mid-October 2002; infrastructure enhancement costs are excluded.
[b] Operations, maintenance, and renewal, including joint industry costs, but excluding performance payments.
[c] Includes train leasing costs but excludes Railtrack/Network Rail charges and performance payments.
[d] 2001/2 data, excluding Railtrack/Network Rail charges.
[e] Freight revenue = 2001/2 data.
[f] Including PTEs, local authorities, and Scottish Executive, but excluding FFG.
Source: SRA, The Strategic Plan 2003: Platform for Progress (2003), p. 37.

services, reviewing fares and a more commercial approach to certain issues'.[62] With a further re-examination on the horizon as part of the 2004 Spending Review, Bowker admitted that the railways faced the 'fight of our lives to make the Case for Rail to Government'.[63] And although the original growth targets of 50 per cent for passenger traffic and 80 per cent for freight were reaffirmed, elsewhere in the plan the SRA revealed that its best estimate of passenger growth to 2010/11 was in fact a more realistic 25–35 per cent, in line with the pessimistic forecast buried in the 2002 plan.[64]

Reception of the second plan matched its tone. Bowker had assured Darling that it demonstrated that the railway 'was getting on with it' and addressing its challenges.[65] But there had been some disquiet within the Department at the inclusion of the infrastructure spending projections (Table 5.3), which threatened to 'bust the 10 Year Plan envelope', and Darling, who had found the tone of the document to be 'overly gloomy', warned the Prime Minister that the

[62] Ibid. p. 10.   [63] Ibid. pp. 4–5.
[64] Ibid. pp. 9, 24. This incongruity was noted by new Board Member David Norgrove: Norgrove–Bowker, 27 January 2002 [Sic: = 2003], SRA.
[65] Bowker–Darling, 29 January 2003, DfT file R78/1/43 Pt. 10.

Table 5.4 Status of 31 investment plans in 2003 Strategic Plan

Project	Priority in 2002 plan	Completion date in 2002 plan	Status in 2003 plan
WCML	s	2005	Descoped; draft strategy Oct. 2002
CTRL Phase I + II	s/m	2003/7	Proceeding
Chiltern	s	2005	Proceeding
Cross Country	s	2005	Proceeding
Mark I replacement + power supply	s	2004	Proceeding
MML extn	s	2005	Proceeding; Parkway stn deferred
TPWS	s	2003	Proceeding
Thameslink 2000	m	2008	Deferred; new enquiry
East London	m	2006	Development work 'affordability concerns'
TransPennine extn	m	2006	Proceeding
West Anglia (London–Stansted)	m	2007	Additional enhancements deferred
ECML	m	2010	Descoped/deferred incremental improvement
South Central	m	2008	Under review
Felixstowe–Nuneaton freight	m	2010	Descoped; gauge work to proceed
Felixstowe–Nuneaton freight			Infrastructure/resignalling deferred
Southampton–West Midlands freight	m	2009	Descoped; reduced gauge work to proceed
Southampton–West Midlands freight			Cherwell Valley section to proceed
South West trains	m	2010	Under review
IOS	s/m	2007	Descoped
ERTMS			Development work
South London Metro			Development work
London Crossrail			Business case in preparation
West Midlands capacity			Development work
Greater Manchester capacity			Under review
Glasgow + Edinburgh airports			Being studied
RPP, RPF, and FFG schemes			Limited scope for new schemes

(cont.)

Table 5.4 (*continued*)

Project	Priority in 2002 plan	Completion date in 2002 plan	Status in 2003 plan
Edinburgh Waverley redevelopment			Development work
DDA			Limited scope
New North–South line			Consultation stage
TransPennine/South Humberside freight			Deferred
CTRL domestic services			Consultation stage

Source: SRA, *The Strategic Plan 2003: Platform for Progress* (2003), pp. 14–16.

reaction to it was likely to be mixed.[66] Officials in general felt that the plan was positive in addressing the massive cost problems facing the industry, and struck 'an appropriate and delicate balance between setting out the difficult issues facing the rail industry and avoiding concern that they are unmanageable'.[67] In the journal *Modern Railways*, Ford complained that for all its length the 2003 plan was less informative on costs and timescales than its predecessor, though in fact this had been an agreed policy. As a DTLR official put it, 'given the interim review and the current funding position [the plan] is deliberately light on numbers'.[68] Under the headline 'Boiling Frogs ate my Strategic Plan', the indefatigable journalist argued that aspirational investment planning was being jeopardized by the inexorable creep of rising rail costs, in much the same way as British Rail's 1991 *Future Rail* prospectus had been treated. *Future Rail* had also provided a 10-year agenda, promising expenditure of £1 billion a year to provide Thameslink 2000, London Crossrail, the CTRL, modernization of the WCML, and more. However, it quickly foundered on the rock of recession, and was soon forgotten when the Conservatives' plans for privatization gathered momentum. Now the various 'de-scopings' appeared to have shaved around £8 billion off the £25.6 billion cost of the enhancement programme.[69] The SRA's ambitions were clearly apparent in the 2003 plan: to engage with all the stakeholders in an improved approach to planning, to stimulate freight traffic via new initiatives such as the company neutral revenue support scheme (see below, p. 165) and to lead in a new series of managerial and structural reforms,

[66] Bronwen Hill–Alan Deighton et al., 4 December 2002, Philip Graham (DfT)–Bowker and Jonathan Barwick (SRA), 23 December 2002, ibid. Pt. 9; Darling–Blair, January 2003, in Matthew Elson (Senior Policy Adviser, No. 10)–Blair, 24 January 2003, Prime Minister's Rail papers, Pt. 9.
[67] Lambirth–Coulshed, 4 December 2002, Fidler–Darling, 10 January 2003, DTLR file R78/1/43 Pt. 9.
[68] Fidler–Lambirth et al., 3 December 2002, ibid. Pt. 8.
[69] Ford, *Modern Railways*, March 2003, pp. 19–21; Gourvish, *British Rail 1974–97*, pp. 312–13. The 'boiling frogs' metaphor refers to the hypothesis that a frog may be boiled alive if the water is heated slowly. Ford applied it to the apparent tendency to ignore escalating rail costs.

including high-level 'G6' meetings and a new Rail Safety and Standards Board. It was also determined to make the case for the railways more broadly. Its most ambitious general statement, *Everyone's Railway* of September 2003, did not impress everyone, however, and Ford dismissed it as a scary document, redolent of Railtrack, despite protestations to the contrary, in holding out the begging bowl.[70] But by this time it was becoming clear that a large funding gap was emerging as rail costs rose, which at prime ministerial level was raising 'fundamental questions about the viability of the existing network and the range of services, about the potential for upgrades, and about the case of rail versus road'.[71] Managerially, the Authority wisely elected to concentrate its attention upon the WCML, Mark I vehicle replacement and the power supply upgrade, together with the development of a capacity utilization policy and the establishment of route strategies. The re-evaluation process produced scepticism about the ECML and South Central upgrades inherited from the Morton period, and there were also doubts as to whether regional railways could be fully supported within the existing service profile. Of course, delivery of an ambitious plan was not in the SRA's hands alone; and the establishment of Network Rail, together with the publication of higher track access charges by the Regulator in October 2003, created pressures reminiscent of those which had produced the Beeching (1963) and Serpell (1983) reports.[72] In April 2003, Bowker presented the DfT and Treasury with three funding scenarios which rang alarm bells by suggesting that rail requirements would be much higher than anticipated. In the following autumn, the departments were expressing serious concerns about the SRA's ability to constrain franchising costs and to control its budgets for 2004/5 and 2005/6.[73] By the time the next strategic plan was due in January 2004, the DfT directed the SRA not to publish ahead of the Government's 2004 Spending Review, a decision that the Authority accepted, since it realized that its third plan could be no more than a holding, transitional statement.[74] The document did not see the light of day in fact.[75] On 19 January, the Government announced that it was to undertake another major review of the railway industry. Soon the SRA would be fully occupied in this lengthy and ultimately cathartic process.

---

[70] Ford, *Modern Railways*, November 2003, p. 7.

[71] Elson–Blair, 20 February and 11 April 2003, Prime Minister's Rail papers, Pts. 9 and 10.

[72] Noted by Ford in *Modern Railways*, April 2003, p. 14.

[73] See, for example, Lambirth–Darling, 9 April 2003, DfT file R73/1/26 Pt. 10, Howells–Bowker, 9 October 2003, R78/1/14 Pt. 11; James Wardlaw (Treasury), Memo. on 'Rail finances: update and options', 16 October 2003, Treasury file (redacted).

[74] SRA Executive Minutes, 11 September 2003, SRA 57/01/01 Pt. 4; SRA Executive Prayers Minutes, 5 January 2004, SRA 57/01/12A Pt. 1; SRA Board Minutes, 15 January 2004; Sue Killen (DG, Rail, Aviation, Logistics, Maritime and Security [RALMS], DfT)–Bowker, 16 January 2004, DfT file R78/1/14 Pt. 11; *Parl. Deb. (Commons)*, 6th ser. (Session 2003–4), Vol. 416 Pt. 2, 19 January 2004, Darling, written answer to Theresa May (Conservative MP for Maidenhead), c. 1009w.

[75] A copy of the draft plan is in SRA file 69/23/99 Pt. 3.

5.4 Franchising Mark II

Bowker inherited a difficult position in relation to franchising. When he arrived, the SRA had just responded to Byers's demand for 'quick wins' by producing a new strategy in August 2001. This established the eight-year, 'enhanceable' concept for nine franchises due to expire in or before 2004 which could be considered either 'opened up', lacking in urgency, or 'heavy loss-makers'; a further six franchises would be re-let on two year extensions (above, pp. 95–6 and Table 4.1). But it was clear that some inexorable problems inherited from the Morton period were still on the table. Five regional franchises—Merseyside, Northern, North Western, Wales & Borders, and Wessex—had encountered financial problems and were being run on temporary, cost-plus, management contracts by Arriva, First Group, and National Express, and a sixth—Anglia—was added in March 2002 after a pre-tax loss of £1.4 million.[76] There were serious problems elsewhere too, with large pre-tax losses being made by National Express's Central (£14.1m.) and ScotRail (£20.8m.) franchises and by Virgin Cross Country (£37.9m.) in 2001/2, and smaller losses being experienced by South Eastern, c2c, and Silverlink.[77] On top of this, there was much to be done with refranchising for some of those where the future had been apparently 'determined', namely, South Central, South West Trains, and TransPennine, the latter a new inter-urban franchise to be carved out of Northern and North Western. Finally, difficulties were evident in the normally secure intercity sector. Although no action had been proposed for the two Virgin franchises, which had been let until 2012, the collapse of Railtrack had thrown the upgrade of the WCML into disarray and moved the franchising goalposts. A two-year extension had been proposed for GNER's franchise, with the acceptance that an ambitious upgrade of the ECML could not be afforded.

Bowker's initial response was to sever the link between 20-year franchises and major infrastructure upgrades and to argue strongly for some rationalization of franchises around the major London termini, beginning at Liverpool Street with the proposed merger of Great Eastern, Anglia, and the West Anglia portion of WAGN to create 'Greater Anglia'.[78] When Bowker wrote to Byers in December, he referred to three types of franchise—'base', 'base flexed', and 'enhanced', and

[76] SRA, *Annual Report 2001/2*, p. 22; *Parl. Deb. (Commons)*, 6th ser. (Session 2002–3), Vol. 395 Pt. 2, 28 November 2002, David Jamieson (PUSS, DfT), written answer to Don Foster (Liberal Democrat MP for Bath), c. 457w; Bowker–Byers, 28 February 2002, SRA. A seventh—Great Northern—was operated on a management contract for a short time in 2001/2 when WAGN was split in anticipation of the establishment of Thameslink 2000. WAGN was reinstated in March 2002 following the portfolio agreement with National Express. A subsequent proposal to combine the GNER and Great Northern franchises worked up under the name 'Project Harry' came to nought: see Ray O'Toole (CEO, National Express) and Garnett (GNER)–Bowker, 6 December 2002, SRA.

[77] TOC accounts, SRA.

[78] This effectively marked the end of the original Wessex franchise concept, which included the transfer of South West Trains's Waterloo–Exeter and Reading–Brighton routes and would have created two domestic companies operating out of Waterloo. Eventually, Wessex was merged into the Greater Western franchise, with South West Trains retaining the Waterloo–Exeter route. SRA News Release, 19

made it clear that a 15-year period was now preferred, with reviews after 5 and 10 years. This squared with the current thinking in Whitehall. The DTLR had been disappointed that Byers's initial statement in July 2001 had been 'widely misinterpreted as a general move towards short-termism' instead of the real intention—to establish 'horses for courses'.[79] In due course, Bowker developed a strategy of his own. Revealed during the autumn of 2002 it was intended to correct some of the perceived defects of 'Mark I franchising' established when the franchises were first let in the mid-1990s. At that time, OPRAF had specified a minimum passenger service requirement—the PSR—and operators were free to add services above this minimum. But this had encouraged an uncoordinated and burdensome pressure upon the existing infrastructure. In addition, there had been an element of 'ORCATS raiding'. Since revenues on jointly operated routes were subject to the ORCATS revenue-sharing formula for allocating tickets to services, there was an incentive for some TOCs to add services in these areas with the principal aim of abstracting revenue from an incumbent.[80] But more importantly, the initial insistence that the franchisees bore the revenue risk had not worked well, and by 2002 it was clear that poor performance was all too frequently a by-product of business pressures. And, in any case, the balance between risk-taking and reward, as so often in relations between the public and the private sector, had become skewed in favour of the latter, since the SRA was increasingly being asked to shore up the system when it failed. The 2003 plan noted that the assumptions built into the first franchise lettings by the successful bidders were that operating losses before subsidy could be cut by nearly £600 million from 1997/8 to 2001/2; in fact only £222 million was achieved.[81] The situation required urgent action, since, as Bowker told Darling in October 2002, no fewer than 17 of the 25 original franchises required action to be taken by the end of 2004 (the first 17 listed in Table 5.5). Whether the broad policy for these had been determined or not, the post-Hatfield difficulties had produced an environment in which the SRA's search for enhanceability was likely to founder on the rock of financial realism.[82] There was evidence of this when the SRA, required to make budgetary savings of £242 million in 2003/4, began to ask operators bidding for new or extended franchises to indicate what could be achieved with subsidy reductions of 10 and 20 per cent.[83] Soon, Bowker

December 2001, and see also HC Transport Committee Report on *Passenger Rail Franchising and the Future of Railway Infrastructure*, 2002, HC239-I, paras. 29–30, annex.

[79] Bowker–Byers, 11 December 2001, SRA; Byers–Bowker, 13 December 2001, DTLR file R73/1/26 Pt. 10, Coulshed–Byers, 13 December 2001, R10/5/56 Pt. 3.

[80] ORCATS = Operational Research Computerised Allocation of Tickets to Services. Cf. Bradshaw–Grant, 28 January 2001, SRA. A good example was the competition between Anglia and Great Eastern for the Ipswich–London traffic in 1997–8: Interview with Newton (2006), and see also *Financial Times*, 29 September 1997, p. 9; *Evening Standard*, 7 May 1998, p. 18.

[81] SRA, *Platform for Progress*, p. 48; Interview with Newton (2006).

[82] Bowker–Darling, 3 October 2002, SRA.

[83] Bowker, dinner with TOCs, 16 December 2002, leaked to *Guardian*, 19 December 2002, p. 25. See Bowker, letters to TOCs, 20 December 2002, SRA.

Table 5.5 Franchise development by the SRA, 2002–4

Franchise	Type	Franchisee	Expiry	Action proposed	Date franchise agreed	Actual progress: Franchisee	Start	Expiry
Those expiring Feb. 2003–Feb. 2004								
Merseyside	R/MC	Arriva Trains	Feb. 2003	Opened up; pass to PTE	Feb. 2002	Serco/Ned Rlys (PTE concession)	July 2003	July 2028
Northern	R/MC	Arriva Trains	Feb. 2003	Opened up; pt to new TransPennine Exp:	Oct. 2004	Serco/Ned Rlys	Dec. 2004	Sep. 2011[a]
					Sep. 2003	First/Keolis	Feb. 2004	Feb. 2012[b]
South Central	LSE	Govia	May 2003	Determined; 20 years	Aug. 2002	Govia (Southern)	May 2003	Dec. 2009
Island Line	R	Stagecoach	Sep. 2003	Re-let to Feb. 2007	Dec. 2003	Stagecoach	Dec. 2003	Feb. 2007
South West	LSE	Stagecoach	Feb. 2004	Determined; 20 years	Oct. 2002	Stagecoach (interim)	Feb. 2004	Feb. 2007
Those expiring in Apr. 2004								
Anglia	R/MC	GB Rlys		Pt of new **Greater Anglia:**	Jan. 2004	LNER/National Exp (ONE)	Apr. 2004	Apr. 2011[c]
Central	R	National Exp		Lossmaker; 2-year extn	Oct. 2003	National Exp	Apr. 2004	Apr. 2006[d]
Great Eastern	LSE	FirstGroup		Re-let as pt of new Greater Anglia (see above)				
North Western	R/MC	FirstGroup		Determined; pt to new TransPennine (see above)	Feb. 2004			
ScotRail	R	National Exp		Lossmaker; re-let	June 2004	First Group	Oct. 2004	Oct. 2011[c]
Thames	LSE	Go-ahead		2-year extn interim	Nov. 2003	FirstGroup (GW link)	Apr. 2004	Apr. 2006
Thameslink	LSE	Govia		2-year extn then **Thameslink/GN**	Feb. 2004	FirstGroup	Apr. 2006	Apr. 2015

Franchise	Sector	Operator	Date	Notes	Date	Operator	Date	Date
Wales & Bdrs	R/MC	National Exp		Opened up Oct. 2001	July 2003	Arriva Trains Wales	Dec. 2003	Oct. 2018
Wessex	R/MC	National Exp		Opened up Oct. 2001; 2-year extn then pt of new Greater Western (see below)			Apr. 2004	Apr. 2006
WAGN	LSE/R	National Exp		Re-let; 2-year extn; WA to new Greater Anglia, GN to Thameslink			Apr. 2004	Apr. 2006
Those expiring Oct. 2004–Dec. 2006								
Silverlink	LSE	National Exp	Oct. 2004	2-year extn; re-let	Sep. 2004	National Express	Oct. 2004	Oct. 2006[d]
East Coast	IC	GNER	Apr. 2005	2-year extn; re-let for upgrade Then re-let to incumbent	Jan. 2002		Apr. 2003	Apr. 2005
Great Western	IC	FirstGroup	Feb. 2006	Core of new **Greater Western** franchise	Mar. 2005	GNER (Sea Containers) FirstGroup	May 2005 Apr. 2006	May 2012[c] Apr. 2016
South Eastern	LSE	Connex	Dec. 2006	2-year extn; terminated To form pt of new **Integrated Kent** franchise (**+domestic CTRL**)	June 2003 Nov. 2005	SRA Govia	Nov. 2003 Apr. 2006	Apr. 2006 Apr. 2014

(cont.)

Table 5.5 (*continued*)

Franchise	Type	Franchisee	Expiry	Actual progress:		Action proposed	Start	Expiry
				Date franchise agreed	Franchisee			
Longer franchises, 2008–21								
MML	IC	National Exp	Apr. 2008			Determined; no action	Apr. 1996	Apr. 2008[d]
c2c	LSE	National Exp	May. 2011			Long term; no action	May 1996	May 2011
Gatwick Ex	LSE	National Exp	May 2011			Long term; no action	Apr. 1996	May 2011
West Coast	IC	Virgin	Mar. 2012			Long term; but additional support/renegotiations	Mar. 1997	Mar. 2012
Cross Country	IC	Virgin	Apr. 2012			Long term; but additional support/renegotiations	Jan. 1997	Apr. 2012[d]
Chiltern	LSE	M40	Dec. 2021	Feb. 2002	New 20-year franchise	Long term; determined; no action	Mar. 2002	Dec. 2021

[a] Plus conditional two-year extn.
[b] Plus optional five-year extn.
[c] Plus conditional three-year extn.
[d] Plans to establish new franchises for West Midlands, East Midlands, and New Cross Country were announced in Oct. 2005 to start in Nov. 2007; in Feb. 2006, it was announced that Silverlink would pass to TfL on the same date.

Source: SRA.

IC = intercity; R = regional; LSE = London & South-east; MC = under management contract ITT = invitation to tender.

8. The SRA announces cuts in off-peak train services, January 2003: Jonathan Pugh, *Times*, 17 January 2003.

had taken up the cause of bus substitution in rural areas, and was being dubbed the new Beeching or 'Bowching'.[84] The Authority then made serious efforts to explore the possibilities for operational savings. The rationalization of a selection of off-peak train services was introduced in May and September 2003.[85] Then, following work by PricewaterhouseCoopers in 2003, the Department asked the SRA to explore the opportunities arising from the wider application of Driver Only Operation (DOO), and cuts in the staffing of stations. This it did with the help of Halcrow and AEA Technology, finding that potential savings of £100 million were identified from DOO, and £108 million from cuts at 510 stations. Leaving aside the personal security implications of such measures, savings of this magnitude had already been included in more sober cost projections under the title MSCR ('minimum support for the continuing railway'), but in any case, by the time these figures were produced the Rail Review of 2004 had already begun.[86]

In 'Mark II franchising', the new deals were to be in essence service contracts. The franchises would specify both the train frequency and the initial timetable to be run; subsequent adjustments would be controlled more tightly. Some good ideas were built into the new template, especially in relation to the fragile franchises which were operating on a cost-plus, management basis. The intention here was that revenue risk should be apportioned on the 'cap and collar' principle, with the operator responsible for a defined revenue band, and the SRA sharing in the outcome whenever revenue rose above or fell below the band. The new approach was defended as 'providing clarity of service specification', enabling the SRA to give effect to its intentions under the capacity utilization and route utilization banners.[87] There was also to be a more comprehensive monitoring of operational performance, embracing not only punctuality and the cancellation rate but also 'quality' measures of train presentation, station environments, information, security, and sales. The SRA was adamant that it was not its intention 'to interfere in day to day management of the franchises, nor ... to stifle private sector flair by micro-managing', but the TOCs disagreed strongly, resenting the implied loss of managerial freedom and lock-in aspects of the new deals.[88] A new template franchise agreement was developed over the period December 2002–March 2003, envisaging a franchise length of 5–8 years. However, achievement lagged behind conceptualization. Only one franchise—Chiltern— was re-let in 2002 on the former 20-year basis, and even here there were not

[84] Cf. *Private Eye*, 7 March 2003, p. 10.

[85] SRA Board Minutes, 5 December 2002–6 February 2003; SRA Press Release, 16 January 2003; Coulshed–Darling, 12 February 2003, DfT file R78/1/14 Pt. 10.

[86] See Dave Bennett (DfT)–Kim Howells (Minister for Transport), 15 April 2004, DfT file R100/1/3 Pt. 1.

[87] Route utilization strategies are medium-term assessments of the potential demands for train services on specified parts of the network.

[88] SRA, *Franchising Policy Statement* (November 2002); Garnett (GNER)–Bowker, 16 October 2002, SRA; Andrew Campbell (Darling's PPS)–Coulshed, 19 September 2002, DfT file R73/1/26 Pt. 12; Interview with Richard Davies (ex-SRA, now ATOC), 3 July 2006.

only problems in unravelling infrastructure plans, specifically the doubling of track between Bicester and Aynho which Railtrack's administrators were unable to progress on the original basis, but also difficulties with the Regulator, who complained vigorously about encroachment and regulatory duplication in the draft agreement.[89] In Bowker's time, that is, to September 2004, only three new franchises were established: Arriva Wales in December 2003, TransPennine in February 2004, and Greater Anglia in April 2004. In addition, in 2003 South Central was re-let for six years to the incumbent operator, Govia, in May, Merseyside was re-let as a 25-year PTE concession to a new entrant, Serco and NedRailways (a subsidiary of Netherlands Railways) in July, and the financially weak Connex South Eastern was taken in-house by the SRA in November (Table 5.5). But taking into account well-developed plans, by early 2004 a new, more rationalized franchise map was firmly in sight (Figure 5.4), and the initial steps had been taken to establish new franchises for ScotRail (which began in October 2004), Northern (December 2004), Greater Western, and an Integrated Kent franchise (both in April 2006, after the SRA had been wound up). Elsewhere, the SRA dealt with the ailing Virgin Group franchises by providing emergency support from July 2002, moving the two contracts onto an agreed budget/management fee basis pending a satisfactory revision of terms. However, the negotiations proved lengthy, stretching beyond the life of the SRA. Stagecoach's franchises, South West and Island Line, were extended until February 2007. Negotiations also began with the East Coast incumbent, GNER, which had been given a two-year extension to April 2005 by the SRA at the beginning of 2002. The franchise was eventually let to GNER on terms advantageous to the Government from May 2005. Short extensions were also agreed for franchises whose long-term future had yet to be determined: Central; Thames (renamed Great Western Link and with First Group substituted for Govia); and Wessex, pending the establishment of Greater Western; WAGN, pending Greater Anglia; Silverlink; and Thameslink (pending Thameslink/GN, which began as First Capital Connect in April 2006) (Table 5.5).

What may be said about the new approach to franchising and its results? The first thing to observe is that while franchise competitions attracted a healthy number of bidders, the process did little to widen the market for franchising. The only new entrants were Serco and NedRail, a joint venture which successfully tendered for the Merseyside concession and went on to win the new Northern franchise; and Keolis, the French transport operator, which joined with First-Group to run TransPennine. Entrants tended to be inhibited in the post-Hatfield climate, but there were institutional barriers too, and NedRail complained that it had encountered a lack of encouragement in its initial efforts (with South West

---

[89] Bowker–Byers, 16 January 2002, SRA; Winsor–Bowker, 1 February 2002, and reply, 20 February 2002, copies in DTLR file R73/1/26 Pt. 11.

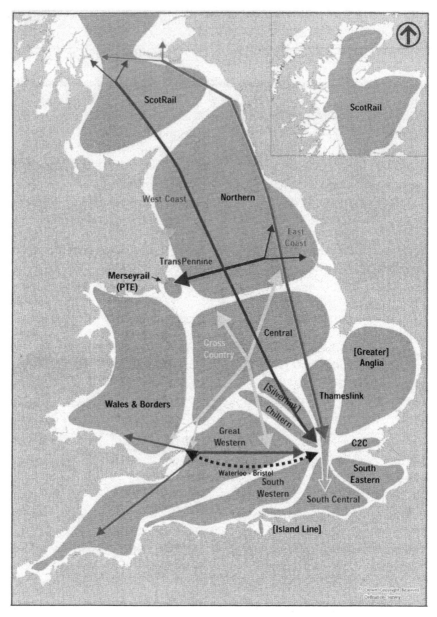

Figure 5.4 SRA franchise map, February 2004

Source: Richard Davies, Memo. to SRA Executive Committee on 'Franchise Map', 10 February 2004, SRA57/01/02 Pt. 50.

Trains and Thameslink).[90] In the unfranchised market, only Grand Central came forward to join Hull Trains in bidding for paths, but its initial efforts were unsuccessful in 2003/4, with the SRA adamant that, as with Hull Trains, its appearance would be 'heavily abstractive' for the incumbent franchisee (it has subsequently gained entry on the ECML to run services from Sunderland to London).[91] As for the rest, it was essentially a matter of shuffling the pack of cards and redistributing them among what Ford called 'the unreconstructed bus bandits'.[92] This tendency, together with the extension of franchises with a poor operating record to existing holders, as in the case of South West Trains and Central, for example, invited the criticism that the SRA was rewarding failure, while the reference of the Greater Anglia (National Express) and ScotRail (FirstGroup) decisions to the Competition Commission did nothing to indicate a vigorous competition in the passenger rail market.[93] It was difficult for the SRA to win the publicity game, however. If the Authority chose a newcomer, it could be attacked for encouraging instability and being unfair to an incumbent. If it chose an existing franchisee, it invited the criticism that it was stifling competition. If the arrangements appeared to reward the franchisee, there were questions about the stewardship of public money; if a franchisee who had signed up to what appeared to be a good deal for the public sector then failed, more criticism would follow. With so many franchises falling due, a legacy of the decisions taken in 1996–7, there was clearly a risk of both 'bidder fatigue' and 'SRA fatigue'. And adding to the complexity of deal-making with bidders were uncertainties about infrastructure funding as Railtrack was replaced by Network Rail, about future fares policy (including the potential liability for VAT), about the exposure to risk (in London and the South-east) produced by the Mark I replacement programme, and about the requirements of a Government increasingly anxious about the affordability of the railways within its spending review mechanism. As infrastructure costs—and consequently the cost of Government/SRA support—rose, civil servants became concerned that some of the new franchising arrangements (e.g. the deal with Govia on South Central) appeared to be increasing the Authority's financial commitments rather than reducing it. Indeed, a paper prepared within the DfT in May 2003 asserted that the SRA's franchising commitments over the following year were 'unaffordable'. Mark Lambirth, the Director, Railways, then wrote to Shaw to ask for a paper showing the affordability implications of the franchise

[90] Patrick Verwer (NedRail)–Byers, 22 November 2001, DTLR file R73/1/26 Pt. 10. On the other hand, Anton Valk was more sanguine: Valk (MD, IBG, NedRailways)–Spellar, 14 October 2002, DfT file R78/1/14 Pt. 9; Interview with Anton Valk, 16 May 2007.
[91] Sunil Gupta, Memo. to SRA Executive, 26 February 2004, SRA file 57/01/02 Pt. 50. A test suggested that for every £1 of new revenue £7 had been abstracted from existing operators by Hull Trains.
[92] *Modern Railways*, September 2002, p. 15.
[93] Competition Commission, *FirstGroup plc and the Scottish Passenger Rail Franchise* (June 2004), and *National Express Group plc and the Greater Anglia Franchise* (November 2004). The Commission sought 'behavioural remedies' from FirstGroup but did not find evidence of any substantial lessening of competition in East Anglia.

programme as a whole.[94] And from this point there was a 'budget/target outcome' approach to future decisions. Any new arrangements required the SRA to assess affordability in relation to an estimate of the MSCR and its own budget, where the pressures intensified, particularly for the year 2004/5. In these circumstances, the holding of franchise competitions was certainly a complicated and time-consuming process. By 2003, the competitions for 'prequalification' (shortlisting) and then 'preferred bidder' status were conducted on a scientific basis, led by Shaw. SRA managers undertook a forensic scrutiny of the documentation. Elaborate matrices weighed up such factors as affordability, value for money and operational integrity, using, *inter alia*, an affordability model which by this time had stretched to iteration '52e'.[95] For the trickier competitions, and for non-competitive renewals, where the incumbent was required to ensure a degree of enhancement, an army of consultants was required to provide specialist expertise. For the problematic South Central case, where a 20-year franchise with Govia had been abandoned in favour of a $6^3/4$ year contract, three consultants were employed: KPMG, Booz Allen Hamilton, and Eversheds. One should not be surprised, therefore, that the cost of the refranchising deals was large. In a response to a parliamentary question, the cost of three of them—Greater Anglia, Wales & Borders, and TransPennine—was put at £10.8 million, with Greater Anglia alone costing £4 million.[96] With three to five bidders for each competition, the total cost of each new franchising process lay between £11.5 and £27.5 million.[97]

The competition for the Greater Anglia franchise, the first of Bowker's new model contracts, attracted considerable attention from rail watchers. Journalists, and ultimately academics, were puzzled about the SRA's decision to exclude FirstGroup, operator of the Great Eastern franchise, from the short list in April 2003. Wolmar made much of the decision, pointing out that the shortlisted bidders, Arriva, National Express, and GB Railways, operators of the Anglia franchise, all had franchises which were in financial difficulty and had been moved onto management contracts. He also pointed out that Great Eastern had a comparatively good operating record, while FirstGroup *was* soon shortlisted for the Northern franchise (in December). Wolmar implied that there was an element of vindictiveness in that FirstGroup had launched a study of the prospects

[94] Jenny Frew (DfT)–Darling, 2 April 2003, Tracey Waltho (Div. Man., Rail Economics & Modelling, DfT), Memo. on 'Scorecard—Franchise Decisions in the next 12 Months', 26 May 2003, Lambirth–Nicola Shaw, 7 August 2003, DfT file R73/1/26 Pt. 13.

[95] On the origins of the affordability model see Caroline Low (KPMG)–Peter Hawthorne (SSRA), 10 November 2000, SRA.

[96] *Parl. Deb. (Commons)*, 6th ser. (Session 2003–4), Vol. 422, 7 June 2004, McNulty, written answer to John McDonnell (MP for Hayes & Harlington), 26 May 2004, c. 72w. McDonnell was also told that the SRA had spent £40.7m on franchise replacement and extensions, April 2001–April 2004: ibid. 4w.

[97] Calculation based on £2.5m. SRA/DfT costs plus £3–5m. per bid. See HC Transport Committee Report on *Passenger Rail Franchising*, P.P.2005–6, HC1354, November 2006, para. 59.

for a high-speed Great Western line, without first referring it to the SRA.[98] Certainly, the eventual winner, National Express, was not immune from criticism on operating grounds, having a number of poor performing franchises in its roster (such as Central and WAGN). Indeed, in 2002, it had appealed to the SRA when it forecast losses (to March 2004) of £115 million on its Central and ScotRail businesses, and had received assistance of £56 million in a financial restructuring. On the other hand, its c2c business was performing almost as well as the Great Eastern.[99] The official SRA view was that the exclusion of FirstGroup from Greater Anglia was a classic case of 'incumbent inertia'. The company had been guilty of complacency during the shortlisting stage, and had provided inadequate documentation. The regulatory discipline imposed by the SRA was heralded as successful in persuading the bidder to raise its game in subsequent competitions.[100] Subsequently, FirstGroup was successful in the competition for ScotRail, this time at the expense of National Express, and was awarded the Thames franchise on a short-term basis pending conversion to the Greater Western franchise, a competition which it also won. Of course, it was more complicated than that. The exclusion of FirstGroup was certainly accompanied by some tension between the franchisee and the SRA. Moir Lockhead was an assertive chief executive, and his company had entered a broader strategic debate by advocating a measure of vertical integration, with the TOCs adding timetabling, signalling, and train regulation to their responsibilities. An initial paper in July 2001 suggesting that the Great Western and Anglia zones be used as trial areas was followed by a more considered paper promoting the idea of an integrated East Anglian franchise. This was sent to the DTLR at the time of Bowker's appointment in December.[101] The company's somewhat aggressive efforts to acquire Thames in 2002 was a further source of irritation, and Bowker was not overjoyed by the actions of its commercial director, Dean Finch, when he sent in an unsolicited proposal to combine Great Western and Thames and then tried to bounce the Authority by appealing to both the Department and the Prime Minister's Delivery Unit.[102] Later on, Lockhead talked to Bowker about

[98] Wolmar, *On the Wrong Line*, pp. 222–3; *Guardian*, 18 October 2002, p. 11; *Daily Telegraph*, 2 January 2003, p. 27. See also Jupe and Crompton, 'A Deficient Performance', 1049–50.

[99] Gary Backler (SRA), Memo. 27 February 2002, Byers–Bowker, 28 February 2002, SRA; SRA Board Minutes, 7 March 2002; PPM performance statistics for 2001/2 and 2002/3, in SRA, *Annual Report 2002/3*, p. 39.

[100] Interviews with Bowker and Newton (2006), and Moir Lockhead, 31 July 2007.

[101] FirstGroup, 'The Case for Vertical Integration', 11 July 2001, Morton's papers, SRA; FirstGroup, 'The Future of the Railways: Proposal for Operational Integration Through a First Great Anglian Pilot', December 2001, enclosed in Moir Lockhead (Chief Executive, FirstGroup)–Byers, 5 December 2001, DTLR file R73/1/26 Pt. 11, and also in Lockhead–Bowker, same date, SRA. National Express and Stagecoach were also advocates of vertical integration. See Richard Brown (National Express), 'Power to the Operators', in Transport 2000, *The Railways: Where Do We Go from Here?* (2001), and Stagecoach, 'A Platform for Change: the Potential for Vertical Integration on Britain's Railways', November 2001, cit. in HC Transport Local Government and Regions Committee Report on *Passenger Rail Franchising*, January 2002, para. 56.

[102] Dean Finch (Commercial Director, FirstGroup)–Bowker, 6 August 2002, and Bowker's annotation, Lockhead–Bowker, 12 and 13 August 2002; Graham Cross (SRA)–Bowker, 14 August 2002, SRA.

a more ambitious plan to acquire a substantial slice of the rail and bus market under the name 'Project Blue'.[103]

FirstGroup did not take the Greater Anglia decision lying down. It complained that GB Railways enjoyed an advantage in the competition due to its management contract with the SRA. Then it secured a takeover of the company, which immediately raised questions of information asymmetry, and the other bidders responded by demanding a level playing field and 'Chinese walls'. Finally, it demanded a judicial review, which was only withdrawn once it became clear that the company would be successful elsewhere.[104] On the other hand, First-Group was scarcely treated diplomatically by Bowker, a regular traveller on the Great Western line, who complained to the company whenever he experienced a bad journey.[105] Personal relations aside, the Greater Anglia decision revealed more about the strategic management of the franchise map by the SRA than anything else. The shortlisting of Arriva, GB Railways, and National Express appeared to present the last with a clear chance for the expanded franchise, since its two rivals were in financial difficulty. There was also a strategic advantage in choosing National Express. While it is difficult to find hard evidence, by 2003, FirstGroup was clearly a frontrunner for the Thames, and ultimately the Greater Western franchise, and it was unlikely that either the SRA or the competition authorities would have been happy with a single owner of the two major expanded franchises operating out of London. It therefore made sense to award one to FirstGroup, and one to National Express.[106] The judging of the competition was carried out with due diligence, assisted by KPMG. Operational integrity, future passenger benefits, and the bidders' intentions in relation to revenue generation, cost control, and the financial premia offered, were all carefully assessed. In fact, the competition was much closer than expected, and it is not at all clear that the data supported the SRA's conclusion, conveyed to the Secretary of State, that National Express was a 'clear winner'. But the decision itself came as no surprise.[107] Similar considerations had operated when

[103] The proposal, which involved the acquisition of National Express by FirstGroup, was not progressed. See 'Strictly Private and Confidential Notes of Meeting between Moir Lockhead and Richard Bowker on 27th May 2003', SRA.
[104] Slaughter & May–SRA, 11 April 2003; SRA Executive Prayers Minutes, 25 June and 9 July 2003, SRA file 57/01/12A Pt. 1; Bob Davies (Chief Executive, Arriva Trains)–Bowker, 17 July 2003, P.M. White (Group CE, National Express)–Bowker, 23 July 2003, SRA.
[105] Bowker–Finch and John Armitt (Chief Executive, Railtrack), 19 February 2002, Bowker–Lockhead, 19 August 2002 and 25 February 2003, SRA.
[106] On SRA–FirstGroup negotiations in relation to Thames and Greater Western see Newton–Bowker, 22 January 2002, Finch–Stuart Baker (SRA), 26 February 2002, Lockhead–Bowker, 12 and 13 August 2002, Cross–Bowker and Newton, 1 October 2002, SRA. Ironically, the fact that National Express operated a substantial bus fleet in addition to rail services in East Anglia led to a reference to the Competition Commission: *Financial Times*, 28 May 2004, p. 3.
[107] Martin Deutz (KPMG)–Peter Wilkinson (SRA), 12 November 2003; Graeme Hampshire, Memo. 14 November 2003, SRA; Bowker–Darling, 24 November 2003, DfT file R73/1/49 Pt. 3. The competition for Northern was also close, though the SRA announced another 'clear winner': John Gilbert (SRA), Memo. to SRA Executive, 12 February 2004, SRA file 57/01/02 Pt. 50, Bowker–Darling, 28 April 2004, SRA.

the SRA strove to decide between Virgin and GNER for an upgraded ECML (above, pp. 89–90). Decision-making was more a case of the 'visible hand' of network planning than the 'invisible hand' of the market, more a case of strategic planning by the Authority than the disinterested verdict of a group of professional assessors.[108]

What of the key issues of cost control and subsidy reduction in the management of franchises? Another plank of the Mark I franchises, as we have seen, was to build in subsidy reductions over time, to reflect the efficiency gains that private enterprise would doubtless capture. But these had proved to be largely illusory, owing to the efficiency gains made by British Rail in the last 10 years of nationalization, the optimism of initial bidders, and the cost pressures produced by increased traffic. Bowker's public approach was to encourage TOCs to secure operational cost savings, and to deal with those which had got into difficulty. The problematic regional franchises were re-let or reorganized, but what was the outcome in relation to the total subsidy paid? Earlier government expectations of future payments proved to be substantially wide of the mark, affected by interventions with ailing franchises and the introduction of 'Clause 18.1' adjustments, whereby TOCs were to be 'held harmless' of changes occasioned by the access charge review mechanism (a 5% increase in charges raised franchise payments by c.£130 million in 2003/4).[109] The total SRA payment to the TOCs, including incentive payments, amounted to £1.4 billion in 1997/8, then fell to £847 million in 2000/1 and £877 million in 2001/2. The pay-out then rose substantially from £907 million in 2002/3 to £1.48 million in 2003/4 (Table 5.6). The SRA portion of the total SRA/PTE bill was almost halved in 2004/5, but the figure of £778 million was the product of adjustments made prior to, and as a result of, the Regulator's access charges review in 2003 (access charges rebates, 're-profiling' (deferral) of Network Rail's income met by additional borrowing, see below, pp. 193–200). With the payments made by the local authority PTEs, the total direct assistance received by the TOCs amounted to £1.9 billion in 2003/4 and £1.2 billion in 2004/5 (Table 5.6). But on top of these sums there was the additional support made directly to Network Rail in the form of network grants, amounting to £1.4 billion in 2003/4 and £2.0 billion in 2004/5, most of it to support the passenger railway. Pressures on the SRA budget were also alleviated by deferring the income due to Network Rail, worth £1.5 billion in 2004/5 alone. When these sums are taken into account, the support given to the railways' passenger operations amounted to a very substantial £3.3 billion in 2003/4 and

---

[108] On 'incumbent inertia' and the 'visible hand' see Alfred D. Chandler, Jr., *The Visible Hand: The Managerial Revolution in American Business* (Cambridge, MA, 1977), and Marvin B. Lieberman and David B. Montgomery, 'First-Mover Advantages', *Strategic Management Journal*, 9 (1988), 41–58.

[109] The TOCs were also protected from the costs of industrial action. Under this heading, the SRA made payments of £15.65m. in 2003 and £7.63m. in 2004: *Parl. Deb. (Commons)*, 6th ser. (Session 2005–6), Vol. 439, Derek Twigg (PUSS, DfT), written answer to John McDonnell (Hayes & Harlington), 24 November 2005, c. 2226w.

Table 5.6 Net franchise payments, 1997/8–2004/5 (£m., current prices)

Year	Net franchise payments SRA only	SRA + PTEs	Central + local government support (published figures)
1997/8	1,425.1	1,836.2	1,804
1998/9	1,195.8	1,582.5	1,533
1999/0	1,032.6	1,392.0	1,343
2000/1	847.2	1,190.1	1,130
2001/2	877.1	1,300.7	1,037
2002/3	907.5	1,336.0	1,239
2003/4	1,484.8	1,884.8	1,773
2004/5	778.2	1,163.7	1,267

Source: SRA, *Annual Reports*; ORR, *National Rail Trends Yearbook 2005/6*, p. 70.

£3.2 billion (£4.7 billion if we include income deferral) in 2004/5.[110] The cause for anxiety was very evident.

Where did the franchising increases arise? The SRA did have to give more support to the ailing Northern, North Western, Central, and ScotRail franchises, providing a total net payment of £371 million in 2002/3 and £439 million in 2003/4, on top of PTE payments of £355 and £376 million (Table 5.7). However, the amounts paid by the SRA were only around 25 per cent higher than the forecasts made in 2000. More significant for the Authority's total budget was the increase in access charges; the additional support occasioned by the replacement of the Mark I slam-door trains; the unexpected level of assistance given to railways in Wales and the west of England; and the rescue operations required for some of the larger franchises where the outturn was well below earlier expectations, namely, Connex South Eastern, and the two Virgin franchises, Cross Country and West Coast. In 2000, the forecast franchise payment for Cardiff and Wales and West in 2003/4 was £57 million. In fact, their successors, Arriva Trains Wales, Wales & Borders, and Wessex, while adding services to the portfolio, consumed £199 million in that year (Table 5.7). Support to the South Eastern franchise in 2003/4, the year of the SRA takeover, amounted to £118 million, compared with a forecast of £30 million in 2000. Here, the operator, Connex, owned by the French conglomerate Vivendi, had revealed in 2002 that it expected a deficit of some £700 million (later revealed to be £820 million) to the expiry of the contract in 2011. It blamed rising costs, and the fact that, in common with other operators in the London commuter market, its pricing was constrained because a high proportion of its fares were subject to

[110] Data taken from SRA, *Annual Report 2005*, pp. 84, 149 (my thanks to Peter Hawthorne (SRA) for guiding me through these accounts). Published figures of total government support to the rail industry (including freight, CTRL, Crossrail, etc.) are £3.7bn in 2003/4 and £3.8bn in 2004/5: ORR, *National Rail Trends Yearbook 2005–6*, p. 71.

Table 5.7 Net franchise payments to individual operators (plus PTE support), 2000/1–2004/5 (£m., current prices)

Franchise	2000/1	2001/2	2002/3	2003/4	2004/5
Northern	109.8	115.2	112.2	122.2	79.7[a]
PTE	59.8	86.4	89.9	107.6	116.2[a]
North Western	78.6	86.6	86.9	88.9	44.7
PTE	68.1	86.7	92.6	96.6	58.6
ScotRail	110.2	81.0	102.2	124.0	72.0[a]
PTE	138.4	133.3	127.9	127.6	146.6[a]
Central	102.9	78.5	70.1	103.5	112.1
PTE	28.7	45.5	44.6	44.7	64.2
Cardiff/Wales & West	68.9	62.4	—	—	—
Wales & Borders/Wessex	—	61.3	141.2	199.0[a]	149.0
South Eastern	43.3	39.6	37.2	117.6[a]	67.6
Virgin West Coast	57.7	190.9	188.8	328.6	113.0
Virgin Cross Country	79.9	118.5	206.3	241.6	118.5
All SRA	847.2	877.1	907.5	1,484.8	778.2

Source: SRA.

[a] New and old franchise data combined.

RPI − 1 per cent regulation. In fact, optimistic forecasts of the potential for cost reduction and therefore the subsidy required lay at the root of the problem. In December, the SRA had agreed to provide additional assistance of £58.6 million for 2003 in return for a reduction of the franchise length to 2006, opening the way to the establishment of an integrated Kent franchise.[111] Within six months, however, the Authority decided to terminate the contract and take the franchise in-house as the 'operator of last resort'. The juxtaposition of a bailout and a termination disconcerted commentators, including the House of Commons Transport Committee, who raised questions about the SRA's command of events.[112] But the fact was that the assistance offered in December 2002 had been made conditional on Connex showing much more transparency about its financial reporting and control systems. PricewaterhouseCoopers, asked by the SRA to report on the situation, found in May 2003 that barely half of the 29 measures required had been put in place. This provided the justification for a change of operator, but it was Connex's further demands for assistance of up to £183 million that provoked the Authority into taking this unprecedented step. Notice of termination was given in June, and public sector operation as South East Trains began in November. The change was hailed by some as a

[111] Bowker–Darling, 21 November 2002, Iryna Terlecky (SRA)–Coulshed, 5 December 2002, DfT file R73/1/45 Pts. 2 and 3. The payment of £58.6m. was in addition to £24m. paid in June 2002 to facilitate the replacement of Mark I vehicles.

[112] HC Transport Committee, Report on *The Future of the Railway*, P.P. 2003–4, HC145-I, April 2004, para. 122.

'renationalization', though the SRA's intention was to operate the franchise on a caretaker basis until it was re-let. And no immediate financial gains were anticipated, which produced more pressure on the SRA's budget for 2003/4.[113] The transfer produced significant additional costs for the SRA, including £2.6 million for consultancy, which were itemized in detail by a subsequent NAO enquiry.[114] However, it also emerged that the return of public sector control was accompanied by financial and operating improvements. The SRA reported a gain of 4.1 percentage points in punctuality, an underspend against subsidy received, and a small operating profit, though it must be said that improvements in the performance of Network Rail was a substantial contributor to the performance of the train operator.[115]

Undoubtedly, the biggest disappointments of all were West Coast and Cross Country, operated by Virgin Rail Group (Virgin 51%, Stagecoach 49%). In July 2002, a 'letter agreement' provided 'holding' support to the company in the form of short-term emergency finance, at a time of considerable uncertainty. Indeed, the agreement stated that it had been 'negotiated in an environment marked by an absence of clarity as to the financial prospects of Virgin West Coast and Virgin Cross Country'. It is clear that there were broader political considerations, not least the very real possibility that unless a deal were reached Virgin might frustrate progress towards securing Railtrack's exit from administration.[116] An equally pressing concern was the faltering position of Stagecoach, which urgently required something positive to include in its annual results.[117] The train operator was expected to constrain operating costs and produce agreed annual budgets, pending the satisfactory renegotiation of the franchises.[118] In the two years to March 2004, overall support to the 'profitable' West Coast amounted to £517 million, and to Cross Country £448 million, a total of £965 million (Table 5.7). And yet in 2000 the expectation was that the two franchises would cost only £37.6 million in that period, with the SRA actually receiving a premium (net

[113] Mike Ainsworth (DfT)–Darling, 26 March and 6 June 2003, PricewaterhouseCoopers, draft report, 1 May 2003, Ainsworth–Rowlands, 9 June 2003, DfT file R73/1/45 Pt. 5; SRA/KPMG Discussion Team, paper, 13 May 2003 [with audit trail], and Bowker–Darling, 16 June 2003, SRA; Elson–Blair, 20 June 2003, Prime Minister's Rail papers, Pt. 11. A subsequent enquiry by the NAO asserted that PwC had found Connex non-compliant with only 5 of the 29 clauses: NAO, *The South Eastern Passenger Rail Franchise*, December 2005, p. 20, P.P. 2005–6, HC457. On Connex's complaints about the allegations made at the time of termination, see Olivier Brousse (CE, Connex Transport UK)–Bowker, 30 July 2003, SRA, and Brousse (CE, Connex North America)–Darling, 26 April 2004, DfT file R73/1/45 Pt. 6.

[114] NAO, *South Eastern Passenger Rail Franchise*.

[115] SRA, *Annual Report 2005*, p. 6. The PPM improved from 80.1 in 2003/4 to 84.2 in 2004/5. A more detailed evaluation of performance trends is given in NAO, *South Eastern Passenger Rail Franchise*. And see also *Parl. Deb. (Commons)*, 6th ser. (Session 2003–4), Vol. 426, 16 November 2004, Darling, oral answer to Clive Efford (MP for Eltham), c. 1145.

[116] SRA Board Minutes, 18 July 2002.

[117] Ibid. 4 July 2002; SRA Executive Prayers Minutes, 22 July 2002, SRA file 57/01/12 Pt. 1. On Stagecoach's problems, the product of its investment in the US bus industry, see *Independent*, 23 July 2002, pp. 15, 17.

[118] KPMG, SRA letter agreement with Virgin Rail Group, 19 July 2002, p. 7, SRA.

payment) of £13 million in 2003/4.[119] It is difficult to criticize the SRA for presiding over this debacle, the origins of which lay in the over-optimism of the initial franchise bids, the nature of Virgin's PUG2 contract with Railtrack for the WCML upgrade, and late delivery of the new Pendolino trains (the subject of litigation with the manufacturers, Alstom).[120] Ironically, it was Bowker who had played a leading role in negotiating the Virgin deal with Railtrack. But while the company may have congratulated itself on its commercial acumen, with hindsight it was probably a mistake to think that advantage would come from squeezing Railtrack's 'pulpless orange'.[121] The period 2002–4 saw further problems, notably difficulties experienced with a new timetable for Cross Country introduced under the name 'Operation Princess', and there were long and often rather unrewarding negotiations between the SRA and Virgin on the latter's budgets, the principles to apply in any refranchising deal, and, above all, the need to demonstrate value for money. The work was complex, with SRA staff supplemented by the consultants Booz Allen Hamilton and Ernst & Young. It had yet to bear fruit when the SRA was effectively wound up.[122] But there is no doubt at all that the impact on its own budgets for 2002/3 and 2003/4 was substantial.

Was this rise in franchise payments a matter of incompetent management by the SRA, inadequate cost control, or revenue generation by the TOCs, or merely the product of the inexorable 'pass-through' of infrastructure costs and penalties, precipitated by the collapse of Railtrack? One may find all these elements present, of course, but it is a tougher task to apportion responsibility with any precision. The SRA presided over larger pay-outs in many instances, but this was not just a matter of bailing out the foolhardy; higher than expected payments were a feature of nearly all franchises in 2002/3 and 2003/4. The SRA certainly wished to avoid hiatus or breakdown within the group of operators. When National Express had asked for assistance in 2002, the 'do nothing' option carried risks that the franchisee would introduce draconian cuts in services, or even 'hand back the keys' on all nine of its franchises. Clearly, a settlement was to be preferred.[123] The same thing applied when the SRA decided to give more support to the Anglia

---

[119] SRA, *Annual Report 1999/2000*, pp. 44–5, *2005*, pp. 148–9. Higher payments were also made to South West Trains and South Central in 2003/4, where the net payments were £92m and £78m, respectively.

[120] Jessica Walters (SRA), Memo. to SRA Executive Committee, 27 May 2004, SRA file 57/01/02 Pt. 53.

[121] On the use of this term in railway history, see Gerald Crompton, ' "Squeezing the Pulpless Orange": Labour and Capital on the Railways in the Interwar Years', *Business History*, 31(2) (1989), 66–83.

[122] SRA Board Minutes, 15 January 2004, Adrian Foster (Booz Allen Hamilton), Memo. on 'Project Euston', 10 February 2004, Jonathan Moseley (SRA), Memo. to SRA Executive, 21 July 2004, SRA file 57/01/02 Pts. 50 and 54, SRA Executive Minutes, 8 and 22 July 2004, 57/01/01 Pt. 4; Shaw, Memo. to SRA Executive Committee, 8 November 2004, 57/01/12 Pt. 10; Iryna Terlecky and Doug Sutherland, Memos. to SRA Executive Committee, 4 May 2005, 57/01/02 Pt. 58.

[123] SRA Board Minutes, 7 February 2002; Peter Austin, Memo. to SRA Executive Committee, 18 February 2002, SRA file 57/01/02 Pt. 30; Backler, Memo. to SRA Board, 27 February 2002, cit.

franchise prior to the establishment of Greater Anglia.[124] And when Darling announced a comprehensive review of the railway industry at the beginning of 2004 and made it clear that only short-term rollovers would be allowed during the review period, the SRA pressed the case for two-year extensions for Wessex, Great Northern, and Thameslink. Although the Treasury and DfT were far from happy with the idea, they accepted the argument that disruption should be avoided.[125] Similar considerations arose with the letting of the Northern contract later in the year. Here the issue was complicated by the fact that the new franchise was to comprise a group of services from parts of the former First NorthWestern and Arriva Trains Northern, making hard commercial information more difficult to gather.[126] In addition, there was the involvement of five PTEs. Despite the uncertainties, the bidding competition between Serco/NedRail and FirstGroup had been a close one. The SRA's preference for Serco/NedRail was communicated to Darling in March 2004, but neither the Treasury nor the Department were inclined to rush the matter. No reply was forthcoming until the end of June, by which time information emerging after the separation of TransPennine from North Western and Northern, and anxieties about the post-Review environment had led the bidder to negotiate an additional subsidy of about £30 million NPV. Further prevarication had the effect of adding further to costs since the arrangements with the incumbent franchisees had to be extended beyond the October expiry date.[127]

What may be said of operators' costs? The TOCs' profit and loss data indicate that while income rose by 26 per cent from 2000/1 to 2004/5, costs rose by 22 per cent, the cost pressures being particularly evident in MML, Silverlink, Chiltern, and the Virgin franchises, where income growth was also higher than average (Table 5.8). The subsidy paid per passenger-kilometre rose sharply in 2003/4, to approach the level paid in 1997/8, at the beginning of the process, and for all the travails of the lossmakers the sector's pre-tax profits rose sharply from the 2000/1 low; affected by the bailout of the Virgin franchises, and the deals done with others, that is, National Express, Arriva, and FirstGroup (particularly re North Western), profits were almost four times higher at £345 million or £13.8 million per franchise, and double the profitability in 1998/9 (Table 5.8 and cf. 3.3, above). It was difficult for the SRA to have a serious impact on cost levels, however hard it may have tried. The outcome was that

[124] Byers–Bowker, 16 March 2002, SRA.

[125] Ian McBrayne (DfT)–Killen and Vivien Bodnar (DfT), 28 January 2004, SRA Press Notice, 13 February 2004, Paul Boateng (Chief Secretary, Treasury)–Darling and Darling–Bowker, both 12 February 2004, DfT file R73/1/34 Pt. 2.

[126] Interview with Valk (2007).

[127] Northern Rail Replacement Franchise Information Supplement, 12 March 2004, SRA; Ben Still (DfT)–Killen et al., 27 April 2004, DfT file R73/1/7 Pt. 3; John Gilbert, Memo. to SRA Executive Committee, 27 May 2004, SRA file 57/01/02 Pt. 53; Bowker–Darling, 16 March 2004, Darling–Bowker, 29 June 2004, Bowker–Darling, 27 August 2004, Bowker–Killen, 2 September 2004, SRA; Shaw, Memo. to SRA Executive Committee, 4 September 2004, SRA file 57/01/12 Pt. 10; Bob Chauhan and David Steele (Treasury), Memo. 7 June 2004, Treasury file (redacted), ref. 040604.

Table 5.8 TOCs' operating costs, pre-tax profits, and government subsidy received per passenger-km, 2000/1–2004/5

	2000/1	2001/2	2002/3	2003/4	2004/5	% change 2000/1–2003/4	% change 2000/1–2004/5
Income (£m.):	4,920.0	5,163.7	5,556.3	6,086.4	6,205.9		
average	196.8	206.5	222.2	234.1	248.2	+19.0	+26.1
Operating costs (£m.):	4,792.5	4,977.3	5,271.7	5,768.0	5,868.5		
average	191.7	199.1	210.9	221.8	234.7	+15.7	+22.4
Pre-tax profits (£m.):	92.5	183.1	293.4	412.6[a]	345.4		
average	3.7	7.3	11.7	15.9[a]	13.8	+329.7	+273.0
Subsidy (£m.)[b]:	1,347.8	1,288.6	1,320.8	2,050.0	1,005.4		
per pass-km (pence)	3.4	3.3	3.3	5.0	2.4	+47.0	−29.4
Individual franchises							
Income (£m.):							
Cross Country (Virgin)	227.6	278.5	383.2	463.8	375.5	+103.8	+65.0
West Coast (Virgin)	392.6	567.0	582.8	664.0	518.4	+69.1	+32.0
MML	113.8	121.1	133.9	150.5	178.0	+32.2	+56.4
Chiltern	63.1	71.5	80.9	91.6	98.4	+45.2	+55.9
South Eastern (Connex, SRA)[c]	368.4	366.5	394.1	441.1	443.2	+19.7	+20.3
c2c	97.9	91.8	94.7	99.4	94.6	+1.5	−3.4
Operating costs (£m.):							
Cross Country	260.8	312.7	409.6	428.6	379.9	+64.3	+45.7
West Coast	367.0	504.1	524.5	635.2	487.5	+73.1	+32.8
Chiltern	63.9	65.4	74.1	84.1	90.0	+31.6	+40.8
MML	103.8	111.3	120.5	131.7	183.1	+26.9	+76.4
South Eastern[c]	362.2	370.2	406.5	447.0	429.0	+23.4	+18.4
Silverlink	104.9	131.1	152.4	163.0	153.0	+55.4	+45.9

(cont.)

155

Table 5.8 (continued)

	2000/1	2001/2	2002/3	2003/4	2004/5	% change 2000/1–2003/4	% change 2000/1–2004/5
Thames/GW Link	105.9	93.7	105.3	109.1	108.5	+3.0	+2.4
ScotRail	354.2	336.5	353.1	387.6	363.0	+9.4	+2.5
Pre-tax profits (£m.):							
Cross Country	−35.2	−37.9	−31.1	126.4[a]	−4.2	–	+88.1
West Coast	26.1	64.9	58.0	28.8	31.5	+10.3	+20.8
South Central[d]	8.8	−0.1	17.8	29.1	23.8	+230.7	+172.0
Central Trains	−18.4	−14.1	−6.3	−6.7	12.8	–	–
Chiltern	−0.6	5.6	7.0	7.8	8.4	–	–
MML	10.6	10.3	13.8	20.0	−1.5	+88.7	–
c2c	10.8	−1.0	0.5	−0.2	−2.1	–	–
Subsidy per pass-km (pence):							
Gatwick Express	−6.0	−3.5	−2.7	−6.6	−8.1	+10.0	+35.0
GNER	0.2	−0.8	−0.7	−0.6	−1.6	–	–
Thameslink	−1.8	−2.6	−3.7	−3.0	−3.5	+66.7	+94.4
North Western	16.8	20.5	22.6	23.9	21.3	−42.3	−26.8
Island Line	33.7	36.9	39.3	46.8	48.2	−38.9	−43.0

[a] Includes exceptional item in 2003/4 of £95.61 (profits before exceptional item = £30.8m.), which also inflates the average profit.
[b] Merseyside data excluded in part of 2003/4 and all of 2004/5.
[c] Includes combined results for Connex SE and SE Trains (SRA) in 2003/4.
[d] Includes combined results for Connex SC and Govia in 2001/2.

Source: SRA.

Notes: Subsidy data include payments by PTEs and exclude incentive payments. For individual TOCs, a rise in subsidy, or a fall in 'negative subsidy', that is, premium, is regarded as a negative result. A reduction in subsidy, or an increase in negative subsidy, is regarded as positive.

operating costs, and particularly labour costs, tended to rise with traffic levels and were difficult to cut without producing a deterioration in performance. A study by KPMG in July 2003, undertaken before the subsidy horrors of 2003/4, underlined the problem. It found that in 2002/3 TOC losses before subsidy were £579 million higher than forecast in the original franchise bids, with much of the underperformance caused by higher than expected operating costs. Output had risen by 15 per cent, but with productivity, here defined as TOC-controllable costs per train-kilometre, the initial gains had been more than cancelled out over the period 1999/2000 to 2002/3. As we have noted earlier, staff numbers proved impossible to cut, while labour costs were rising with traffic volumes. By 2002/3, the TOCs were employing 45,700, 14,000 (44%) more than expected, and an increase of 15 per cent on staffing in 1997/8. Costs per head had risen from £21,900 in 1997/8 to £26,700 in 2002/3.[128] By 2003/4, it was evident to the SRA that it was unrealistic to expect too much from the TOCs in relation to cost reduction.[129] A study by the economist Andrew Smith, though limited to the period to 2001/2, has underlined the importance of TOC operating costs, arguing that they accounted for 38 per cent of the post-Hatfield rise in railway costs to 2001/2. He blames the pressures exerted by a more intrusive and risk-averse safety culture, but an equally appealing hypothesis is that there were general cost pressures produced by catering for a 9 per cent increase in demand (2000/1–2004/5, Table 5.9) within a private sector environment, on a relatively unchanged network and with trains that (whether old or new) did not become cheaper to operate.[130] A more sophisticated evaluation of the various factors affecting TOC costs, in a recent paper by Nash and Smith, provides some support for this view. The authors consider the significance of aggressive bidding in the initial stage, together with the impact of management contracts with the SRA, health and safety requirements, service quality pressures, and changes in the responsibility for train maintenance, during a period of considerable turbulence. They suggest that the renegotiation activities and cost-plus contracts of the SRA may have weakened incentives for cost control in the affected TOCs, but concede that it may have been those TOCs which were failing to contain costs which got into trouble. Exogenous factors, such as rising fuel prices, tighter health and safety requirements, disability discrimination legislation, and general demands for higher quality, should not be discounted.[131]

---

[128] Thomas, 'Overview of TOC Financial Performance', July 2003, cit.; Interview with Richard Brown, 26 October 2007. Cf. also the analysis of TOC costs in KPMG, 'Analysis of historic TOC financial performance', 2002, and Chris Nash and Andrew Smith, 'Passenger Rail Franchising—British Experience', paper for ECMT workshop, Paris, 12 January 2006, subsequently published in ECMT, *Competitive Tendering of Rail Services* (Paris, 2007), p. 21.

[129] Interview with Richard Davies (2006), and see also SRA, 'Why are Franchise Payments Projected to Rise?', 25 April 2003, SRA.

[130] Smith, 'Are Britain's Railways Costing Too Much?', 2006, cit. 37–8.

[131] Nash and Smith, 'Passenger Rail Franchising—British Experience', pp. 7–34.

Table 5.9 Rail performance, 2000/1–2006/7: traffic, passenger quality, and safety indicators

Year	Traffic		Passenger performance: PPM %	Passenger		Total passenger delay minutes (million)	Responsibility for delay: Railtrack's share (%)—passenger only	Accidents	
	Passenger national rail (bn km)	Freight (bn net tonne-km excl. infrastructure)		Complaints to rail users' committees (no.)	Complaints to TOCs (no.) per 100,000 journeys			Passengers killed in train incidents (national rail) (no.)	Signif. train incidents national rail (no. per million train-km)
1997/8	34.7	16.9	89.7	14,735	n.a.	12.7	53	7	0.12
2000/1	38.2	18.1	79.1	14,129	131	23.8	60	10	0.14
2001/2	39.1	19.4	78.0	14,628	110	22.4	50	0	0.11
2002/3	39.7	18.5	79.2	11,192	128	21.9	56	6	0.09
2003/4	40.9	18.9	81.2	7,363	79	20.6	55	0	0.08
2004/5	41.8	20.4	83.6	9,274	71	18.0	51	5[a]	0.09[a]
2005/6	43.2	21.7	86.4	—	74	15.6	53	0[a]	0.04[a]
2006/7	46.1	22.6	88.1	—	69	14.6	57	0[a]	0.06[a]

[a] Calendar year 2004, 2005, 2006.

Source: SRA, National Rail Trends Yearbook 2004–5, pp. 3, 15, 20, 28; ORR, National Rail Trends Yearbook 2006/7, pp. 8, 23, 28, 38; RPC, Annual Report 2004/5, p. 50; HSE, Railway Safety 2001/2–2003/4, ORR, Railway Safety 2005–7 and information from DfT, ATOC, RSSB, and Network Rail.

As support to the passenger railway increased again, and the media made much of the more eye-catching bailouts, improved train performance and quality remained a firm government objective. In June 2001, Tony Blair established a Delivery Unit at Number Ten, headed by Professor Michael Barber, from the University of London's Institute of Education. For the railway industry, where the Prime Minister was anxious to achieve a 'real customer push',[132] the aim was to secure first, a year-on-year improvement in performance, then (from 2003) a specific target of 85 per cent for the reliability/punctuality (PPM) measure by September 2005.[133] However, in spite of this additional tier of monitoring added to the SRA's and Department's oversight of performance, improvement in rail travel was hard to achieve in the years after Hatfield. Matters were scarcely helped by the delay in setting up Network Rail. Then there was the impact of the Potters Bar accident, which not only produced a dip in operating perform-ance (though nothing like that which followed Hatfield) but also challenged the competence and managerial effectiveness of infrastructure maintenance and renewal.[134] The Prime Minister was provided with a detailed analysis of punctu-ality and reliability on a weekly basis, then from May 2002 on a monthly basis, and the Department produced its own delivery plan.[135] But when the SRA held a special seminar to 'drive performance improvement' on 27 May, there was some disappointment in Whitehall at the slow pace of change.[136] Government disappointment intensified six months later when Bowker told Lambirth at the DfT that notwithstanding a raft of initiatives designed to analyse and correct operating weaknesses,[137] the PPM would remain 'flat' at around 80 per cent over the next three years. Blair expressed surprise at this news, and was told that a 'stretched' SRA was unable to give performance the necessary priority.[138] By December, Barber was expressing doubts about whether the SRA was an appropriate body to drive performance improvement, and Blair, having enthusi-astically endorsed Bowker's appointment, was now showing some irritation with the performance of his rail chief.[139] Performance continued to run in line with Bowker's pessimistic trajectory in 2003–4. In May 2003, a 'vigorous discussion'

[132] Blair, annotation on Hackland–Blair, 6 July 2001, Prime Minister's Rail papers, Pt. 1; *Independent*, 23 June 2001, p. 10.

[133] That is, a moving annual average [MAA] score of 85% at end Q2/2005/6: Michael Barber (Head of PMDU)–Blair, 6 February 2002, Cabinet Office file R14/6 Pt. 3; Barber–Blair, 11 July and 3 October 2003, ibid. Pt. 11. The target was subsequently extended to March 2006 [MAA at end Q4/2005/6].

[134] Elson–Blair, 21 June 2002, ibid. Pt. 7.

[135] John Larkinson (SRA)–Bowker, 30 April 2002, Lambirth–Bowker, 3 May and 17 September 2002, SRA, and see also DfT file R100/4/2 Pt. 1.

[136] Bisson–Rachel Evans (DTLR), 29 April 2002, Elson–Blair, 24 May and 18 July 2002, ibid. Pts. 6 and 7.

[137] Including RADAR [a report commissioned from AEA Technology analysing the reasons for deteri-orating train performance, September 2002], attention to right time train departures, adoption of the NRPP [National Rail Performance Plan], rolling stock reliability, establishing a 'virtual general manager' to reduce delays when incidents occurred.

[138] Bowker–Lambirth, 21 November 2002, copy enclosed in Elson–Blair, 29 November 2002, with Blair's annotations, ibid. Pt. 8.

[139] Michael Barber (Head of PMDU)–Blair, 20 December 2002 and 24 January 2003, ibid. Pts. 8 and 9.

between Barber and Bowker was followed by a joint review of ways to improve the SRA's performance planning work. A new performance management system to guide SRA monitoring of the TOCs was established in November, and the worst performers were visited by Kim Howells, the Transport Minister, and the SRA. This was followed in March 2004 with a priority review of rail performance by the Department, the SRA, and the Delivery Unit.[140] There were no 'quick wins' with performance, however, and it was not until the summer of 2004 that clearer signs of sustained improvement emerged. But by this time the announcement had been made that the SRA was to be abolished, and Bowker had tendered his resignation.[141] The published annual figures indicate the extent of the gulf between expectation and reality. In 1997/8, the measure was 89.7 per cent. After falling to 79.1 in 2000/1 and 78.0 in the following year, it improved slowly, but at 83.6 in 2004/5 it remained below Government expectations (Table 5.9).

Some measures gave comfort to the Government. Passenger traffic, at 41.8 billion km, was 20 per cent higher than in 1997/8, and freight traffic, at 20.4 billion tonne-km, had risen by 21 per cent (Table 5.9). After the immediate post-Hatfield difficulties, passenger complaints were falling in volume, and overcrowding, though scarcely measured with precision, appeared to have fallen and then stabilized, with the PIXC measure below the SRA's target for the London commuting peaks of 3 per cent in the period 2002–5.[142] The safety record, measured either in passenger fatalities or in train accidents per million train-km, remained good (Table 5.9). But, as we have observed, it was the PPM which remained stubbornly below past achievements. The less publicized data on delay minutes, and on incentive payments paid by the TOCs to the SRA, underline the sluggishness of the industry's recovery from Hatfield. The total number of delay minutes increased from 14.0 million in 1999/2000 to 23.8 million in 2000/1, but still amounted to 21.9 million in 2002/3 and 20.6 million in 2003/4. It was not until after 2004/5 that something approaching pre-Hatfield standards obtained (Table 5.9 and 3.1).[143] Incentive payments made to the SRA, amounting to £3.3 million in 1999/2000, rose sharply to £92.5 million in 2000/1, and remained high until the performance benchmarks were modified by the Regulator in 2003/4.[144] It was also evident that the financial pressure

---

[140] Barber–Bowker, 18 June 2003, SRA; Barber–Blair, 14 February-28 November 2003, 9 January 2004; DfT, SRA and PMDU, Final report of Joint Rail Priority Review, 25 March 2004, Elson–Blair, 26 March 2004, Prime Minster's Rail papers, Pts. 9–12.

[141] Barber–Blair, 28 May and 22 July, 1 and 29 October 2004, 11 March and 8 April 2005, ibid. Pts. 11–14.

[142] 2002: 2.9%; 2003: 2.7%; 2004–5: 2.9%: SRA and ORR, *National Rail Trends Yearbooks*. On the limitations of the PIXC measure see Paula Crofts (SRA), Memo. to SRA Executive Committee, 27 May 2004, SRA file 57/01/02 Pt. 53. Crofts argued that operators were running more trains, but passengers were also tending to spread themselves across the morning and evening peaks.

[143] Delay minutes data, DfT.

[144] The net payments were 2000/1: £92.5m.; 2001/2: £82.5m.; 2002/3: £80.2m. SRA, *Annual Report 2000/1*, p. 113; 2002/3, p. 48.

felt by the SRA, Network Rail, and the TOCs would translate to pricing in the passenger market. From January 1999, regulated fares (chiefly savers, weekly season tickets, and most London commuter fares) had been subject to a restriction of RPI − 1 per cent. The SRA argued, in a report on fares in June 2003, that with the rising cost of rail operations the burden had fallen disproportionately upon the taxpayer. The latter now met 45 per cent of the industry's costs, in comparison with only 25 per cent in 1999. With passengers buying regulated tickets enjoying a 6.6 per cent reduction in the real price since privatization, the pain fell on those London-serving TOCs whose regulated fares made up a substantial and inflexible proportion of their fare structures, and especially those who were committed to declining subsidy levels or rising premia.[145] The SRA's draconian solution, involving an increase of RPI + 7 per cent in London and the South-east and the removal of regulation from savers, was resisted by the Government. But from January 2004 RPI − 1 per cent was replaced by RPI + 1 per cent for regulated fares for a three-year period; a more flexible form of fare regulation was introduced based on 'fare baskets' instead of individual fares; and the FIAP incentive scheme (which linked performance and fare increases in the London area and was found not to have worked well) was abandoned.[146] Some TOCs began to price more aggressively where they could, introducing 'yield management systems' and ticket quotas, and adjusting ticket availability and the margin between regulated and unregulated fares.[147] The published data on rail fares indicate that the overall effect was upward. Taking January 1997 as a baseline, by January 2003 real fares were 3.8 per cent higher, and by January 2006 the increase was a more substantial 10.5 per cent. For unregulated long-distance journeys, first and standard class fares in January 2006 were in real terms 52 and 28 per cent higher than they were nine years earlier (Table 5.10).[148] There were some very cheap deals for those able to book well ahead on 'Easyjet' principles, but pricing complexity increased, and on the whole the real cost of rail travel continued to rise. Walk-on fares also remained high in comparison with those in many other countries in Western Europe where rail services were more heavily subsidized.[149]

By the time of the Rail Review in early 2004, the advantages and disadvantages of passenger rail franchising had clearly emerged. The TOCs had arguably

---

[145] SRA, *Fares Review Conclusions 2003* (June 2003); Darling–Blair and Elson–Blair, 13 June 2003, Prime Minister's Rail papers, Pt. 11. See also Heather Whicker (DfT), e-mail–Andrew Price (DfT) et al., 19 January 2004, DfT file R101/1/3 Pt. 2.

[146] SRA Special Board Minutes, 9 April and 3 July 2003, SRA; Bowker–Darling, 14 May 2003, SRA; Elson–Blair, 9 May and 13 June 2003, Prime Minister's Rail papers, Pts. 10 and 11.

[147] HC Transport Committee Report on *How Fair are the Fares? Train Fares and Ticketing*, P.P. 2005–6, HC700-I, 19 May 2006, esp. paras. 77–86, 101–8; Barry Doe, *Rail*, 5–18 July 2006, p. 48, 13–26 September 2006, pp. 46–7.

[148] The HC Transport Committee provided similar findings for 1995–2005: *How Fair are the Fares?*, para. 45.

[149] Barry Doe, *Rail*, 1–14 February 2006, pp. 50–1; UBS study, cit. in *Financial Times*, 29 August 1997, p. 5; HC Transport Committee, *How Fair are the Fares?*, paras. 1–2, 28–31, 45–7, 57–9.

Table 5.10 Real fare increases, 1997–2006 (Jan. 1997 = 100)

Fare	Jan. 1997	Jan. 2001	Jan. 2003	Jan. 2006
London & South East regulated standard	100.0	95.5	92.5	96.9
Long distance first	100.0	125.7	137.4	151.9
Long distance unregulated standard	100.0	110.4	115.6	128.3
All tickets	100.0	103.1	103.8	110.5

Source: ORR, *National Rail Trends Yearbook 2005/6*, p. 64.

provided customer focus and new services, but it was doubtful whether an appropriate balance had been struck between the encouragement of competition and the maintenance of stability in the industry. Normal economic models for regulating business were difficult to apply to railway franchises, where operating losses were a characteristic. The competitions for refranchising were expensive to administer and, for the TOCs expensive to enter, a point put forcefully to the SRA whenever there was a failure to pre-qualify.[150] The SRA seems to have exhibited more pragmatism and opportunism in the process than its strategic plans had promised, and outsiders were disconcerted by decisions such as the extension of Stagecoach's tenancy of South West Trains, where vigorous lobbying groups of disgruntled commuters had been formed, and the successful contractor had the lowest PPM of all the London and South-east operators in the period 2001–3. Pragmatism was certainly evident here, with the SRA determined not to under-mine the commissioning of new trains to replace the slam-door stock, which it was obliged to fund, and therefore agreeing terms which some commentators felt were relatively generous.[151] There was a fine line to be trod between extracting value for the taxpayer through the premia paid by franchisees and ensuring that the business plans they offered up were realistic, deliverable, and stable. The record of the SRA under Bowker, then more briefly under his successor, David Quarmby, and the subsequent 'micromanagement' by the Department for Transport suggest that this line has yet to be identified with precision.[152] The SRA itself was also under more pressure. The House of Commons Transport Committee, chaired by the redoubtable Gwyneth Dunwoody, had undertaken its own assessment of the industry, and its report in April 2004 on *The Future of the Railway* was scathing in many of its attacks, though the mud was distributed

---

[150] Note Go-Ahead's reactions when failing to pre-qualify for the Greater Western and Thames-link/Great Northern competitions: Chris Moyes (Chief Executive, Go-Ahead Group)–David Quarmby (Chairman, SRA), 3 May, 13 June and 3 July 2005, SRA.

[151] Frew–Darling, 2 July 2003, Darling–Boateng, 4 July 2003, DfT file R73/2/1 Pt. 9; Wolmar, *On the Wrong Line*, p. 267. The internal documentation shows that the SRA's decision was supported by a due diligence report from KPMG and a comparator report from Booz Hamilton. Peter Albertini and Bob Wharton (SRA), Memo. to SRA Executive, 27 March 2003, SRA file 57/01/02 Pt. 42; SRA Board Minutes, 3 April 2003, SRA.

[152] Cf. *Private Eye*, 1 September 2006, p. 10.

pretty evenly at a structure that was regarded as 'not fit for purpose'. On franchising, the Committee produced a long list of criticisms, condemning the 'woefully poor' management of the South Eastern franchise, the large number of risk-free management contracts and the short-termism of franchise extensions. Finding little evidence of the leadership demanded of the SRA by its predecessor committee in 2002, it concluded that the SRA had been deficient in 'imagination, focus and performance'.[153] The attack may have been somewhat unfair in that the Authority could not be expected to shoulder all the burdens produced by operator over-confidence and failure, where transaction costs proved to be high, but there was clearly much for Darling's Rail Review to address in relation to the railway's main interface with the public.

5.5 The aspirations for freight

Passenger traffic took much of the limelight in railway policy-making, but freight traffic, if something of a Cinderella in revenue terms, had a potentially critical role to play in broader policies embracing congestion and the environment in a country which had been dominated by road transport for over half a century. The challenge was considerable. The railways' share of inland freight transport was disappointing, a mere 7 per cent in 2000/1.[154] Market research at the turn of the century confirmed that under the existing regulatory environment the future lay with those limited traffics where rail transport wielded a strong competitive advantage, namely, coal, aggregates, metals, and deep-sea container traffic. Inland flows of coal for use in power stations were increasing with the rise in imported coal from countries such as Poland and Australia, bringing a substantial business to ports such as Immingham and Hunterston. With an 85 per cent share of the market the major rail operator, EWS, commanded a business where the average length of haul was now much longer than the traditional 'merry-go-round' flows from, for example, the Yorkshire pits to nearby power stations.[155] There were also opportunities arising from the booming container market, particularly the large consignments shipped through ports such as Southampton, Felixstowe, Tilbury, and Thamesport. Although competitiveness was constrained when the length of haul was short and additional transhipment was required, the railways' share of this business grew from about 17 to 25 per cent in the 10 years after

---

[153] HC Transport Committee, *The Future of the Railway*, 2004, paras. 112–31; HC Transport Committee Report on *Passenger Rail Franchising*, para. 12.

[154] DfT, *TSGB 2005*, p. 64.

[155] Chris Rowley (SRA), Memo. to SRA Executive Committee, 9 December 2004, SRA file 57/01/02 Pt. 56; SRA Freight Team, Coal Operations Study—Conclusions (February 2005); Gourvish, *British Rail 1974–97*, pp. 63–5, 283–8; *Modern Railways*, October 2005, p. 48.

privatization.[156] Despite the efforts of a generation of British Rail ayatollahs, rail freight was stubbornly specialized in these bulk, train-load cargoes, and the more prominent (by volume) general merchandise or 'wagon-load' business was essentially a road-based one. Wagon-load traffic, more prominent in countries such as France, Germany, and Italy, had all but disappeared in the UK and the disappointing record of freight train traffic through the Channel Tunnel was a further testimony to this decline, notwithstanding the substantial public support given to EWS operations as a result of the Railway Usage Contract signed with Eurotunnel in 1987 and the privatization of Railfreight Distribution in 1997.[157] Further evidence of the railways' weakness in the market was provided by the fact that despite the dictum that freight should be a wholly commercial activity, the deepsea intermodal container business of the other main operator, Freightliner, was loss-making and dependent on regular grants: on privatization the company negotiated a block grant worth about £77 million over the five years to March 2001.[158] On top of this, all operators benefited from a situation where on mixed (passenger + freight) lines the track access charges for freight were based on variable cost, even though some traffics created more substantial track wear than these payments implied. In 2001, following the charges review of the previous year, the Regulator halved the access charges payable by freight, the shortfall being made up in direct SRA grants to Railtrack totalling about £500 million in the existing control period.[159] The aspirations of Government, and consequently the SRA, inserted in the 10 Year Plan, were to achieve an 80 per cent growth in freight traffic by 2010/11, that is, 32.6 billion tonne-km, and £4 billion had been earmarked for the sector, but the SRA's strategic planning documents warned that this objective would be difficult to attain after the disruptions caused by the Hatfield accident. The traffic carried in 2005/6, 22.1 billion tonne-km, was at its highest level since the oil crisis of 1973, but with only five years left in the planning cycle it was likely to fall way short of the objective for 2010.[160]

In May 2001, the freight department within the SRA produced a strategy document, which set out a framework to achieve a significant modal shift from

[156] DETR paper on 'Rail Freight in Great Britain: Background and Current Issues', March 2000, pp. 4–5, citing work carried out for Railtrack by McKinsey, DETR file R10/5/66; Iain Dewar (SRA), draft memo. On 'Freightliner Ltd.', September 2006. Deepsea container traffic increased by 61%, 1991–2001, and container traffic through Felixstowe and Southampton increased by 88% and 129%, respectively. SRA, 'Long Term Plans and Prospects. A SRA Legacy/Handover Document' (June 2005), pp. 75–6. Rail's market-share was c.30–34% at Southampton and c.21–23% at Felixstowe.

[157] Gourvish, Britain and the Channel Tunnel, pp. 297–305.

[158] Richard Threlfall (DETR)–Lord Macdonald, 19 June 2000, DETR file R10/5/66 Pt. 1; Freightliner Ltd P&L accounts [my thanks to Iain Dewar (SRA) for this information]. In December 1999, Freightliner sought a 15-year grant of £475m.; the Department/SSRA agreed a 'rollover' provision amounting to £46m. for the next 3 years.

[159] ORR, Review of Freight Charging Policy: Consultation documents (May–November 2000), Provisional Conclusions (April 2001), Final Conclusions (October 2001); SRA, 'Long Term Plans and Prospects', p. 63; Glaister, 'British Rail Privatisation', p. 29; Interview with Riley (2006).

[160] ORR, National Rail Trends Yearbook 2005–6; Gourvish, British Rail 1974–97, p. 473.

road to rail and aimed to raise the latter's market share from 7 to 10 per cent. The strategy rested on a four-pronged approach: investing in infrastructure; providing targeted grant assistance and revenue support; supporting innovation; and reducing constraints on rail access to markets, for example, at ports and terminals. The intention was to encourage operators to capture a larger share of the market for larger containers. Here the main planks of the policy were a substantial investment in infrastructure to enable the railways to handle the larger 9-foot 6-inch high containers, notably the upgrading of routes to the WCML from Felixstowe and Southampton; and the introduction of a more imaginative grant-aid scheme, called Company Neutral Revenue Support (CNRS), where assistance would not be company-specific, as earlier grants were, but would be aimed at sectors of the market which were 'economically marginal' but 'environmentally worthwhile'.[161]

What progress was made in the relatively short time that the SRA was in charge of freight strategy? In February 2001, the Authority assumed responsibility for the two grant schemes which had been operated by the Transport Department. Freight Facilities Grants (FFGs), capital expenditure grants for freight customers contemplating shifting from road to rail transport, were introduced in Section 8 of the Railways Act of 1974. They were designed to cover the capital costs of providing new rail infrastructure, that is, sidings, terminals, and loading and unloading equipment. Historically support was modest, about £4 million a year in the two decades to 1994, but their scope was extended by the Railways Act of 1993. Track Access Grants (TAGs) were provided for in the same Act in order to provide revenue support from 1995 for traffics which were vulnerable to a switch from rail to road.[162] In the two years to March 2003, a total of £54.5 million was awarded in the form of FFGs, with the private sector making commitments amounting to £31.6 million. At the same time, TAGs were awarded to the extent of £13 million. The CNRS funding, intended to replace TAGs and start in 2002, was not introduced until April 2004, with European Commission clearance until March 2007. Expressed in pounds per container moved, the scheme applied to the intermodal container market and was tied to the traffic moved rather than the individual operator. In 2004/5, 58 services were supported at a cost of £22.2 million, with most of the money effectively reserved for the specialist container operator, Freightliner (28 services, £16.4 million).[163] Less discretionary were the significant sums paid in support of Channel Tunnel freight services. Payments amounted to £125 million in the period 1998–2001, and £102 million in 2001–5, and considerable uncertainty was caused by the imminent expiry of the commitments, under the 1987 Railway Usage Contract with Eurotunnel, to

---

[161] SRA, *Freight Strategy* (May 2001), pp. 3–4.   [162] Gourvish, *British Rail 1974–97*, pp. 13, 418.
[163] SRA, *Company Neutral Revenue Support* (February 2004), and *Annual Report 2002/3–2005*. Note some additional support was initiated in Scotland and Wales under devolved powers.

pay a Minimum Usage Charge until 30 November 2006.[164] Of course, these payments, while not inconsiderable, were small in comparison with those made to the passenger businesses. The freight sector was also affected by the post-Hatfield disruptions, then from 2003 by cuts in grant as rail costs rose. The FFG and TAG schemes were halted in 2003/4 as an economy measure, a move criticized by the Commons Transport Committee,[165] the three-year budget for the CNRS was committed shortly after it was launched, and only very limited sums were available for a hastily re-launched TAG (£0.2m. to EWS in 2004/5).[166] Freight also suffered from the truncation of the incremental output schemes (IOS). And working against the railways was the Government's decision to permit larger and heavier lorries on British roads: 40-tonne vehicles from January 1999, then 44-tonne vehicles from February 2001.

One must have some sympathy for the SRA freight managers, who were frustrated by the slow progress with infrastructure investment and often exasperated by the emphasis on passenger franchises, the latter of course evident in the SRA's work on capacity and route utilization. Furthermore, the Authority's work on the specification of network outputs also disturbed freight operators, who challenged the assumption that freight lines could automatically be maintained to lower standards.[167] In fact, the real efforts had to come from the private sector operators, and indeed from customers, who needed to be persuaded that investing in a shift of mode was worthwhile. The Rail Freight Group, the Freight Transport Association and (from 2005) the Rail Freight Operators Association proved to be effective lobbyists, but given the fundamental economics of trans-shipment, 'growing the market' was a tough call, whether the railways were in public or private hands.[168] The largest operator, EWS, was acquired by Canadian National Railway in 2001, a move followed by a programme of rationalization and risk reduction. If the SRA was exhorting the industry to enter new markets, EWS

---

[164] The commitments were transferred to the SRA in January 2001. BRB was committed to pay EWS's charges until April 2005, and was further liable to November 2006 if EWS ceased operations. BRB, *R&A 1998/9–2000/1*; BRB(R), *R&A 2001/2–4/5*; Gourvish, *Britain and the Channel Tunnel*, pp. 303–5. EWS threatened to withdraw from this unprofitable traffic after April 2005, and was able to secure an extension of the support until 30 November 2006. See Allan Bennett (SRA), Memos. to SRA Executive Committee, 27 March 2003, SRA file 57/01/02 Pt. 42, and 5 May 2005; Jonathan Riley (Executive Director Freight, SRA)–Lambirth, 18 August 2004, SRA file 57/01/12 Pt. 10; EC, *State aid N159/2005—United Kingdom EWSI Channel Tunnel Freight Support Funding* (22 June 2005), C(2005) 1816.

[165] HC Transport Committee, *The Future of the Railway*, para. 141. On the impact of the cuts, see Steve Armstrong (SRA), Memo. to SRA Executive Committee, 17 June 2004, SRA file 57/01/02 Pt. 53.

[166] Armstrong, Memo. to SRA Executive Committee, 17 September 2004, SRA file 57/01/12 Pt. 10. A new, all-encompassing grant, the Sustainable Distribution Fund, was announced by Darling in July 2005: *Parl. Deb. (Commons)*, 6th ser. (Session 2005–6), Vol. 436, 19 July 2005, c. 72–4ws.

[167] Cf. Herbert Smith (for EWS)–Bowker, 2 December 2003, SRA; Duncan Shrubsole (Darling's PS)–Ian Corfield and Ed Cullen, 25 February 2004, reporting views of Keith Heller (Chief Executive, EWS), DfT file R101/1/25 Pt. 1; Interview with Clarke, 2006.

[168] The RFG in particular was a trenchant advocate of freight in its press releases: cf. 'Bowker stabs freight in the back', 4 December 2003 [sic: 2002], ' "Platform for Progress" or "Smokescreen for Failure?" ', 5 February 2003, SRA.

was tending to consolidate in its established core business.[169] Railtrack's decision to open up infrastructure train services to competition encouraged a measure of diversification in Freightliner, which had been affected by the shift from block grant to the CNRS. The company, owned by its venture capitalist investors, 3i and Electra, from 2005, reorganized its services and began to compete with EWS for some 'heavy haul' traffics. The smaller incumbents, Mendip (aggregates), DRS (Nuclear flasks), and GB Railfreight also responded to market opportunities, the last taking some intermodal business and winning a contract from Royal Mail. The SRA also referred to the appearance of new entrants, for example, Advenza–Cotswold Rail, Fastline (Jarvis), FM Rail, and AMEC SPIE, but their activities were marginal. Operators certainly invested in new locomotives and wagons, but on the whole they focused on tried and tested markets, since both barriers to entry and buyer switching costs were high.[170]

There was no shortage of planning activity at the SRA. The freight team undertook some valuable work in assessing the environmental impact of rail transport, notably via the Sensitive Lorry Miles analysis, which placed monetary values on the external benefits of moving freight from road to rail to assist investment decision-making. The SRA's revised assessment of May 2003 provided a much more sophisticated measurement of the benefits.[171] The team's work on freight interchanges (March 2004) and market studies (2004/5) was also important, though this had hardly had time to bear fruit before the Authority was faced with closure.[172] On the other hand, the focus on container traffic, which was undoubtedly a sound strategy, was hindered by the tardy progress with key enhancement schemes. The Felixstowe–Nuneaton route was cleared for 9-foot 6-inch containers, but only using the more circuitous route via the congested North London line.[173] The initial, 'gold-plated' proposal for Southampton–WCML was also abandoned in favour of a more realistic scheme priced at £53 million, though at the time of writing this has yet to be implemented. In the meantime Freightliner's share of the growing container traffic passing through the port fell from 34 per cent in 1999/2000 to 31 per cent in 2004/5.[174] At 55

---

[169] SRA, 'Long Term Plans and Prospects', p. 64. Canadian National acquired Wisconsin Central, which held a 42.5% stake in EWS.

[170] Ibid. pp. 64–8, 72; *Modern Railways*, October 2005, pp. 50, 52. FM Rail was forced into receivership in December 2006: *Modern Railways*, April 2007, pp. 74–5.

[171] In 1991, the value was 10p per lorry-mile, in 1996 20p for motorways, £1 and £1.50 for single carriageway and urban roads. The SRA's 2003 revision provided values ranging from 4.1p–173.8p, with a weighted average of 51.1p.

[172] Interchange opportunities were progressed at Birch Coppice (Warwickshire, opened October 2006), Alconbury (later abandoned), Castle Donington, Telford and Sheffield: SRA, 'Long Term Plans and Prospects', pp. 79–81; *Modern Railways*, October 2005, pp. 62–3; Interview with Riley, 2006.

[173] The argument here is not clear-cut. The cleared route was longer, but it was also faster and electrified. Interview with Iain Dewar, 11 October 2006.

[174] SRA, *Annual Report 2005*, p. 45; information from Keith Gray (Freightliner). The Government's intention to progress both the Felixstowe–Nuneaton and Southampton–Nuneaton schemes was announced in October 2007, with grants of £123m.: DfT press release, 30 October 2007.

Victoria Street, missionary zeal tended to outweigh caution. Assumptions made on the basis of top-down models inevitably produced optimistic forecasts of the potential for a switch from road to rail. Each new traffic gained was heralded in the SRA's annual reports—for example, the use of rail by the supermarkets Safeway and Asda (2002), and the award of a large (£11.7m.) grant to Buxton Lime in support of its cement traffic in 2001/2; and each innovatory response was trumpeted in quarterly briefings.[175] But good news was often countered by bad, for example, Royal Mail's exit from its rail contracts with EWS in 2004, and the evidence that innovatory competitions and imaginative grant schemes lead to sustainable traffic flows over the longer-term was to say the least mixed, with the Blue Circle and Minimodal innovation winners in 2000 (Chapter 2, p. 50) failing to achieve a significant take-off, for example.[176] Of course, tonne-kilometre data tended to downplay the importance of traffics with a low weight-to-volume ratio, and new measures were produced to highlight the railways' contribution in environmental terms, such as lorry journeys saved and lorry-kilometres avoided. Thus, rail operations were calculated to have avoided 5.89 million lorry journeys in 2003/4 and 7.20 million in 2004/5, when the CNRS scheme was reckoned to have removed 650,000 HGV road journeys. In 2004/5, the railways saved a total of 1.43 billion lorry-km, and the share of the market rose to 11.7 per cent.[177] But road haulage clearly continued to dominate. When responsibility reverted to the Department, there was little to suggest that a breakthrough was imminent in the non-bulk sector where the scope for growth was largest.

5.6 Conclusion

Bowker was appointed to the SRA to give it clarity of purpose, drive, and enthusiasm. This he did; but while there were undoubted achievements,[178] in the areas of planning and franchising his personal management style was a mixture of charm and the offensive, a cocktail which tended to put people 'off side'. On the surface pleasant and engaging, he quickly revealed a combative style, exhibiting a desire to do it all, to lead the industry. Inevitably, he trod on toes

[175] SRA, *Annual Report 2001/2*, p. 16, 2002/3, p. 52; *SRA Freight Quarterly*, 1–8 (Winter 2001–Summer 2005).
[176] *Modern Railways*, October 2005, p. 50.
[177] SRA, *National Rail Trends 2004/5*, p. 33; SRA, *Annual Report 2005*, p. 46. Downward adjustments were made to the 2004/5 data [journeys saved 6.95bn, lorry-kms saved 1.20bn] in ORR, *National Rail Trends 2005/6*, pp. 45–6.
[178] The SRA's role in establishing Network Rail, and its project management of the WCML, Mark I stock replacement, and Southern power supply upgrade is discussed in Chapter 6.

and was resented by the other main players, the TOCs, DfT, Network Rail, and the Regulator, especially in relation to some of his more radical plans for the reorganization of the industry.[179] Of course, there were pluses in his personal scorecard. Planning received encouragement and impetus, and no-one could now criticize the SRA, as they had in Morton's day, that it had no strategies. On the other hand, turning aspirations into reality was more difficult, and however much the SRA may have protested that its new approach to franchising was not 'micromanagement', the TOCs resented Bowker's more prescriptive approach to new contracts. They were also uncomfortable with his more bullish management style, and were irritated to receive acerbic letters whenever the SRA chairman had a bad train journey. The competitions for short-listing and preferred bidder status were tense, expensive affairs, and some of Bowker's more defensive reactions to criticism fed the belief within ATOC that he was sometimes patronizing, and even dictatorial, in his approach. When the SRA opened a dialogue with the TOCs about the new franchise concept, Christopher Garnett of GNER warned him that the approach was 'leading a number of companies to wonder whether there is a long-term financial future in franchising. At the same time, the tone of the meeting was frankly quite patronising and implying less and less being done by TOCs and even more control going to the SRA.'[180] As railway costs rose and frustrations ran high, Bowker, chosen as an antidote to Morton, in fact appeared to metamorphose into his predecessor, complete with Mortonesque pronouncements, hyper vigilance, and inquests into leaks to the media.[181] These tensions were inevitable, perhaps, particularly in the charged environment surrounding the Rail Regulator's further access charges review, the work for the 2004 spending round, and the DfT's rail review (see below, pp. 189–201, 219 ff.). By the autumn of 2003, a somewhat beleaguered Bowker was seeking to defend his position by telling his Minister that he had 'inherited a shambles', in which there had been 'simplistic analysis, no discipline, contempt for the Department and HM Treasury and an SRA strategy based entirely on throwing money at problems'.[182] But in Whitehall officials were beginning to ask whether there had not been a return to some of the old bad habits.[183] However, the SRA's increasing difficulties with costs should not be used to conceal the more positive legacy of its activities in the period 2001–4. Planning and franchising activities were now more in tune with an industry which had clearly moved from planned decline to year-on-year growth. Passenger and freight traffics had increased, new trains had been ordered, and operational performance was beginning to improve again,

[179] See notes taken during the SRA Executive Directors' Away Afternoon, at the Work Foundation, n.d., SRA. Proposals such as Project PD are discussed in Chapter 6.

[180] Garnett–Bowker, 16 October 2002, SRA.

[181] Bowker–Lockhead, 19 August 2002, cit.; Bowker, SRA Board Minutes, 3 July 2003; Bowker–Winsor, 28 October 2003, SRA file 57/01/12 Pt. 8.

[182] Bowker–Darling, 6 October 2003, SRA.   [183] Wardlaw, Memo. 16 October 2003, cit.

though uncertainties remained in relation to the future level of subsidy, which had obvious implications for service levels and the contribution to come from the fare-box. And at last there were some solid and more realistic plans for the enhancement of both the passenger and freight railway, even if the increased burden falling on the public sector was making the prospects of early achievement more and more remote.

6

The Strategic Rail Authority and the Railway, 2001–4

Network Rail, Cost Escalation, the Regulator's 2003 Review, and Project Management

6.1 Taking Railtrack out of administration

The SRA, while not a party to the Government's decision to place Railtrack in administration, was very much involved in the considerable work undertaken to take it out again. Thus, at an early stage, the Authority was represented on a steering group chaired by David Rowlands of the DTLR, along with the Treasury, the No. 10 Policy Unit and a cluster of financial and legal advisers. When Bowker became Chairman the Department asked the SRA to sponsor the bid team which would work up the proposals for a Company Limited by Guarantee (CLG), initially known as 'Newco' or 'Newtrack'.[1] A strong group was assembled, including Nicola Shaw, Jon Bevan (seconded from Allen & Overy), and executives from Booz Allen Hamilton, KPMG, Lazards, Linklaters, and First

---

[1] SRA Board Minutes, 1 November and 20 December 2001; Bowker–Rowlands, 14 and 21 December 2001, SRA.

Class Partnerships. The process proved to be tricky for a variety of reasons. More particularly, as the initial, over-optimistic assumptions about the length of time administration would operate began to fade, anxieties about rising infrastructure costs began to intrude into every aspect of the debate about structure and organization.

At the time of the administration order, both the Department for Transport and the Treasury had been in a hawkish mood.[2] As we have seen, Byers had been given confidence by a supportive tripartite meeting with Blair and Brown on 19 September 2001. A few days after the Court's decision in October he told Robin Cook, the leader of the Commons, that the SRA and ORR would be merged. The proposed successor to Railtrack, a CLG, would have no equity and would therefore only require a single regulator.[3] The approach was initially uncompromising in relation to Railtrack's shareholders. Both privately and publicly, Byers declared it to be wrong to provide compensation, quite apart from the 'prohibitively expensive' charge it would make upon the public purse.[4] The holders of Railtrack's debt were of course quite another matter, since the treatment of these creditors might have a wider impact upon the Government's PFI and PPP initiatives. The period of administration was also expected to be short. In September 2001, the thinking in Whitehall was that the process would be over in three to six months and certainly no later than the end of the financial year, that is, 31 March 2002.[5] However, it was not long before a more realistic appraisal was evident. The industry's major players had all been bruised by events and were disinclined to behave passively. Railtrack was smarting from the decision itself and anxious to fight its corner. The Rail Regulator, Winsor, who had been personally hurt by events (above, pp. 105–6) was making loud noises about having been threatened with removal and was determined to defend the regulatory parameters within which he operated.[6] The TOCs were concerned about the perceived threat to economic regulation. Finally, the SRA was annoyed about having been kept in the dark.[7]

While there were some public statements of support for administration, initially much energy was consumed in inquests into how the decision had been taken, and in defending the Government's action.[8] There were numerous debates in Parliament, two calling for the annulment of the administration order, and the Transport Committee was able to extend its current enquiry into franchising

---

[2] Atter–Brown, Adonis–Blair, both 14 September 2001, cit.

[3] Hackland–Campbell, 21 September 2001, cit.; Byers–Cook, 12 October 2001, Cabinet Office file R14/6 Pt. 3.

[4] Byers, DfT News Release, 7 October 2001; *Parl. Deb. (Commons)*, 6th ser. (Session 2001–2), Vol. 372, Byers, statement, 15 October 2001, c. 954–6.

[5] Atter–Brown, 14 September 2001, cit.

[6] His sense of injustice ran deep: cf. Winsor–ORR, 4 July 2004, released under FOI.

[7] SRA Board Minutes, 16 October 2001.

[8] SRA Press Release, 8 October 2001; Byers, statement, 15 October 2001, cit.; Railtrack News Release, 15 October 2001; Hackland–Blair, 8, 9, 10, 11, and 12 October 2001, Prime Minister's Rail papers, Pt. 3.

to embrace the future of Railtrack. In such an environment, a fully cooperative response from the industry was difficult to obtain.[9] On the regulation issue, several factors worked against the simple removal of Winsor. The Regulator naturally resisted attempts to discharge him, but in fact many of his arguments carried substantial weight. The TOCs and Freight Train Operating Companies (FOCs) had the right of veto in relation to any transfer of Railtrack's responsibilities, and they soon made it clear that they were opposed to any dilution of the existing framework of economic regulation.[10] Winsor was also able to draw comfort from the more guarded wording of Byers's Commons statement on 15 October, which while stating that the existing structure should be streamlined and that Railtrack's successor would require 'far less intense regulation', conceded the point that 'there will be a continued need for some form of economic regulation'.[11] Furthermore, the Government itself realized that an ORR/SRA merger would require a very competent chief executive to combine a wide range of skills, both economic and managerial, and be able to work well with Whitehall. Given the earlier experience of recruitment to the SRA chair, the prospects of finding such a super-executive seemed to be fairly remote.[12] Blair was personally keen on reforming the regulatory system and favoured a single independent body, combining both economic and safety functions. This was in line with the views expressed by Tony Grayling and Dieter Helm, who had suggested that the SRA and ORR should be merged, with the further option of transferring responsibility for rail safety regulation from the HSE to the new body.[13] The SRA undertook preparatory work in conjunction with the consultants NERA and Mercers.[14] But by December, with the options for regulatory reform still being studied, the Department fully accepted that 'the co-operation of the existing Regulator is needed in getting Railtrack out of administration'. In these circumstances, officials accepted that the relationship with Winsor, who

---

[9] On further inquests in Parliament, see HC Transport Committee, *Report on Passenger Rail Franchising: MOE*, HC239-II, March 2002, esp. Winsor, 7 November 2001, QQ.732–811, and Byers, 14 November 2001, QQ.820–934; *Parl. Deb. (Commons)*, 6th ser. (Session 2001–2), Vol. 374, Theresa May (MP for Maidenhead), private notice question, 5 November 2001, c. 20–9; Vol. 375, Byers, oral answer to Gwyneth Dunwoody (MP for Crewe & Nantwich), 20 November 2001, c. 173; Opposition debate, 13 November 2001, c. 715–71; Eric Pickles (MP for Brentwood & Ongar), debate seeking annulment of the order, 22 November 2001, c. 547–60; Vol. 376, Opposition debate, 3 December 2001, c. 24–79. There were similar debates in the Lords.

[10] ATOC and EWS, letter to Byers, 12 October 2001, Winsor archive; Tim Reardon (SRA)–Ariel Steering Group, 5 December 2001, Mercer Management Consulting, 'Informal Consultation' draft, 6 December 2001, SRA; Bisson–Blair, 21 December 2001, Prime Minister's Rail papers, Pt. 3.

[11] Byers, Commons statement, 15 October 2001, cit.; ORR, File Note, 16 October 2001, Winsor archive.

[12] Atter–Brown, 14 September 2001, cit.

[13] Transport Stocktake, 13 November 2001, reported in Bisson–Campbell, 15 November 2001, Prime Minister's Rail papers, Pt. 3; Dieter Helm–Geoffrey Norris (Special Adviser, No. 10 Policy Unit), enclosing 'A Note on the Concordat between the SRA and the Rail Regulator, and the Case for Merging the Two Bodies', March 2001 [sic: actually 2002], ibid. Pt. 5; and Grayling, *Getting Back on Track* (2001), p. 30.

[14] O'Donnell–Grant et al., 29 November 2001, SRA.

was opposed to any modifications to the existing regime, required 'very careful handling'.[15] The intervention of the recently appointed SRA Chairman, Bowker, was also a factor. The idea that he might take over the responsibilities of the Regulator had been put to him in early discussions. But he immediately told Rowlands that it was 'overly simplistic and populist' to argue that regulation had failed the industry. Furthermore, it was 'some of the very constituents who now suggest regulation is overly complex that have contrived to limit its effectiveness. During my time as a Train Operator, I was continually disappointed at TOCs inability to energise themselves and enforce the rights that have always existed in law.' On the other hand, he thought that a change in the relative roles of the ORR and SRA was needed since 'the wider public interest duty' should rest with the funder, that is, the Government. 'One has to recognise', he wrote, 'that many of the powers conferred on the ORR were first established in a world where prevention of contraction rather than facilitation of growth was considered the primary objective.' In the new world, it was only 'right that the SRA should take the lead in analysing and prioritising the use of existing capacity, what network enhancements go forward, and the balance of expenditure between enhancement and renewals'. This 'significant change' would require legislation, but was for the future; the immediate task was to get Railtrack out of administration, which meant that it was 'imperative that an effective working relationship with Tom Winsor is established now'. The Department fully accepted this, and while the preference was for a 'slimmed down economic regulator and a strengthened SRA' the attention turned to encouraging Winsor and Bowker to pursue a policy of mutual cooperation.[16] Byers also sought to improve his relationship with the Regulator at a private dinner in early February 2002.[17]

Attitudes inside Railtrack Group also changed. The company was initially regarded as having almost invited administration, and Robinson, the Chairman, had been cooperative to the extent of being prepared to accept the Government's offer to lead the not-for-profit successor to his company.[18] But once it was made clear by his fellow directors that this would produce a clear conflict of interest, he hastily turned down the offer, and made his decision public. There was also the possibility that shareholders might hold the directors personally liable. Marshall resigned as Chief Executive, though he agreed to stay on until he was succeeded by Harding, the Finance Director, in March 2002. From an early stage, then, Robinson, Marshall, and Harding led the fight to obtain adequate compensation

---

[15] DTLR, 'The Future of Railways Regulation', December 2001, enclosed in Byers–Blair, 21 December 2001, and Bisson–Blair, 21 December 2001, ibid.

[16] Bowker–Rowlands, 11 December 2001, SRA and see also Hackland-Blair, 7 December 2001, Prime Minister's Rail papers, Pt. 3, and DTLR, 'The Future of Railways Regulation', December 2001, cit. Bowker has argued that if he had accepted the proposal to assume the Regulator's responsibilities, the SRA would not have been wound up: Interview with Bowker, 2006.

[17] ORR, File Note, 6 February 2002, Winsor archive.   [18] Hackland–Blair, 8 October 2001, cit.

for their shareholders.[19] With Railtrack concentrating on the shareholder issue, the Government's uncompromising attitude to compensation quickly evaporated. The company had some strong arguments in its armoury. It was the subsidiary company, Railtrack plc, which had been placed in administration, and the parent company, Railtrack Group plc, could continue to trade, along with its non-regulated businesses, for example, property, and, more importantly, its interest in Section 1 of the CTRL.[20] The parent company faced serious liquidity problems, of course, but its non-regulated interests might be sold for the benefit of share-holders. Directors immediately announced that the company's cash holdings withheld by HSBC, amounting to £372 million, were alone worth 70p a share, while its interest in CTRL was worth another 70p. The Government then offered Railtrack Group short-term funding of £7–10 million to enable it to meet its obligations in relation to its cash deposits.[21] With Railtrack Group pressing for a shareholder settlement of £3.60 a share, the price paid on privatization, the treatment of equity holders was again not a simple matter. The Treasury was inclined to resist compensation, being more concerned about the implications for the Government's ambitions for PFI and PPP of the treatment of holders of the £4.4 billion of unsecured Railtrack debt, who had been unsettled by a downgrading from the credit rating agency Standard & Poor. However, as an official conceded, if lenders were seen to have been bailed out by the Government then it would be difficult to refuse to help the shareholders: 'fat cat city bankers get 100p in the pound and grannies…lose their blouses'.[22] In his Commons statement, Byers had reassured debt holders by offering them the option of transferring their debt to the new company with no loss of principal or interest. On the other hand, he argued that 'it would be wrong' to pay shareholders £3.60, which would require £1.5 billion in new money from the taxpayer.[23] But this approach involved 'a facile distinction between bondholders "good" and shareholders "bad" '. Financial institutions often held both types of paper, and it was a dangerous game to seek to advantage one element in their portfolio while penalizing another.[24] The Prime Minister clearly did not share the sanguine stance of some of his advisers and, only 10 days after Byers's statement, said that

---

[19] Hackland–Blair, 9 October 2001, cit.; Railtrack News Releases, 9, 10, and 12 October 2001; Harding, thesis, p. 164. Robinson was succeeded as Chairman by Geoffrey Howe, an insolvency lawyer and Managing Partner of Clifford Chance, also in March 2002.

[20] Though the operating concession was held by Railtrack plc, the liability rested with Railtrack Group.

[21] Hackland–Blair, 9 October 2001, cit.; Railtrack News Releases, 10 and 16 October 2001; Harding, thesis, pp. 162–3, who suggests that the Government may have been keen to keep Railtrack Group in existence in order to provide a buffer between it and Virgin in relation to the WCML upgrade. But there was also the issue of reforming the rail safety organization, some of which resided in Railtrack Group via its not-for-profit subsidiary, Railway Safety.

[22] Adonis–Brown, 14 September 2001 and Hackland–Blair, 11 October 2001, cit.; Ian Kemsley (Treasury)–Brown, 17 September 2001, DfT, Weir doc. vol. K11.

[23] Byers, statement, 15 October 2001, cit.

[24] These points were put to Blair: Derek Scott (Policy Adviser, No. 10)–Blair, 18 October 2001, Prime Minister's Rail papers, Pt. 3. Scott wrote about his time in Number Ten in Off Whitehall (2004). Railtrack is not mentioned.

the shareholders would receive something.[25] Byers quickly conceded the point that the Group's assets would be available to them.[26]

Administration proved to be not only an expensive but a protracted process. The role of the administrators was to transfer the business to ensure the management of the railway network was 'properly carried on', and, equally critically, to manage the network in the interim period. Alan Bloom, leader of the Ernst & Young team, certainly had the requisite experience, having been involved in the rescues of both Olympia & York at Canary Wharf and Barings Bank. But such expertise did not come cheap, and it remained to be seen whether the administrators could cast a judicious eye upon the complexities, financial demands and safety considerations presented by railway infrastructure renewal and maintenance. Contrary to the allegations in some quarters, government officials *did* make a rudimentary risk assessment, and in particular rehearsed the implications for public expenditure of a long interregnum. In September 2001, for example, Lewis Atter, head of the transport team at the Treasury, advised the Chancellor that it would cost £150 million a month to make up Railtrack's revenue shortfall and that there would also be restructuring costs. Over a six-month period, this implied a bill of at least £1 billion, though of course most of these costs would be returned to the public purse when the new company was established and able to borrow.[27] How many months would be required was a matter of speculation at the outset. The administration order required the administrators to present a comprehensive restructuring plan within 90 days, but this was a tall order and, in any case, was not the same thing as a completed transfer.[28] Winsor was quick to pooh-pooh early DfT assumptions that three months would be sufficient to complete the work. When he met Mottram on 10 October, he made it clear that a 90-day objective was 'completely unachievable'. The work, he said, would be 'complex and difficult', would cost hundreds of millions, and divert management attention away from running the railway.[29] It was not long before Winsor's opinion was shared more widely. On 26 October, Blair had been briefed that a six-month target to get Railtrack out of administration would be 'very challenging indeed'. The administrators had concluded that the state of Railtrack plc was such as to make the due diligence aspects of the transfer a 'major task'. The complexities of the overlapping regulatory jurisdictions were a further concern. Alan Bloom therefore made strong hints of 'potential slippage'.[30] A

[25] Blair, interview in *Daily Telegraph*, 25 October 2001, p. 40; Railtrack News Release, 25 October 2001; and cf. annotation on Hackland–Blair, 10 October 2001, cit.

[26] Byers–Blair, 19 October and 14 December 2001, Cabinet Office file R14/6 Pt. 3 and Prime Minister's Rail papers, Pt. 3.

[27] Atter–Brown, 14 September 2001, cit.; Iain Ure (DfT)–Darling, 10 October 2002, DfT file R95/1/1 Pt. 4.

[28] Insolvency Act 1986, s. 23 and cf. 'Railtrack Management Strengthening and Funding Recommendations', 12 October 2001, SRA.

[29] ORR, File Note, 10 October 2001, Winsor archive.

[30] Hackland–Blair, 26 October and 2 November 2001, Byers–Blair, 2 November 2001, Prime Minister's Rail papers, Pt. 3.

few weeks later, Byers told Blair that the process would definitely take longer than six months. He hoped to be able to announce a preferred bidder by March 2002, though a formal exit from administration would be unlikely before the summer.[31] By the end of January, the administrators were sufficiently gloomy about the prospects to suggest that there might be no end to the matter until the autumn of 2003.[32]

It was not until 25 March 2002 that Network Rail, which had been formally constituted three days earlier, submitted its bid for Railtrack plc, and a further seven months was required before the transfer took effect. In the first period, October 2001–March 2002, it was considered important to open up the bidding process to competition. In fact, there were enquiries from parties other than the SRA-supported bidding group, though in the end they came to nothing. Westdeutsche Landesbank—WestLB—was the most serious of these, and as early as 9 October the Government was made aware of its interest. Mottram was informed that the Bank was interested in participating in a financing strategy for Railtrack, and 'for some months' had been looking at the prospects of making a formal bid for the company.[33] Bank representatives then met Morton on 7 November. Interest was also expressed by Babcock & Brown, who met Bowker five days later. WestLB, which was well versed in debt-led corporate restructuring, had some experience of utilities through its acquisition of Mid Kent Water. It formed a consortium called SwiftRail and expressed a willingness to work within a CLG framework. However, its primary interest lay in refinancing, and it expected the 'core asset management functions' to be fulfilled by a private sector company. Babcock and Brown, in contrast, were more interested in providing financial advice, in particular on the concept of funding through the securitization of passenger revenues ('farebox securitization').[34] The appearance of these companies gave rise to a possible conflict of interest in the role of the SRA, which was to sponsor, that is, pay for, the CLG bid team's costs and lead the negotiations on the funding package, including a contract for differences,[35] but had also to provide a level playing field for other potential bidders.[36] The two roles were clearly defined and separated, but at a comparatively early stage it emerged that only the Government's CLG proposal was in play. With its

---

[31] Bisson–Campbell, 23 November 2001, ibid.

[32] O'Donnell–Bowker et al., 25 January 2002, SRA. Reference to 2003 does not appear to be a misprint. The comment may have been intended to encourage more urgency within government.

[33] Robin Saunders (MD, Asset Securitisation, WestLB)–Mottram, 9 October 2001, Prime Minister's Rail papers, Pt. 3.

[34] 'Note of Meeting with West LB, 7th November 2001', 'Note of Meeting with Babcock & Brown 12th November 2001', Saunders–Bowker, 20 November 2001, SRA; HC Transport Committee Report on *Passenger Rail Franchising*, para. 48.

[35] A contract for differences stipulates that the seller will pay the buyer the difference between the current value of an asset and its value when the contract takes effect.

[36] SRA Board Minutes, 10 January and 7 February 2002; SRA, 'Role of SRA in relation to all bidders and in relation to CLG', January 2002; SRA, 'Railtrack (in Administration): SRA Ground Rules and Procedures', February 2002; and Bowker–Alan Bloom (Joint Special Railway Administrator), 17 January 2002, SRA.

costs being met by the SRA, it enjoyed a considerable advantage, and neither WestLB nor Babcock & Brown was prepared to make a comprehensive bid for Railtrack plc.[37]

More time-consuming was the need to draw up a detailed framework for the new body. While the basic constitution and governance structure of the CLG were formulated relatively quickly, drawing on the model provided by Glas Cymru (Welsh Water),[38] it is clear that many fundamentals, not least the regulatory apparatus, the funding mechanisms and status (private or public) of the new body were in a rudimentary state when the administration order was obtained.[39] It was also necessary to revisit the whole question of performance and incentives. The Department did make good progress in staffing the proto-CLG with business heavyweights. At the end of November, it was announced that Ian McAllister, Chairman and MD of Ford UK, who had been a candidate for the post of SRA chairman, had been appointed to head up the team. He had converted losses into profits at Ford and enjoyed wide support in Whitehall.[40] McAllister was joined by Adrian Montague as Deputy Chairman and Iain Coucher as Managing Director. Montague was the leading PFI specialist and a former director of the SSRA; he was expected to focus on Whitehall and City issues. Coucher was an engineer with extensive experience of London Underground's PFI and was subsequently Chief Executive of Tubelines, a PPP contractor. He was appointed to drive the bid.[41] Meanwhile the administrators took steps to strengthen the management of the insolvent company, Railtrack plc, with John Armitt of Costain appointed Chief Executive in December 2001, and Jim Cornell, a British Rail engineering stalwart, becoming a non-executive director. Armitt had an impressive CV, having managed the Sizewell B and second Severn Bridge projects when with Laing. He had also been Chief Executive of Union Railways, the company responsible for the CTRL before London & Continental. Most important of all, he had turned round the ailing Costain business from 1997.[42] His presence was certainly required since the existing Railtrack staff were suffering from a loss of morale, and the offer by Bechtel to bring in 30–50 executives in order to strengthen the senior management had done nothing to alleviate the

[37] Hackland–Blair, 7 December 2001, Byers–Blair, 14 December 2001, cit.; SRA Board Minutes, 7 and 18 March 2002.

[38] Grant–SRA Executive et al., 17 October 2001, David McMillan (Director Rail Restructuring Directorate, DTLR)–Ian McAllister (CLG), 20 December 2001, Adrian Montague (CLG)–Bowker, 4 January 2002, SRA; *Parl. Deb. (Commons)*, 6th ser. (Session 2001–2), Vol. 373, Byers, written answer to Mark Hendrick (MP for Preston), 23 October 2001, c. 195–7w.

[39] ORR File Note, 10 October 2001, cit.; HC Transport Committee Report on *Passenger Rail Franchising*, para. 12.

[40] Hackland–Blair, 16 November 2001, Prime Minister's Rail papers, Pt. 3; Bronwyn Hill (DfT)–Ian McAllister (Ford), 27 November 2001, SRA; DfT News Release, 29 November 2001; Interview with Rowlands, 2007.

[41] Hackland–Blair, 7 December 2001, cit.; SRA–Coucher, 28 January 2002, SRA; SRA Press Release, 16 January 2002. By this time, a group of substantial advisers had been found: Linklaters (legal), UBS Warburg (financial), and Jarvis Rail and Arup (technical).

[42] *Times*, 15 December 2001, pp. 25, 48; *Observer business*, 16 December 2001, p. 12.

situation.[43] But a strong team could not be assembled cheaply—Armitt's salary alone was reported to be £450,000 a year—and concern was expressed in some quarters, notably by Chris Grayling, a Conservative member of the Commons Transport Committee, about the cost of the rescue operation.[44]

6.2 The creation of Network Rail

By the end of March 2002, the work on organization, outputs, and financing had reached the stage where a proposal from the CLG team could be submitted. This took the form of a pre-emptive bid, obviating the need for a competition (though there was precious little sign of one) and thereby offering the quickest route out of administration. Unsurprisingly, the team proposed to establish a private, non-equity CLG, with the Government as funder of last resort.[45] However, the details had been thrashed out in a somewhat hectic atmosphere. Much had to be put in place simultaneously: an output specification from the SRA; funding arrangements acceptable to Government; an outline organizational structure and governance framework; a business plan for the successor company; arrangements to enable the Government through the SRA to exercise a measure of control over the company; and determination of the regulatory environment. The situation was far from ideal, and the anxiety to speed up the process meant that some matters were dealt with hastily which in a more settled period might have been handled differently. For example, the CLG team formulated its draft business plan without being able to get inside Railtrack plc, since the administrators preferred an arms-length relationship. Instead the team employed consultants, Jarvis and Arup, and the documentation could not pretend to provide specific and detailed action plans to overhaul the renewal and maintenance business.[46] In addition, there was much anxiety within the Department and the Treasury about whether the proposed control arrangements would enable the new company to be regarded as a private sector company and thus remain off the Government's balance sheet. For its part, the SRA Board was clearly anxious about the implications for its existing commitments of sponsoring a new owner. The deal agreed

[43] Hackland–Blair, 12 October 2001, Bisson–Campbell, 23 November 2001, Byers–Blair, 14 December 2001, cit.; Marshall–Hackland and Marshall–Blair (private letter), both 21 November 2001, Prime Minister's Rail papers, Pt. 3. Bechtel's offer was not taken up: Interview with John Armitt, 31 May 2007.
[44] Grayling was MP for Epsom & Ewell. See *Parl. Deb. (Commons)*, 6th ser. (Session 2001–2), Vol. 379, 30 January and 6 February 2002, c. 316w, 1005w; Vol. 380, 12 and 25 February 2002, c. 213w, 784w. Armitt's salary on joining Network Rail in October 2002 was £450,000 p.a. (Table 6.1).
[45] Network Rail, offer to Railtrack Group, 25 March 2002; and see also Elson–Blair, 8 March 2002, Prime Minister's Rail papers, Pt. 5.
[46] Cf. Montague–Bowker, 26 April 2002, SRA; Ford, in *Modern Railways*, May 2002, p. 19; SRA Board Minutes, 6 June 2002.

179

in March was based on the future securitization of track access charges by the CLG. But in the short term, the CLG, now known as Network Rail, would raise bridging finance to repay Railtrack's £7.5 billion debts,[47] provide short-term working capital of up to £2 billion, and buy the Railtrack shares. The proposed purchase price was £500 million. The Government, 'in recognition of the benefits of an early exit from administration', would provide the funding via an SRA grant of £300 million, together with £2 billion as a stand-by loan, which would enable Network Rail to borrow the additional £200 million required, and under-pin the existing support to Railtrack from the European Investment Bank (EIB) (£800 million drawn) and Kreditanstalt für Wiederaufbau (KfW) (£250 million). The exit grant enabled Network Rail to offer a sum for Railtrack plc that was equivalent to comparatively generous compensation for shareholders of about £2.45–2.55 a share, with the Government contributing a sum sufficient to bridge the gap between the assets available for distribution (cash, CTRL interest [to be sold to London & Continental and Network Rail for £375 million], property, etc.) and a sum sufficient to ensure shareholder approval for the deal.[48] Shareholders were paid £2.00 a share in December 2003, and two years later had received payments totalling £2.605, 93 per cent of the value (£2.805) on suspension.[49] The Government shared in its own largesse since it held over 1 million shares in the company.[50]

There were clearly risks in entering into these arrangements, and the SRA Board was anxious to be held harmless against the financial consequences. In order to provide the 'highly confident' letter about financing which the CLG team required, the SRA had first to convince itself that an early exit from administration was financially important. A calculation was made which valued the transaction at between £150 and £650 million (2001/2 NPV).[51] Then there was the matter of the stand-by support to be provided by the SRA, which amounted in the first instance to £9 billion to support the acquisition. On top of this, further sums were required: £1 billion to support the EIB and KfW loans; £7 billion to finance 'legacy costs', that is, the 'known unknowns' associated with the WCML upgrade and post-Hatfield expenditure implications; and £4 billion

[47] Estimate of Railtrack Group plc for 30 September 2001, News Release, 27 June 2002. Network Rail's accounts stated the acquired debt of Railtrack plc to be £7.7bn: Network Rail Ltd, *R & A 2003*, p. 7. Note that the *restated* accounts of the subsidiary put the starting debt in 2002/3 as £6.3bn; Network Rail Infrastructure Ltd, *R & A 2003*, pp. 2, 11.

[48] Railtrack Group News release, 27 June 2002; SRA Board Minutes, 2 May 2002.

[49] RT Group plc, letter to shareholders, 4 December 2006, www.rtgroup.co.uk. A final distribution of c.1p a share is expected to be made in 2008–9.

[50] *Parl. Deb. (Commons)*, 6th ser. (Session 2001–2), Vol. 380, John Spellar, written answer to Christopher Chope (MP for Christchurch), 12 February 2002, c. 214w.

[51] SRA Board Minutes, 18 March 2002. A share purchase scheme was held to offer time savings of 6–9 months, yielding earlier efficiency savings, reduced performance penalties, and faster delivery of major projects: Byers–Blair, 12 March 2002, Prime Minister's Rail papers, Pt. 5, and HC Transport Committee Report on *Government Response to the Committee's First Report on Passenger Rail Franchising and the Future of Railway Infrastructure*, P.P. 2001–2, HC756-i, MOE, 10 April 2002, Byers, supplementary note, 30 April 2002.

as a 'long-term contingency buffer' that is, guarantee of last resort. Thus the extent of the possible exposure amounted to £21 billion. In providing Network Rail with the 'highly confident' letter, the SRA in turn sought reassurances from the Government on the matter of affordability and contingent liability. It wished any disbursements made under the funding framework and credit facilities arrangements for Network Rail to be regarded as additional to the SRA's existing budget and 10 Year Plan provision. It also asked the DTLR and Treasury to endorse the confident letter, together with the calculation of the benefits of an early exit from administration.[52] The Authority certainly had grounds for concern, since in January the Treasury had been arguing that if the loan were ever drawn, it would produce a call on the SRA's fixed budget and thus 'crowd out' other railway expenditure.[53]

Mottram was able to give Bowker *some* comfort. In his letter of 18 March, he assured the SRA that adequate funds would be available to meet the financial obligations incurred by the bridge financing, and more generally in relation to the proposed support package. He and Andrew Turnbull, Permanent Secretary to the Treasury, were also happy to endorse the 'early exit' benefit estimates. However, he noted that the 'discretion of ministers' could not be 'fettered' in respect of future funding for the railways, and could not anticipate the approval of the Office for National Statistics (ONS) of the proposal that the new company be classified as a free-standing private company. Bowker then sent Montague the comfort letter with these revisions.[54] The initial assumption was that Network Rail's accounts would be kept separate from those of the SRA and off the Government's books, but assurances provided to the SRA by the Department and Treasury proved premature.[55] While the ONS intimated that it would regard Network Rail as a private company once its board was in place, its attitude to the Government's financial support rested on whether the liabilities were contingent or not.[56] The National Audit Office (NAO), on the other hand, reached an unequivocal position. Applying generally accepted accounting principles, Sir John Bourn, the Comptroller and Auditor General, viewed the Government/SRA relationship with Network Rail as akin to a shareholder's. The right to nominate a board member who would sit on both the nomination and remuneration committees, and the extent of the financial support, including the contingency buffer, were deemed sufficient to require the treatment of the company as an SRA subsidiary, together with consolidation of the accounts in accordance with

---

[52] Bowker–Mottram, 15 March 2002, SRA Board Minutes, 18 March and 11 April 2002. See also Network Rail Ltd, *R & A 2003*, pp. 8, 62.

[53] David Thomas (SRA)–Bowker, 5 January 2002 and annotations, SRA.

[54] Mottram–Bowker, 18 March 2002, Bowker–Montague, 25 March 2002, SRA.

[55] SRA Board Minutes, 11 April and 6 June 2002; Byers, Directions and Guidance letter to SRA, 22 March 2002, McMillan, e-mail–SRA, 24 March 2002, SRA; Atter, telephone conversation with Thomas, 24 March 2002, and Rowlands–Bowker, reported in SRA Board Minutes, 2 May 2002.

[56] Martin Kellaway (ONS)–Jeff Golland (Treasury), 19 March and 26 June 2002, Treasury (released under FOI).

financial reporting standards. The decisive factor here seems to have been a change of opinion on the part of PricewaterhouseCoopers, who were acting for the NAO as the SRA's auditors.[57] The divergent views of the NAO and ONS, in large measure the product of their very different remits, were the subject of a joint statement on 24 October, and the Network Rail accounts were duly incorporated into those of the Authority from the year 2002/3. Whatever the Treasury may have wished, the extent of the support to be provided by the SRA, its participation in the management, and the Government's position as guarantor and lender of last resort were sufficient to position Network Rail as a subsidiary of this public sector body. And whatever the explanation, a situation where the ONS and NAO could take opposite views of the status of the company was both confusing and unsatisfactory.[58]

The matter of railway regulation had also to be addressed. By early March, it was clear that the DTLR had retreated from its promise to undertake a fundamental review. Inside Number Ten, there were fears that after administration no changes would be made at all.[59] Instead, faith was being put in a 'concordat' signed by Bowker and Winsor in February, essentially a memorandum of understanding in which the SRA and the Rail Regulator agreed to 'work constructively and effectively together', share information and ensure that their respective roles were aligned and coherent. Evidence of this may be found in Bowker's letter seeking Winsor's endorsement of the CLG structure set out in the bid.[60] While there were hopes that the existing system might be made to work, the Treasury was far from happy with it given the uncertainties about future funding requirements. In January, officials had suggested that the contract for differences accompanying the CLG might be used to 'neuter' the regulatory system by clawing back regulatory income following any interim review. In March, they continued to press for a regulatory review, fearing that the Government would be faced with a large bill, together with insufficient levers over Railtrack's successor.[61] But Byers reminded his colleagues that Winsor's cooperation was essential to a successful outcome,

---

[57] SRA Board Minutes, 17 May and 6 June 2002; *Parl. Deb. (Commons)*, 6th ser. (Session 2001–2), Vol. 389, Darling, written answer to Jane Griffiths (MP for Reading), 19 July 2002, c. 568–9w. At Number 10, Matthew Elson found PwC's decision 'extremely irritating': Elson–Blair, 17 May 2002, Prime Minister's Rail papers, Pt. 6.

[58] ONS Press release, 24 October 2002. The ONS regarded Network Rail as a private company from 16 August 2002 (subsequently amended to 1 April 2003, the implementation date for the directors' incentive scheme: ONS Press release, 27 February 2004). See also evidence to HC Treasury Select Committee, 4 December 2002, QQ.125–247; Interviews with Lewis Atter (Treasury), 22 February 2007, Bob Chauhan (Treasury), 3 April 2007, and Nicola Shaw (SRA), 2 May 2007. For a more trenchant criticism of Network Rail's classification, see Stephen Glaister, 'Chairman's Comments', in Colin Robinson (ed.), *Regulating Utilities and Promoting Competition: Lessons for the Future* (Cheltenham, 2006), pp. 28–9, and Robert Jupe, 'Public (Interest) or Private (Gain)? The Curious Case of Network Rail's Status', *Journal of Law and Society*, 34:2 (June 2007), 244–65 and esp. 259–60.

[59] Elson–Blair, 4 and 8 March 2002, Byers–Blair, 12 March 2002, Prime Minister's Rail papers, Pt. 5.

[60] SRA and ORR Concordat, 25 February 2002 (sent to Byers on 28 February and published on 7 March); Bowker–Winsor, 18 March 2002, and see also Bowker–SRA Executive Group, 23 May 2002, SRA.

[61] Thomas–Bowker and Elson–Blair, 8 March 2002, cit.

since he retained the ability to frustrate any progress with the CLG.[62] Eventually, the Government retained a measure of reforming zeal, with Byers's successor, Darling, announcing in June that a statutory regulatory board would replace the Rail Regulator on the expiry of Winsor's term of office in 2004. Winsor then issued a statement indicating that he would conduct an interim review of access charges, opening the way to an exit from administration.[63] But the new proposals fell far short of earlier aspirations to streamline the structure, and the Treasury and Number Ten were accused of having 'flip-flopped' on the matter.[64] The franchisee Virgin was also treated with kid gloves for the same reason. When the SRA reached a relatively generous settlement with the company over its franchises in July, the possibility that the latter might frustrate an early exit from administration was an important element in the negotiations.[65]

Funding details were also finalized. Network Rail was able to secure the £9 billion of bridge financing from the commercial banks, but the SRA continued to express anxiety about the extent of the company's cash requirements. As early as 18 March it had noted that in Control Period 2 these were expected to be some £5 billion more than allowed for in the Regulator's review. In May, it observed that the company's 'emerging forecasts' were 'considerably in excess of earlier indications', and in June it reported that the cash required was £6–7 billion more than the £16 billion allowed by the Regulator.[66] But with Network Rail's the only bid on the table, and the Government intent on getting the infrastructure company out of administration as quickly as possible, the only way forward was to reach an agreement with the bidder. The Government's initial funding support was limited to the period to December 2004 instead of 2006, and an agreement was signed by the SRA on 21 June.[67] On the previous day, Darling was able to tell his Cabinet colleagues that agreements would be signed that week. He attributed the progress made to the improvement in relations between the SRA, the Rail Regulator, and Railtrack.[68] At the same time, he warned that the industry still faced enormous problems, highlighted once again by a serious accident, this time at Potters Bar on 10 May, where faulty track was quickly

---

[62] Byers–Blair, 12 March 2002, cit.; Winsor–ORR, 4 July 2004, cit.

[63] *Parl. Deb. (Commons)*, 6th ser. (Session 2001–2), Vol. 386, Darling, Written Answer to Bob Blizzard (Labour MP for Waveney), 12 June 2002, c. 1262–3w and see also Vol. 387, Darling, Statement, and Oral Answer to Anne McIntosh (Conservative MP for Vale of York), 27 June 2002, c. 979; ORR, *The Proposed Acquisition of Railtrack plc by Network Rail Ltd: A Statement by the Rail Regulator and Proposed Licence Modifications*, 14 June 2002. On the background to the rapprochement, see Interview with Winsor, 2006, referring to a meeting between Winsor and Mottram on 7 May 2002, and Darling–Blair, 10 June 2002, Elson–Blair, 7 and 14 June 2002, Prime Minister's Rail papers, Pt. 7.

[64] Jeremy Heywood (Blair's PPS), e-mail to Elson, 9 June 2002, ibid. Pt. 7. The case for retaining an independent economic regulator was of course strengthened by the decision to incorporate Network Rail's accounts into those of the SRA: Elson, e-mail reply to Heywood, 10 June 2002, ibid. On the Chancellor's agreement to the policy change, see Brown–Darling, 11 June 2002, ibid.

[65] See above, p. 152.   [66] SRA Board Minutes, 18 March, 17 May and 6 June 2002.

[67] Ibid. 13 June and 4 July 2002.

[68] On evidence of greater cooperation in the industry, see SRA/Railtrack Level 1 meetings, 11 July and 26 September 2002, SRA; G6 Meetings from 2002 (SRA, NWR, ORR, ATOC, EWS, HSE).

identified as the cause. 'Real long-term improvement', he said, 'would take a very long time.'[69]

Railtrack Group accepted the offer and on 27 June announced that they would recommend it to shareholders. A sale and purchase order was signed subject to obtaining the necessary clearances. A write-down of Railtrack plc capital of nearly £2 billion was required.[70] Protesting shareholders complained that the purchase price of £500 million was not based on a proper valuation of the company, and refused to withdraw their action against the Government for misfeasance. Nevertheless, an overwhelming majority of shareholders (97%) voted to approve the deal in July.[71] Time was also taken up in obtaining the endorsement of the European Commission to both the Government's grant and the purchase of Railtrack's interest in the CTRL.[72] While the Department worked towards an application to the Court to have the administration order lifted, anxieties about increasing costs and commitments remained. Eyebrows had certainly been raised in May when Coucher, Network Rail's MD, revealed that he thought the new company should be able to work within the financial limits set by Winsor's earlier charges review.[73] This view was soon dispelled, as we have seen, and in September Network Rail gave the SRA substantially revised financing data following a reassessment of the expenditure required for the WCML upgrade. This showed that the company's net debt would rise by a further £1.2 billion at 31 March 2004, and by £3.7 billion at 31 March 2006. Unsurprisingly, SRA Board members, prompted by the non-executives, David Quarmby and Jeremy Mayhew,[74] continued to express concerns about the deal and especially the danger that an increase in Network Rail spending would jeopardize the Authority's existing functions. Reassurance was provided by the Department, but only until 2004, after which funding would be subject to the outcome of the Regulator's interim review.[75] In common with several PFI projects, the Government could take comfort in the fact that revenue spending had been avoided by an encouragement to Network Rail to take on additional borrowing. On top of this, the company introduced a significant change in the way renewals expenditure was treated, electing to capitalize it over the life of the asset. This had the effect of reducing the depreciation charged by £1.6 billion in 2001/2 and £1.45 billion in 2002/3. With the network now being valued at depreciated replacement cost, the effect of this adjustment was to improve the

[69] Cabinet Conclusions, 20 and 27 June, 4 July 2002, Cabinet Office.

[70] Railtrack News Release, 27 June 2002. The final purchase price was £510m., including acquisition costs: SRA, *Annual Report 2002/3*, p. 75.

[71] Railtrack Group plc EGM, 23 July 2002, as reported in *Rail Politic*, 26 July 2002, and SRA Board Minutes, 1 August 2002.

[72] Consent was given on 17 July and 18 September, respectively.

[73] As reported by Ford, *Modern Railways*, May 2002, p. 19.

[74] Quarmby and Mayhew, the non-executives on the Board's Investment and Procurement Committee, were members of a special committee set up to scrutinize the deal.

[75] David Quarmby (Dep-Chairman, SRA)–Jon Bevan et al., 27 September 2002, Trewin, File Note, 3 October 2002, Stephen Hatch (DfT), Note, cit. in SRA Board Minutes, 3 October 2002.

Profit & Loss Account for 2001/2 by £1.05 billion.[76] But accounting alterations could not disguise the fact that infrastructure costs were rising, as was evident when the purchase of Railtrack plc finally took effect on 3 October. Furthermore, with Winsor having announced another interim review, the determination of these costs was not in the Government's hands. By this time, the costs of administration itself were becoming apparent, though the final figure was not agreed until June 2003. The bill was not cheap. The administrators' fees alone exceeded £20 million, and with advisers' costs the total amount was £51 million.[77] If we include the cost of the advice taken by the Department, together with the SRA's own costs, then the direct costs of administration amounted to at least £81 million.[78]

The new company, Network Rail, was organized on private sector lines with a main Board, a holding company, Network Rail Ltd., and an operating subsidiary, Network Rail Infrastructure Ltd. Appointed members substituted for the shareholders. At the top a board of twelve, led on a non-executive basis by McAllister and Montague, was strengthened with the appointment of non-executives drawn from the transport industry. There was Cornell, who had prepared British Rail's infrastructure units for privatization in 1993–6,[79] and recently retired managers from the United States (Hoppe) and Australasia (Sayers). At executive level, Armitt retained the Chief Executive's role he had had at Railtrack plc, with Coucher becoming his deputy. Finance and Engineering were entrusted to Ronald and Peter Henderson, executives with substantial experience in the engineering industry. Chris Leah, the safety director, was the only survivor from pre-administration days (Table 6.1). The SRA's non-executive nominee was David Bailey, an experienced procurement and logistics manager and former Commercial Director of London Transport. His 'special rights' included membership of four Board committees—nominations, remuneration, audit, and safety, and he was also asked to ensure that satisfactory management incentives were created for executive directors via a performance-related bonus scheme, which was eventually introduced on an interim basis for the six months to 31 March 2003.[80] The structure and governance of Network Rail centred on the 115 members of the company. They were made up of 30 industry members, who

[76] Network Rail Infrastructure Ltd, *R & A 2003*, pp. 49–50. The revised treatment of renewals also had the advantage of limiting the company's exposure when it overspent on renewals, since the overspend could be added to capital.

[77] The administrators' expenditure on advice amounted to £30m., with bills of £13.9m. from Deutsche Bank, and £8.0m. from Slaughter & May. Roy Martin (Network Rail)–Alison Munro (DfT), 4 March 2003, Tom Oscroft (DfT)–Munro, 4 July 2003, and accompanying statements in DfT file R95/1/1 Pts. 4 and 9.

[78] In October 2002, DfT spending on advice was put at £21.5m. and the SRA's bid team costs at £8.6m. Iain Ure (DfT)–Darling, 10 October 2002, ibid. Pt. 4.

[79] Gourvish, *British Rail 1974–97*, pp. 403–4.

[80] Network Rail News Release, 3 March 2003; Network Rail Ltd, *R & A 2003*, pp. 14, 19–23, 30–1; SRA Board Minutes, 5 September and 5 December 2002, 16 January and 6 March 2003. A revised incentive plan, linked to the company's business plan, with potential bonuses of up to 160% of baseline salary, applied from 1 April 2003: Ibid. 1 May 2003.

Table 6.1 The Network Rail Board, March 2002–November 2004

	Age[a]	Salary[a]	Appointed[b]	Resigned	Background
Ian McAllister, Chairman	59	£210,000	Mar. 2002		Motor industry: Ford UK
Adrian Montague, Dep Chairman	55	£70,000	Mar. 2002	Dec. 2004	Finance: British Energy; PFI Task Force; SSRA; Kleinwort Benson/Dresdner
Executive directors					
John Armitt, Chief Executive	57	£450,000 + b	Oct. 2002		Railways: ex-CE Railtrack plc; Costain; Union Railways; Laing
Iain Coucher, Dep Chief Executive	41	£400,000 + b	Mar. 2002		Railways/IT: ex-MD Network Rail; Tubelines; London Underground; EDS
Peter Henderson, Projects/Engineering	49	£300,000 + b	Oct. 2002		Engineering: Bechtel
Ronald Henderson, Finance	57	£300,000 + b	Aug. 2002		Engineering: BICC, Balfour Beatty
Chris Leah, Safety/Compliance	55	£300,000 + b	Oct. 2002	Dec. 2004	Railways: ex-Railtrack
Non-executive directors					
David Bailey, SRA nominee	63	£35,000	Aug. 2002		Transport: London Transport
Jim Cornell	63	£35,000	Oct. 2002		Railways: British Rail
Charles (Chuck) W Hoppe	68	£35,000	Aug. 2002		Railways: US Railway Association; Booz Allen & Hamilton
Ross Sayers	61	£35,000	Aug. 2002		Transport: Assoc British Ports; NZ Railways; NSWales Rail Authority
Sir Robert Smith	58	£35,000	Aug. 2002	Sep. 2003	Finance: Weir Group; Morgan Grenfell/Deutsche Asset Management; RBOS; ICFC
Rob den Besten	63	£35,000	Sep. 2003		Railways: NedRail

Appointed after Nov. 2004: Michael Firth (HSBC), Dec. 2004; Yvonne Constance (National Electricity Consumers' Council), May 2005; Chris Green (Virgin), June 2005; Ian Buchan (National Express), Feb. 2006.

b = bonus

[a] As reported in R & A 2003 (den Besten reported in R & A 2004).

[b] Date of first appointment to Network Rail (formed 22 March 2002).

Source: Network Rail, R&A.

were representatives of railway licence holders and in effect self-appointing; the SRA member; and 84 public members, who were representatives of stakeholder groups and private individuals, these being selected by an independent panel chaired by Sir Malcolm Field, former Chairman of the Civil Aviation Authority.[81] Members were expected to 'hold the Board accountable for the stewardship of the Company', though from the beginning doubts were expressed within the Government and elsewhere that they would be able to wield much power.[82] Indeed, the independent think tank New Economics Foundation published a report criticizing the Government for not having been more adventurous in its governance proposals. The selection and appointment of two tiers of members, insisted upon by Montague and the CLG team,[83] fell far short of elected, multi-stakeholder representation, it argued. Its conclusion was that the chosen model was 'even less accountable than the shareholder ownership structure that it is supposed to replace and is far less democratic than either shareholding or nationalisation'.[84] Similar thinking was evident in the DfT, where it was suggested that the members were more interested in performance rather than cost, and would not subject the company to the kind of 'cross-cutting scrutiny' that institutional investors and City analysts would apply to a conventional PLC, a view shared by the Transport Select Committee.[85]

Network Rail's general strategy, articulated in the company's business plan, was to secure stability over the period 2002–4, concentrating on the core OMR function (operations, maintenance, and renewals), but also developing arrangements with the SRA for a specified enhancement programme.[86] Initially, the climate was optimistic. Armitt and Coucher immediately got to work, with Armitt promising to get to grips with the network, investigate work processes, and drive costs down. A review of the organizational structure began with the aim of providing more centralized control over the regional zones, while giving due attention to local initiatives. The executives undertook to reform managerial incentives and effect a transformation of the organization and corporate culture. Given Railtrack's record, this seemed a tall order, but by the end of the financial year changes had been made. A business plan was launched. Railtrack's zones, which had been criticized for behaving independently, were being

---

[81] Numbers from Hazel Walker (Group Company Secretary, Network Rail)–Bowker, 3 December 2002, and SRA Board Minutes, 5 December 2002. Network Rail reported 116 members in *R & A 2003*, p. 11.

[82] Elson–Blair, 8 March 2002, Prime Minister's Rail papers, Pt. 5.

[83] Montague–Bowker, 4 January 2002, SRA.

[84] New Economics Foundation, *A Mutual Trend: How to Run Rail and Water in the Public Interest* (September 2002), cit. in *Rail Politic*, 20 September 2002.

[85] Lambirth, Note on 'Network Rail', n.d. (2004), Treasury file on 'NR' (redacted); HC Transport Committee, *The Future of the Railway*, 2004, para. 59. Later on, Montague conceded the point that there was 'no real accountability to Members for financial performance': Montague–Rowlands, 9 February 2004, enclosing draft Memo. on 'Network Rail: Repositioning for accountability', 5 February 2004, DfT file R101/1/1 Pt. 3. See also NAO, *Network Rail—Making a Fresh Start*, P.P. 2003–4, HC532, 14 May 2004, paras. 3.1–3.3.

[86] Network Rail, *Business Plan 2003*, 31 March 2003, pp. 3–10.

recast as regions with a standardized structure and reporting line to Coucher, and area delivery groups were established to encourage local initiative.[87] Reassuring noises were made about getting a grip on asset management. The first steps were taken to exercise a greater central control over maintenance policies and the use of contractors, accompanied by the decision to take a limited amount of maintenance in-house in order to assist the control process.[88] Integrated planning units were also created to improve possessions management. On the other hand, it is more difficult to assess the impact of the consultant-led 'employee engagement programme' and executive team-building exercises, while staff numbers rose by 9 per cent, from 12,610 at 31 March 2002 to 13,774 a year later.[89]

The SRA, which had Bailey as a director, and deputy chairman Quarmby as an industry member, expected to be closely involved in Network Rail's operations. It assumed that it would need to exercise a considerable influence over the new company's output, costs, and performance, particularly in the period leading up to Winsor's forthcoming access charges review. The Authority saw its role as to specify; the ORR would price; and Network Rail would deliver. In this defined environment, it was obviously imperative for the three parties to work closely together.[90] However, from the start, outsiders perceived that there might well be tensions in their continuing relationship.[91] The SRA Board shared this view, and continued to nurse fears that its own core activities might be threatened if Network Rail experienced a substantial cost overrun. To prevent this it would need to act as a leading decision-maker in relation to both the core network and enhancements in the period to 2004. Joint meetings of executive directors were organized, together with monitoring of the company's performance via a series of periodic reports. Welcoming the new management's undertaking in its business plan to cut costs by 20 per cent by March 2006, the SRA expected Network Rail to move fairly quickly to a securitization of its access revenue stream, and transfer as much risk as possible to the private sector via SPVs.[92] The first six to nine months of the new infrastructure company's life were therefore rather tense. The new management increasingly looked to Winsor, the economic regulator, as the major influence in their planning. In contrast, they came to regard the SRA as an irritating complication in terms of day-to-day management, in much the same way as Railtrack had done, and notwithstanding the latter's new position

[87] Plans were advanced to break up the Eastern Region into two, and to establish a WCML Unit.

[88] The Paddington–Reading contract was the first contract to be identified for in-house conversion. In October 2003, Network Rail announced its decision to bring all maintenance work in-house.

[89] Network Rail, *Track Record* (January 2003), and organizational announcement, 3 October 2002, SRA; McAllister and Armitt, statements, 4 June 2003, in Network Rail Ltd, *R & A 2003*, pp. 3–6 and in Network Rail Infrastructure Ltd, *R & A 2003*, pp. 3–10 and see also p. 55, and SRA Board Minutes, 5 September, 7 November, and 5 December 2002, and 3 April 2003.

[90] Ibid. 6 June and 3 October 2002.   [91] Cf. Elson–Heywood, 10 June 2002, cit.

[92] SRA Board Minutes, 6 June 2002; Ian Gilbert (SRA)–Bowker et al., 25 April 2003, Cassandra Meagher (SRA)–Nicola Shaw et al., 19 May 2003, SRA.

as shareholder-banker. The SRA, on the other hand, had cause to believe that its relationship with Network Rail should be closer. It was sceptical about the ability of the senior managers to immediately transform the company's 'strong regional autonomy', and by the end of the 2002/3 financial year there was evidence that no magic wand had been waved in relation to operating performance. The report for the last four weeks of the year revealed that the delay minutes attributable to Network Rail (affecting passenger and freight operators) were 23 per cent worse than the target and 11 per cent worse than in the previous year.[93] However, the SRA Board accepted that there were boundaries which should not be crossed. In April 2003, it noted that the SRA's role 'in assisting NR' was part of its remit to exercise industry leadership, but acknowledged that it should not overstep 'the line to shadow directorship'.[94] This was a perceptive assessment of the situation. The evolving relationship between the two institutions was to be a critical element in the industry's changing fortunes in the period to 2004.

6.3 The escalation of infrastructure costs and the Regulator's Interim Access Charges Review 2003

By the end of March 2003, there was more evidence that the challenge of containing rail infrastructure costs within the envelope of government funding was becoming ever greater. Roger Ford had already warned his readers of creeping rail costs—the 'boiling frog' syndrome. 'Someone has to get a grip of Network Rail', he warned.[95] But when Network Rail published its business plan on 31 March it revealed that the core functions would require expenditure of £18.8 billion—£6.3 billion per annum—in the three years to 31 March 2006.[96] This figure, which excluded contingencies and enhancements, was £1.8 billion higher than the 'worst case' projections which the company had offered in September 2002, and 90 per cent more than the amount allowed for by the Regulator in his earlier review in 2000 (£3.3 billion p.a., 2001/2–2005/6). At the Treasury, alarm bells began to ring. Broadly, the cost of the rail infrastructure looked set to rise by around £3 billion a year. The transport team noted that the

---

[93] Network Rail, 'Summary Report for Period 13' (2–31 March 2003), SRA, and see also SRA Board Minutes, 5 June 2003. The delay minutes for the full year 2002/3 were provisionally given as 14.6m. (later confirmed as 14.7m. Network Rail Infrastructure Ltd, *R & A 2003*, p. 7), 29% worse than target and 9% worse than in 2001/2.

[94] SRA Board Minutes, 3 April 2003.   [95] *Modern Railways*, February 2003, p. 18.

[96] £6.06bn, 2003/4; £6.32bn, 2004/5; £6.45bn, 2005/6: Network Rail, *Business Plan 2003*, p. 45.

company might save up to £1 billion a year from its cost reduction programme, while the decision to fund renewals by additional borrowing might enable it to accommodate a cost increase of a further £1 billion a year. But this would still leave a shortfall of £1 billion, thereby threatening both the integrity of the 10 Year Plan, which had envisaged spending of only £3.2 billion p.a., and the 2002 Spending Review (2003–6).[97] The plan also provided a considerable challenge for concurrent financial planning in Whitehall, and in particular the preparations for the 2004 Spending Review (for 2005–8). As things stood, Network Rail's plan appeared to be both 'unsustainable and unaffordable'.[98]

The Prime Minister was quickly briefed about the rise in rail costs. He was told that cost inflation had swallowed up the allocation under the 10 Year Plan and had produced a funding gap of £1.5 billion a year. His response was a simplistic one: 'This is pretty depressing. But what has suddenly driven up costs? It's surely the safety issue.'[99] Safety was a pressing matter, of course, and costs had been affected by the decision to adopt the Train Protection and Warning System. At the same time, the Government became convinced that the existing safety organization was expensive and had suggested that responsibility for safety regulation be removed from the Health & Safety Executive (HSE) and transferred to the new Rail Safety and Standards Board, which had succeeded Rail Safety in April. McAllister had influenced the Prime Minister's beliefs when he criticized the proliferation of bodies responsible for safety, and condemned the complexity, risk aversion, and detachment from cost considerations of the existing environment. He was an enthusiastic advocate of the proposed reform.[100] However, the railway industry's 'cost drivers' were more numerous. Anticipating the work of the ORR, SRA, and Network Rail on the interim access charges review, Matthew Elson and Stephen Fidler rehearsed the possibilities for Blair's benefit. In a paper entitled 'Where Has All the Transport Money Gone?', they noted that the major cause of rising rail costs was a projected £21 billion increase in infrastructure costs to 2010/11, which would all but wipe out the provision for network enhancement. Safety expenditure was but one element in this. A backlog in infrastructure renewals, traced by Network Rail to reduced spending on track relaying from 1985, inefficiency in the use of track possessions, and an excessive bureaucracy in the setting of technical standards, were some of the items highlighted. 'But much of the increase', it was suggested, 'is simply the consequence of combining a number of uncoordinated and unchallenged decisions.'[101] However, there was

---

[97] HMT, *Opportunity and security for all: Investing in an enterprising, fairer Britain. New Public Spending Plans 2003–2006*, July 2002, Cm.5570, ch. 8.

[98] Atter and Wardlaw–Boateng, 28 March 2003, Treasury file on 'NR business plan' (redacted).

[99] Elson–Blair, 11 April 2003, enclosing revised annex on 'The Challenge for Rail', and Blair's annotation, Prime Minister's Rail papers, Pt. 10. Blair's concerns about the cost and excessive risk aversion of the safety bureaucracy are also referred to in Elson–Blair, 4 April 2003, and Heywood–Campbell, 16 April 2003, ibid.

[100] McAllister–Elson, 8 May 2003, and see also Heywood–Campbell, 21 May 2003 and Elson–Blair, 23 May 2003, ibid. Pt. 11.

[101] Cf. Elson and Fidler–Blair, 16 May 2003, ibid. Pt. 11.

little more to be done within central government but await Winsor's interim review.

The Regulator's review was a tripartite affair. The principal players—ORR, Network Rail, and the SRA—were expected to work hard together, though much of the impetus seems to have come from the ORR.[102] It was logical to embark on an iterative process in which bottom-up engineering plans were benchmarked centrally, and then exposed to top-down assessments of both the available resources and the opportunity for efficiency improvements.[103] At the root of Network Rail's savings programme was the intention to identify and tackle the several cost drivers. As the Department, the Treasury, and Number Ten watched on anxiously, a series of papers was published which led from Network Rail's tentative business plans of March 2003 to the Regulator's final conclusions in December. The main steps were as follows. In June, Network Rail produced a further business plan, with 10-year expenditure projections as required by its network licence (Condition 7). This gave some comfort to those who wished to see the company exercise some control on costs. At this stage, the projected spend for the five years from 2004/5 to 2008/9—£29.5 billion—was apparently £5.5 billion lower than the 'pre-efficiency' assumptions used in the March business plan. However, the immediate benefits would be comparatively small—a reduction of only £300 million in 2004/5 (Table 6.2). In September 2003, Network Rail produced a cost submission which was effectively its final request for funding. Several iterations were offered, including pre- and post-efficiency calculations. The baseline, 'post-efficiency' estimate indicated an expenditure of £24.5 billion, an improvement of £5 billion on the June estimate. First, the company had taken into account the SRA's draft Network Output Specification, published in July, which indicated savings that might arise from reducing the maintenance and renewals work on the lightly used routes. The calculation also envisaged a reduction in spending on the WCML upgrade. Then expenditure was trimmed by a further £500 million by taking into consideration the Regulator's third consultation paper, also published in July. This had suggested that savings could be made in the renewals programmes for both 2004/5 and 2005/6 by deferring some of the work. However, Network Rail argued that deferrals would have a deleterious impact on performance, and indeed this was the reason given for rejecting the last option, an 'illustrative assessment' of the effect of extending renewal deferrals over the rest of the five-year period. A further cut of £1.2 billion would be possible (see Table 6.2), but the effect on performance would be significant, and the target punctuality rate of 90 per cent would not be attained until 2012/13 instead of 2008/9. The company's preferred choice, the baseline option with efficiency savings, was heralded as offering a programme which was

[102] Cf. Ford, *Modern Railways*, December 2003, p. 15.
[103] Cf. SRA Board Minutes, 13 June 2002.

Table 6.2 Estimates of Network Rail's expenditure requirements for 2004/5–2008/9 (£bn, 2002/3 prices)

Date	Operations	Maintenance	Renewals[a]	OMR[a]	West Coast	Total 2004–9	Total 2002/3 actual	Total 2003/4	Total 2004/5
June 2003 plan 'pre-efficiency'	6.3	6.6	17.8	30.7	4.3	35.0	4.9	6.1	6.4
June 2003 plan 'post-efficiency'	5.2	5.5	13.9	24.6	4.9	29.5	4.9	6.1	6.1
September 2003 cost submission 'post-efficiency'									
(i) NOS option[b]	5.2	5.6	10.5	21.3	3.7	25.0	4.9	6.1	5.8
(ii) Baseline	5.2	5.6	10.0	20.8	3.7	24.5	4.9	6.1	5.5
(iii) 'Further deferral'	5.2	5.7	8.6	19.5	3.7	23.3	4.9	6.1	5.5
October 2003 Regulator's draft conclusions	5.3	5.2	9.5	20.0	2.6	22.6[c]	/	/	5.4
December 2003 Regulator's final conclusions	5.2	5.2	9.6	20.0	2.2	22.2	/	/	5.2

[a] Excluding WCML.

[b] Taking into account SRA's draft Network Output Specification, July 2003.

[c] Originally £22.7bn, but included errors in calculating maintenance spending in 2007/8 and 2008/9 and was amended to £22.6bn in the ORR web version of Draft Conclusions. My thanks to Paul Plummer (Network Rail) for explaining the discrepancy.

Source: Network Rail, Interim Review of Track Access Charges: Cost Submission, Sep. 2003, pp. 64–7, 72–3, 78–9, 84–5; ORR, Interim Review of Track Access Charges: Draft Conclusions, Oct. 2003, Table 8.1, and Final Conclusions, Dec. 2003, Table 8.1.

£10.5 billion less costly than the pre-efficiency estimate of £35 billion made known in June, a saving of some 30 per cent (Table 6.2).[104]

Winsor's draft conclusions followed in October. As in the previous exercise, the Regulator assessed the company's revenue requirements by estimating expenditure and adding in an overall return and an allowance for amortization. This time, however, the process was not entirely straightforward. Winsor's requests to the SRA to reveal its rail budget had been met with 'radio silence', and in the circumstances he could do no other than work to the assumption that the existing pattern of services would be supported.[105] Expenditure requirements for the five-year period were therefore put at £22.6 billion, beginning with £5.4 billion in 2004/5 (Tables 6.2 and 6.3).[106] The main difference with the new review was that since renewals expenditure was now being treated differently (see above), a proportion of the spending could now be financed by borrowing, instead of being charged in the year in which it was incurred. Thus, Winsor added £12 billion of renewals expenditure to the RAB (Regulatory Asset Base) over the five years. And in establishing the base figure he was also prepared to include the debt accumulated by Railtrack/Network Rail as a result of overspending in the period 2001–4 (some £5.6 billion) and £1.9 billion to cover 'revenue shortfalls' over the same period. The RAB was therefore provisionally set at £17.5 billion at April 2004, more than double the figure (£7.3 billion in 2002/3 prices) set in 2000, rising to £23.8 billion by 31 March 2009. Nevertheless, the raising of the RAB did not mean that all renewals and enhancements should be financed by borrowing—Winsor thought that around half of the renewals programme might be handled in this way. This meant that access charges would have to rise to £18.7 billion in 2004–9 (Table 6.3), leaving the Government with an additional funding requirement of £1.5 billion a year from April 2004 and busting the existing budgets. Nor had Network Rail much cause for comfort. After pitching in at £35 billion, more than double the level envisaged in Winsor's 2001 review, and then trimming the fat down to £24–25 billion, it had secured an offer of something under £23 billion. But this was not a generous settlement in the circumstances. Indeed, Winsor insisted that activity levels should rise, suggested that the scope for achieving efficiencies was considerable, and indicated that gains of 8 per cent per annum were feasible over the first three years. Steering a course between the 10 Year Plan projections and Network Rail's planning, he indicated that expenditure should fall from £5.4 billion in 2004/5 to £3.7 billion in 2008/9. He also expected the company to deliver 'very material improvements in operating performance', setting provisional targets for infrastructure delay minutes

---

[104] Network Rail, *Interim Review of Track Access Charges: Cost Submission*, September 2003, pp. 3–8, and News Release, 23 September 2003. See also ORR, *Interim Review of Track Access Charges: Third Consultation Paper*, July 2003, and SRA, *The SRA's Specification of Network Outputs. Consultation on the SRA's Draft Strategy* (July 2003).

[105] Cf. Winsor–Bowker, 1 September 2003, SRA, and Wolmar, *Rail*, 14–27 September 2005, p. 30.

[106] Here, we are using the corrected figure of £22,599m. and not the £22,689m. quoted in October 2003. See Table 6.2 for details.

Table 6.3 Main steps in the Regulator's Interim Charges Review, December 2003 (data for 2004–9 unless otherwise stated, £bn, 2002/3 prices)

	ORR draft conclusions Oct. 2003	ORR final conclusions Dec. 2003
Expenditure		
Operating	5.3	5.2
Maintenance	5.2	5.2
Renewals		
WCML	2.6	2.2
Other	9.5	9.6
Total	12.1	11.8
Total OMR	22.6	22.2
2004/5 only	5.4	5.2
RAB additions		
Overspending debt 2001–4	5.6	5.7
Revenue shortfall 2001–4	1.9	1.9
Renewals	12.1	13.9}
Enhancements	0.8	
RAB: March 2004	17.5	17.7
RAB: March 2009	23.8	24.7
Amortization	6.7	6.9
Return on RAB	6.9	7.1
Gross revenue requirement	24.8	24.9
Net revenue requirement	21.1	21.4
To be met by		
Grants	2.4	2.5
Track access charges	18.7	18.9

Source: ORR, *Interim Review of Track Access Charges: Draft Conclusions*, Oct. 2003 (ORR web version), *Final Conclusions*, Dec. 2003.

(12.3 million for passenger and freight in 2004/5, falling to 9.1 million by 2008/9, a reduction of 38 per cent on the figure of 14.7 million in 2002/3), network capability, and asset condition (broken rails, temporary speed restrictions, etc.).[107] Winsor conceded that his draft conclusions would take spending 'beyond that which can be accommodated' in the SRA's existing budget, but could not see 'any realistic alternative to this outcome'. Network Rail might undertake some 'prudent' borrowing, but at the same time the Government would need to increase its support substantially.[108]

[107] ORR, *Interim Review of Track Access Charges: Draft Conclusions*, October 2003, paras. 9.3–36.
[108] Ibid. paras. 2.8; Elson–Blair, 28 November 2003, Prime Minister's Rail papers, Pt. 11.

After further discussions between the parties, the Regulator published his final conclusions on 12 December 2003. Some ground was conceded after last-minute manoeuvring. Once the draft conclusions had been made known, Darling had sought to persuade Winsor that he might allow Network Rail to borrow more. Elson informed Blair that Darling had 'pointed out to Tom Winsor that if he confirms his (currently draft) conclusions he will be seen not as the regulator who stood up to Government in defence of the rail industry, but as the regulator who brought the industry to its knees'.[109] And certainly the prospect of some adjustment had been mentioned by Winsor, who in the draft conclusions had referred to the possibility raised by the SRA that it might extend some credit facilities due to expire in 2005, thereby encouraging the Regulator to revise his opinion on the amounts that Network Rail could borrow.[110] His *Final Conclusions* referred to further pressure:

Three weeks before the publication of this document, the SRA...requested that certain enhancement schemes which it had previously asked to take forward under separate contracts with Network Rail should be included in the RAB...Ten days before the publication of this document, the DfT and the SRA made a joint submission...in which they explained that for accounting reasons it would be desirable for the SRA in future to increase the amount of money that it pays in grant to Network Rail, allowing access charges to be set at a lower level...[111]

In fact, Winsor's adjustments to the basic calculations were comparatively small. The RAB was now fixed at £17.7 billion, after responding to the SRA's request for the inclusion of enhancement items, mainly the upgrade of the Southern Region's electric power supply (see below).[112] Projected expenditure was shaved by about £400 million to £22.2 billion, primarily as a result of reassessing the spending on the WCML upgrade. Here, the Regulator announced that he required further savings of £640 million, bringing spending down to £2.8 billion, a figure 22 per cent lower than Network Rail's cost submission of £3.6 billion in September.[113] This was to be achieved by postponing some of the works for 18–24 months, most of it on the Trent Valley line (Rugby–Stafford). The cuts also enabled the opening OMR expenditure, for 2004/5, to be reduced from £5.4 to £5.2 billion.[114] The gross revenue requirement was increased by £100 million to £24.9 billion, net revenue (after property, freight income, etc.) was estimated as £21.4 billion; and after grants of £2.5 billion, this left £18.9 billion to be found from track access charges,

[109] Ibid.; Interview with Alistair Darling, 31 January 2007.

[110] ORR, *Draft Conclusions*, 2003, para. 11; Winsor–Bowker and Ron Henderson (Network Rail Infrastructure), 11 November 2003, SRA.

[111] ORR, *Access Charges Review 2003: Final Conclusions*, December 2003, paras. 10, 18, 12.12–19.

[112] Ibid. paras. 14, 12.13–19. The amount allowed was £717m. in 2004–7 (power upgrade £528m., CTRL blockade £108m., new trains for Southern Region £49m., and £32m. for Thameslink 2000).

[113] That is, from £3.613bn to £2.803bn (excluding regional WCML renewals). With regional renewals spending was to be 18% lower, that is, £3.749bn cf. £4.559bn. Ibid. paras. 10, 7.2–3, 7.18, 7.38.

[114] Ibid. paras. 7, 9, 7.3–4, 7.32, 7.38, 8.2. See also Winsor–Armitt, 5 November 2003, SRA.

£200 million more than in the draft conclusions. Otherwise, the calculations were little altered. Amortization was raised by £200 million to £6.9 billion, and returns by a similar amount to £7.1 billion. However, the interest rates remained the same: 7.0 per cent, 2004–6 and then 6.5 per cent, 2006–9, lower than the 8 per cent allowed to Railtrack in 2000.[115] The performance regime set out in the draft conclusions was also confirmed.[116] On the important matter of government funding, Winsor declared that it was too late to respond to the Department and SRA's last minute request to change the profiling of Network Rail's income between grants and track access charges. However, while fixing the charges at £18.9 billion, he did agree to consider a subsequent submission by Network Rail to a new schedule of grants, giving the company a deadline of 29 February 2004 to produce it.[117] Network Rail accepted the conclusions on 5 February, and a proposal was submitted to re-profile its revenue stream, by increasing its initial borrowing and altering the balance between grant and access charges. The Regulator accepted the proposal on 10 March. Network Rail undertook to borrow a further £3.14 billion, and access charges were frozen for the first two years of the control period. Network Rail's revenue requirement of £21.45 billion for 2004–9 was to be provided by direct SRA grants of £9.35 billion (43%); £8.96 billion in access charges (42%); and additional borrowing (15%).[118]

What was the Government's response to the Regulator's review? On receiving the draft conclusions, the view in Number Ten was that the ORR's cost analysis was 'robust and well argued', but that at the same time the Regulator, by allowing OMR expenditure and access charges to rise, had set the Government a 'terrific problem'.[119] In Whitehall, there was little room for manoeuvre in this contract-driven, regulated, post-privatization world, where there was clearly an in-built, institutionalized tension between the economic regulator and the strategic allocator of public money. Winsor's regulatory apparatus, in common with that for other British utilities, was a hybrid of British and American regulatory approaches: he not only agreed the capital base and fixed the rate of return, as an American regulator might do, but also set expenditure and (effectively) prices, and presided over the access contracts between operators and the infrastructure company.[120] This was a considerable responsibility, and it also put the

---

[115] ORR, *Access Charges Review 2003: Final Conclusions*, paras. 11, 15, 17, 13.3, 15.4, 15.7.

[116] Ibid. paras. 13, 9.3 ff.

[117] Ibid. paras. 21, 15.8–13. The Regulator also said he would look at two further areas of uncertainty before the next review in 2009: expenditure on signalling renewals and possessions compensation, and the WCML upgrade, should costs rise (or be likely to rise) by 15% or more than expected. Ibid., para. 37.

[118] Network Rail news release, 5 February and 1 March 2004; ORR press notice, 10 March 2004.

[119] Heywood–Blair, annotation on Elson–Blair, 28 November 2003, cit.

[120] On the respective strengths and weaknesses of US and UK regulation, see C. D. Foster, *Privatization, Public Ownership and the Regulation of Natural Monopoly* (Oxford, 1992), esp. pp. 186–225, Matthew Bishop, John Kay, and Colin Mayer (eds.), *The Regulatory Challenge* (Oxford, 1995), pp. 1–17, 358–85, and Mark Armstrong, Simon Cowan, and John Vickers, *Regulatory Reform: Economic Analysis and British Experience* (Cambridge, MA, 1998), esp. pp. 165–94.

Government on the back foot. In British Rail's day, the management would simply have been told to make do with a reduced budget, although in such circumstances complaints would have surfaced, as with Peter Parker's bitter references to the 'crumbling edge of quality' during the period of financial constraint in 1976–9.[121] But Winsor had a duty to ensure that the rail network was properly maintained, as well as determining the price for access. And any attempts by the Government to intervene would almost certainly bring Network Rail back onto its balance sheet. Nor would a draconian approach to fares and marginal services have made much of a dent in the £1.5 billion shortfall. Some radical ideas for tackling the funding problem were floated, including the hypothecation of revenue from an increase in petrol duty. There was also a Treasury proposal to 'wipe the slate clean' by writing off Network Rail's legacy debt, which was worked up under the name 'Project Elephant'. However, this was later rejected, and in any case, the chances of something radical being implemented were remote given the need for urgent action.[122] But higher access charges presented a very real budgetary problem. For the period 2001/2–2005/6, the Regulator expected OMR spending to rise from £16 billion to £24 billion, with a corresponding increase in access charges. As we have seen (above, p. 149), higher charges would be passed on by the TOCs to the SRA to meet via the Clause 18.1 mechanism, and would be classed as current expenditure (revenue), but the SRA's budget was already overstretched. In the interval between Winsor's draft and final conclusions (October–December 2003), a 'heavy lifting group', consisting of representatives from the DfT, Treasury, SRA, Network Rail, and ORR, met to discuss a package to support Network Rail during the 2004 Spending Review period. The SRA pressed for interim funding, based on a definition of the MSCR (Minimum Support for the Current Railway), and Winsor belatedly made it known that he was willing to assist in the process.[123] However, the discussions between the parties were far from easy. There were arguments between the SRA and the DfT over what should be included in the MSCR. Many kites were flown, including a suggestion from the Department that Winsor might postpone his final determination and defer higher access charges for three years, and another from Network Rail that £800 million might be shaved off the WCML upgrade by adding five minutes to London–Glasgow journey times.[124] The most intractable difficulty, of course, was that of finding a funding solution which did not fall foul of the Government's fiscal rules preventing borrowing to cover current expenditure over an economic cycle. It was only at the eleventh hour that the 'lifting group' came up with the idea of paying a higher proportion of Network Rail's income in the form of direct grant, which could be counted as capital

---

[121] Parker, cit. in Gourvish, *British Rail 1974–97*, pp. 47, 85.

[122] Elson–Blair, 28 November 2003, cit.; Information from Peter McCarthy (DfT) and Lewis Atter (KPMG).

[123] SRA Executive Committee Minutes, 23 October and 13 November 2003, SRA 57/01/01 Pt. 4.

[124] Ibid. 27 November 2003, and see also SRA Board Minutes, 6 November 2003.

expenditure, thereby making it possible to reduce track access payments. Winsor insisted that this should be a stop gap measure, and that Network Rail should receive the full revenues no later than April 2006.[125]

What was the SRA's verdict on the review? How well had they worked with Winsor and Network Rail? There had been many meetings, but it is not possible to say that the relationship between the bodies was close. It was an open secret that there had been fundamental disagreements between the Regulator and the strategic body whose financial position he was supposed to take into account, and these were picked up by the Commons Transport Committee in its contemporaneous report on *The Future of the Railway*. The Committee also noted that Network Rail had acted independently of the SRA in its decisions on maintenance.[126] Despite the SRA's intention not to 'micromanage' the new company, Bowker pressed McAllister in a series of meetings in the summer and autumn of 2003 to improve the strength of railway operating experience at the top of the company, a perceived shortcoming which ATOC also shared.[127] Performance may have been tackled over the course of 2003/4, but there were evident glitches, notably on the WCML, where a limited track possession on 30 May 2003 produced 'one of the worst non-Hatfield results ever recorded'.[128] The pressure may have had some effect. A revised functional organization was introduced, with an attempt to align management more closely with the TOCs via joint operational control centres. About 650 jobs in senior and middle management were shed (Project Violet), and an experienced operator was appointed as an adviser: Graham Eccles, Chairman of both South West Trains and Virgin Rail. On the other hand, Network Rail did not consult the SRA before deciding to take all of its maintenance in-house. The much older McAllister tended to look upon Bowker as something of an earnest sixth former, while Armitt and Bowker were very different personalities. By the beginning of 2004, general relations between the two bodies were reported to be 'more difficult'.[129]

More significant, perhaps, were the clashes between the SRA and the Regulator over the areas for which they had a 'dual key', namely, enhancement expenditure. The Regulator did not confine himself to determining how much the Railway should cost; he was also intimately involved in what Network Rail should do, which brought him into potential conflict with the Authority as 'specifier' of the network. Two areas of disagreement were publicized by the two

---

[125] SRA Executive Committee Minutes, 27 November 2003, 57/01/01 Pt. 4; Bowker–Winsor, 5 December 2003, SRA; ORR, *Final Conclusions*, 2003, paras. 21–4; Ford, in *Modern Railways*, January 2004, p. 5.

[126] HC Transport Committee, *Future of the Railway*, April 2004, paras. 39, 41, 145, 153–62. Evidence was taken from June 2003 to January 2004.

[127] SRA Board Minutes, 7 August, 4 September and 2 October 2003; Garnett (Chairman, ATOC)–McAllister, 14 May 2003 and reply, 28 May 2003, SRA.

[128] Chris Green (Chief Executive, Virgin Trains), fax to Robbie Burns (Regional Director, Midlands, NWR), 2 June 2003, and reply, same date, SRA.

[129] SRA Board Minutes, 6 November, 4 December 2003 and 15 January 2004.

parties. First, there was the costing of the WCML upgrade; second, there was the issue of the spending on transitional enhancements which the SRA had asked to be included in Network Rail's asset base. As we have seen, the Regulator, while taking the SRA's strategy as his benchmark, decided that savings could be extracted from the WCML project by delaying the rate of implementation by 18–24 months. This displeased the SRA, which made its disagreement with the decision public, while privately noting that the expenditure profile would be 'impractically skewed' and that the Rugby, Trent Valley, and Stafford renewals would be 'out of synchronisation', constraining the number of train paths and London–Glasgow journey times.[130] Winsor's handling of the SRA's request for the treatment of enhancement expenditure also caused resentment. Receiving the proposal at a very late stage—2 December 2003—the Regulator was concerned about both the costing of the elements and the revelation that the SRA had agreed to indemnify Network Rail against project costs and liabilities. He therefore rejected the request to add £1,067 million to the RAB, which included an allowance of 50 per cent for contingencies, and instead fixed the increase at £717 million. The decision was accompanied by some withering remarks about a report from the SRA on the principal component, the Southern power upgrade project, submitted on 20 November. Here Winsor criticized 'the apparent lack of robustness of the cost estimates', 'the very high level of contingency', and the 'inefficient risk allocation agreed between the SRA and Network Rail'.[131] Winsor was required to have regard to the SRA's finances, but that did not mean that he had to constrain his statutory responsibilities as custodian of the rail network to find a solution which lay within the SRA's and the Department's budgetary scope. In fairness to all the parties, some tension was inevitable given the speed with which major policy was being determined. But by the autumn of 2003, the 'concordat' had been all but torn up. This had been clear from somewhat acrimonious correspondence between Bowker and Winsor in October. Winsor was irritated that the SRA was finding it difficult to set out its financial position in full as he prepared to finalize his review, and he refused to be bounced on the profiling of access charges. Thus, when Bowker told him that 'we agreed that we had all been working on the understanding that any access charges increase...would only impact from 1st April 2006', he replied: 'It is emphatically not the case that we have agreed this.' And when Bowker complained about a leaked letter to the *Daily Telegraph*, implying that the ORR had been responsible, Winsor not only refuted the allegation but added some trenchant words about the SRA going beyond its jurisdiction in relation to network outputs and projects such as the WCML: 'So much for our separate, discrete and

---

[130] SRA press release, 19 December 2003; SRA Executive Committee Minutes, 8 January 2004, SRA 57/01/01 Pt. 4. See also SRA/ORR High Level Meeting Minutes, 3 November 2003, SRA.
[131] ORR, *Final Conclusions*, 2003, paras. 12.15–19.

complementary jurisdictions...The SRA has consistently engaged in precisely the regulatory overlap and competition which you and I said should not take place.'[132]

By January 2004, anxiety levels in Whitehall had been raised significantly. The Regulator's award had created substantial doubts about whether the railway could be funded by the Government, and the SRA had been encouraged to refine its affordability analyses under pressure from the Department. Some of the calculations produced by Winsor's team failed to gain acceptance in either Network Rail or the SRA, and the Regulator's insistence on applying his remit to the letter irritated those who felt that a more flexible approach was required.[133] However, the position in which he had been placed was scarcely straightforward. He had not wished to be party to a fudge caused by the impact of Railtrack's earlier failings on the Government's balance sheet. On the other hand, the difficulties created by applying a wide-ranging element of economic regulation to Britain's railway industry had become all too evident. The access charges determination of 2003 was reminiscent of some of the shortcomings of the American regulatory approach, that is, allowing the capital base to rise, and protecting a rate of return, but in this instance with a company, now quasi-public, which provided the infrastructure for an activity requiring a very significant degree of public subsidy. More than this, the seriousness of the crisis surrounding rail finances had begun to have an impact upon the position, and even credibility, of the SRA. Prodded by the Treasury, the Department had issued the Authority with numerous warnings about the need to pull in its belt. On 16 January, Sue Killen, Director General of the DfT's RALMS group,[134] informed Bowker that Ministers were asking the SRA to work with a non-Network Rail budget that was £175 million less than set out in its MSCR calculation. Ministers did not 'wish to see any expenditure on enhancements, or grants towards the cost of enhancements, which is not already unavoidably committed until it is clear that the railway as a whole is delivering the required efficiencies and that further work on these schemes is affordable'. They also asked the SRA to look carefully at its running costs, expecting to see 'a significant reduction in the level of spend on external advice'. In these circumstances, 'It has been agreed that it would not be sensible for the Authority to publish its 2004 strategic plan.'[135] A much warmer letter, sent to Doug Sutherland on 5 February, indicated that the SRA had made strenuous efforts to meet departmental requirements.[136] But by this time the fundamental rationale for such a body was about to come under scrutiny. The

---

[132] Bowker–Winsor, 2 and 28 October 2003, and replies, 8 and 30 October 2003, SRA. There was a further exchange over Winsor's correspondence with Philip Mengel of EWS, in which the Regulator expressed his views on the 'work of the SRA': Bowker–Winsor, 21 November 2003, SRA.

[133] Thus Roger Ford: 'A Rail Regulator Whose Approach to his Powers makes Ozymandias Look Reticent': *Modern Railways*, December 2003, p. 4.

[134] RALMS = Rail, Aviation, Logistics, Maritime, and Security.

[135] Killen–Bowker, 16 January 2004, cit.

[136] Killen–Sutherland, 5 February 2004, DfT file R78/1/14 Pt. 11.

DfT had undertaken a review of the 10 Year Plan, and Darling had produced a vision for the next 20–30 years. With an earlier, 'blue skies' enquiry into transport having been entrusted to John Birt by Tony Blair, Whitehall was full of review mania, and major reform was clearly in the air.[137] However, the SRA had not helped its cause by publishing *Everyone's Railway: The Wider Case for Rail* in September. Whatever its intentions, and however much it may have been presented as a 'reminder for all parties of the advantages and benefits of rail rather than as a specific bidding document', it looked like a request for more money and in this context clearly irritated the Government.[138] Furthermore, there was abundant evidence that the aspirations of the SRA–ORR Concordat had not been satisfied, while the relationship between the SRA and Network Rail was far from cordial. Bowker had begun to articulate his frustration with the status quo, and had drawn up plans to merge the Authority with Network Rail, under his leadership, using the codename 'Project Proper Delivery' or 'PD'. Responding to the SRA's lack of operational authority and the absence of a single 'controlling mind', Bowker suggested that the Authority should take immediate control of Network Rail, leaving the Regulator to jettison economic regulation and concentrate on Competition Act powers. The proposal would have effectively reconstituted the British Railways Board, and resembled Birt's thinking, which had been put to the Prime Minister in the previous year.[139] How realistic such ambitions were is not difficult to determine. A merger was scarcely likely given the problems it would have created for the classification of a company already perilously close to, if not part of, the public sector. The idea was shared with Rowlands at the DfT, but given the emerging dissatisfaction with the SRA was given short shrift.[140] A further example of discord was the failure to produce a revised brochure setting out the respective roles of Network Rail, the ORR, and SRA. Bowker's wish to see such a document was expressed in November 2002, and by July 2003 Nicola Shaw had produced a draft for consideration. However, there was no response from the Regulator, and by January 2004 the SRA Board agreed to wait until he had stepped down.[141] Thus, by the time that Darling announced a major review of the industry and its institutional arrangements on 19 January 2004, against a backcloth of rising costs, there were reasons to doubt the viability of existing arrangements, including the position of the SRA, and all options were on the table.[142]

---

[137] Elson–Blair, 11 April 2003, and Elson and Fidler–Blair, 16 May 2003, cit.; Elson–Blair, 20 June 2003, Darling–Blair, 3 October 2003, Prime Minister's Rail papers, Pt. 11. On Birt's inquiry, see Elson–Blair, 8 March 2002, cit. and 18 October 2002, ibid. Pt. 8.

[138] SRA Board Minutes, 3 September 2003; Interview with Mayhew, 2006, and Rowlands, 2007.

[139] Elson–Blair, 18 October 2002, cit.

[140] Memo. to SRA Executive on 'Project PD', 13 June 2003, Shaw, e-mail to Bowker et al., 18 June 2003, SRA; Interview with Rowlands, 2007.

[141] SRA Board Minutes, 7 November 2002–15 January 2004.

[142] Elson–Blair, 14 January 2004, Prime Minister's Rail papers, Pt. 12.

6.4 Enhancement projects and railway investment

It is important here to remind ourselves that the work of the SRA was not confined to making contributions to the Regulator's charges review and coping with the financial consequences. Aside from franchising, fares, and the other policies described in Chapter 5, it had made a determined effort to get to grips with what enhancements could be contemplated in the midst of the difficulties of the transition from Railtrack to Network Rail. The main projects which required urgent attention were the WCML upgrade, where the SRA felt it could act as the badly needed project champion; the replacement of the slam-door, Mark I stock in use south of the Thames, due to be completed by 1 January 2005; the associated financial transactions surrounding the procurement of new rolling stock; and the upgrading of the electric power supply south of the Thames to enable the new trains to run effectively. All this required additional resources, initially referred to as the 'Glass Elevator', then as 'TPFA' (Transitional Projects Funding and Implementation Arrangements).[143]

Turning first to the WCML, we have seen how this major project was re-launched with the ambitious 'PUG2' upgrade contract between Railtrack and Virgin Rail in October 1997. The contract provided for badly needed additional capacity and an increase in maximum speeds from 125 to 140 mph by 2005, and was intended to enable Virgin to meet the terms of its West Coast franchise, which promised substantial premium payments from 2002/3 to 2012/13.[144] We have also noted that estimated costs rose substantially, from £2.2 billion in June 1998 to £5.85 billion in November 1999, and £7.2 billion in April 2001.[145] From 1999, relations between Railtrack, on the one hand, and the Regulator and the SRA, on the other, had deteriorated as serious shortcomings in the company's project management had surfaced. The misplaced choice of signalling technology (see above, p. 49), the separation of work on track, signalling, and power lines, and the uncertain boundaries between the renewals and enhancement elements in the project were potent examples of this, and confidence in the ability to contain costs had evaporated.[146] But it was also clear that the PUG2 deal, which Bowker had

---

[143] The 'Glass Elevator' was a funding mechanism comprising Network Rail debt supported by SRA credit. Its origins lay in 'headroom' funding of up to £1.6bn agreed in early 2002 and predicated upon Railtrack's successor moving to depreciation accounting for renewals. However, it was subsequently replaced by adding project costs to Network Rail's RAB. Cf. Linnard–Bowker, 18 December 2001 and 2 January 2002, SRA.

[144] Grant–Mottram, 22 October 2001, SRA. A history of the project to 2000 is provided in ORR, *Interim Review of Track Access Charges: West Coast Route Modernisation: A Consultation Document* (July 2003), pp. 37–43.

[145] See above, p. 49, 77. Data in current and constant 2005/6 prices are provided by the NAO in its report on *The Modernisation of the West Coast Main Line*, P.P. 2006–7, HC22, 22 November 2006, Appendix 1 and Table 10 [here we prefer Railtrack's unpublished estimate of £7.2bn in April 2001 to the publicized figure of £6.3bn in December 2001 (report, p. 27)].

[146] Interview with Chris Green, 15 October 2007.

negotiated for Virgin, with Winsor's help, had exposed Railtrack to considerable risk, as had its commitments in relation to capacity for other users of the line, which were enforceable by the Regulator.[147] In May 2000, the Regulator took enforcement action against the company in relation to the upgrade, and matters were made worse by the latter's panicky response to the Hatfield accident, and by slippage in Virgin's procurement of new, tilting, 'Pendolino' trains. By late 2001, with Railtrack in administration and Bowker about to be installed as SRA Chairman, a complex renegotiation was in progress, involving the Department, Virgin, Railtrack, and the SRA. As we have seen, the waters were muddied by concerns over Bowker's potential conflict of interest as a former Virgin manager and by the Department's efforts to determine the matter itself. But the events of December 2001–January 2002 fully demonstrated the difficulties faced by the project owing to: the lack of a strong project champion; Railtrack's ineffectual grasp of costs; conflicts between Virgin and other users of the line (encouraged by the Regulator's ruling on train paths for freight and non-Virgin passenger services when endorsing the PUG2 deal); disagreements within the SRA between advocates of intercity passenger and freight; and the Department's efforts to conclude a deal which was advantageous to Virgin. The story was as follows. In the summer of 2001, Railtrack reviewed the project and concluded that it was foundering. Not only would the work on Phase I (125 mph by May 2002) be late and cost twice as much as anticipated, but there was no implementation plan or firm costing in place for Phase II (additional capacity and 140 mph by May 2005). Talks between the Department and the contracting parties resulted in heads of terms being signed in October, just after the administration order had been made. It was conceded that Phase I would be delayed (until at least May 2003), while the Phase II ambitions were considered no longer feasible. The putative agreement comprised two elements: the 'Hartwell accord', which left much of Phase II as an option for the SRA to consider, and embraced a revised compensation package of £330 million to be paid to Virgin by Railtrack for breach of PUG2; and the 'Omega' proposals, which sought to constrain access to the WCML for users other than Virgin. Maximum speeds were to be lowered to 125 mph, and Virgin would retain train paths at the expense of freight operators (principally EWS) and other TOCs (e.g. Silverlink). In the meantime, the SRA had conducted its own review, with the help of Booz Allen Hamilton, KPMG, and Linklaters. The conclusion was that Phase I should be delivered as soon as possible, but that in Phase II the route's capacity should be optimized for *all* users. Opposition to Hartwell and Omega was communicated to Byers by Morton, shortly before his departure, and subsequently confirmed by the SRA Board. Morton was concerned that the deal might prejudice the position of his successor. 'The current agreement', he wrote, 'is too

---

[147] ORR, *The Regulator's Conclusions on the Proposed Tenth Supplemental Agreement to the Track Access Agreement between Railtrack plc and West Coast Trains Ltd (The 'PUG2' Agreement)* (June 1998).

favourable to Virgin. Richard Bowker simply would not survive the "Caesar's wife" test.'[148]

In January 2002, after both the SRA and the Rail Regulator had expressed opposition to Byers's proposal to determine the allocation of capacity himself and give Virgin 10 train paths an hour, the idea was shelved. Alternatives were then evaluated, with Bowker now fully involved in the SRA's deliberations.[149] The matter was urgent. Virgin, experiencing financial difficulties with its Cross Country franchise and unable to secure the revenue growth it had forecast for West Coast, was pressing for renegotiated track access rights to be concluded by the end of May, while at the same time EWS was pursuing its own ambitions for track access. Both, of course, required the endorsement of the Rail Regulator.[150] The situation again stretched the capability of the privatized railway structure, exposing the shortcomings of the SRA's intrusion into the industry's 'decision tree'. All parties except the Regulator appealed to the SRA while seeking to retain freedom of action. Thus, Railtrack was anxious that the SRA bear the risks and costs involved in accommodating Virgin's passenger ambitions and those of other operators after October 2004.[151] Freight interests continued to express concern that an advantageous deal for Virgin would result in fewer freight paths.[152] Virgin voiced strenuous opposition to the SRA's actions in opposing the Hartwell deal, while GNER complained that timetabling plans, which apparently included five Euston–Edinburgh trains a day, would abstract traffic from its King's Cross–Edinburgh services. The SRA could not stand aside. It had responsibilities for a franchise that appeared to be failing, and had been given the role of securing the optimum strategic use of the network. However, as Bowker conceded, 'to a very large extent this role is executed through the decisions of others'.[153] In fact, the SRA quickly decided to prioritize intercity and long-distance freight services, thereby endorsing a 10-path solution for Virgin, but with 'flighting' (closer timings) of West Coast trains on the congested sections, and adjustments outside the peak.[154] But on one thing most agreed with the Authority's diagnosis. The project required clear sponsorship as a commercial and customer-led project, instead of one 'where the project programme management and delivery

---

[148] Morton–Byers, 31 October 2001, SRA; SRA Board Minutes, 1 November and 6 December 2001.

[149] Ibid. 22 January 2002; Kent–Byers, 16 January, 2002; Kinchin-Smith, Memos. on 'West Coast Route Strategy', 10 and 28/9 January 2002, SRA.

[150] Kinchin-Smith, Memo. on 'West Coast Route Strategy: Virgin Rail Group issues', 28/9 January 2002, SRA.

[151] Stephen Bull (Finance Director, Railtrack plc [in railway administration])–Kinchin-Smith, 6 February 2002, and reply, conceding responsibility, 8 February 2002, SRA.

[152] Cf. Lord Berkeley (Rail Freight Group)–Bowker, 12 February 2002, Richard Turner (Chief Executive, Freight Transport Association)–Byers, 15 February 2002, SRA.

[153] Tony Collins (Virgin Trains)–Bowker, 25 January 2002, and reply, 6 February 2002; Garnett–Bowker, 18 February 2002, SRA.

[154] Kinchin-Smith, Memo. on 'West Coast Route Strategy', 7 February 2002, SRA Board Minutes, 7 February 2002. David Quarmby was a dissentient. He preferred an 8/9-path solution, expressing concern that the 10-path solution carried too many attendant risks: Quarmby, 'Notes' from Bombay, 7 February 2002, and see Bowker–Quarmby, 12 February 2002, SRA.

defines [sic] both the outputs and the implementation options'.[155] To that end, and given that Railtrack was in administration, the SRA sought to 'de-scope' and 'de-risk' the upgrade. With the Department's encouragement it led a high-level Steering Group (later called Project Board) charged with the task of producing a draft route utilization strategy for the WCML. This would facilitate the submission by Virgin and Railtrack of a revised track access agreement to the Regulator.[156]

The work was far from easy, and it quickly emerged that the task of reconciling the requirements of passenger and freight trains was a challenging one.[157] Nevertheless, there was a genuine attempt by all parties to get to grips with the project, and the presence of Bechtel in reviewing Railtrack's infrastructure programme provided a further stimulus.[158] By the time Network Rail had made an offer for Railtrack in June, the timetabling work had been completed. It had proved possible to reconcile most of the operators' demands, though capacity was constrained on the Trent Valley line and north of Crewe. On the other hand, Bechtel's work had revealed that the cost of the project would be much higher, and the timescale longer, than anticipated. It was hoped that 125 mph running would be possible by the autumn of 2004, but addressing the backlog of renewals would create operational problems in the form of longer track possessions.[159] In the following month, as we noted in Chapter 5, the SRA provided emergency support to Virgin's ailing franchises. The loss-making Cross Country franchise had been cross-subsidized by West Coast profits, but this arrangement was jeopardized by the delay in delivery of the new trains and the over-optimistic schedule of franchise premia which Virgin had agreed to meet.[160] Under the 'letter agreement', the two contracts were effectively moved onto a management contract basis pending resolution of the outstanding issues surrounding the WCML upgrade and the procurement of new trains. The Authority then proceeded to pay Virgin a total of £965 million over the next two years.[161]

After this, the SRA, headed by new recruit Jim Steer and a small team led by Stuart Baker, worked up its route utilization work and WCML strategy, with due consultation.[162] In September, timetabling work had been refined to accommodate significant improvements in service levels from 2004, and full delivery in 2007/8. Adjustments to off-peak services meant that Virgin could have

---

[155] Note on 'West Coast Project Issues 12.2.02', SRA.

[156] Andrew Murray (DTLR)–Linnard et al., 15 February 2002, West Coast Steering Group Agenda and papers, 18 February 2002, SRA; SRA Board Minutes, 7 March 2002. Initial members were Bowker, Armitt, Collins, Graham Smith (EWS), Bob Goundry (Freightliner), with David Rowlands (DTLR) as an observer.

[157] Ibid. 11 April 2002; Stuart Baker (SRA), Memo. to SRA Executive Committee, 15 April 2002, SRA.

[158] SRA Board Minutes, 2 May 2002. The Bechtel review was commissioned by Armitt.

[159] Ibid. 13 June 2002.

[160] The West Coast franchise envisaged a subsidy of £56.5m. in 2001/2 moving to a premium of £60.3m. in 2003/4.

[161] Ibid. 18 July 2002, Coulshed–Darling, 12 July 2002, SRA, and see above, p. 152.

[162] The SRA also engaged Oakleigh Consulting to report on lessons from the project's earlier phase.

11–12 trains in the peak, while freight operators could have something close to the 'PUG2' commitment of 42 additional paths, though not north of Crewe. As to the infrastructure programme, the SRA noted that the Bechtel review of May 2002, while an excellent piece of work, reflected Railtrack functional specifications, and did not match the customer-driven timetable requirements. If implemented as planned the project would cost £13.2 billion (with no provision for contingencies), more than twice the figure agreed by the Regulator for CP2, and would not be completed before 2012. Its own review envisaged a cost of £9.9 billion, a reduction of over £3 billion to be achieved by deferring some renewals, and postponing the introduction of the signalling and train control innovation, ERTMS.[163] A consultation document for the West Coast strategy was published in October, and a final document appeared in June 2003. This sought to define the objectives and outputs for the route, including production of a specification of future use and a business case. In doing so, the SRA had assumed responsibility as client and sponsor of the work. Spending had been estimated at £9.9 billion (£7.6bn for renewals, £2.3bn for enhancements), though the intention was to secure additional economies as the work proceeded. The key objective was to deliver 125 mph running on 'Europe's longest, busiest mixed traffic railway', with capacity for 80 per cent more long-distance passenger trains, and 60–70 per cent more freight traffic. Journey times would be reduced: London–Birmingham in 80 minutes, London–Manchester in under 2 hours, London–Glasgow in 4 hours 15 minutes. A punctuality target of 90 per cent was set for 2007/8. All this would mean considerable disruption to services, and the Authority worked hard to sell the implementation package to operators. Engineering work was to be concentrated in the period May 2003–September 2004, using 'blockade' strategies, that is, temporary line closures, allowing significant progress to be made by September 2004, with completion in December 2008. Working closely with Network Rail and the train operators, the SRA claimed to have made a real difference to project management, retaining much of the thrust of the 'PUG2' agreement, but with reduced costs.[164] In the meantime, Bechtel signed a £160 million contract with Railtrack to provide the necessary project management, with a team led by Tom McCarthy.[165] Both the DfT and the Treasury endorsed the SRA's strategy. In September 2002, Darling assured Paul Boateng, the Treasury Chief Secretary, that the cost–benefit calculation for the SRA's proposals was superior to a 'do-minimum' alternative in which the enhancements would be stripped out, and expressed the hope that the project, which would be financed by Network Rail, could still be accommodated within

---

[163] 'Progress Report', ibid. 5 September 2002; SRA, *Annual Report 2003/4*, p. 14.

[164] SRA Board Minutes, 1 May 2003; SRA, *West Coast Main Line Strategy: Refreshing a Prime National Asset* (June 2003). In 2003, unit renewal costs were found to be 60% higher than average. Booz Allen Hamilton, Report to ORR on 'WCRM Review of Efficient Costs' (December 2003), para. 46; ORR, *Final Conclusions*, 2003, para. 7.35.

[165] Railtrack plc and Bechtel Ltd, 'Programme Management Services Agreement for the West Coast Route Modernisation Programme', draft, 4 September 2002, SRA.

the resources earmarked for the 10 Year Plan. The proposals were duly endorsed, though the Treasury's concerns about the railways' 'disturbing' cost trends and 'ineffective' project management were fully articulated.[166]

By this time, of course, Winsor was busy with his track access charges review, and as we have seen, the two bodies eventually clashed over the project. The SRA may have been the project's 'client', taking responsibility for the specification of the enhancement work and the desired outputs, but it was accepted that it was for the Regulator to determine the project's efficient cost and its impact on track access charges. The manner in which this duty was discharged was another matter, of course, and the exchanges became increasingly adversarial on both sides. While accepting the SRA's strategy document of June 2003, Winsor raised serious questions about the efficiency and phasing of the project as set out, and the risks to delivery. Armed with the powerful regulatory tool, Condition 7, together with a scoping report from Booz Allen Hamilton, he articulated his concerns in a consultation document in July, at meetings of the Project Board, and in his draft conclusions in October. He came up with alternatives to the Network Rail/SRA's base option: 'minimum initial cost', saving £2.4 billion, and 'radical restructuring', saving £1.1 billion.[167] Network Rail was then told that the Regulator was particularly concerned about the promise to deliver 125 mph running south of Crewe and Manchester by September 2004. He suggested that the work that was critical for the increase in line speeds had not been properly programmed, and the highest priority work had not been done. There were thus doubts as to whether the work would be completed on time, while the accelerated timetable was likely to encourage overspending (work done by the ORR's consultants, Mouchel Parkman, had already revealed that the WCML's unit costs were much higher than average). Winsor expected Network Rail to demonstrate that it was doing all it could to achieve economies in the post-September 2004 phase, including a firmer justification of the need for 'condition-based renewal'. The company was therefore asked to respond to a suggestion that expenditure be cut by £200 million in 2004/5 and by £400 million in 2005/6.[168] When Winsor published his final conclusions in December, he assumed that efficiencies totalling £863 million could be achieved over the review period, producing a cost of £2.8 billion (excluding regional renewals) for the remainder of the work. Since £3.1 billion had been spent to 2002/3, and the expenditure for 2003/4 was £1.7 billion, this indicated a total cost for the upgrade of £7.6 billion, £2.3 billion below the SRA's estimate of £9.9 billion in June 2003.[169] Winsor's intervention, as we have seen, prompted some acrimonious exchanges. The Regulator was adamant that

---

[166] Darling–Boateng, 27 September 2002, and reply, 7 October 2002, Prime Minister's Rail papers, Pt. 8. The 'do-minimum' proposal would have cost over £8bn.

[167] See ORR, WCRM Consultation Document, 2003, paras. 3.1 ff. and Table 5.1, and WCRM Project Board Minutes, 22 September 2003, SRA.

[168] Winsor–Armitt, 5 November 2003, SRA.

[169] ORR, Final Conclusions, 2003, para. 7.39; Progress Report, March 2004, SRA. See also Booz Allen Hamilton, Report, December 2003, Table 8.

the SRA should not seek to use the Project Board as the 'governance structure' for the project. In January 2004, he told Bowker that Network Rail, not the SRA, was in charge of the project, and was accountable for its specification and delivery to the train operators and the Regulator. He wrote: 'The SRA persists in asserting a jurisdiction which it does not have. When will you stop doing this?'[170] Bowker's response conveyed his exasperation. He reiterated his difficulties with the final conclusions. The project was not deliverable with the funding and programme which the Regulator had outlined. Furthermore, the SRA was upset by the Regulator's intention to deal with WCML enhancements within the regulatory framework, since it much preferred to handle these by means of direct contracts with Network Rail.[171] Winsor's interventions may have been resented in some quarters, and Bowker has argued that the ORR had failed to master all the complexities of the upgrade,[172] but the fact is that he provided a catalyst for further activity to control and review the project. By March 2004, a substantial revision of the delivery profiles had been drawn up, with some elements brought forward (in comparison with the Regulator's suggested profile) and others postponed further. And the reduced project cost figure of £7.6 billion was confirmed.[173]

Notwithstanding the arguments over the implementation and costing of the upgrade, and the limitations of the blockade 'windows' set for the substantial engineering work, the project milestones were then achieved. New Class 390 Pendolino trains began to come into service from April 2002, with a London–Manchester service from January 2003. In September 2004, with the completion of Stage 1A, Virgin were running to Manchester in 2 hours 15 minutes (fastest train: 2 hours 6 minutes), with London–Birmingham in 83 minutes.[174] The Crewe/Liverpool/Preston upgrade, Stage 1B, was completed in June 2005, after which the SRA handed over responsibility for the project to the DfT. In December, 125 mph running to Glasgow was provided, with a $4^1/_2$ hour journey time (Stage 1C).[175] By this time, some £6.5 billion of the *c.*£8 billion budget had been spent.[176] The new timetables were not introduced without some difficulties,[177]

---

[170] Winsor–Bowker, 5 January 2004, SRA.

[171] Jim Steer (SRA)–Michael Beswick (Network Rail), 12 December 2003, Bowker–Winsor, 22 January 2004, SRA; Interview with Paul Plummer, 7 March 2007.

[172] Interview with Bowker, 2006.

[173] 'Progress Report', March 2004, and briefing documents from SRA and Network Rail, 25 March 2004, SRA.

[174] SRA, Report to Ministers and DfT on 'West Coast Project', September 2004, SRA. A record time of 1 hour 54 minutes for London–Manchester was also achieved.

[175] A record run in September 2006 was made in 3 hours 55 minutes, beating the Advanced Passenger Train's 1980s record by 20 minutes.

[176] Mike Adams (Bechtel)–Peter Henderson (Network Rail), 29 October 2003, SRA; SRA, *Annual Report 2005*, pp. 30–1; *Rail*, 7–20 December 2005, p. 6.

[177] Cf. Green–Burns and John Conway (Network Rail), 23 July 2004, complaining about putative adjustments to the September 2004 timetable, and note complaints from Milton Keynes commuters, SRA, report, September 2004, cit.

and the media coverage of train failures and teething troubles with air conditioning and toilets was predictably shrill.[178] However, the overall verdict has been favourable. With only the final series of upgrades—Rugby, Nuneaton, Trent Valley, Stafford, &c.—to complete, the NAO's report of November 2006 concluded that the SRA had turned round the project. Its intervention had provided a clear direction, enabling project milestones to be met with a firmer grip on costs. This said, the NAO also observed that the project was likely to exceed Winsor's cost estimate by some 10 per cent, achieving only about 70 per cent of the 'efficiencies' he had outlined in his charges review.[179] The current position appears more favourable. In May 2007, Network Rail reported efficiency savings of 24 per cent, stating that it was on course to achieve the Regulator's target of 31 per cent, though the news was overshadowed by an earlier train derailment on the WCML at Grayrigg.[180] The impact of the upgrade on traffic has been more equivocal. Virgin was able to report that in 2005/6 passenger numbers on its West Coast services were 38 per cent higher than in 1997/8, while its Cross Country services had seen a growth of 62 per cent. However, passenger *mileage* has exhibited a more modest growth, at under 10 per cent on the West Coast since 1993/4.[181]

The replacement and/or modification of British Rail's 'slam door' Mark I passenger fleet was a policy of long vintage. The use of new or modified stock had been recommended by the Hidden enquiry into the Clapham accident of 1988, and the issue resurfaced when the old stock was involved in further accidents, for example, at Purley (1989) and Cowden (1994). In 1992, British Rail found the cost of a modification programme to be prohibitively expensive: over £200 million, about £3.4 million per life saved. Because BRB expected to replace all but about 300 of the vehicles by the year 2000, no further action was taken. However, in the dog days of nationalization, the rolling stock investment programme was curtailed, and in 1995, when 2,700 of the vehicles were still in use, it was anticipated that at least half would still be operating 5 years later.[182] The HSE, which had been slow to pronounce on the matter, eventually acted in May 1998, issuing a consultative document which proposed, *inter alia*, that unmodified Mark I stock

[178] Cf. *Financial Times*, 30 March 2005, p. 4; *Daily Mail*, 18 March 2005, p. 39; SRA, Report on 'West Coast Project', March 2005, pp. 2, 5, June 2005, p. 1. On earlier teething troubles, see Gwyneth Dunwoody–Darling, 2 August 2004, and Bruce Witham–Virgin Trains, 6 July 2004, in DfT file R73/1/6 Pt. 17.
[179] NAO, *Modernisation of the West Coast Main Line*, pp. 7–8, 18. See also DfT, *West Coast Main Line Progress Report* (May 2006).
[180] Network Rail Infrastructure Ltd, preliminary results for 2006/7 (24 May 2007). The Grayrigg accident was on 23 February 2007.
[181] Virgin Trains Press Release, 24 April 2006. Roger Ford provides data for 1993/4 and 2005/6 showing a 54% rise in West Coast passenger journeys, but only a 9.3% increase in passenger miles: *Modern Railways*, February 2007, pp. 20–1.
[182] Gourvish, *British Rail 1974–97*, pp. 354–5. British Rail's modification programme proposed fitting vehicles with crashworthy ends and anti-climb buffers.

should be withdrawn early, but that modified vehicles be permitted to remain in use until 2007, by which time new franchise contracts would have provided for replacement.[183] In August 1999, new Railway Safety Regulations provided for the removal of Mark I stock by 1 January 2003. However, there was to be a short moratorium (until 1 January 2005) for vehicles which had been modified, with central locking, and a 'cup and cone' device to prevent overriding in the event of a collision.[184]

The principal lessees of the stock were the three main franchisees south of the Thames: Connex South Eastern, Connex South Central, and South West Trains. Together they were operating with about 1,700 vehicles in 2000–1.[185] Although the Mark Is clearly performed badly in collisions and there were an uncomfortable number of train incidents involving inappropriate use of the doors, they were mainly deployed during the morning and evening peak periods to supplement more modern trains. Furthermore, the cost of the revised modifications seemed expensive, especially given the short operating period envisaged and the fact that they were unlikely to give effective protection at speeds over c.35 mph.[186] The investment could also be challenged in relation to the number of lives that might be saved.[187] Doubts about the need for modification inhibited action, and, in any case, the franchise periods were short. Although Connex had a 15-year franchise for South Eastern, with a commitment to replace all its Mark Is by October 2006, the South West and South Central franchises were due to end in February and May 2003, respectively. During the SRA's 'shadow' period, 1999–2001, the target for modification or replacement began to look increasingly unrealistic. By November 2001, the three southern franchises had informed the HSE that they considered the proposed 'cup and cone' modification to be 'inappropriate' and 'unnecessary'. They argued that it would produce additional safety concerns, while the introduction of the Train Protection Warning System (TPWS) across the network would greatly improve the operating environment.

---

[183] HSE, *Railway Safety 1996/7*, pp. 47–9; Roger Ford, *Modern Railways*, July 1998, pp. 438–40. The draft regulations also embraced the fitting of all trains with a protection system, and fitting of all bi-directional line signals with train stops and speed traps.

[184] S.I.1999 No. 2244, 10 August 1999. The regulations came into effect in April 2000.

[185] Numbers were stated to be 1,781 and 1,743 in SRA presentations in April and November 2002, respectively. A figure of 1,738 'at the start of the programme' was published in SRA, *Annual Report 2003/4*, p. 23. In addition, there were about 400 vehicles in use elsewhere on the network, for example, on c2c, Great Eastern, and ScotRail.

[186] *Parl. Deb. (Lords)*, 5th ser. (Session 2001–2), Vol. 631, Lord Falconer, replies to Lord Berkeley, 7 February 2002, wa116–17. Cup and cone modifications were estimated to cost c.£7–11,000 a vehicle, and central locking c.£25–30,000 a train: Ford, *Modern Railways*, July 1998. Ford later thought that there might be a financial case for modification: ibid. February 2001, p. 24.

[187] The number of fatalities per fatal accident was 5.7 for Mark I stock cf. only 2.1 for post-Mark I stock, 1967–96: analysis by Prof. A.W. Evans, reported in HSE, *Railway Safety 1997/8*, pp. 47, 49. However, the annual death rate in significant train accidents was low, and deaths caused by falls from slam-door trains while running averaged only 2.5 p.a., 1996/7–2001/2: *Railway Safety 1999/2000*, p. 38, 2001/2, pp. 56, 58.

Consequently in May 2002 they applied to the HSE for an exemption from the regulation.[188]

The SRA's role was in theory somewhat tangential. However, under Section 54 of the 1993 Railways Act, the franchising authority was empowered to take steps to encourage railway investment, principally by giving guarantees that new trains would be used by successor franchisees, and in handling the refranchising process it could insist that operators procure additional rolling stock. On the other hand, it was for the ROSCOs—HSBC, Porterbrook, and Angel Trains—to purchase the trains from manufacturers, and for the TOCs to lease them. Nevertheless, once the Authority had emerged from its 'shadow' status, it developed a more proactive rolling stock strategy. It sought to encourage the manufacturers, Railtrack and the operators to address the comparatively leisurely response to the introduction of new trains, something which had caused the Minister for Transport, John Spellar, to convene a series of meetings with the manufacturers Alstom, Bombardier, and Siemens in 2001–2.[189] The matter was complicated by a number of factors: the need to re-let the short franchises; the emerging financial difficulties of incumbent franchisees such as Connex South Eastern; and the fact that the impact of the new trains on the electric power supply had not been considered when Mark I replacement had been insisted upon by the HSE. Once again, with Railtrack in administration and in some disarray, the SRA took the initiative in a project which involved seven interrelated elements: vehicle supply; vehicle acceptance; enhanced power supply; provision of train depots; driver training; responses to longer trains (either platform extensions or selective door opening [SDO]); and *pro tem* modifications to the Mark Is. Aside from the realization that there was a considerable time lag between ordering a new vehicle and putting it into service, the failure to perceive that the power supply would need to be upgraded to handle the new, power-hungry trains was a substantial one. It was not until the summer of 2001 that Railtrack began to voice its concerns, prompted by the order which South West Trains had placed for 785 Desiro units from Siemens in April. The company then engaged W. S. Atkins and AEA to undertake an 'OSLO' modelling exercise, funded under the 'Project Endeavour' arrangements. And it was only in November, the month after the administration order, that the SRA's executive committee debated the issue for the first time, when Railtrack revealed its opinion that a minimum investment of £300–500 million would be needed to run the new trains on their lowest power settings.[190]

[188] HSE Press Release, 22 May 2002; Mike Parker (SRA), Memo. to SRA Executive Committee, 30 November 2001, SRA 57/01/02 Pt. 29; SRA Executive Committee Minutes, 20 December 2001 and 20 June 2003, 57/01/01 Pt. 3; John Self, Memo. 20 June 2002, 57/02/02 Pt. 35.

[189] See DfT file R73/1/6 Pts. 10–11.

[190] Parker, Memo. on 'Power Supply South of the Thames', SRA Executive Committee Minutes, 9 November 2001, SRA 57/01/01 Pt. 3, 57/01/02 Pt. 28. See also Railtrack, 'Mk.I Rolling Stock Power Supply Issues Discussion Paper' (n.d.), SRA, and Bowker, evidence to HC Transport Select Committee, P.P. 2002–3, HC125i, 26 November 2002, Q.199.

It is easy to criticize Railtrack for neglecting the power supply requirement, but the failing was shared by the manufacturers, the TOCs and the SSRA, and to a lesser extent by the HSE and ORR.[191] As Roger Ford noted, it was 'a huge problem which has slipped in under everybody's radar'.[192] When Richard Bowker became SRA Chairman in the following month, he was told that the arrangements for replacing the Mark I stock were 'far from robust'.[193] An industry summit was then convened in January 2002 to encourage a serious response to replacement. A steering group consisting of representatives from the SRA, Railtrack, the three TOCs, and three train manufacturers (Bombardier, Alstom, Siemens) was set up in February. Railtrack then assembled a power supply team, and in May David Bailey was appointed as the SRA's project sponsor.[194] A 'credible' plan was drawn up, focusing upon the prioritization of routes and the creation of support mechanisms for train orders.[195] The SRA's main responsibility under the 'Southern Region New Trains Programme' was to ensure that funding was in place to cover the work on the power supply and other costs. While Railtrack was in administration, the SRA was responsible for funding both the project management and the initial work, though over the longer term the costs were expected to pass to Railtrack's successor. In October 2002, the costs were put at £915 million for the power upgrade, and £1,210 million for the project as a whole, including the provision of depots, train storage, and compensation. At this stage, Bowker was able to obtain Darling's agreement that the additional funding for this be provided on an emerging cost basis via the so-called Glass Elevator. However, in December 2003, the Regulator agreed to add only £528 million to Network Rail's RAB to cover the upgrade, and, in fact, a concerted review process by the SRA, Network Rail, and the TOCs produced a redefinition of the works, reducing estimated costs to £709 million.[196]

Then there was oversight of the £2.5 billion train procurement process. By July 2002, the final replacement orders had been made, allowing the SRA to assess the prospects for delivery. The Authority facilitated the process by giving Section 54 assurances to the incumbent TOCs and providing underwriting to the ROSCOs, Angel Trains (for South West Trains), and Porterbrook (for South Central). Stagecoach ordered 785 Siemens 'Desiros' for South West Trains; Govia

[191] Roger Ford recalls that there was some frustration in Railtrack's Southern Region because the manufacturers (except Alstom) were unable to provide it with the necessary current characteristics until 2001: communications with author, 25 May 2004 and 15 February 2007.

[192] Roger Ford, in *Modern Railways*, January 2002, p. 26.

[193] Parker, Memo. 30 November 2001, cit.

[194] SRA Executive Committee Minutes, 7 and 20 December 2001, 11 and 22 January 2002, SRA 57/01/01 Pt. 3; SRA Board Minutes, 22 May and 4 July 2002. Bailey had been charged with the task of developing a safety investment strategy for the SRA: SRA Board Minutes, 11 April 2002. The SRA was also assisted by Professor Brian Mellitt (adviser) and Opteama (UK) (consultants).

[195] SRA, 'Mark I Replacement: Summary of the Holistic Plan', April 2002, and 'Industry Plan Issue 1', 31 December 2002, SRA. See also SRA, *Rolling Stock Strategy* (December 2003), pp. 1–2, 9–10.

[196] Bailey, Memo. 22 October 2002, SRA Executive Committee Minutes, 24 October 2002, SRA 57/01/01 Pt. 4, 57/01/02 Pt. 38; SRA Board Minutes, 5 December 2002, 3 April 2003; SRA, *Annual Report 2003/4*, p. 24. On the Regulator's review see above, p. 195.

ordered 700 Bombardier 'Electrostars' for South Central (later renamed South-ern); and Connex ordered 618 'Electrostars' for South Eastern, where HSBC Rail was the lessor.[197] Here, the Authority faced a number of problems with each of the three franchises which had an impact upon the procurement process. As we have already observed, the operating performance of South West Trains had given cause for concern. Stagecoach pressed for a longer franchise, but was able to negotiate only a one-year extension to February 2004, followed by a three-year extension to February 2007 on terms which many regarded as generous. One of the effects of the changes was Stagecoach's decision to withdraw from 120 of the 785 'Desiros' it had ordered. The SRA played a strategic, facilitating role in negotiating an imaginative response to this news. It worked with all the parties concerned—the manufacturer, Siemens, the ROSCO, Angel, and the franchisee, National Express, which urgently required additional rolling stock for its Silverlink and Central franchises on the WCML. The redirected stock—30×4-car Class 350s—was then modified by Siemens for dual-voltage working north of the Thames. The cost implications for the SRA were not insignificant—at least £30 million—but this bill for modifying the order and re-marketing the trains was preferable to the £100 million-plus bill it would have had to bear if there had been a cancellation.[198]

South Central's difficulties had been met in part by taking the franchise from Connex and transferring it to Govia, but the latter's aspiration for a 20-year franchise stalled and a more realistic $6^3/_4$-year term (to December 2009) was eventually agreed. Finally, the financial difficulties experienced by Connex South Eastern produced a request in 2002 for additional subsidy to compensate it for having to meet an earlier replacement deadline. Further requests for assistance in 2003 culminated in the SRA taking the franchise back in November. There were also difficulties with the manufacturing and acceptance processes. The acceptance procedures proved to be unduly lengthy—nearly two years—for both Alstom's Class 458 'Juniper' trains for South West Trains, and the Adtranz/Bombardier 377s. Dissatisfaction was expressed about the quality and reliability of the 458s, where the failure rate was comparatively high, prompting Stagecoach to switch to Siemens, who undertook to provide vehicles which had been tested more fully before entering service.[199] Bombardier also disappointed the SRA when it sought

---

[197] These are vehicle numbers, not train sets. The South West Trains order was subsequently reduced to 665 vehicles. Govia took on Connex's order of 240 vehicles for South Central, while the Connex total for South Eastern included 210 vehicles ordered in 1997.

[198] SRA Executive Committee Minutes, 9 January–27 May 2003, SRA 57/01/01 Pt. 4; Andrew Hudson (SRA), Memo. 19 May 2003, Graeme Hampshire (SRA) et al., Memo. 28 August 2003, SRA 57/01/02 Pts. 43 and 46; SRA Board Minutes, 1 May 2003.

[199] At Period 4, 2004/5, the moving annual average figure for miles per technical casualty was only 4,412 for the 458s, compared with 14,510 for Alstom's Gatwick Express 460s and 31,415 for Bombardier's c2c Class 357s (both of which experienced early teething troubles), and 23,021 for the less complex Mark Is: ATOC data in DfT file R73/1/6 Pt. 17. By Period 10 the figures were 7,734, 16,137, 31,149, and 21,997: SRA. See also Andy Barr, Memo to SRA Executive Committee, 21 May 2004, SRA 57/01/02 Pt. 53 (for Period 12 2003/4 data), and *Rail*, 26 May–8 June 2004, p. 45.

to slow down train delivery in 2003–4. Here, the company was clearly intent on smoothing out the rate of production at its Derby plant, but it was justified in raising questions about the power supply, claiming that both Connex and Govia had asked it to adjust delivery dates. It was also anxious to avoid a repetition of the situation in 2000–1, when over 200 vehicles were produced but were unable to enter service with Connex South Eastern and c2c. However, Bombardier's actions did nothing to dispel uncertainty about the completion of the overall programme.[200]

The procurement and commissioning process for the trains had to be linked in with the upgrade of the power supply, thereby encouraging a considerable amount of manoeuvring. The SRA worked on the development of a strategic reserve of rolling stock, and at various stages the swapping of trains, and the concentration of new trains on particular routes were considered.[201] Considerable savings were achieved by adjusting the balance between platform lengthening and the use of SDO.[202] The timetables were eased by extracting concessions from the HSE. First, exemption from the requirement to modify the stock was duly obtained in October 2002.[203] At this point, it became clear that the 1 January 2005 deadline for replacement could not be met. The necessary work to reinforce the power supply would not be completed in time, which meant that around 350 of the 2,000 + new vehicles would not be able to gain network acceptance.[204] Thus, in March 2004, the three TOCs applied for a further exemption to operate Mark Is beyond the deadline. This was granted in October, the exemption running until 30 November 2005. Inevitably, the activity was concentrated in the period 2004–5, but by the time of the SRA's demise most of the programme had been delivered. At the end of 2004/5, 85 per cent of the Mark Is had been withdrawn, and 83 per cent of the new vehicles were in service. Enhanced power had been secured at 58 of the 90 DC sites, and 50 per cent of the high voltage feeder routes had been completed. Of the 116 short station platforms, 82 had been cleared for SDO working, and 28 of the 34 remaining platforms had been lengthened (the remainder following in the summer).[205] By the agreed deadline of 30 November 2005, all the slam-door trains had been replaced.[206] The outturn

[200] Per Staehr (Bombardier)–Bowker, 18 February 2003, Bowker–Spillar, 4 March 2003, Pierre Lortie (Bombardier)–Bowker, 22 August 2003, SRA; *Sunday Times*, 17 August 2003, business p. 2; SRA Board Minutes, 15 January 2004.

[201] Cf. SRA Executive Committee Minutes, 13 and 27 February, 22 May and 26 June 2003.

[202] Ibid. 13 May 2004. Savings of c.£160m. were achieved.

[203] HSE Press Release, 24 October 2002. The exemption was made conditional on the fitment of TPWS by 31 March 2003.

[204] SRA Board Minutes, 3 October 2002; Bailey–Newton et al., 15 October 2002, SRA.

[205] At the end of 2004/5, 1,472 vehicles had been replaced by 1,690 new vehicles: SRA, *Annual Report 2005*, p. 32. Cf. the position in October 2004, when only 858 (49%) Mark Is had been scrapped, SRA Executive, Report to Board, 25 October 2004.

[206] That is, 1,738 scrapped, 2,025 new vehicles: Ibid. *2006*, p. 28. A special exemption was made for the six units used on the Lymington branch: SRA Board Minutes, 6 October 2005. Mark Is also continued to operate north of the Thames on the Aylesbury–Princes Risborough branch and on the Cardiff Bay branch.

cost of £652 million for the additional infrastructure was comfortably below the estimate.[207]

Despite the prevailing gloom about the burgeoning cost to the Exchequer of the railway industry, the SRA was able to fulfil the expectations made of a central strategic body in relation to projects such as the West Coast Main Line and the Southern Trains Programme. The likely counterfactual in the absence of the Authority as project champion was that the WCML upgrade would have cost much more and been further delayed; while it is difficult to see how anyone, whether the ROSCOs, TOCs or Railtrack, would have taken up the baton of project development as the SRA was able to do. The inevitable result would have been a failure to meet HSE deadlines, accompanied by much finger-pointing and legal wrangling. The Authority was also effective in encouraging Network Rail to embark on a limited programme of minor enhancements, including Probus–Burngullow, Filton Jnc., and Swindon Platform 4.[208] Thanks to its technical director, David Waboso, it also advanced other elements of planned capital expenditure, for example, ERTMS (signalling) and GSM-R (digital train radio communication system).[209] Bowker was right when he claimed that these projects represented a real achievement by the SRA. Here, at least then, was a situation where a directing mind, even if lacking full executive authority, was able to produce significant results within a fragmented institutional framework.

6.5 Conclusion

The West Coast Main Line and Mark I replacement programmes were two of the more visible demonstrations of the railway investment process, as were new trains for Virgin's West Coast and Cross Country franchises. How extensive, then, was railway investment during the SRA period, and how did the record compare with that of the past? The published data reproduced in Table 6.4 indicate, as we would expect, the rising cost of infrastructure investment, supported by direct government grants to Railtrack and Network Rail, as well as the accounting change which saw renewals expenditure charged to capital account over the asset's life instead of to revenue account in the year in which the expenditure occurred. This said, infrastructure spending increased in real terms

---

[207] Jim Hailstone (SRA), Memo. to SRA Executive Committee, 19 December 2005, SRA 57/01/02 Pt. 61; SRA, Southern Region New Trains Programme Completion Report (final draft), 24 December 2005, SRA Board Minutes,12 January 2006.

[208] SRA, *Annual Report 2003/4*, pp. 63–4. These schemes were apparently extracted from a reluctant Network Rail after a protracted meeting known as the 'pizza night': Interviews with Steer and Sutherland, 2007.

[209] SRA, *Annual Report 2003/4*, pp. 56–9, 2005, pp. 33–4.

Table 6.4 Railway investment, 2000/1–2006/7 (£m., in constant 2000/1 prices)

Year	Investment			Grants to Railtrack/ Network Rail	Grants to CTRL	Average age of rolling stock (Q1) (years)
	Infrastructure	Rolling stock	Total			
1996/7	1,286	51	1,338	–	–	/
2000/1	2,404	554	2,958	–	–	20.7[a]
2001/2	3,075	900	3,975	487	181	20.1
2002/3	3,557	536	4,093	750	354	19.7
2003/4	4,346	712	5,058	1,333	204	19.3
2004/5	3,173	803[b]	3,976[b]	1,843	279	16.0
2005/6	2,842	489[b]	3,331[b]	1,742	279	13.6
2006/7	3,218	279	3,497	–	–	13.3
Annual average 1996/7–2000/1	1,825.2	229.4	2,054.6			
Annual average 2001/2–2005/6	3,398.6	688.0	4,086.6			

[a] Q2.
[b] In the 2005/6 Yearbook, incorrect figures are given for rolling stock and total investment: in constant 2000/1 prices, 2004/5: £1,722m. and £4,895m.; 2005/6: £435m. and £3,278m. My thanks to Michael Lee (ORR) for confirming the error.

Source: ORR, *National Rail Trends Yearbook 2005/6* and *2006/7*; Treasury, GDP deflator, market prices, 2007. Data for National Rail. Note comparisons are affected by changes of definition and in particular the allocation of maintenance (and renewals) to first revenue, then capital account by Railtrack/Network Rail.

by 52 per cent from £2.40 billion in 2000/1 to £4.35 billion in 2003/4 (in constant 2000/1 prices), but then fell back to £3.2 and £2.8 billion in 2004/5 and 2005/6. Investment in rolling stock fluctuated more sharply, much of the lumpiness being the product of the investment in Mark I replacement vehicles. However, the quinquennial averages point up the increase in investment. Over the period 2001/2–2005/6, rolling stock investment was three times that in the previous five years (1996/7–2001/2), and infrastructure investment was 86 per cent higher. However, much of the activity was in fact necessary to rectify problems caused by the period of comparative neglect between c.1994 and the Hatfield accident in October 2000. For example, the average age of the passenger rolling stock may have been progressively reduced (Table 6.4), but the figure for the first quarter of 2004/5, 16 years, was the same as that when Hambros undertook its valuation of British Rail stock in 1994. It was only in the following year, when the impact of the substantial Mark I replacement programme was being felt, that the figure fell below this.[210] With c.4,000 passenger vehicles procured between 1999 and 2005, most of them inevitably more sophisticated and expensive than the trains they replaced, the record appears to have been a distinct improvement on the modest investment activity undertaken by British Rail. In addition, private sector investment in freight facilities has been impressive since privatization. The companies acquired about 400 new locomotives and 3,000 wagons to 2003, and total investment in the sector has reached about £1.5 billion, according to the Rail Freight Group.[211] However, in overall terms, it is difficult to say that investment has met the expectations of the privatizers. The Mark I programme was an obligation that would have to have been met by the railways, whether private or public; as Roger Ford put it, it was 'not a triumph of privatisation but the result of realpolitik'.[212] If we exclude this enforced programme, then the number of vehicles procured under 'normal circumstances', under 300 a year, was comfortably exceeded by 'constrained' British Rail in the period 1979–90, who introduced more vehicles in the recession years of 1979–82 than the privatized railway has done in more favourable economic conditions.[213]

On the eve of another extensive rail review, what could be said about the way in which rail institutions had responded to the challenge of the post-Hatfield trauma? Railtrack had been replaced by Network Rail, but costs had escalated, the new body's borrowing had risen steeply, and the Regulator's access charges review in December 2003 rung alarm bells in the Department, the Treasury, and Number Ten. The SRA, which had been effectively marginalized in most of the reorganization work surrounding Railtrack and Network Rail, had focused single-mindedly on project management during the hiatus caused by Railtrack's administration in 2001–2 and had had some success with the WCML and Mark

[210] Gourvish, British Rail 1974–97, p. 420.

[211] Lambirth, Memo. on 'Rail Review: Freight', 16 April 2004, Treasury (redacted) file; Berkeley–Gourvish, e-mail, 4 June 2007.

[212] Ford, Modern Railways, April 2003, p. 16.   [213] Gourvish, British Rail 1974–97, p. 219.

I projects. On the other hand, its budget remained under pressure, causing questions to be asked about its ability to control spending, particularly in relation to franchises. Furthermore, its attempts to fill the leadership vacuum, while laudable in theory, in practice trod on the toes of both the Regulator and the fledgling Network Rail. With hindsight, it seems curious that no-one appears to have anticipated the nature of the problems that would arise by injecting the SRA into the railway mix, but by the end of 2003 the discord this had produced was fully understood in Whitehall. The outcome was another major review, and a further period of radical reorganization.

7

The Rail Review and its Aftermath, 2004–5

Cost and performance, what is new?
2004, the Rail Review!

The SRA, only two years old,
Abolished for something yet to unfold.

But the question in this case
Is 'where is the power base?'

Is it the DfT with its strategy?
Or the Chancellor fighting a spending spree?

Network Rail claims industry leadership,
Which brings us maybe from a flood to a drip.

Engineering led systems may be one way,
But who will give the passenger a say?

> [Extract from seasonal doggerel from
> NedRailways for Sinterklaas 2004, in
> Valk–Gourvish, 3 December 2004]

7.1 Origins

The Departmental review of the railway industry, announced in January 2004, was provoked by increasing concerns about the cost to the Government of infrastructure maintenance and renewal, enhancement projects, and franchising

Table 7.1 Government support to the railway industry, 2000/1–2006/7 (£m., in constant 2000/1 prices)

Year	Passenger revenue support			Direct support (grants)		Total support including other elements[a]
	Central government	Local government	Total	NWR	CTRL	
1996/7	1,975	318	2,293	0	0	1,169
2000/1	847	283	1,130	0	0	1,250
2001/2	714	299	1,013	487	181	1,839
2002/3	885	287	1,172	750	354	2,497
2003/4	1,251	381	1,632	1,333	204	3,363
2004/5	786	348	1,135	1,843	279	3,418
2005/6	772	292	1,063	1,742	1,214	4,061
2006/7	1,244	267	1,512	2,904	911	5,416

Source: ORR, National Rail Trends Yearbook 2006–7, pp. 62–3; 1996/7 figure from Table 3.2.
Columns may not sum due to rounding.
[a] Includes freight grants, BRB external funding requirement, SRA project development, etc.

operations in the financial year 2003/4. As we have seen, the environment in which Winsor's access charges review was conducted in late 2003 had been extremely charged. A 'heavy lifting group' had been required to find an acceptable solution to Network Rail's funding requirements in the period covered by the 2004 Spending Round, and the SRA had been encouraged to make a concerted search for economies in the operation of the passenger franchises. Despite these efforts, the level of government support rose sharply. As Table 7.1 indicates, the published data revealed an increase in overall support of 169 per cent in real terms, from £1.25 billion in 2000/1 to £3.37 billion in 2003/4 (in 2000/1 prices). While the greater part of this increase was explained by grants to Network Rail and, to a lesser extent, to the Channel Tunnel Rail Link project, central government support to the passenger franchises was 48 per cent higher in 2003/4, at £1.25 billion compared with £0.85 billion in 2000/1. Franchise support was reduced in 2004/5 and 2005/6, but total support remained at a high level in 2004/5, and exceeded £4.0 billion in 2000/1 prices in 2005/6 (Table 7.1). At these levels, the taxpayer was being asked to contribute something like 45 per cent of total railway costs. The evidence indicates that inside the Treasury there was a belief that the SRA was (i) failing to keep the cost of its refranchising deals within its agreed budget and (ii) showing more commitment to putting up a strong 'case for rail' as part as the 2004 Spending Round than to dealing with the Regulator's review and the problem of cost pressures. The Treasury also felt that the Department was failing to control its NDPB effectively and had been slow to recognize that Winsor's review might have a serious impact on its own budget.

The railways' emerging financial crisis, which was presenting a challenge to the Government's 'golden rule' on borrowing,[1] was also taken to demonstrate the failure of the industry's existing institutional arrangements.[2] The DfT, by raising the question of the need to increase railway funding, revealed that there was little 'discretionary resource' expenditure available in its other transport budgets, and there was already a 'capital/revenue' problem, not only with Network Rail but also with the classification of road schemes. In this situation, it could scarcely resist the *quid pro quo* for short-term support demanded by the Treasury—a tough set of departmental reforms, accompanied by a broader review of transport strategy, asking questions such as 'what rail network should we support?' and 'how can the transport spend be funded?'[3] But in any case Darling had become frustrated with the railways' existing arrangements, evident in the conflicting views of the SRA, ORR, and Network Rail on the WCML upgrade, and the emergence of a 'blame culture' whenever operating performance was discussed.[4] Early thinking about a major review included the Treasury notion that it would be accompanied by the write-off of Network Rail's £7 billion legacy debt, a proposal welcomed by the Department (see Project Elephant, above, p. 197). The idea was later abandoned,[5] but when, just before Christmas 2003, Darling secured Gordon Brown's agreement to a way forward on transport spending, he was told that it would be accompanied by a 'credible rail reform package', to be produced as a joint Treasury/DfT exercise.[6]

Darling's Commons announcement on 19 January 2004 promised to build on the creation of Network Rail with 'more fundamental reform' 'to streamline the remaining structure of the railway and to examine the way the industry works together'. Repeating the familiar mantra of increased demand for rail services and 40 years of substantial underinvestment, the Secretary of State provided a scathing criticism of Railtrack for losing control of its costs. He expressed his determination to end the problems caused by the lack of investment, 'compounded by an ill thought out privatisation', which had produced 'a fragmentation, excessive complication and dysfunctionality'. Costs and choices

---

[1] The 'golden rule' limits the government to borrowing for investment, not to finance current spending, over an economic cycle.

[2] Interviews with Atter and Steer (2007); Wardlaw, Memo. on 'Rail finances: update and options', 16 October 2003, cit.

[3] Elson–Blair, 28 November 2003, cit.

[4] Lambirth, 'chronological run through', 29 July 2004, in Steer, 'Note of Meeting', SRA; Interview with Mark Lambirth, 2 May 2007. SRA insiders have suggested that there were other immediate stimuli for the Review, including a Network Rail briefing for Darling, which undermined the SRA by stating that it was possible to shave £1 billion off the cost of the WCML upgrade, and a direct approach by Bowker to Blair, indicating that he would have to take over Network Rail to deliver the required objectives for the industry, which infuriated the DfT. Hard evidence for these events is naturally elusive.

[5] Alison Munro (DfT, for Lambirth)–Atter, 9 December 2003, enclosing draft terms of reference for a rail review, and Lambirth, Memo. on 'Forward March: Project Overview', 17 December 2003, DfT file R101/1/15 Pt. 1; Interview with Lambirth, 2007.

[6] Brown–Darling, 22 December 2003, Prime Minister's Rail papers, Pt. 11.

about public transport should be more transparent and the scope for devolution explored. Renationalization was firmly rejected, since the private sector (with the exception of Railtrack) had brought increased investment and innovation. In pursuing reform, two principles had to be satisfied: the Government's right to determine public expenditure; and the importance of public–private partnership. The first conveyed a somewhat contradictory message. The railways had to 'operate in the public interest, while protecting the legitimate interests of investors', and it was 'for Government to decide how much public money is spent on the railway and to determine priorities'. However, this assertion rested uneasily with the affirmation that the principle of independent economic regulation was 'essential'. 'No Government department can or should attempt to operate the railways', said Darling, and here there should be 'a single point of decision-making', though it remained to be seen whether that 'single point' could be a private sector institution. Safety regulation and standard setting were more straightforward. These were to be re-examined; they should focus on the 'real risks to passengers and employees and should not be an obstacle to providing reliable services'. The reform process was intended to produce a structure that would enhance rail performance, facilitate investment, and the control of costs. It would run in parallel with the decisions on the Spending Review to 2008, which were to be finalized in the summer.[7] The SRA could derive some comfort from two paragraphs in the statement. The first of these noted that Bowker and the SRA had 'worked extremely hard with the industry to bring greater leadership and strategic direction to the railway—and they will do so with our full support'. The second explained that Darling had asked Bowker and the SRA to coordinate and evaluate emerging solutions for reform 'as they come forward' from the railway industry, and then provide the Secretary of State with advice based on these views.[8]

The Conservative opposition was scathing in its denunciation of Darling's announcement. 'This statement heralds the fifth change in the structure of the railways in nearly seven years of this Labour Government', said Theresa May. She was able to point up the shortcomings of the existing provision: 'One in five trains run late', passenger targets cut, work on new lines abandoned. The treatment of Railtrack had undermined private investment, and Network Rail's borrowings had been underwritten by the taxpayer; expansion plans had been abandoned or deferred; commuters faced 'inflation-busting increases'. The Government, she pointed out, were 'tearing up the very structure that they created less than four years ago'. Darling had declared that there were 'too many organisations, some with overlapping responsibilities'. But 'Who created the Strategic Rail Authority? It was the brainchild of the Deputy Prime Minister. Who created Network Rail? It was the Right Hon. Member for Tyneside, North (Byers).'

[7] Darling, statement, *Parl Deb. (Commons)*, 6th ser. (Session 2003–4), Vol. 416, c. 1075–8.
[8] Ibid. paras. 32 and 53.

'Little wonder', she asserted, 'that Mr. Bowker is worried about his job.'[9] Outside the Commons, the statement merely confirmed rumours that had been circulating since the New Year. Thus, Barrie Clement, writing in the *Independent* on 5 January, had revealed that 'rail bosses' were to be 'stripped of much of their power by ministers', and that power would be concentrated in Darling's hands by taking it away from the SRA.[10] Christian Wolmar has suggested that the piece was inspired by a DfT leak. It certainly produced a variety of responses from interested parties.[11] Anthony Smith of the Rail Passengers Council defended the notion of an 'arm's length' SRA, but Tony Grayling, of the Institute for Public Policy Research, welcomed the idea of changing the Authority's status, arguing that there was a strong case for merging it with the ORR and the rail safety arm of the HSE to create a single strategic regulator.[12] Wolmar himself welcomed the Government's U-turn and the review as 'the first step in the long march towards common sense'. He questioned the idea of asking the industry to respond through Bowker, since 'there are many in the industry who argue that he and his organisation are a big part of the problem'. Nevertheless, Darling's action merited 'a couple of cheers' for recognizing that change was required, even if 'sorting out the mess' would 'require a forensic brain, the courage to attack vested interests and, possibly, an acceptance that some form of renationalisation is inevitable'.[13] Roger Ford accused the Secretary of State of 'sleight of hand' in his presentation of the prospects for higher rail investment under the 10 Year Plan. He found the rest of the statement 'horribly confused', lacking in coherence, and 'according to a mix of rumour and informed sources rewritten over a weekend to placate Richard Bowker'. But he too welcomed the Government's belated acknowledgement that there was much wrong with the industry's structure and organization. His guess was that the outcome might be 'bye bye SRA', which made the Minister's intention that industry views be channelled through the Authority an odd one.[14]

In approaching the review, Bowker told his staff: 'this is a great challenge and a really good opportunity to demonstrate our leadership'. But he also warned that the exercise should not distract executives from day-to-day concerns. There should be no loss of focus on 'delivery'.[15] He went on to invite the industry's stakeholders to take 'an open and objective look at the options', one of the

---

[9] *Parl. Deb. (Commons)*, 6th ser. (Session 2003–4), Vol. 416, May, c. 1079.

[10] Clement, *Independent*, 5 January 2004, p. 1. Bowker dismissed the press speculation as 'exaggerated and in many cases, completely wide of the mark': Ritchie (for Bowker), e-mail–SRA staff, 19 January 2004 12.08, SRA.

[11] Wolmar, *On the Wrong Line*, p. 228.

[12] Reported by Clement in *Independent*, 6 January 2004, p. 2.

[13] Wolmar, *Independent*, 20 January 2004, p. 15. Much the same message was conveyed by Robert Galbraith, *The Business*, 25 January 2004, p. 9.

[14] Ford, *Modern Railways*, March 2004, pp. 18–19. Ford also queried the assertion that the TOCs had *in many cases* brought innovation to services.

[15] Margaret Ritchie (for Bowker), e-mail–SRA staff, 19 January 2004, 17.14, and 21 January 2004, 17.17, SRA.

questions being 'the future role of the SRA'. Characteristically, he proposed that 'informal get-togethers, maybe over dinner' be arranged in addition to the presentation of formal papers. A number of subjects were suggested: accountability; simplicity; performance; affordability; sustaining growth; compatibility with EU legislation, existing and proposed; devolution; and the avoidance of hiatus.[16] At Victoria Street, two parallel workstreams were required: the first to coordinate and present the views of the industry; the second to develop the SRA's own thoughts. A small executive team would be required for the exercise, referred to internally under the title 'Project Bold', but Bowker also wished to involve Board members in the process.[17]

Meanwhile it was quickly evident that the Department's decision to undertake a review had not been preceded by detailed work on how it might be conducted. When Bowker and Nicola Shaw met Sue Killen and Mark Lambirth from the DfT shortly after the announcement, it emerged that the Department was 'at a fairly early stage of thinking'. Killen and Lambirth made it clear that they wished to 'engage the SRA closely', given the latter's operational and commercial experience, but 'it was less clear quite how we would engage or when'. However, it was understood that this was to be a DfT/Treasury review, which Bowker felt was 'perfectly proper'. At the Treasury, some papers were assembled on industry costs and the financing of Network Rail. The DfT was also concerned about Network Rail, and had begun to explore its relationships with the TOCs and the idea of some element of vertical integration. It had also accepted the Treasury's view that some control had to be imposed on SRA spending. Thus, as we have seen, Killen wrote to Bowker three days before the announcement of the review to ask the SRA to work with a budget lower than that set out in its MSCR calculations, imposed a moratorium on further enhancement spending, and asked the Authority to pursue economies in its running costs (above, p. 200). Within the Department, Lambirth sent Howells some 'yuletide' reading on Network Rail and the structural issues it raised.[18] Some early thinking was also undertaken by Chris Bolt, who had just been appointed to succeed Winsor in the reconfigured post of Non-executive Chairman of the Board of the Office of Rail Regulation from the following July. Bolt promised David Rowlands, the DfT's Permanent Secretary, that he would put down some thoughts about possible changes to the industry and these were sent to the Department on 31 December 2003 under the title 'Structure and Regulation of the National Railway in Great Britain'. Here, Bolt rehearsed the principal issues, including those affecting the SRA. The Authority, he argued, was unable to control the subsidy budget for franchises, and could not assess the financial impact of service changes. Network Rail's

---

[16] Bowker–industry members, 29 January 2004, and SRA Board Minutes, 5 February 2004.
[17] Bowker, e-mail–SRA Board members, 21 January 2004, 18.06, Chairman's file on 'Project Bold', SRA.
[18] Lambirth–Howells, 23 December 2003, DfT file R101/1/15 Pt. 1. His thoughts were fed into later discussions on the industry's structure.

knowledge of its assets was insufficient to allow it to minimize lifetime costs, and the contractual structure might also be adding to financial or economic costs. TOC costs were being affected by an imperfect knowledge of 'cost and revenue drivers'. Finally, risk aversion following accidents was also contributing to cost increases. Turning to possible solutions, Bolt was scarcely radical. He assumed that Network Rail would remain a CLG, that train services would continue to be operated by private companies, and that the 'broad shape of the contractual matrix' would continue. The budgetary problem might be addressed, he thought, by enabling the SRA to undertake a review of rail passenger services, in order that they could be aligned more closely with the available subsidy budget when costs changed.[19] The role of the ORR might be expanded to embrace the cost implications of safety changes. The SRA might be given the determining role in specifying services, and the network required to support them, via a more direct contractual relationship with Network Rail. Bolt pointed out that more sweeping changes, such as the transfer of the SRA's functions to the DfT, or the transfer of the Railway Inspectorate from HSE, were clearly possible, though the thrust of his initial position was for an expanded and clarified role for the SRA.[20] It is not clear how this contribution was received, but its last point was not in tune with departmental thinking.[21]

On 7 January, a 'brainstorming' meeting was convened under the title 'Project Forward March'. Here a joint DfT/Treasury group began by discussing network scope and finances, regulation, and industry structure. The latter was aided by revisiting the proposals to reform the regulatory framework drawn up in Byers's time in 2001–2, which had flirted with the idea of making radical changes to the territory occupied by the SRA and ORR.[22] Confusingly, a second review group was set up at the same time (January 2004) to address the performance issue. Consisting of representatives from the Prime Minister's Delivery Unit, DfT and SRA, a 'Priority Review' team was given the task of evaluating the prospects of delivering improved operating performance by September 2005.[23] The group reported that it was reasonable to aim for the Government's goal of achieving an 85 per cent PPM target by September 2005, but conceded that this would require the TOCs to exceed their existing forecasts and Network Rail to

---

[19] Bolt was presumably unaware of the SRA/Steer Davies Gleave Franchise Specification Review of September 2003.
[20] Bolt–Rowlands, 31 December 2003, DfT file R101/1/3 Pt. 1. Bolt's appointment was announced on 8 January 2004: DfT Press Release.
[21] There were other early drafts, including one from Matthew Elson of Number Ten: Elson–Killen, 17 December 2003, DfT file R101/1/15 Pt. 1.
[22] Mike Fawcett–Sue Killen, 6 January 2004, DfT file R101/1/3 Pt. 2; Note on 'March Forward—Brainstorm', n.d., R101/1/15 Pt./1.
[23] The principal team members were Lucy Chadwick (PMDU), John Aspinall (DfT) and Iryna Terlecky (SRA), with the work overseen by Peter Thomas (PMDU), Bodnar, and Shaw. DfT, Draft memo. on 'Proposed Rail Joint Priority Review', 7 January 2004, ibid. Pt. 1, Barber–Blair, 9 January 2004, Prime Minister's Rail papers, Pt. 12.

improve on the Regulator's targets.[24] With current performance running at only 81 per cent, this was clearly a tough ask, as was conceded at a 'rail stocktake' meeting at Number Ten on 6 April. Nevertheless, the Prime Minister was given optimistic assurances about future possibilities. Michael Barber, head of the Delivery Unit, expected performance to reach 87 per cent by the end of 2006, and Rowlands suggested that 90 per cent might be a 'realistic benchmark' in the longer term.[25]

7.2 The review process, January–March 2004

For the main task, the rail industry review, the DfT and Treasury assembled a high-level steering group to oversee operations. Co-chaired by Sue Killen, DG of RALMS, and Nick Macpherson, MD of Public Services at the Treasury, it first met on 9 January. The other members were Lambirth, Vivien Bodnar (Director of Rail Performance) and Willy Ricketts (DG, Strategy Finance & Delivery) from the DfT, with Lewis Atter (Head of Transport Team) and Shriti Vadera (Economic Adviser), from the Treasury. They were later supplemented by Bolt as Regulation Consultant, and Chris Muttukamaru, head of legal services at the DfT. Three subgroups were established to handle the specific workstreams: network size and funding; regulation and strategy; and industry structure. In February, these were combined into a 'lead group' co-chaired by Lambirth and Atter. Advice was taken from KPMG, who were asked to examine industry structure and testing options, and from the consultants Mercers and Jacobs, who were asked to work on money flows and options for savings.[26] The intention was to gather information and formulate recommendations to enable ministers to determine the parameters of politically acceptable action. It quickly became apparent that the SRA was to be kept very much at arm's length from the process. Notwithstanding the wording of Darling's statement, the DfT immediately agreed that the invitation to gather the industry's views was 'to RB personally not SRA as an organisation'. Bowker, while evaluating the work of others was to provide the Department with the raw submissions also, and to do so as an iterative process, 'not presenting proposals towards its conclusion'. His input should be concerned with operational matters, where the Department was short on expertise. The SRA itself should not produce its own consultation documents.[27] In addition, Darling wanted railway

[24] Elson–Blair, 26 March 2004, ibid.
[25] Elson–Scott McPherson (Darling's PPS), 29 April 2004, ibid.
[26] Sandy Bishop and Phil Graham, 'Rail Review Project Management Plan', 25 February 2004, DfT file R101/1/13 Pt. 1, and Bowker, Memo. on 'SRA input to Rail Industry Review', 6 February 2004, SRA. See also DfT files R101/1/9 Pt. 1 and R101/1/10 Pt. 1.
[27] Duncan Shrubsole (Darling's PS)–Killen, 21 January 2004, DfT file R101/1/31 Pt. 1.

stakeholders to be encouraged to submit their views direct to the DfT, instead of channelling them through Bowker.[28]

Notwithstanding these apparent constraints, the SRA's work proceeded on the official line that nothing had been ruled in and nothing had been ruled out. A 'fairly loose' project team was assembled in January 2004, including Bowker, Steer, Jonathan Riley, Richard Davies, and David Thomas. 'Scenarios' and 'models' were identified, and a series of dinners was planned to enhance engagement with the rest of the industry.[29] By this time, there was a fair body of recent work on which Bowker and his team could draw: the Franchise Specification Review of September 2003, the culmination of the work on franchise cost efficiencies, which had been passed to the DfT and Treasury; an examination of the industry's increased overhead costs, which had been initiated in December 2003 and had resulted in a draft report in the following month; and the results of a survey of the industry's stakeholders in October 2003. The Franchise Review was a technical piece of work, intended to be a major contribution to the work for the 2004 Spending Review. It had concluded that £19.6 billion was required for franchises over the 10 Year Plan period, an increase of £8.5 billion over the SRA's estimate in January 2002. This overspend might be cut by £1.0 billion through cost efficiencies (more competition for franchises, DOO, etc.) and by a further £1.2–1.6 billion with service cuts and fares increases (RPI + 3%).[30] If there were any pointers to structural reform, they were that operations would benefit from stiffer competition for longer franchises. But the Treasury took the exercise to demonstrate 'the failure of the existing franchise regime to anticipate or adjust to cost increases', and that part of the problem was that the SRA's work had not been informed by 'a set of internally consistent [guideline] budgets'.[31] The initial analysis of industry overheads, led by Stephen Bennett, indicated that these costs had risen from 15 per cent of turnover in British Rail's time in 1987/8 to 30 per cent in 2002/3.[32] Some important insights emerged: overhead costs had been cut in 1983–91 when determined management attention had been focused on controlling them; the disaggregated privatized railway produced a 'mismatch between authority, accountability and responsibility'; increased supervision had contributed most to the cost escalation—there were no fewer than 15 supervisory organizations regulating or planning railway activities. Opportunities were

---

[28] Shrubsole–Sandy Bishop (DfT) et al., 3 February 2004, ibid. Darling's view reflected the anxiety in some quarters about submitting candid comments about the industry via the SRA.

[29] Bowker, Memo. 4 February 2004, cit.

[30] Powerpoint Presentation on 'Franchise Specification Review, Issue 2: 15 September 2003', slide 108, and summary in Davies, Memo. to SRA Executive Committee on 'PwC: 8 Week Review', 11 September 2003, SRA 57/01/02 Pt. 46.

[31] Wardlaw, Memo. 16 October 2003, cit.

[32] Andrew Nock, Memo. to SRA Executive Committee on 'industry overheads', 19 January 2004, SRA 57/01/02 Pt. 49. 'Overheads' were defined as 'any costs above direct operation and equipment installation'. The calculation was rudimentary and did not include ROSCO and FOC overheads.

identified for radical action to lower overheads in areas such as supervision, pensions, and insurance, in work that was also designed to feed into the Spending Review process.[33] The stakeholder perception survey, however, was something of a curate's egg. Undertaken by Cap Gemini Ernst & Young, the report indicated that the role and objectives of the SRA were widely understood. On the other hand, most respondents believed that there was much still to do to improve the Authority's internal organization, to streamline and drive through the refranchising bidding process, to clarify and improve its relationship with Network Rail, and to change the tone and style of its engagement with the rest of the industry. The perception was that the SRA was exhibiting too much of a procedural culture, instead of a 'results focused culture'. Thus, at the time when the SRA was assembling material for the review, it was evident that its partners in the rail industry were far from happy with key elements of its interaction with them.[34]

Whatever the prevailing climate of opinion, the SRA pressed on with its programme of engagement. The first of four industry dinners was held on 9 February with representatives from TOCs, FOCs, ROSCOs, and other bodies, where the response to reform was predictably diverse.[35] No fewer than 56 written submissions eventually crossed Bowker's desk,[36] but one that caught his eye was from Chris Green of Virgin Trains, who had been encouraged to produce something by the Transport Minister, Kim Howells. Green's personal view was that reform would be best achieved by a more integrated, regional approach, building on the eight regions of Network Rail, and via a strengthened SRA, operating as a UK Rail Board with 'single focus authority'. This body would determine the outputs of Network Rail and the train companies, let and manage contracts with train companies and contractors, and provide centralized train planning. By joining together the SRA and Network Rail, an end would be made to the 'complex and expensive Track Access Regime'; TOCs would instead enforce their rights through the command structure of the new Board.[37] Bowker found the approach to be in tune with his own. The SRA's conception for the future was clear by mid-March. It was for the Government to specify outputs

---

[33] Stephen Bennett (SRA), Discussion draft on 'Spending Review 2004—Industry Overheads', 20 January 2004.

[34] Cap Gemini Ernst & Young, 'Strategic Rail Authority External Stakeholder Survey—Final Report', 12 September 2003; SRA Board Minutes, 2 October 2003, and Bowker–Vernon Barker (MD, TPE), 26 January 2004, SRA.

[35] 'Note of key points from 1st Industry Dinner', n.d., SRA.

[36] Chairman's stakeholder files, SRA. There were 14 submissions from rail lobby groups, 11 from ATOC/TOCs, 7 from local authorities/PTEs, etc., 4 from FOCs, 3 from the unions, 2 from ROSCOs, 2 from contractors/manufacturers, 1 each from Network Rail, RSSB, ICE, Danish State Railways, CIT, and 8 from individuals. Those received by 5 April 2004—52—were summarized in SRA, 'Rail Industry Review: Analysis of Industry Submissions March 2004', SRA.

[37] Green–Bowker, 27 February 2004, Bowker–Howells, 5 March 2004, SRA. A similar structure was proposed by Chiltern/Laing Rail: Adrian Shooter–Darling, 15 March 2004, DfT file R101/1/2 Pt. 2. Richard Brown (CEO, Eurostar) saw the SRA as the only body which could get to grips with industry costs by adopting a resource allocation and rationing role: Brown–Begg, 11 March 2004, copied to SRA.

(network size, service frequency, performance, safety, investment for growth, fares, and subsidy), and this would best be done through a Railways Agency within Government, following the model of the Highways Agency (though with an enhanced role for devolved bodies in Scotland, Wales, London &c.). Delivery would be simplified by establishing a single, National Rail Company operating as a private sector CLG, which would combine the SRA's franchising responsibilities with Network Rail's responsibilities for infrastructure operations, maintenance, renewal, and enhancement (these functions to be exercised through separate Track and Train subsidiaries to comply with EU regulations). The new company would also manage safety and standards. In this way, commercial choices would be aligned with engineering choices, and the Government's relationship with it would be contract-based not licence-based. Independent economic regulation would be retained, but the role of a new Office of Economic and Safety Regulation would be limited to that of policing access and acting as arbiter of the Government–National Rail contract.[38] By the end of March, these ideas had been firmed up in a 53-page document sent to the DfT and Treasury. Entitled 'Everyone's Railway—Ensuring Britain's Railway Delivers for its Customers and Taxpayers', the report noted that private sector respondents to the Review had failed to address the critical areas of ministerial requirements, the need to control Network Rail from a public policy perspective, the limitations of the existing structure in relation to enhancements, the impossibility of transferring Network Rail's debt to the PSBR, and the need for affordability. It was conceded that the establishment of a National Rail Co. to combine much of the SRA with Network Rail posed some challenges in relation to ONS requirements for private sector status, but the unification of output specification and the simplification of delivery mechanisms would, it was claimed, produce savings of 'at least £2.5bn' by 2011.[39]

The SRA's efforts were largely wasted, of course. Before it had made its first thoughts known, the joint DfT/Treasury group had already reached a fair measure of consensus on the 'emerging issues', and, in any case, Darling, in a parliamentary answer on 9 February, had reassured third parties that their rights would remain unchanged.[40] As early as 17 December 2003, Lambirth had noted that ministers wanted 'a single point at which the key decisions on rail strategy and funding come together ... These decisions need to be taken by the Secretary of State, not by NMGDs [Non-Ministerial Government Departments] or NDPBs'.[41] Then in mid-January sub-group B, charged with the task of

---

[38] SRA, 'Project Tidy: Summary of Proposals', 19 March 2004, SRA Board Minutes, 25 March 2004.

[39] Bowker–Darling, 30 March 2004, enclosing SRA, 'Everyone's Railway—Ensuring Britain's Railway Delivers for its Customers and Taxpayers', March 2004, SRA. The submission, which was refined by Board members such as Quarmby, Mayhew, and Gallagher, was also circulated to Howells, Killen, and Vadera.

[40] *Parl. Deb. (Commons)*, 6th ser. (Session 2003–4), vol. 417, Darling, reply to Lawrie Quinn on the role of economic regulation, c. 1237w.

[41] Lambirth, Memo. 17 December 2003, cit.

identifying a 'simpler, more effective structure for central government involvement in the railway',[42] had circulated a paper which noted that

logic would suggest that Ministers would be best served by being directly in control of rail
strategy. Yet the present Government chose to create the Strategic Rail Authority with
an explicitly strategic role (and name) and to promise its Chairman a considerable degree
of autonomy. The result has been a tension with the SRA behaving as if the autonomy
existed but Ministerial reaction and the controlling documentation saying otherwise...If
there is perceived to be a problem currently with lack of Ministerial control, the obvious
solution would be to bring the functions into the Department.[43]

This was not the only option which presented itself, of course, and there was
much discussion of solutions, the most promising of which appeared to be an
executive agency or a 're-populated or re-educated SRA'. But it was obvious that
if the preferred option was to reduce or remove the SRA's statutory responsibilities, then primary legislation would be required. The sub-group went on to
recommend that strategic direction and procurement would be best carried out
by the Department and that the SRA should be abolished.[44]

By the time a Rail Review 'Awayday' was convened with ministers on
23 February, officials and consultants had produced a range of models for both
the 'wheel–rail interface' ('what happens at the bottom?') and government oversight and regulation at the national level ('who determines strategy?'). At the
'coalface', that is, the relationship between train operators and the infrastructure provider, KPMG advanced a series of options, each of which was evaluated
according to cost, performance, and safety requirements (Table 7.2). Preliminary
thinking was that the continental model suggested by experience in Holland and
Denmark, in which there was a publicly owned infrastructure company and a
dominant train company, should be abandoned. A 'functional' model, in which
the Government would contract separately with a network company, train companies, and commercial agents appeared to offer the greatest direct control and
transparency, while models of 'vertical integration' and 'network procurement',
which envisaged an expanded role for Network Rail, ran the risk of amplifying
existing problems.[45] At the awayday, the idea of full vertical integration was
rejected, though it was conceded that there might be an opportunity to make
a trial of integration by joint venture on a local basis. Ministers expressed an
a priori preference for network procurement, in which Network Rail would
handle both infrastructure and operating, leaving the TOCs to fulfil commercial responsibilities (Table 7.2). But the waters were muddied by the introduction of another variant. Howells, after talking to Bowker, suggested that the

---

[42] See Ian McBrayne (DfT)–Vivien Bodnar (DfT), 23 January 2004, enclosing draft paper on 'Central
Government Structure', 23 January 2004, DfT file R101/1/20 Pt. 1.

[43] McBrayne, Memo. on 'Role of the SRA', 15 January 2004, DfT file R101/1/20 Pt. 1.

[44] Memo. on 'Central Government Structure', 23 January 2004, cit.

[45] KPMG, paper on 'Commercial Structures', 23 February 2004, DfT file R101/1/6 Pt. 1; DfT, paper
on 'Rail Review Industry Structure', n.d., R101/1/31 Pt. 1.

Table 7.2 Options for the 'Wheel–Rail interface', February 2004

Option	Description
Status quo	Government pays TOCs to buy access from Network Rail and lease trains from ROSCOs
	TOCs provide customer service, accept a measure of revenue risk
Functional procurement	Three entities: Network Rail; regional train companies; regional service companies (commercial agents)
	Government contracts separately with each to buy access, trains, customer service + revenue generation
Vertical integration	Single entity: Regional Rail companies combining infrastructure, operation, and services (sales &c.)
	Government buys all-in service from regional companies (cf. Japan)
Network procurement (i)	Single entity combining infrastructure and operation (organized regionally)
	But separate regional service companies
	Government contracts directly with both
Network procurement (ii)	Two entities: Track Company; Train Service Company (operation and services) (organized regionally)
Continental model	Publicly owned infrastructure company, and a dominant train company (cf. The Netherlands, Denmark)

Source: KPMG, paper on 'Commercial Structures', 23 February 2004, and earlier drafts, 4 and 12 February, DfT file R101/1/16 Pt.1 and R101/1/10 Pt.1.

Government might also contract with a track company, which would then sub-contract to train companies.[46] And although there was an intention to separate discussion of the 'coalface' with that concerned with the choice of a 'national specifier' of rail strategy, in fact, it became necessary to evaluate these together as options emerged.

In relation to the national structure, the search for consensus was more pro-tracted. The main intention of the review team was to establish government control and reduce regulatory overlap: to deal on the one hand, with the 'overlapping and sometimes conflicting role' of the ORR and the SRA, and on the other, with the antagonistic relationships between the ORR and Network Rail, and between the TOCs and Network Rail. All this meant that neither the Government nor the SRA had direct control over how their funding for the railway was spent. Faced with deciding between the Secretary of State and a 'super-SRA' as the 'national specifier', it was agreed that the SRA should be abolished, leaving the Secretary of State to act as the sole national-level decision-maker. Assisted by a DfT Rail Strategy Unit (RSU), the Minister would determine the trade-off

[46] Shrubsole–Killen, 25 February 2004, ibid.

between subsidy and the fare-box, and the balance of spending on operations, infrastructure maintenance and renewals (OMR), enhancements and subsidy.[47] But how exactly the new structure would work in practice remained uncertain. Once again a series of options was drawn up, and by the time of the awayday, two retained an appeal: an 'executive agency' model, in which a rail strategy unit would be located in the DfT, and procurement would be carried out by an executive agency of the Department; and a 'private agency' model, in which many of the procurement and RSU functions would be carried out by a private sector body (see Figure 7.1). The latter was quickly dismissed by the Treasury and KPMG, but the executive agency alternative had clear weaknesses too. It did not provide a single industry interlocutor, and would place a considerable burden on the Secretary of State and the RSU, which would require greater commercial acumen and delivery expertise within the Department. This gave an opportunity for both Bowker and Dieter Helm, the transport economist from Oxford University, to enter the lists. Bowker's National Rail Co. model (see above) was passed to the Review Team before its formal submission at the end of March.[48] It was joined by another option advanced by Helm, with additional input from Shriti Vadera. This last, which took its brief in part from the model adopted by the Civil Aviation Authority, was essentially a hybrid version of the executive agency and Bowker models. The procurement function was distanced from Government by locating it in a NMGD in the form of an enhanced ORR, produced by a merger with the SRA. The new body, to be renamed the Strategic Rail Regulatory Office (SRRO), would price and regulate the OMR, passenger service, and enhancement outputs (Figure 7.1).[49] Both were deemed to be sufficiently interesting to merit serious consideration alongside those produced in Whitehall. Darling had made it clear that whatever the elegance of the various models, the proposals should be tested against the key considerations of safety, performance, cost, and the reassertion of Government control, and should work in practice and not merely in theory. In particular, he was attracted to the Bowker model, because it did create a single industry interlocutor and brought service specification and infrastructure provision together. He asked that it be evaluated with the others.[50]

When officials prepared for more serious discussions with ministers on 24 March and a Blair–Brown–Darling 'stocktake' meeting on 6 April, no fewer than 18 structural options had been identified, grouped under three headings:

[47] Mike Fawcett (DfT)–Bodnar, 27 January 2004, DfT file R101/1/20 Pt. 1; Lambirth and Bodnar, awayday presentation on 'Oversight and Regulation', 23 February 2004, R101/1/6 Pt. 1; Lambirth, 'chronological run through', cit.
[48] SRA Executive Committee Minutes, 11 March 2004, SRA 57/01/01 Pt. 4.
[49] Graham–Darling, 9 March 2004, DfT file R101/1/31 Pt. 1; Dieter Helm, 'What to do about the Railways', 17 March 2004, and Powerpoint slides, 23 March 2004, SRA. See also Ian Bartle, 'The 2004 Rail Review—Towards a New Regulatory Framework', CRI Occasional Paper 24 (2005), 25–6.
[50] Shrubsole–Killen, 25 February 2004, cit.; Bishop–Darling, 9 March 2004, Shrubsole–Bishop et al., 16 March 2004, Shrubsole–Lambirth, 24 March 2004, DfT file R101/1/31 Pt. 1.

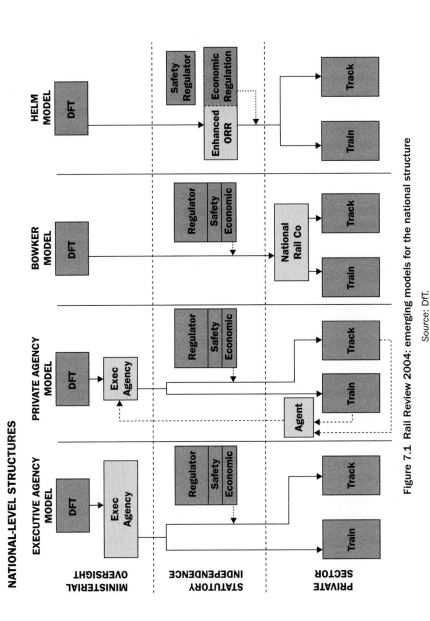

Figure 7.1 Rail Review 2004: emerging models for the national structure

Source: DfT.

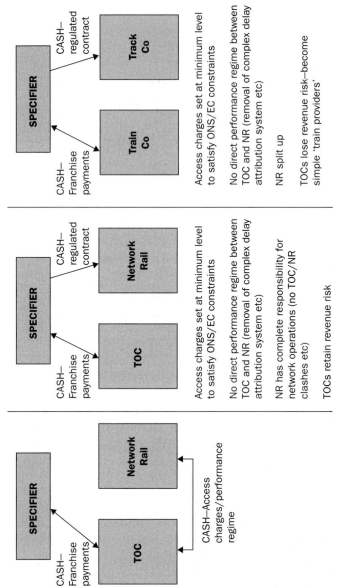

Figure 7.2 Rail Review 2004: emerging models for the train/track interface

Source: DfT.

vertical integration; reform of Network Rail; and reform of the SRA.[51] However, those under serious consideration were as shown in Figures 7.1 and 7.2. Although a great deal remained to be done in determining precisely what was required, the crystallizing approach was that the 'coalface' might best be handled by enhancing the existing structure along 'network procurement' lines, while at the national level some form of executive agency would be introduced. Here, options were narrowing because Treasury (and to a lesser extent DfT) officials had raised serious concerns about the practicalities of both the Bowker and Helm models. Bowker's National Rail Co., a private sector monopoly supplier, would confine the Government's role to that of budget setting. There was no reason to believe that it would be better placed to drive down cost and improve performance than Network Rail. Helm's model carried the risk of producing serious conflict between the regulatory and the policy objectives of government, while European Community regulations would rule out the combination of infrastructure management and safety regulation in the same body.[52] In late March, Network Rail was invited to comment on three models: an enhancement of the existing structure; the Bowker model; and a 'hybrid' model. The last of these proposed an enlarged role for Network Rail as the single body for rail delivery, including franchise management, and with a greater involvement in franchise specification. The company responded by rehearsing the pros and cons of each, and although no conclusions were offered, the thrust of its response was that the hybrid solution would have fewer disadvantages, although it was thought that the TOCs might resist it.[53] However, the Treasury was opposed to the idea, feeling that if Network Rail took on the monitoring of TOC performance it would limit the Government's sphere of influence as well as distracting the infrastructure company from its prime responsibilities.[54]

The rest of the consultation process proved equally frustrating for the review team. Here, of course, it is important to remember that this was not a formal affair, and there was no obligation on the Government to take account of the responses.[55] The Department organized a series of seminars with the industry, the first in London on 23 March, the others in Glasgow, Cardiff, and York. They may have been useful as a public relations exercise, but in practical terms were

[51] DfT, 'Potential Options for Policy and Structural Changes', n.d., DfT file R101/1/20 Pt. 1; Graham–Darling, 24 March 2004, R101/1/31 Pt. 1.

[52] Graham–Darling, 9 March 2004, Lambirth–Bolt et al., 24 March 2004, ibid.; Killen–Macpherson, 26 March 2004, DfT file R101/1/15 Pt. 1; Piers Bisson (Transport Team, Treasury)–Brown and Boateng, 29 March 2004, Treasury [redacted] file on 'Rail Review'; Interview with Lambirth, 2007.

[53] DfT, paper on 'The Rail Review: Proposed Hybrid Structure', n.d., DfT file R101/1/15 Pt. 1; Killen–Bishop and Bodnar, 26 March 2004, enclosing Network Rail, 'Discussion Paper 5: Alternative Railway Industry Models', 26 March 2004, DfT file R101/1/11 Pt. 1. The discussion papers were drafted by Paul Plummer, the Director of Corporate Planning and Regulatory Affairs.

[54] Killen–Macpherson, 26 March 2004, DfT file R101/1/15 Pt. 1; Bisson–Brown and Boateng, 29 March 2004, cit.

[55] Cf. Darling–John Thurso MP, 7 April 2004, DfT file R101/1/2 Pt. 3.

later reckoned to have been a 'Grade A waste of time'.[56] By 19 March, 25 papers had been gathered in, by 1 April over 40. The submissions from the rail industry were analysed by KPMG and the civil servants, who predictably concluded that they had produced a wide range of views. Contrary to expectations, most had been also sent to the SRA, but a few had not, including that from Lord Bradshaw, the former SRA board member, which made the firm recommendation that the Authority should be abolished.[57] The SRA's own analysis of 52 submissions revealed that most accepted that it was for the Government to set the overall policy framework and determine the amount of public funding. But there was no consensus on delivery mechanisms, and the contributions from the major players had been predictably self-serving.[58] But while Bowker maintained that most submissions had failed to address the fundamental issues, civil servants drew comfort from the fact that some common ground was evident in: criticisms of the Network Rail–TOCs relationship; a limited appetite for full vertical integration; and support for a closer alignment of Network Rail and passenger service boundaries.[59] Bowker's own model, while self-serving in retaining an important role for the SRA, nevertheless had its attractions for DfT officials because it accepted that the Government should set the agenda and budget for the railways, and proposed that ministers should be supported by a 'Railways Agency'.[60] However, this certainly did not mean that the central thrust of the model, namely, the establishment of an integrated National Rail Co. in the private sector, had been accepted, anymore than Robinson's 'Project Rainbow' had been accepted when Railtrack's fate was being determined three years earlier. Lambirth, in a subsequent and rather flattering (to the SRA) summary of events, suggested that '80/90% of SRA's analysis [was] shared by DfT/KPMG, except the bit in the middle'. But this was a rather large middle, generating 'a lot of heat and light'. Darling may have wished to establish a single player, but the National Rail Co. concept proved 'unsaleable to HMT' and was opposed by both Network Rail and the TOCs.[61]

At the stocktake meeting on 6 April, the Prime Minister was informed that certain elements of the review had been determined. The SRA would be abolished,

---

[56] Interview with senior official.

[57] DfT, Note on 'Industry Submissions to the Rail Review' (as at 1 April 2004), n.d., DfT file R101/1/3 Pt. 3. Bartle's analysis of the review submissions identifies 78 responses: 'The 2004 Rail Review', 81–5.

[58] SRA, Rail Industry Review Analysis, March 2004, cit., and Bowker, Letter to Industry, n.d. [April 2004], SRA; Rosie Snashill (Rowlands's APS)–Killen et al., 19 March 2004, DfT file R73/1/7 Pt. 3. ATOC and Graham Eccles of Stagecoach had pressed for the consideration of vertical integration, which was opposed by Network Rail, who otherwise offered little on structural change. See Armitt–Killen, 8 March 2004, Keith Ludeman (Chairman, ATOC)–Killian [sic], 12 March 2004, SRA, and James B. Sherwood (President, Sea Containers)–Darling, 12 March 2004, DfT file R101/1/2 Pt. 3.

[59] Lambirth–Bolt et al., 24 March 2004, and DfT, Note, cit. Some important submissions arrived after 1 April, notably from the Commission for Integrated Transport, 7 April 2004, and the Rail Regulator, 6 May 2004. See also Bartle, 'The 2004 Rail Review', 26–7, 46.

[60] Lambirth–Darling and Howells, 31 March 2004, DfT file R101/1/3 Pt. 3.

[61] Lambirth, 'Chronological Run Through', cit.

with most of its responsibilities reverting to the Department; the HSE would lose its responsibility for rail safety regulation; and this would probably be transferred to the ORR, which would be reconstituted as a Board under the chairmanship of the 'sensible and pragmatic' Chris Bolt. Network Rail would be retained and built upon as the only plausible candidate for the job of delivering the Secretary of State's strategy and outputs. It would remain in the private sector, since it was difficult to see how its debt—equivalent to 2 per cent of GDP—could be carried by the public sector. The new structure, now clearly the result of merely tinkering with the existing one, would therefore seek to align Network Rail and TOC boundaries, and introduce a 'more appropriate' contractual relationship between them to incentivize performance.[62] There was no alternative but to run with Network Rail, in spite of the universal criticisms of the company which had been reported to the review consultants.[63] By this stage, clearly, pragmatism, rather than 'blue skies' thinking, was driving the process.

7.3 From review to White Paper, April–July 2004

In April and May, the review team moved towards final conclusions and the drafting of a White Paper. There were of course issues other than the structural to be addressed: for example, costs and performance; franchise remapping; regulation and safety; market participation/open access; ROSCO leasing, where the costs for ex-British Rail stock were found to be almost three times higher than for new stock;[64] and devolution. Much time was taken up with the consideration of the cost problem, involving contemplation of a 'Beeching Mark II or III', building on the SRA's franchise specification review.[65] Debate also extended to the best way of managing train company performance, and the need to correct the 'perverse incentives' given to TOCs to introduce additional services as a

---

[62] DfT, Note on 'Rail Review—Update on Progress', 26 March 2004, DfT file R101/1/3 Pt. 2; Elson–Blair, 26 March 2004, cit.; Bishop–Macpherson, 29 March 2004, R101/1/31 Pt. 2; Bisson–Brown and Boateng, 29 March 2004 and Elson–Macpherson, 29 April 2004, cit.; Bisson–Gus O'Donnell (Permanent Secretary, Treasury), 19 April 2004, Treasury file [redacted] on 'permsec brief on review'.

[63] Network Rail was seen by respondents as a company with 'very deep and pervasive problems of management, skills, working practices, [and] culture', its project, operational and engineering practices were 'very poor', as was its management of the supply chain: KPMG, 'Network Rail: Governance, Membership, Targets and Incentives', 16 April 2004, and 'Update', 12 May 2004, DfT file R101/1/15 Pt. 1. At least one official criticized the KPMG's 'market intelligence' as 'extremely partial': Mike Fawcett (Rail Finance Divn, DfT)–Lambirth, 12 May 2004, R101/1/11 Pt. 1, but see the defence in Timothy Stone (KPMG)–Lambirth, 13 May 2004, ibid.

[64] Graham–Darling, 1 December 2004, DfT file R13/4/29 Pt. 4.

[65] Cf. KPMG, 'Overview of Franchise Remapping', 12 March, 'Overview of Participation Issues', 19 April, 'Update', 20 April, and 'Rail Review update', 12 May 2004, DfT file R101/1/15 Pt. 1. On Beeching (Mark I, 1963) and Serpell (Mark II?, 1983), see above, p. 135, and Gourvish, *British Railways 1948–73*, p. 305 ff. and *British Rail 1974–97*, pp. 151–81.

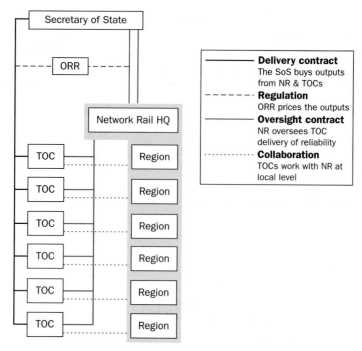

Figure 7.3 Rail Review 2004: the integrated model

Source: DfT.

result of the ORCATS revenue allocation regime (see above, p. 137).[66] But on the industry's structure an accepted view was emerging, with attention focused on an 'integrated' model, in which an executive agency within the Department would define outputs, let franchises, and contract with Network Rail. The latter would act as the 'controlling mind', taking responsibility for performance and the day-to-day aspects of franchise operations through the Network Code and local output agreements (Figure 7.3).[67] Neither the conclusions of the House of Commons Transport Committee, nor the recommendations of the Rail Regulator, nor the wider publicity given to Bowker's model could deflect the review team from these relatively modest intentions. The Transport Committee, reporting on 1 April, had recommended that both the SRA and Network Rail should be abolished and their responsibilities transferred to a new public sector agency. The media response was that this was far too radical a notion for the Government to accept.[68] Winsor's contribution of 6 May was, in contrast, more conservative, since he noted that Darling's parliamentary statements had already ruled out

---

[66] Bisson–O'Donnell, 19 April 2004, cit.   [67] KPMG, 'Updates', 20 April and 12 May 2004, cit.
[68] HC Transport Committee, *The Future of the Railway*, para. 218; *Financial Times*, 2 April 2004, p. 5.

radical options. He challenged the idea that the state should assume 'command and control' of a private sector industry, argued that the industry already had a single directing mind for operating in Network Rail, and felt that the proposal to move safety regulation from HSE to ORR should be given 'very careful consideration'. And unsurprisingly he suggested that the SRA should be brought more firmly under government control and stick to its franchise procurement brief.[69] Given departmental interest in the National Rail Co. model, revelation of the SRA's submission was potentially more influential. On 19 April, the *Daily Telegraph* ran a story on Bowker's proposals, prompting a press release from the SRA which was reported widely on the following day. However, these press reactions were scarcely favourable. The consensus was that this prescription was too radical for the Government's review, and it was a straightforward process for journalists to gather criticisms of the model from the train operators and the Rail Regulator.[70]

In the preparations for meetings between the Department and the SRA in April, ministers were briefed to the effect that the SRA could not survive in its present form. The Secretary of State was reported to be 'hugely attracted by a BR Mk2', but here a 'Catch 22' situation obtained: a National Rail Co. did not work as a private company, but the Government could not afford to have it in the public sector.[71] Nevertheless, in meetings with officials between 29 April and 12 May, Darling continued to pursue his interest in the National Rail Co. model, and the SRA was drawn into the discussions.[72] At the same time, Darling's Transport Minister, Howells, expressed concerns about the emerging role for Network Rail by compiling a list of requirements for the new structure. He was worried that the preferred integrated model would fail to rectify either the prevailing blame culture surrounding the TOCs' operations or the 'SRA–ORR friction problem', and do little to improve incentives.[73] However, by 6 May, Darling seemed to have been persuaded that the integrated model should be supported.[74] And when Bowker met Macpherson a week later, he realized that his

[69] ORR press release, including '2004 DfT Rail Review: Submission by the Rail Regulator', 6 May 2004. Cf. also Tom Winsor, 'The future of the railways in the light of the government's rail review 2004', in Colin Robinson (ed.), *Regulating Utilities and Promoting Competition: Lessons for the Future* (Cheltenham, 2006), pp. 11–12.

[70] *Daily Telegraph*, 19 April 2004, p. 32, 20 April 2004, p. 27, and 24 April 2004, p. 30; *Financial Times*, 20 April 2004, p. 4; *Times*, 20 April 2004, business p. 21; *Guardian*, 20 April 2004, p. 19. See also Bowker, letter to industry correcting *Daily Telegraph* error, 20 April 2004, SRA, and article in *Sunday Times*, 25 April 2004, business p. 13.

[71] Lambirth, Memo. 8 April 2004, DfT file R101/1/3 Pt. 3; Sarah Dudgeon (DfT)–Darling, 26 April 2004, R73/1/7 Pt. 3; SRA Executive Committee Minutes, 22 April 2004, SRA 57/01/01 Pt. 4. While Bowker met Rowlands on 27 April, it is not clear that he also met Darling as originally envisaged.

[72] Shrubsole–Bishop, 27 April 2004, Bishop–Darling, 30 April 2004, Shrubsole–Killen, 13 May 2004, DfT file R101/1/31 Pts. 2–3; SRA Board Minutes, 6 May 2004, SRA Executive Committee Minutes, 13 May 2004, SRA 57/01/01 Pt. 4.

[73] Howells, 'Living with the Hybrid Model', 6 May 2004, and Howells, Note on 'Main Concerns and Questions on the Integrated Model', n.d. in Deborah Heenan (DfT)–Shrubsole et al., 25 May 2004, ibid. Pt. 3.

[74] Shrubsole–Killen, 13 May 2004, cit.

model was unlikely to be adopted. This was confirmed on 18 May in discussions with Darling. The Secretary of State had been briefed to indicate the 'downside' of the SRA's model and the 'upside' of the review team's alternative.[75] Bowker refused to concede the argument, and by tweaking his model sought to persuade Darling and Howells that it was possible to give ministers control over a national rail company while retaining its inherent attractions: a single point of accountability, simplified structure, and the clarity created by public sector specification and private sector delivery.[76] Exploiting the fact that reservations were still being expressed in some quarters about the virtues of the integrated model, Bowker pressed the point further in subsequent meetings with Darling and his officials, advisers such as Vadera, and representatives of the TOCs.[77] Of course, there were naturally some anxieties inside Whitehall about the extent to which Network Rail as a monopoly supplier could be controlled by government within the CLG framework, about the infrastructure company's ability to respond positively to its expanded role, and about the impact on the TOCs, where some unease was evident.[78] But on 8 June, when Bowker and Steer met Darling and Howells, the SRA executives were left in no doubt that the Government's mind had been made up.[79]

In subsequent correspondence with the Department, Bowker continued to argue that there were significant drawbacks in what was being proposed. He was particularly concerned about the involvement in the process of Armitt and Coucher from Network Rail, and Graham Eccles (Stagecoach) and Keith Ludeman (Go-Ahead Group and ATOC Chairman) from the TOCs. Writing to Killen on the 14th, he expressed unease about both the direction of the work on the proposed contract between the Government and Network Rail, and the latter's proposed new relationship with the TOCs.[80] Then, in a seven-page diatribe on the 20th, effectively the last throw of the dice, he identified three 'show-stopper' issues facing the review: the nature and role of the DfT as client; the TOCs' understanding of what was being proposed; and the risks of disintegration during the transition period following the publication of the White Paper. The first was the most important. Here, Bowker challenged the way in which the public interest responsibilities would now be discharged by the DfT and not by the SRA and ORR. Consolidation was not by itself a problem, but rather 'the way that it

[75] Bowker–Killen, 5 May 2004, SRA; SRA Executive Committee Minutes, 13 May 2004, SRA 57/01/01 Pt. 4; Bishop–Killen, 18 May 2004, DfT file R101/1/3 Pt. 4.

[76] Bowker–Darling, 19 May 2004, SRA; Killen–Darling, 7 June 2004, Shrubsole–Killen on 'Rail Review—Meeting with Richard Bowker', 13 June 2004, DfT file R101/1/31 Pt. 3.

[77] SRA Executive Committee Minutes, 27 May 2004, SRA 57/01/01 Pt. 4.

[78] Cf. Fawcett–Bishop, 2 April 2004, DfT file R101/1/11 Pt. 1; Bob Davies (CE, Arriva Trains)–Darling, 25 May 2004, R101/1/2 Pt. 6; Shrubsole–Bishop, 30 June 2004, R101/1/31 Pt. 3; Bowker, 'Project Bold' notes, n.d., SRA.

[79] Shrubsole–Killen on 'Meeting with SRA on Rail Review', 13 June 2004, DfT file R101/1/31 Pt. 3; SRA Board Minutes, 10 June 2004.

[80] Bowker–Killen, 14 June 2004, SRA. On Network Rail/TOC involvement in the review process, see Shrubsole–Killen, 14 June 2004, DfT file R101/1/31 Pt. 3.

is proposed to be done that has fatal flaws'. The appointment of Network Rail as 'client for the railway as a whole' would not work:

No one can be both client and contractor, both judge and jury. Offering a major supplier, for that is what Network Rail is, the opportunity to tell you what they'd like to sell you, as opposed to telling them very precisely what you want to buy and then managing their delivery of such, is to abdicate responsibility. Network Rail is a monopoly supplier, and moreover one which is problematic to manage. No doubt it will be argued that the proposed model shows Government specifying the outputs to be delivered but examination of the documents we have seen shows this to be very high level and rather detached with Network Rail taking the lead on a great deal of client work.

There was more. Bowker argued that Network Rail as a private company could not discharge the client role satisfactorily and the result would be higher costs. The idea of the company managing industry planning, analysis, route strategies &c. was also condemned:

this will result in production-led planning, lack of customer focus and increased costs and will be horribly reminiscent of the Marsh-led British Rail of the early 1970s. The reasons why I place so much emphasis upon getting the clienting of procurement right is because every grain of my experience and every ounce of my knowledge of this Industry in practice tells me that the delivery of anything in the modern context requires highly objective, smart and effective client management.

The Government's desire to avoid micromanaging the industry was understand-able, but by passing so much down to Network Rail there was a very real danger of recreating Railtrack with a model in which the Government exer-cised only a 'light touch'. Bowker also felt that the TOCs had been misled into thinking that there would be a joint venture approach to performance management, when the reality was that matters would be directed by Network Rail. In conclusion, he told Darling that it was 'enormously risky to ask a department of central Government to promote the kind of commercially aware, timely and risk based decision making and judgement that is absolutely essential for the effective operation of organisations such as SRA, Network Rail and the TOCs.'[81]

These trenchant criticisms were rebuffed by the Department. Replying on 25 June, Darling maintained that 'the model can and will work'. The role of intelligent client would not be delegated to Network Rail: 'DfT will be responsible for the specification and will be held accountable.' The Department would act as the client for major enhancement projects, and although it would commission the development of route utilization strategies, a 'challenge focus' would continue. Furthermore, the TOCs were fully aware of what was being proposed, and the transition process required 'clear leadership' and would therefore be led by the

---

[81] Bowker–Darling, 21 June 2004, SRA. Bowker continued to press Darling to establish an 'arm's length' NDPB to effect its client role.

Department.[82] The Cabinet had been informed of the results of the review on the previous day. Predictably, the existing and 'hopelessly inadequate' organization of the railways was blamed on the previous administration. 'Radical change' was needed to regain control of costs, where a significant element was attributable to inefficiency and capacity problems. The preferred option, with the Department controlling strategic decisions and exercising 'effective control over the cost of rail to the taxpayer', was endorsed. However, some concerns were expressed about the handling of safety responsibilities, and the future financing of the industry, and in particular the proposal to reduce costs by service thinning and line closures.[83] The SRA Board was briefed about the results of the review on 1 July, and gave full support to its Chairman's critical response on the issue of the 'engaged and informed client'.[84]

A White Paper entitled *The Future of Rail* was duly published on 15 July, accompanied by a Commons statement. The Department reaffirmed that the railways were a public–private partnership, specified by government and delivered by the private sector. The SRA was to be wound up. The Government would now set the overall strategy and objectives of the industry, including the size and shape of the network, 'key timetable outputs', performance requirements, regulated fare levels, enhancement priorities, and so on, and the DfT would award passenger franchises. At this stage, it was not certain exactly how this would be done, that is, whether there would be a DfT railway directorate to determine strategy *and* a separate rail agency ('mini-OPRAF') to award franchises, or whether the two functions would be combined.[85] What was clear was that some of the decision-making in relation to service requirements would be devolved to the regional transport bodies, particularly in Scotland, Wales, and London. The ORR would continue to price outputs and provide economic regulation, and would in addition take on the safety brief from the HSE. However, it would no longer act independently to define Network Rail's outputs. Network Rail would assume overall responsibility for the network, including planning, timetable setting, and performance, and would be free to reinvest its profits in enhancements.[86] The company would deliver a reliable service via a contract with Government, and would transform its management and governance apparatus to reflect its new responsibilities. The number of franchises would be reduced and brought into line with Network Rail regions. Network Rail and the train operators would work together much more closely with 'aligned incentives' and new operational arrangements, including joint control centres, on the basis of a pilot scheme tried with South West Trains. The penalty regime would also be reformed and

[82] Darling–Bowker, 28 June, faxed on 25 June 2004, SRA.

[83] Cabinet Conclusions, 24 June 2004.

[84] SRA Board Minutes, 1 and 2 July 2004; Bowker–Darling, 2 July 2004, SRA.

[85] Cf. Killen–Darling, 7 July 2004, DfT file R101/1/31 Pt. 3.

[86] This was something the DfT and SRA had resisted when Network Rail was created: SRA, 'draft article', 2004.

simplified.[87] The voice of consumers was to be strengthened. Somewhat against the trend of devolved responsibility, the SRA-sponsored Rail Passengers Council and the nine independent regional committees were to be replaced by a single national body reporting to the Secretary of State. Finally, Darling revealed that Bowker would be standing down in September. David Quarmby would take his place until the SRA finally closed its doors, probably in the second half of 2005. But the assumption was that this was a small price to pay for the reintroduction of 'clarity of purpose and responsibility'.[88]

The Rail Review may be seen as a demonstration of John Kingdon's theoretical evaluation of the several streams inherent in the policy process. By converging, problem streams, solution streams, and political streams move an issue onto the public policy agenda and thence towards government action. In this instance, however, there was a linear progression, in which agendas were set, the policy options were explored with the help of specialists, and were then narrowed down when the more creative solutions foundered on the rock of political imperatives.[89] The outcome was in fact close to a simple triangular formulation—the DfT at the top, Network Rail and the TOCs at the lower apices, and the ORR in the middle—which had been sketched out in the Treasury several months earlier.[90] For the Government, the removal of the SRA was the only thing that could be done without disturbing the other players. The decision was taken not because the Authority had been a failure, but because its remit had proved impossible, and complexity and antagonism had accompanied its efforts to effect change in the industry.[91] Whatever aspirations Bowker may have nursed, and however much he may have drawn encouragement from his meetings with the Prime Minister, the SRA did not have, and could not be given, sufficient autonomy to become the single decision-maker. And yet it was far from clear that Network Rail had grasped the full implications of their new role. They had tended to approach reform from an operational stance, and already possessed most of the responsibilities (timetabling, operational control, etc.) which they were being asked to discharge. Strategic planning and route utilization work would be new, of course, but here Quarmby, having discussed the situation with McAllister and Armitt, drew the conclusion that the company was not fully cognisant of

---

[87] The intention was to 'professionalize' the measurement process, and relate the compensation paid to revenue lost, with TOCs receiving less than the full amount to preserve incentives. Cf. Rachel Evans (DfT)–Darling, 7 July 2004, ibid.

[88] DfT, *The Future of Rail*, 15 July 2004, Cm6233; *Parl Deb. (Commons)*, 6th ser. (Session 2003–4), Vol. 423, Darling statement, 15 July 2004, c. 1548–50. On the detailed discussions leading to the White Paper, see DfT file R101/1/31 Pt. 3.

[89] John W. Kingdon, *Agendas, Alternatives and Public Policies* (2nd edn., New York, 2003), pp. viii, 20–3, 86–9, 143–4. Inside DfT, the rail review was seen to rest on four phases: briefing the stakeholders about the need for reform; engaging in genuine consultation; testing emerging conclusions on the key players; and securing cooperation in the transition period. Lambirth, Memo. on 'Stakeholder Strategy', 7 May 2004, DfT file R101/1/31 Pt. 3; Interview with Lambirth, 2007.

[90] Interviews with Atter and Chauhan, 2007.

[91] Cf. Bartle, 'The 2004 Rail Review', 75; Winsor, 'The Future of the Railways', pp. 12, 21.

what it was taking on. Certainly, it initially saw little need to tap into the expertise of SRA staff or to make changes to its governance structure.[92] Nor was there room for Bowker in the developing structure.[93] The SRA continued to express its reservations about the new regime in private discussions, but had no alternative but to knuckle down and make it work.[94] An inquest on the rail review convened by executives after Bowker's departure reached the conclusion that the Authority might have tried to gain the support of other stakeholders and worked more cooperatively with the key departments and civil servants, but it is difficult to see how such an approach would have made any difference to its fate.[95] The SRA now faced a long and managerially challenging period of 'transition', with much detailed work to be done. Although most of its functions were transferred to the DfT by July 2005, the HQ at 55 Victoria Street was not vacated until March 2006, and a residual element limped on until final closure in November.

Undaunted by the patent fragility of Prescott's *10 Year Plan* of July 2000, Darling published a White Paper on *The Future of Transport* five days after his paper on *The Future of Rail*, on 20 July 2004. Seeking to establish a network for 2030, the document repeated the familiar observation that there had been 'decades of under-investment' without giving any confidence that the post-SRA Department would be any more successful in aligning planning and delivery. It was of course the case that 'ageing and over-stressed networks' were being asked to handle ever rising levels of traffic. Linked to the outcome of the 2004 Spending Review (see below, p. 250), the DfT's strategy embraced 'sustained investment over the long term', 'improvements in transport management', and 'planning ahead'. But with the strategic planning function for railways to be taken in-house, it remained to be seen how far the rail component of the DfT's aspirations would be addressed. And given the fact that so much of the Rail Review discussions had been taken up with the need to control costs, and the demise of the SRA had been provoked in part by its bolder plans for railway investment, the aspirations of this White Paper must have produced more than a

[92] Quarmby, 'Notes from the Network Rail AGM', n.d. [July 2004], SRA; Interview with David Quarmby, 1 May 2007. The failure of Network Rail Members, led by Cllr Philip Davis of the West Midlands Regional Assembly, to establish a proactive members' forum was a further demonstration of governance difficulties. See Davis–McAllister, 18 July 2003 [my thanks to David Quarmby for this ref.]; Davis–Network Rail Members, 2 June 2004, SRA; Davis–Killen, 2 July 2004, Fawcett–Killen, 7 July 2004, DfT file R101/1/11 Pt. 1; SRA Board Minutes, 5 August 2004.

[93] Philip Graham (DfT)–Lambirth et al., 7 June 2004, DfT file R101/1/31 Pt. 3.

[94] See Shaw–SRA Executive, 19 July 2004, enclosing a critical review of the White Paper; SRA Executive Committee Minutes, 22 July 2004, SRA 57/01/01 Pt. 4, SRA Board Minutes, 16, 20, and 22 July 2004, Bowker, speaking note, draft article, and correspondence for SRA Board's meeting with Darling, 22 July 2004; DfT, 'Note of Meeting between Alistair Darling, Secretary of State for Transport and the SRA Board at Marsham Street, 22 July 2004', n.d., SRA; Bowker–Blair, 13 July 2004, Fidler–Blair and Darling–Blair, 14 July 2004, Prime Minister's Rail papers, Pt. 13; Bowker–Robert Wilkins (East Sussex Co. Co.), 26 July 2004, and Bowker–Richard Turner (Freight Transport Association), 28 July 2004, SRA.

[95] SRA executive directors' meeting at the work foundation, 2004, cit.

few wry smiles among those whose contribution was no longer required.[96] It is to the issue of costs, funding, and financing that we now turn.

7.4 Addressing the railway: costs and Network Rail

As we have noted, an important element in the Rail Review had been the issue of cost control. And the process of review had been accompanied by the final settlement of the Rail Regulator's interim charges settlement in December 2003, and with the Government's broader Spending Review of 2004. The first issue, a reprofiling of Network Rail's income with more borrowing in the first two years of Winsor's settlement (2004–9), was resolved in March 2004. With income for Network Rail set at £8.8 billion over the two years 2004/5–2005/6, track access charges were set at £2.4 billion, 27 per cent of the total income required, with the remainder provided by grants and borrowing. An additional £3.1 billion in debt was to be taken on, making around £7.6 billion in all. The company's total debt was therefore set to rise from £12.8 billion at the beginning of 2004/5 to about £20.5 billion by the end of 2005/6.[97] The negotiations were not without difficulty. As a *quid pro quo*, Winsor wanted a 'bonfire of the covenants'—the removal of those controls on Network Rail imposed by the SRA as lender of last resort which, he contended, duplicated those available through his jurisdiction as Regulator. The SRA, on the other hand, complained that it was being required to review the controls in haste, and in particular was minded to resist the removal of one of the controls: Clause 4.2 of the Cooperation Agreement with Network Rail, which required the latter to 'facilitate and implement' the SRA's strategies subject to adequate reward.[98] In the event, the Government wished to settle the matter to the Regulator's timetable, and were not disposed to challenge his position.[99] However, the episode gave further encouragement to officials who had been insistent that a resolution of the SRA–ORR arguments over jurisdiction was clearly required.

With the income reprofiling resolved, at least for the time being, Government attention turned to the refinancing of Network Rail's debt. As we have seen, the initial intention had been to handle the long-term debt by securitizing the company's income from track access charges and grants. The sums involved were large. During the review period, any notion that the legacy debt might be

[96] DfT, *The Future of Transport: a network for 2030*, 20 July 2004, Cm6234.
[97] ORR Press Release, 10 March 2004, and see also Fawcett–Darling, 12 February 2004, DfT file R101/1/3 Pt. 2. Debt figures of £13.0bn (beginning 2004/5) and £20.3bn (end 2005/6) were given in R93/1/3 Pt. 7. Network Rail's actual debt at the end of 2005/6 was £18.2bn.
[98] SRA Executive Minutes, 26 February 2004, SRA57/01/01 Pt. 4; SRA Board Minutes, 4 and 9 March 2004; Bowker–Darling, 4 and 9 March 2004, SRA.
[99] ORR, *Annual Report 2003/4*, pp. 1–2; Interview with Lambirth, 2007.

written off was finally rejected by the Treasury. In addition, complications were encountered in organizing a securitization. Given the fact that the private sector required an unconditional financial indemnity from the Government to support the loans advanced, the risk would reside with the Government, and therefore the ONS advised that the amounts borrowed would have to be added to public sector debt.[100] There was also a governance issue, and at the SRA Shaw made the point that securitization, which would increase the involvement of financial institutions, was likely to reinforce the prevailing culture within Network Rail.[101] Instead, after having embarked on the issue of medium term notes in March 2004 (£6.5 billion of a £10 billion programme was quickly raised), the longer-term debt was handled via a £20 billion debt issuance programme (DIP), agreed in October. Here, current financing would be continued via a larger stand-by credit facility.[102] This was not only a more straightforward procedure, but it would also reduce the cost of capital, and the debt would not score to the public sector, although there remained some concern that the change might reopen the debate about the status of Network Rail as a private company. At this stage, neither the DIP operation, which left the Government with a 'remote' contingent liability, nor the demise of the SRA and transfer of debt guarantees to the Department altered the ONS's initial decision to classify the company as a private sector one.[103] And £2.25 billion was raised in the second half of November 2004, with a further £1.35 billion added by the end of 2004/5.[104] However, commentators continued to express concerns about the status of the company, prompted by the decision of the ONS to reclassify London & Continental Railways (Channel Tunnel Rail Link) as a public sector company in February 2006. The interest burden, which involved rates which were higher than those charged in the public sector, and the absence of any significant transfer of risk, were elements which attracted particular criticism.[105]

---

[100] Bisson–O'Donnell, 19 April 2004, cit.; Fawcett–Darling, 11 June and 2 July 2004, DfT files R101/1/11 Pt. 1 and R101/1/31 Pt. 3. Additional arguments against securitization were (1) after the Rail Review track access charges were likely to form a smaller proportion of Network Rail's total income and (2) given higher interest charges payable under securitization, handling the legacy debt in this way represented poor VfM.

[101] SRA Executive Prayers Minutes, 14 June 2004, SRA 57/01/12A Pt. 2; Interview with Shaw, 2007.

[102] Treasury, Memo. on 'Network Rail Financing', June 2004, in Fawcett–Darling, 2 July 2004, cit.; Darling–Quarmby, 4 October 2004, SRA; Network Rail Ltd, *R & A 2004*, p. 7; ORR, *Network Rail's Long Term Debt Issuance Programme. A Statement by the Office of Rail Regulation, and a Proposed Network Licence Modification* (October 2004).

[103] See Russell Coleman (Treasury)–Martin Kellaway (ONS), 9 July 2004, DfT, *Departmental minute in respect of certain changes to the contingent liabilities arising from Government support for Network Rail borrowing* (August 2005), ONS, *The National Accounts classification of Network Rail: note by the Office for National Statistics* (28 November 2005), and Robin Lynch (Chairman, National Accounts Classification Committee)–Michael Romberg (Treasury), 4 February and 30 November 2005, ONS website.

[104] Ron Henderson (Network Rail), Presentation to Members, 1 December 2004, SRA; Network Rail Ltd., *R & A 2005*, p. 8.

[105] Cf. NAO, *Network Rail—Making a Fresh Start*, 2004, paras 3.18–3.23; Glaister, 'British Rail Privatisation', 38–9; Jupe, 'Public (Interest) or Private (Gain)?', 255–6, 263–5.

246

Table 7.3 DfT estimate of spending requirements, provisions, and 'pressures' for the current railway, 2004/5–2010/11 (£m., 2004 prices)

	2004/5	2005/6	2006/7	2007/8	2008/9	2009/10	2010/11
MSCR							
Resource	1,661	1,599	2,409	2,249	2,332	2,497	2,347
Investment	2,388	2,966	3,646	2,793	2,583	2,019	2,031
Total	4,049	4,565	6,055	5,042	4,905	4,516	4,378
Provisions							
Resource	1,349	1,284	1,487	1,435	1,566	1,489	1,514
Investment	2,537	3,099	2,731	2,672	2,259	2,599	2,575
Total	3,886	4,383	4,218	4,107	3,825	4,088	4,089
Pressures							
Resource	−312	−315	−922	−814	−756	−1,008	−833
Investment	+149	+133	−915	−121	−324	+580	+544
Total	−163	−182	−1,837	−935	−1,080	−428	−289

Source: Bishop–Macpherson, 29 March 2004, DfT file R101/1/31 Pt.2.
Assumptions: MSCR = existing (2003/4) service levels + contracted enhancements (WCML, CTRL), with Network Rail achieving 30% efficiency gain required by Rail Regulator, SRA producing efficiency gains on franchising via DOO, etc., and uncommitted enhancements (ECML, East London Line, Thameslink 2000, etc.) not delivered.
Provisions = existing + diversion of unallocated capital reserve to railways.

The major challenge in 2004/5, of course, was to square the industry's financial needs with available resources, over the period of the Spending Review, the period of the 10 Year Plan, and beyond. More specifically, savings were required to peg back escalating costs, so that the gap between the minimum spending requirements for the current railway (MSCR) and the available public provision might be closed. In March 2004, the Treasury was supplied with an indication of the 'pressures' or shortfall over the remainder of the 10 Year Plan period (i.e. to 2010/11), divided into 'resource' (revenue) and 'investment' (capital) spending (Table 7.3). As the table indicates, the shortfall amounted to £1.8 billion in 2006/7, attributable to revenue and capital deficiencies in equal measure; and to £0.9 and £1.1 billion in 2007/8 and 2008/9, respectively, attributable mainly to revenue. The SRA's near contemporaneous submission to the 2004 Spending Review on 6 April offered little comfort to the would-be cost cutters. It produced seven spending scenarios over the 10 Year Plan period, ranging from £36.4 billion for a fully compliant option working within the original parameters of the Plan, to £41.0 billion for the MSCR, and £43.0 billion for a higher investment option (Table 7.4). Increasing demand for rail services meant that 'some tough choices [were] unavoidable'. 'Crowding', performance, and economic value had been examined in some detail. The exercise revealed that simply retaining the status

Table 7.4 SRA submission to 2004 Spending Review: rail industry subsidy scenarios

Scenario	Cost over 10YP £bn	Description	Fares (RPI + 1% to 2006)	Thinning (%)	Cuts	Projects
Compliant	36.4	Affordable within 10YP allocation	RPI + 20% 2006 RPI + 2% 2007–11	30	30% network and station closures	As MSCR
Semi-compliant	38.3	Most affordable option avoiding route closures	As compliant	20	—	As MSCR
MSCR	41.0	Efficient cost of maintaining current outputs[a]	RPI + 1% 2006–11	None	—	WCML, CTRL, ERTMS, SRNTP, DOO, DDA, etc.
Optimized-MSCR	41.0	Better value	RPI + 2% 2006–11	7.5	—	As above + ECML, FFG, RPP, Thameslink
Extra-optimized MSCR	40.8	Bolder combination	RPI + 7% 2006 RPI + 2% 2007–11 (LSE, London I-City, PTE)[b]	10	Minor network and station closures	As above + East Coast strategy, Soton–WCML
Investment	43.0	Meets wider objectives; £2.2bn extra investment	As extra	10	—	As above + Olympic bid, airports, GW upgrade, etc.
SRA preferred	42.5	Avoids high fare increases and substantial closures	RPI + 5% 2006 RPI + 2% 2007–11 Saver deregulation	5	—	As Extra + Crossrail, ELL, major stations, Olympic bid, Felixstowe–Nuneaton, etc.

Source: SRA, 'SR04 Submission', 6 April 2004, SRA.

[a] Assumes £60m. p.a. savings from de-staffing of lightly used stations and implementation of DOO, Network Rail achieving target efficiencies and returning £1.6bn rebate to TOCs, and only contractually committed enhancement projects undertaken.

[b] Other routes = RPI + 2% 2006–11.

quo (MSCR) was 'not a sustainable proposition', since restraining fare increases would lead to severe overcrowding and poor performance. The other scenarios combined price hikes with additional network enhancements (see Table 7.4) to produce a range of estimated effects. The SRA's 'preferred' option was close to the upper bound of suggested spending. Priced at £42.5 billion (Table 7.4), it was defended because it would secure a performance result (PPM) some 2–3 per cent better than the MSCR by 2011, and produce 25 per cent less overcrowding by 2016, with a relatively modest fare increase (RPI + 14% to 2010/11) and with only minor cuts in routes and service levels.[106] Related to such calculations, of course, was the immediate programme of passenger franchise savings that the SRA expected to extract from DOO and station de-staffing, part of the passenger franchise specification review, and further savings which the Authority hoped to achieve with the belated introduction of franchise budgetary targets. The details were sent to Howells a few days before the spending review submission.[107] What was the reaction in Whitehall? Earlier in the review process, the joint team had examined a range of actions to raise fares and prune services under a 'Beeching Mark II' banner. Initial calculations were certainly reminiscent of the Beeching exercise some 40 years earlier. They indicated that a significant proportion (c.60–75%) of the regional network might not be justified by 'social benefits', though it was conceded that the little used stations—60 per cent contributed only 5 per cent of total patronage—cost very little to retain.[108] The Treasury argued that there were sound value for money reasons for a draconian response to the situation, closer to the SRA's semi-compliant option (see Table 7.4), namely, a 10 per cent real increase in fares in 2006 followed by 2 per cent thereafter, removal of 20 per cent of intercity services, together with the most heavily subsidized regional services, and closure of 10 per cent of the network. But these 'controversial' steps, producing savings of around £0.5 billion by 2007/8, would still leave significant revenue and capital pressures.[109] It should not be assumed that political expediency necessarily ruled out such radical policies. The Prime Minister, briefed by one adviser to the effect that getting the railway industry to stay within the 10 Year Plan budget would be 'politically disastrous', was told by another that it was 'not obvious ... that we can afford *not* to cut some bits of the network'.[110] During the 'stocktake' meeting on 6 April, Blair agreed that there were no easy solutions and that some 'tough decisions' were required. At least one adviser favoured a more generous, 'high investment' approach to the long-term funding of transport, but the consensus was with Brown, who

---

[106] SRA, 'SR04 Submission', 6 April 2004, SRA. In contrast, the fully compliant scenario would achieve a PPM 0.8–1.4% better than the MSCR, and 20% less overcrowding, but would require a 30% hike in real fares, a 30% network cut, and 30% service thinning.

[107] Bowker–Howells, 1 April 2004, SRA.

[108] Tracey Waltho et al., 'The Cost of the Railway', paper for awayday, 23 February 2004, DfT file R101/1/6 Pt. 1.

[109] Bisson–O'Donnell, 19 April 2004, cit.   [110] Annotation on Elson–Blair, 26 March 2004, cit.

stressed the need for a solution to the immediate financial pressures facing the industry.[111]

The DfT, without further discussion with the SRA, made its own submission to the Treasury, pricing the MSCR at £41.3 billion over the 10 Year Plan period.[112] The Spending Review decisions in July involved an overall allocation to transport of £37.6 billion over the three years 2005/6–2007/8, including cash additions of £1.6 billion in 2006/7 and 2007/8, an additional £1.7 billion 'reform package' to meet 'immediate pressures' in 2005/6 and 2006/7, and a permanent 'uplift' of £0.5 billion per annum over the 10 Year Plan figures from 2006/7.[113] The share that was destined for the railway industry was not determined at this stage, and there was much 'divvying up' to do within the Department.[114] When Darling revealed the allocation in a written statement in February 2005, it emerged that £12.2 billion (32%) was earmarked for rail, £15.0 billion (40%) if the support to the CTRL were added.[115] Behind the published figures, it was clear that the Treasury's decisions in SR04 required some major savings from the Department on the rail budget. The initiative had begun with the SRA's work, but responsibility for the considerable work that was to follow— identifying the rail budget, determining what was to be cut and how, and further changes to the capital/resource apportionment, i.e. the balance between track access charges and government grants to Network Rail—passed to the DfT. The SRA was informed that capital/resource adjustments would be required for both 2004/5 and 2005/6, and the battle to reconcile projected expenditure with the SR04 allocation continued over the autumn of 2004 and into the spring of 2005.[116] At this point, the SRA was informed that savings to bridge a funding gap of about £200 million were required for 2005/6.[117] This required attention, but one thing was patently clear. The main problem for the railways was the doubling of infrastructure costs from about £3 billion to £6 billion. In comparison with this, the effort to shave sums off the passenger operating budget, which in any case would be likely to elicit a massive public outcry, was small beer.

The Rail and Spending Reviews of 2004 could be judged positive steps in that the Government formally recognized that the railways' privatized structure

[111] Elson–Macpherson, 29 April 2004, cit.; Birt–Jonathan Powell (Policy Adviser, No. 10), 2 April 2004, and see also a later intervention, Birt–Blair, 10 June 2004, Prime Minister's Rail papers, Pt. 12.

[112] This from SRA Board Minutes, 6 May 2004.

[113] Figure of £37.6bn taken from Annex A of *The Future of Transport*, cit. Cf. departmental expenditure limit of £38.0bn in Treasury, *2004 Spending Review. New Public Spending Plans 2005–2008. Stability, security and opportunity for all: Investing for Britain's long-term future*, July 2004, Cm6237, p. 106.

[114] Cf. Rickett–Robert Devereux and Lambirth, 22 July 2004, DfT file R75/1/54 Pt. 1.

[115] *Parl. Deb. (Commons)*, 6th ser. (Session 2004–5), Vol. 430, Darling, written statement, 10 February 2005, c. 94–5w. Cf. total identified in Lambirth–Killen, 1 September 2004, DfT file R75/1/54 Pt. 1.

[116] Cf. SRA Executive Prayers Minutes, 8 and 19 July, 11 August 2004, Chairman's Review meeting, 21 September 2004, SRA 57/01/12A Pt. 2; SRA Board Minutes, 13 January and 3 February 2005.

[117] Darling, statement, 10 February 2005, cit.; SRA Executive Prayers Minutes, 17 January 2005, SRA 57/1/12A Pt. 3.

needed reform, and that a higher level of public spending was required. On the other hand, the reviews merely highlighted a perennial aspect of the 'railway problem' from the 1950s. Thus, the examination of ways of achieving higher levels of investment went hand in hand with serious discussions of ways to achieve major cuts in the current provision. Here, the fare-box was already set at a high level compared with many European countries, and this meant that unless pricing were used to choke off demand, a higher level of public subsidy was necessary. After 'decades of under-investment', the level of support required was much higher than successive governments were prepared to supply, and indeed a case could be made for restraint on social grounds, given the use of railways by the comparatively better-off. On the other hand, the increasing public concern with the environmental impact of transport has caused rail travel to be regarded more favourably. It remains to be seen whether the exercises of 2004, which were full of good intentions to provide sustained investment over the longer term, will prove any more successful than Robertson's Modernisation Plan of 1955, Parker's electrification report of 1981, and Prescott's 10 Year Plan of 2001, in transforming Britain's rail infrastructure.

7.5 Winding up the SRA

A long interregnum followed the White Paper of July 2004. Although the Department for Transport lost no time in establishing initial plans for the transitional period, that period was to prove longer than anticipated. In DfT–SRA meetings in June, the talk turned to issues of 'transition', and early in July a Transition Steering Group was set up. It was chaired by Bodnar, with Newton the SRA's nominee as Chief Executive-elect in place of Bowker, and Coucher representing Network Rail. It subsequently became known as the Industry Review Group.[118] Soon afterwards a high-level Programme Board was added, with Killen in the chair, and Quarmby the SRA's representative.[119] At the same time, the DfT engaged KPMG to undertake a functional mapping exercise of the SRA (500 employees) and the DfT's Rail Directorate (90 employees), together with an

---

[118] Killen–Darling, 7 June 2004, cit.; McBrayne–Darling, 14 June 2004, DfT file R101/1/31 Pt. 3; Killen–Bolt, 6 August 2004, SRA; SRA Board Minutes, 16, 20 July and 5 August 2004, SRA Press Release, 30 July 2004. Below the Industry Review Group, a Transition Managers Forum met monthly to handle more detailed issues.

[119] SRA Executive Prayers Minutes, 14 July 2004, SRA 57/01/12A Pt. 2. Other members included Lambirth and Bodnar (DfT), Ian McAllister (NWR), Suzanne McCarthy (ORR), Keith Ludeman (ATOC), Nick Starling (HSE), Stewart Francis (RPC), and John Ewing (Scottish Executive): Industry Programme Board Agenda, 15 September 2004, SRA. McCarthy resigned as Chief Executive of ORR in October, and was replaced by Keith Webb.

outline implementation plan.[120] Preparations were made in parallel for the legislation that would be required. A Railways Bill was introduced into the Commons on 25 November. It reached the committee stage on 14 December, received a third reading on 27 January 2005, and obtained royal assent on 7 April. Passage of the legislation was comparatively smooth, the only major challenge being an unsuccessful Lords amendment requiring the Secretary of State to formulate a long-term strategy for the railways.[121] On the other hand, it took some time before the DfT was able to determine the precise nature of its new organizational structure. Four months elapsed before it decided, in November, to establish a central rail organization inside Great Minster House. Whether this would be an executive agency like the Highways Agency or an internal division remained a matter for argument within the Department.[122] The issue was not resolved in favour of the latter until January 2005, and the decision to appoint Dr. Mike Mitchell of FirstGroup to lead 'DfT Rail' as Director General was not made until May. In many ways, this timescale was not surprising. The reform agenda touched all parts of the railway industry, and its fragmentation made implementation of the new arrangements a protracted affair, necessitating numerous 'quadrilateral' meetings of DfT, ORR, Network Rail, and the TOCs. The SRA portion of the overall work appeared at first sight to be comparatively small. After all, closure of the SRA and the transfer of its responsibilities represented only one item in a 30-strong list of objectives, and the DfT's Transition Plan of October 2004, worked up by PricewaterhouseCoopers as Programme Managers, contained references to the SRA in only 3 of the 27 identified workstreams. Nevertheless, abandonment of the Government's rail NDPB was clearly the key change in the structural firmament, and in fact there were implications for the SRA in nearly all the other areas of the work, including safety, devolution, franchise remapping, network management, economic regulation, performance, and freight. New Directions and Guidance from the Secretary of State were also required, not least to produce a revision of the SRA's business plan. The document was eventually issued in October.[123]

The SRA had to a certain extent anticipated events. On 1 July the Board agreed to establish its own transition committee; chaired by Pen Kent, it began meeting in early August.[124] Within the executive, special transition meetings

---

[120] KPMG, drafts of 'DfT/SRA Function Mapping', 7–30 July 2004, SRA [figures are 91 staff for DfT rail directorate, 493–516.5 for SRA]; SRA Board paper on 'Strategic Rail Authority: Rail Review to Closure', n.d. (November 2005), SRA.

[121] Darling–Prescott, 13 January and 21 February 2005, and reply, 10 March 2005, DfT file R101/1/27 Pt. 2 and Prime Minister's Rail papers, Pt. 14. The amendment, introduced by Lord Bradshaw (in Committee) and Viscount Astor, was defeated by 136 votes to 120: *Parl. Deb. (Lords)*, 5th ser. (Session 2004–5), Vol. 671, 4 April 2005, c. 484–95. Another issue, the insistence on parliamentary scrutiny of rail closures guidance, was introduced in committee. See below, p. 256.

[122] Newton–Transition Executive et al., 6 August 2004, SRA.

[123] Darling–Quarmby, 7 October 2004, enclosing 'Direction and Guidance to the Strategic Rail Authority', SRA. Draft D&G had been given to the SRA in early July: Shrubsole–Bowker, 9 July 2004, SRA.

[124] SRA Board Minutes, 1 and 20 July, and 5 August 2004.

were convened, and a transition team was created, subsequently organized as a transition steering group led by Riley.[125] Much of the attention at both board and senior management level was focused on obtaining adequate rights for SRA employees and maintaining staff morale. After all, there was still a business to run. The SRA was heavily engaged in important franchising negotiations (East Coast, Kent, Greater Western, Gatwick Express, West Coast, Midland, and Northern), and in drawing up route utilization strategies for several parts of the network. There were capital projects to manage (WCML, East London Line, and Thameslink 2000), policy inputs were required on issues such as freight and standard-setting, and the 2004/5 budget needed attention, not least in relation to expenditure in Scotland, where the Scottish Executive was to assume responsibility for the ScotRail franchise, together with the specification and funding of the country's infrastructure.[126] These several responsibilities, which were later set out in a series of SRA disposition statements, could not be transferred wholesale to the Department overnight.[127] Nor, of course, could the SRA's relationships with Network Rail and the newly established Office of Rail Regulation (following the expiry of Winsor's contract on 4 July). From the Authority's perspective, it was thus essential to maintain the Executive's cohesiveness, mount an effective communications strategy, manage the relationship with the DfT, and ensure that the transition itself was adequately resourced.[128] The Board's transition committee led the process, drawing on experience elsewhere, notably with the establishment of the Office of Communications (OfCom), which had taken on the responsibilities of five bodies in 2003.[129]

From early September 2004, the SRA was led by Quarmby as Chairman and Newton as Chief Executive and Board Member. Their brief was to ensure that the Authority's statutory functions were fulfilled while effecting an orderly wind-down of activities.[130] Secondments aided the process: Waboso went to the DfT, Rob Andrews, the SRA's Director of Safety Development, went to the ORR.[131] The protection of employment rights was a major concern. The SRA's initial stance in July 2004 had been that most, if not all, of its employees would be required in the new structure.[132] The Authority had been promised that the

---

[125] SRA briefing note, 13 August 2004, in SRA 57/01/12A Pt. 2.

[126] DfT, Directions and Guidance to the SRA, 7 October 2004, para. 3.4. Similar arrangements were to be put in place in Wales: ibid. para. 3.5.

[127] John Larkinson (SRA), Memo. to Executive on 'Decisions, Milestones and Timelines for next 18 months', 7 July 2004; SRA Executive Prayers Minutes, 16 July 2004, SRA. For disposition statements see SRA 57/01/02 Pt. 60.

[128] Jonathan Riley–Bowker, 30 June and 2 July 2004, enclosing drafts of 'Structure for Executive discussion on transition', SRA.

[129] SRA Board Transition Workshop Minutes, 3 November 2004, SRA.

[130] Quarmby, letters to rail industry, 23 September 2004, SRA.

[131] David Waboso (Director), Memo. on 'SRA's "safety role" following the White Paper', 31 August 2004, SRA 57/01/12 Pt. 10; SRA Executive Prayers Minutes, 13 and 17 September 2004, SRA57/01/12A Pt. 2.

[132] Julia Evans (Director, Human Resources, SRA)–SRA Nominations and Remuneration Committee, 24 June 2004; Bowker–Darling, 22 July 2004, SRA ['There is no organizational 'fat' at the SRA'].

rights established under the Transfer of Undertakings (Protection of Employment) Regulations (TUPE) of 1981 would be applied, providing similar terms
and conditions, continuity of employment, and so on.[133] On 29 July, Howells
informed Bowker that

in planning the transfer of functions to the department, we shall act as if the TUPE
Regulations applied. I understand that it is open to debate whether in strict law the
Regulations do apply, but it is the Government's policy (encapsulated in COSOP, the
Cabinet Office Statement of Policy in this area) to treat transfers within the public sector
as if they did.

But there remained some uncertainty about the position, and Howells also made
it clear that he rejected the idea that the Department would 'need to retain
as many staff as are currently carrying out the functions'.[134] It later emerged
that the process of dealing with the staff would be less accommodating. The
Department rejected the option of a block transfer of staff, and elected to design
the new DfT Rail from first principles. There was clearly a danger that disgruntled
leading managers might be poached by other organizations,[135] and with the
Department intent on recruiting a much smaller number of staff for its Rail
division, no more than half of the 600 or so staff holding positions in the SRA
and the DfT's old rail directorate, it was accepted that there would be a fairly
substantial number of redundancies. Newton, who had taken an interest in staff
matters when an assistant director with OPRAF, led the transition process. He
was particularly critical of the quality of the Department's human resources management, and the approach it took towards employees of the NDPB. Although a
human resources managers' forum was established to focus on personnel issues,
the SRA failed to convince the DfT that a code of practice for dealing with the
staff was required, and the latter was criticized for making little effort to lead or
direct the process.[136] A matching exercise was undertaken, with job descriptions
for new DfT posts compared with those of the SRA and existing DfT staff. If
there was a 'match' of 80 per cent or greater, the incumbent would be offered
the position.[137] At first, the DfT made it clear that rejection of a matched post
would not prejudice the rights of SRA staff to redundancy terms. However,
a major source of dissatisfaction was its subsequent decision in May 2005 to
withdraw the redundancy option for those who rejected the offer of departmental
posts. The change, introduced shortly after Mitchell's appointment, was made

[133] Killen, reported in 'Note of meeting . . . 22 July 2004', cit.
[134] Howells–Bowker, 29 July 2004, and see Newton–Killen, 4 August 2004, SRA. On uncertainty, see
SRA Board Minutes, 13 January 2005.
[135] SRA Executive Prayers Minutes, 23 July 2004, SRA 57/01/12A Pt. 2.
[136] SRA Executive Minutes, 23 September 2004, SRA 57/01/01 Pt. 4; SRA Board Minutes, 3 March
2005; Interview with Newton, 2006. On OPRAF cf. OPRAF Executive papers, 1995, DfT file SRA2/15/1
Pt. 1.
[137] SRA, 'Rail Review to Closure', cit. If there were more matches than available posts, a closed
competition would be held.

because there had been a disappointing take-up rate by SRA executives.[138] A factor here was undoubtedly the generous terms and conditions they enjoyed in comparison with their counterparts in the civil service. An example of this was the fact that when six senior DfT Rail posts (reporting directly to the Director General) were made known in January 2005, no fewer than 116 SRA employees were qualified by grade to apply for them. Other difficulties were created by Network Rail's unwillingness to embrace a TUPE-related approach, though it subsequently offered generous terms to SRA entrants, and by the reluctance of the ORR to commit itself to functional responsibilities until these were clarified with the DfT.[139]

How many people were required? By the end of 2004, the SRA's more realistic appraisal was that around 300 staff would go to the Department, while another 60 would join other organizations within the rail industry. A phased transfer over the period June–October 2005 was implemented by the DfT in preference to the SRA's suggestion of a 'big bang' transfer in September.[140] In the event, only 179 SRA employees transferred to the Department, most of them going to DfT Rail in Great Minster House. This represented 36 per cent of the SRA's headcount for 2004/5 (493). The most significant transfers were 90 from Operations, 40 from Finance and Commercial, and 27 from Strategic Planning (Table 7.5). Senior executives took up three of the six posts reporting directly to Mitchell: Gary Backler (Rail Service Delivery), Graham Dalton (Rail Projects), and Richard Horton (Rail Procurement).[141]

In addition, the reconstituted Rail Passengers Council, operating from 24 July 2005 and subsequently using the operating name Passenger Focus, took 26 staff from the SRA-sponsored body. Earlier, 14 employees had moved to Network Rail, to handle route utilization, performance management, and enhancement projects, and smaller numbers found their way to the ORR, TfL (East London Line project), the Scottish Executive and the TOCs.[142] Some of the senior managers joined TOCs: Bowker (National Express), Shaw (FirstGroup), and Riley (Serco).[143] This left about 150 staff to be made redundant. Most had left by the time 55 Victoria Street was vacated in December 2005. A reduced board and a handful of executives were retained to handle residual matters, which continued

[138] SRA Executive Committee Minutes, 9 December 2004, 6 January and 12 May 2005, SRA 57/01/01 Pt. 5; Terlecky–Quarmby and Newton, Quarmby–Newton, both 18 May 2005, SRA Board Transition Committee Minutes, 19 May 2005, Riley, Memo. to SRA Board, 27 May 2005, SRA Board Minutes, 2 June 2005. Part of the difficulty was the product of the higher salaries paid by the SRA. Staff who transferred to DfT posts with lower salaries were required to 'mark time' until the grade salary band 'caught up'. Several potential recruits failed to find this an attractive proposition.

[139] SRA Executive Committee Minutes, 6 January 2005, SRA 57/01/01 Pt. 5.

[140] Nigel Thomas (SRA), Memo to SRA Executive Committee, 26 May 2005, SRA 57/01/02 Pt. 59; SRA Board Minutes, 7 April and 5 May 2005.

[141] Ibid. 3 March 2005.

[142] SRA, 'Rail Review to Closure', cit.; Riley, Memo. to SRA Board, 6 October 2005.

[143] Bowker joined National Express as CEO after a two-year interval. Of the other senior executives, Waboso joined London Underground and Reardon went to the DfT.

Table 7.5 Transfer of SRA staff, June–October 2005

Function	Headcount July 2004	Number transferred	Destination	% of headcount
Strategic planning	88	27	DfT Rail	31
		3	TfL[a]	3
		4	DfT, ORR, ScE	4
Operations	163	90	DfT Rail	55
Finance and Commercial (incl. Projects)	119	40	DfT Rail	34
Legal	13	7	DfT Rail	54
Technical	11	3	DfT Rail	42
Freight	22	3	DfT LMT	14
		1	DfT Rail	4
Total SRA (incl. other functions not listed above)	493	171	DfT Rail	35
		8	DfT	2
		179	Total DfT	36
		6	Elsewhere	1
		185[b]	All[b]	38[b]
RPC	69	26	New RPC	38

[a] Transfer November 2004.
[b] Excludes 14 staff transferred to Network Rail, the majority in February–March 2005, other non-transfer moves, for example, to ORR, TfL, and Scottish Executive, and subsequent moves, for example, to TOCs.
Source: KPMG, 'DfT/SRA Function Mapping', July 2004, SRA; SRA Board paper on 'Strategic Rail Authority: Rail Review to Closure', n.d. (November 2005), SRA.

into 2006. The most important of these were management of the Mark I replacement programme; management of the South East Trains franchise, which was to remain in public hands until the Integrated Kent Franchise started; and responsibility for the rail closures procedures, following difficulties in effecting a speedy handover to the Department.[144] New closure procedures were included in the 2005 Act, but these required consultation on, and parliamentary scrutiny of, draft guidance on the criteria for considering rail closures before they could be introduced. The consultation period did not begin until 26 January 2006, and the process was not completed until November.[145] The retained staff were Quarmby, Newton, Kent, and Mayhew, at board level, and Sutherland, Trewin, Peter Hawthorne, and Cedric Pierce. This skeletal complement found a home at the offices of British Railways Board (Residuary), Whittles House, in Pentonville

[144] SRA Executive Committee Minutes, 12 and 26 May, 14 July and 29 September 2005, SRA 57/01/01/ Pt. 5; Riley, Memo. to SRA Board, 3 November 2005; Mark Rose (SRA), Memo. on 'Closure—conversion of existing North London Line (NLL) between Stratford and North Woolwich', 19 October 2005, SRA 57/01/02 Pt. 61.
[145] McBrayne–Newton, 24 October 2006, SRA; DfT et al., *Railways Closures Guidance* (18 October 2006). See also DfT file R18/1/14 Pts. 1–8.

Road.[146] The residuary body, which had been established as a subsidiary of the SRA, thus outlived and indeed swallowed up its parent. The British Railways Board also remains in existence.[147]

The transition from SRA to DfT had not been an entirely smooth affair. There was some criticism inside the SRA of the fact that its exclusion from the Rail Review process had to some extent been continued in the transitional phase, reinforced by the critical stance which it had adopted to the reform proposals when the White Paper was published. More importantly, the Authority expressed frequent complaints about the slow pace of change in designing and populating DfT Rail.[148] To some extent, this was a product of the 'linear' approach taken by DfT—dealing first with the White Paper, then with the design of the new directorate, then with staffing, and finally with implementation—instead of providing strong overall project direction and management from the beginning of the process. Having been initially excluded from the organizational design work for DfT Rail, the SRA was then required to work closely with the Department in developing the design.[149] There was clearly frustration when the Department initiated moves to posts for which the detailed description had yet to be completed, and in the end much reliance was placed on the SRA-generated 'disposition statements' to guide the process.[150] At least the announcement and conduct of a general election, held on 5 May 2005, provided no more than a passing distraction for the railway industry on this occasion, with the Railways Act having obtained its royal assent in the previous month. Labour won a third term, with its overall majority falling from 167 to 65. However, the Conservatives continued to disappoint, and alternative transport strategies were thin on the ground.[151] And whatever the transitional frictions, there was clearly a substantial ex-SRA presence in the newly constituted DfT Rail division, and a presence elsewhere in the industry, in the ORR, Network Rail, and the TOCs. It certainly could not be said that the wholesale experience of the former NDPB was cast aside, in areas such as planning, franchise letting, and performance. Indeed, of the eight directors in the DfT's new Rail and National Networks organization of April 2007, three are former ex-SRA executives.[152]

Franchising continued to consume a substantial amount of the SRA Executive's time. The White Paper set the tone for the future DfT-led regime, when it

---

[146] Quarmby–SRA Board, 6 July 2005, SRA. Pierce managed South East Trains until June 2006. Others, for example, Philip O'Donnell and Iain Dewar, transferred to BRB (Residuary).

[147] Under French Law, BRB remains responsible for the obligations in the Channel Tunnel Usage Agreement and related agreements.

[148] Cf. SRA Chairman's Review Meeting Minutes, 8 February 2005, Quarmby–Executive Directors, 22 February 2005, SRA 57/01/12A Pt. 3; SRA Board Minutes, 3 February, 3 March 2005.

[149] SRA Board Minutes, 3 March 2005; SRA Executive Committee Minutes, 9 December 2005, SRA 57/01/01 Pt. 5.

[150] SRA, 'Rail Review to Closure', cit.

[151] Labour 355, Conservatives 198, Liberal Democrats 62, Others 30.

[152] DfT, Organization charts, 1 April 2007. The ex-SRA directors are Graham Dalton, Gary Backler, and Jack Paine (who succeeded Richard Horton as Head of Rail Procurement).

promised that the number of franchises would be reduced. The TOCs were now expected to work more closely with Network Rail, a consistent view of performance and service frequency would be applied, and the penalty regime would be simplified and made less adversarial. In future competitions, operators would bid to operate a defined timetable, and would not be able to take independent decisions to add extra services. Bidders would be judged not only on price but also on past performance and reliability. New contracts would include stipulations about train and crew availability; the balance of risks between the Government and the franchisee would be 'sensible'; if financial difficulties were encountered, 'surrender' of the franchise would be preferred to a 'bail-out'.[153] The intention in the reforms was to impose a tighter grip on the passenger train operators and encourage a more cooperative approach to operating performance to flourish, free of adversarial compensation-chasing, and perverse incentives such as 'ORCATS raiding'. Franchise agreements would normally run for 7–10 years. The erosion of 'moral hazard', through the assistance given to franchisees in distress and the use of cost-plus contracts, would be halted.[154] The White Paper was followed by a statement from Darling on 19 October, in which he revealed that the number of franchises would be reduced from 24 to 19 with the establishment of a Greater Western franchise, a merger of the Great Northern and Thameslink franchises as the precursor to 'Thameslink 2000', a break-up of the Central Trains franchise, and a new franchise combining South West Trains and the Island Line. The SRA would complete the route utilization strategies for the Brighton Line, East Coast, Great Western, and West Midlands; thereafter the responsibility for this work would pass to Network Rail.[155]

We must not exaggerate the significance of the change of policy. As we have seen, since 2003 the SRA had been engaged in altering its approach to franchising in line with much of the Department's thinking, and privately the latter conceded that the introduction of route utilization strategies had been 'one of the SRA's most effective innovations'.[156] It was the SRA that introduced further improvements to the franchising methodology, including the use of business plans and performance improvement planning, assessments of performance, and cost control in bidding competitions, and compliance with the requirements of the Office of Government Commerce's gateway review procedures.[157] And since DfT Rail did not assume responsibility for franchising until July 2005, while

[153] DfT, *Future of Rail*, paras. 4.3.24 ff.
[154] Cf. DfT, Discussion Draft on 'Rail Industry Restructuring', 14 July 2004, Treasury [redacted] file. A more radical proposal, to replace individual TACs with a 'bulk payment' by government direct to Network Rail, was rejected. The idea was not new: cf. Linnard–Morton and Bolt–Morton, both 14 April 1999, Morton's papers, SRA.
[155] *Parl. Deb. (Commons)*, 6th ser. (Session 2003–4), Vol. 425, Darling, written statement, 19 October 2004, c. 35–6w.
[156] Discussion draft, July 2004, cit.
[157] Cf. SRA Executive Prayers Minutes, 14 October 2004, SRA 57/01/12A Pt. 2; Jack Paine (SRA), Memo. to SRA Executive Committee, 28 April 2005, 57/01/02 Pt. 58; SRA, *Annual Report 2004/5*, pp. 26–7; Interview with Shaw, 2007.

eight franchises were due for renewal by April 2006, it fell to the SRA to take some key decisions under the aegis of Nicola Shaw, who remained in post as MD Operations until she joined FirstGroup as MD of UK Bus in May.[158] The work was not inconsiderable. The franchises requiring attention handled about a third of passenger journeys and consumed half of the total government subsidy.[159] Of course, the Authority's freedom of action was circumscribed. The amended Directions and Guidance of October 2004 required the SRA to obtain the agreement of the Secretary of State to any franchise 'variations, extensions or replacements'. One of the most important of these was the award of the re-let East Coast franchise to the incumbent operator, GNER, in March 2005. Notwithstanding pressure exerted by GNER's American parent company, Sea Containers, to obtain a single tender extension, the SRA organized a bidding competition for the franchise, which was to run until 2015.[160] By October 2004, four pre-qualified bidders had emerged: GNER, Danish Railways, FirstGroup, and Stagecoach/Virgin.[161] Assessment of the bids was undertaken with the help of Peter Wilkinson of First Class Partnerships, in January–March 2005. Two of the bidders submitted proposals satisfying the 60 per cent minimum requirements for operational integrity, and were found to be affordable. Of these, GNER's bid clearly stood out. The company had submitted the most aggressive revenue forecasts and promised to pay a high premium of £1,265 million to the public sector over the course of the franchise, substantially more than its nearest rival.[162] The SRA Board noted that GNER's forecasts were 'credible' though 'challenging', and endorsed the Executive Committee's concerns that arrangements should be made to maintain liquidity. Further negotiations involved a package of improvements to be provided, notably an increased number of London–Leeds services.[163] The final terms not only committed the franchisee to pay the Government a substantial £1.3 billion over the period 2005–15, but also included an undertaking to invest £125 million.[164] However, the gains to the public sector soon proved to be nugatory. GNER's difficulty in meeting the premium conditions became evident in the wake of the London bombings in July 2005. Its problems were also revealed during its opposition to the entry of an 'open access' company, Grand Central Railway, which culminated in an unsuccessful appeal to the High Court in July 2006.[165] There was a further challenge to the franchisee when its parent filed for Chapter 11 bankruptcy in the following October.[166] Two months

---

[158] SRA Executive Minutes, 24 March 2005, SRA 57/01/01 Pt. 5; SRA Board Minutes, 5 May 2005.

[159] SRA Executive Minutes, 20 January 2005, SRA 57/01/01 Pt. 5.

[160] Cf. Shrubsole–Killen, 12 July 2004, DfT file R101/1/15 Pt. 1; Bowker–Sherwood, 14 July 2004, SRA.

[161] Quarmby–Stephen Nicol (Minister for Transport, Scottish Executive), 7 October 2004, SRA.

[162] David Borchard and Pete Wilkinson, Memo. on 'InterCity East Coast Replacement', SRA Executive Committee Minutes, 10 February 2005, SRA 57/01/02 Pt. 57, 57/01/01 Pt. 5.

[163] SRA Board Minutes, 15 February and 7 April 2005.   [164] GNER Press Release, 22 March 2005.

[165] See White & Case, 'Open Access Operations—Charging and Competition', Railway law & policy briefing [my thanks to Tom Winsor for this reference].

[166] *City A.M.*, 17 October 2006, pp. 2, 12–13.

later, the franchise was surrendered, with GNER directed to continue operating on a management contract basis until a new competition was concluded.[167] It is difficult to argue that either the impending demise of the SRA or the urgency of the negotiations—a new franchise had to be in place by 1 May 2005—made any difference to the decision-making process. However, one outcome of the change of regime was postponement of the publication of the SRA's route utilization strategy for the East Coast line. Somewhat perversely, this followed, rather than preceded, the award of the franchise.[168]

Other work undertaken before July 2005 included the re-letting of the Northern franchise in December 2004, negotiations concerning the new Integrated Kent franchise, and the specification of new franchises for Greater Western and Great Northern/Thameslink, where pre-qualified bidders were announced in April 2005. The Northern franchise negotiations were probably the most complex undertaken by the SRA. Not only were there two incumbent operators—First North Western and Arriva Trains Northern—but a new franchise—TransPennine Express—was to be carved out of the new combination. The reshaped Northern franchise was both large and commercially problematic, and a further complication was the involvement of no fewer than five PTEs. As we have noted (above, p. 154), the competition between Serco/NedRail and FirstGroup had been close, and the award of the franchise was clearly hindered by the lack of hard commercial information and the delay produced by the Rail and Spending reviews. An SRA recommendation that Serco/NedRail be selected as preferred bidder was put to the Secretary of State in March 2004, but Darling's agreement was not obtained until the end of June, by which time the successful bidders had revised their calculations and were now seeking a substantial increase in subsidy over the $8^{3}/_{4}$-year period. This had the effect of re-opening the matter, and the SRA was at one stage inclined to turn to the runner-up, FirstGroup.[169] However, agreement was quickly reached with Serco/NedRail, and on 27 August, a fortnight before he stepped down, Bowker informed Darling of the SRA's proposal to provide an additional subsidy. The discussions with Serco and NedRail, he reported, had been 'fraught', but he believed their concerns were genuine.[170] Darling was scarcely happy with this request for additional funding, but his failure to respond quickly produced further costs, since the arrangements with the incumbent franchisees had to be extended beyond the October expiry date.[171]

[167] *Times*, 15 December 2006, p. 59, 16 December 2006, p. 11; *Financial Times*, 15 December 2006, p. 3. The shortlisted bidders, announced in February 2007, were Arriva, FirstGroup, Stagecoach/Virgin, and National Express: *Financial Times*, 21 February 2007, p. 4.

[168] Peter Northfield (SRA), Memo. to SRA Executive Committee, 9 June 2005, SRA 57/01//02 Pt. 59; Interview with Steer, 2007.

[169] SRA Board Minutes, 23 August 2004; SRA Executive Prayers Minutes, 25 August 2004, SRA 57/01/12A Pt. 2.

[170] Bowker–Darling, 27 August 2004, SRA.

[171] Bowker–Killen, 2 September 2004, Shaw, Memo. 4 September 2004, cit.; SRA Executive Prayers Minutes, 6 September, 4 and 8 October 2004, SRA 57/01/12A Pt. 2.

The new franchise agreement was eventually signed on 16 October, taking effect on 12 December. It committed the Government to pay a subsidy of £2.5 billion, the highest level of all the existing franchises, although an attempt was made to 'improve affordability' with the provision for a re-specification within the first two years.[172]

The Integrated Kent franchise was awarded to Govia, a subsidiary of Go-Ahead Group, and began under the name 'Southeastern' in April 2006. Its development involved the handing over of the South East Trains franchise, and more importantly, determination of the vexed question of CTRL commuter services, where there was a lively debate about abstraction from existing services, and a careful evaluation of the business case given London & Continental's proposed track access charges, which were higher than expected. Both the DfT and the Treasury took a close interest in the SRA's work in specifying the franchise, since it was by no means certain that the inclusion of commuter services produced an affordable option.[173] At the end of November 2004, the business case and affordability plan for the franchise were approved by Darling, despite the fact that the subsidy projections exceeded those given in the earlier calculation of the MSCR. He agreed that the fares base should be calculated on the basis of a real 3 per cent increase for five years from January 2006. The invitation to tender document was then approved in January 2005.[174] Contracts with HSBCR, selected as the preferred ROSCO in October 2003, and Hitachi, selected, after some prevarication by HSBC, as the preferred manufacturer for new commuter trains in October 2004, were finally concluded in May 2005. Complicating features here included lengthy negotiations with the parties in relation to the procurement of an associated investment in new depot facilities at Ashford and Ramsgate, which were not completed until September 2005.[175]

The SRA also drew up the specifications for the Greater Western and Thameslink/Great Northern franchises, the competitions for which proceeded in tandem. Each attracted seven applicants by the February 2005 deadline, and the only newsworthy element was the exclusion of the Thameslink incumbent, Govia, from the list of pre-qualified bidders, which numbered three and five,

---

[172] Andrew Nock and Charlotte Hickman (SRA), Memo. on 'Re-specification of Northern Franchise', 25 November 2004, SRA 57/01/12 Pt. 10. Subsidy represented c.70% of franchise income.

[173] SRA Executive Committee Minutes, 8 July 2004, SRA 57/01/01 Pt. 4; Shaw–Rachel Evans (DfT), 21 July 2004, DfT file R73/1/45 Pt. 6. At this stage, the DfT rejected the SRA's assumption that there should be a one-off 3% real increase in fares, a cap on TACs, and that the franchisee should operate the Ebbsfleet station.

[174] Phil West (DfT)–Shaw, 30 November 2004, Darling–Newton, 14 January 2005, SRA. Bidders were asked to bid for two price levels: RPI + 1%; and RPI + 3% for the first 5 years. Rachel Kelley–Tony McNulty, 24 January 2005, DfT file R73/1/45 Pt. 9.

[175] Shrubsole–Killen, 12 July 2004, cit.; Mike Parker (SRA), Memos. to SRA Executive Committee, 24 February and 24 March 2005, SRA 57/01/02 Pt. 58; SRA Board Minutes, 3 March, 7 April and 5 May 2005; SRA Chairman's Review Meeting Minutes, 19 and 26 July and 6 September 2005, SRA57/01/12A Pt. 3. The cost of the depot investment rose from £50m. to £88m. during the negotiations.

261

respectively.[176] Production of the invitation to tender documents was not straightforward. In the Greater Western case, the SRA devoted much time to the identification of service cuts, including removal of the London–west of England sleeper service and the Newquay branch, and rationalization of Bristol/ Exeter/Plymouth/Penzance and Oxford–Bicester services.[177] These specifications were of course subject to further evaluation by the Department and the bidders before the franchise was let, and in the event the sleepers were retained.[178] With the expanded Thameslink franchise, there was the associated matter of the utilization of the Brighton Main Line. The SRA's route utilization strategy, published as a consultation document in September 2004, recommended ending the dedicated Gatwick Express franchise and combining the services with those provided by Govia (Southern). In this way, supply and demand imbalances would be corrected. The Gatwick Express trains took a third of the train paths but delivered fewer than 10 per cent of total passengers. During the morning peak, the service from Gatwick to Victoria (every 15 minutes) was running with low loadings, while there was severe overcrowding on the adjacent Brighton– Victoria services.[179] Negotiations then began with Govia and National Express. The latter was prepared to consider the early surrender of Gatwick Express, whose financial position had deteriorated, in return for modifications to its agreement for the equally problematic Midland Main Line, but the proposals for Gatwick Airport were hindered by opposition from the British Airports Authority.[180] In February 2005, the SRA produced a revised route utilization document which sought to address BAA's concerns, and reached commercial agreement with the two companies. The deals were interdependent; that with National Express was conditional on the SRA receiving at least £43 million from Govia. The agreement with the latter also provided for the cascading of 14 train-sets to Thameslink/Great Northern.[181] The Secretary of State's early

---

[176] Steve Hoskins (SRA), Memo. on 'Greater Western Franchise', 1 March 2005, James Smith (SRA), Memo. on 'Thameslink/GN Franchise', 9 March 2005, SRA Executive Committee Minutes, 10 March 2005, SRA 57/01/02 Pt. 57, 57/01/01 Pt. 5; SRA Board Minutes, 22 March and 7 April 2005. On the exclusion of Govia, see newspaper comment, 2 April 2005. FirstGroup, National Express, and Stagecoach were shortlisted for both franchises: for Thameslink/GN MTR/John Laing and Danish railways/EWS were added.

[177] Andrew Nock and Steve Hoskins (SRA), Memos. 28 April and 5 May 2005, SRA Executive Committee Minutes, 28 April, 5 May and 23 June 2005, SRA 57/01/02 Pt. 58, 57/01/01 Pt. 5; SRA Board Minutes, 5 May 2005.

[178] The Newquay branch was also retained.

[179] Quarmby–Stakeholders, 16 December 2004, and Quarmby–Tessa Jowell (SoS for Culture, Media and Sport), 13 January 2005, SRA; SRA Board Minutes, 13 January 2005.

[180] The proposal was that National Express would hand back the MML franchise on 31 December 2007 instead of 29 April 2008, with negotiations focusing on the fate of the East Midlands Parkway station project and the provision of Meridien train-sets for MML. Stuart White (SRA), Memo. on 'MML and Gatwick Express: Proposed NX deal', 23 December 2004, SRA Executive Committee Minutes, 8 July and 16 December 2004, Executive Prayers Minutes, 24 December 2004, SRA 57/01/12 Pt. 10, 57/01/12A Pt. 2, 57/01/01 Pts. 4–5.

[181] White, Memo. to Executive Committee, 21 February 2005, Richard Cantwell and Annette Smith (SRA), Memo. 22 February 2005, SRA 57/01/02 Pt. 57.

approval was sought so that the new arrangements could be introduced with the December 2005 timetable. However, this was not forthcoming, and the issues had not been resolved by the time of the handover to DfT in July.[182] The fundamental decisions on Greater Western and Thameslink/Great Northern were also taken by the Department. The successful bidder for these franchises—FirstGroup—was announced in December and the new franchises began in April 2006. Initial operations have not been without controversy. On Greater Western, there have been complaints from passengers about how the successful bidder has approached the task of making the franchise work commercially, given its commitment to pay £1.131 billion in premia over the 10-year term. Overcrowding in the Bristol–Bath corridor has been singled out for particular criticism.[183] The SRA was also involved in trying to resolve the uncertainties surrounding the business case for the combined Great Northern/Thameslink franchise.[184] FirstGroup, operating as First Capital Connect, has promised premia totalling £808 million over nine years, but criticisms of its pricing changes during the evening peak are a further demonstration of the tension between private sector profit-seeking, government insistence on value for money, and the impact on commuters and leisure passengers.[185]

Virgin's West Coast and Cross Country franchises continued to provide headaches for the SRA in 2004–5. A lengthy period of negotiation for a long-term deal for the West Coast resumed in September 2004, but the position in November was that the parties were some distance apart.[186] On top of this, the SRA was also unable to agree Virgin's subsidies for 2005/6, its position being justified by the fact that the company had exceeded its 2003/4 and 2004/5 budgets for the two franchises by £110 million and £68 million, respectively. After failing to reach agreement by March 2005, the SRA imposed the subsidy budgets for 2005/6. At £86 million for West Coast and £126 million for Cross Country, they were £70 million and £42 million below the company's bids. The two parties continued to argue over the next four months. The SRA took the view that in the past the company had produced pessimistic revenue forecasts and had persistently overstated its subsidy requirements, and criticized it for taking a dividend payment of £22 million from Cross Country in 2003/4.[187] Having imposed a lower budget on Cross Country, the Authority then faced the prospect that the franchise would soon be insolvent—Virgin said that it would have a negative cash balance by 1 July 2005. The possibility of re-profiling the subsidy

[182] SRA Executive Prayers Minutes, 13 September 2005, SRA 57/01/12A Pt. 3; SRA Board Minutes, 7 April, 5 May and 4 August 2005; SRA, *Annual Report 2004/5*, p. 17, *2005/6*, p. 24.
[183] *Rail*, 21 December 2005–3 January 2006, pp. 6–7; *Modern Railways*, February 2007, p. 6; *Rail*, 31 January–13 February 2007, pp. 3, 12, 26–7.
[184] Cf. SRA Board Minutes, 5 May 2005.   [185] *Times*, 12 August 2006, p. 28, 20 March 2007, p. 3.
[186] Shaw, Memo on 'Virgin West Coast', 8 November 2004, and on 'West Coast Trains', 23 November 2004, SRA 57/01/12 Pt. 10; SRA Board Minutes, 13 January 2005.
[187] Paul Rodgers (SRA), Memo. 4 May 2005, SRA Executive Committee Minutes, 24 February, 10 March, 4 and 12 May 2005, SRA 57/01/02 Pt. 58, 57/01/01 Pt. 5; SRA Board Minutes, 5 May 2005.

payments to Cross Country in 2005/6 was still being discussed when the baton passed to Great Minster House. It was left to the Department to announce, in October, that the franchise would be re-let in 2007.[188]

While franchising became the DfT's responsibility from July 2005, some aspects remained to be dealt with by the SRA, notably the handover of ScotRail and Arriva Trains Wales to the Scottish and Welsh Assemblies. On 17 October 2005, the Scottish franchise was handed over to the Scottish Executive, to be supervised by Transport Scotland and its first chief executive, Dr. Malcolm Reed; oversight of the Welsh franchise passed first to the joint administration of DfT Rail and the Welsh Assembly until the latter assumed full responsibility on 1 April 2006.[189] When the SRA relinquished South East Trains on the same date, it was able to derive considerable comfort from the fact that it had operated the South Eastern franchise on a breakeven basis in the years 2004/5 and 2005/6.[190] Of course, the work done by the SRA before its closure was undertaken with the full knowledge of the Department, but in the year following the publication of the White Paper the indications were that the new world of fewer franchises would not prove to be a problem-free solution to the overall requirements for successful franchising: stable conditions for passengers; minimizing public sector subsidy and risk; and encouraging the private sector to deliver customer benefits without passing on the burden to them in higher fares, overcrowding, and a worsening quality of service. At the time of writing (October 2007), it is far from clear that these objectives have been satisfied. FirstGroup clearly underestimated the difficulties when it made changes to Greater Western services in 2007, and its predicament was exacerbated by problems with the infrastructure. Echoing railway company nicknames in the nineteenth century, complainants dubbed First Great Western 'Worst Late Western'. Protests about pricing changes in the London area introduced by First Capital Connect and South West Trains have produced further adverse publicity. The discontent has spilled over into the national passenger survey of Spring 2007, which recorded a decline in satisfaction both in these franchises and nationally.[191] At the same time, the passengers' voice became more centralized with the transformation of the Rail Passengers Council. In July 2005, this was reconstituted as a single national body, operating subsequently as Passenger Focus; the regional committees were then dissolved. The intention to give greater clout to the lobby was a persuasive argument in

---

[188] Rodgers, Memos. 12 May and 23 June 2005, SRA Executive Committee Minutes, 23 June, 14 and 18 July 2005, SRA 57/01/02 Pts. 58 and 60, 57/01/01 Pt. 5; SRA Board Minutes, 7 July and 4 August 2005; DfT Press Release, 18 October 2005. The shortlisted bidders for the new Cross Country franchise were Arriva, FirstGroup, National Express, and Virgin: DfT Press Release, 19 September 2006.

[189] SRA Prayers Minutes, 19 October 2005, SRA57/01/12A Pt. 3; www.information.wales.gov.uk.

[190] SRA, *Annual Report 2005/6*, pp. 13, 79. Operating profits before tax were shown as £4.2m. in 2004/5, and £1.3m. in 2005/6 [after an unsubsidized FRS17 charge of £2.7m.].

[191] *Times*, 8 May 2007, p. 8; *Financial Times*, 1 June 2007, p. 4; Passenger Focus, *National Passenger Survey Spring 2007* (2007); *Rail*, 26 September–9 October 2007, pp. 3, 12; Interview with Anthony Smith (RPC), 10 July 2007. Some of the pricing adjustments were a matter of applying London Transport's zonal fare structure to national rail: *Modern Railways*, December 2006, p. 8.

favour of the changes, but the loss of regional representation (outside London, Scotland, and Wales) was interpreted in some quarters as a move to dilute local and regional opposition to service adjustments. The Council's creation of 'passenger link managers' to handle individual franchises was presented as a way of maintaining local representation, but this was far removed from the approach of the local committees.[192]

Finally, in the months before it handed over the reins, the Authority continued to fulfil a number of strategic planning tasks. It published important policy documents on community railways and on cycling in November 2004, accessibility in March 2005, and gauging (loading gauge) in June.[193] And in the last months, executives kept busy developing a simplified franchise agreement, conducting the initial work on a series of regional planning assessments, completing the route utilization work for the Great Western and West Midlands, developing the specification for a combined South West Trains/Island Line franchise and the separation of Greater London 'metro' services from Silverlink, and continuing with useful work in the area of technological investment, for example, ERTMS and GSM-R. Encouragement was also given to work on standard-setting via a cross-industry strategy group set up by the SRA, and to the development of a replacement strategy for the High Speed Trains first introduced in the 1970s.[194] That there was a need for such a body in the privatized structure, a fact which had inspired universal agreement that it should be set up in 1999, was in some ways more evident towards the close of its period of existence than it had been at the beginning. One thing was clear. Many of its activities were essential to the modern railway industry and were retained by its successors.

7.6 Conclusion

The situation in 2004/5 was reminiscent of that some 40 years earlier, when in circumstances of rising rail costs and worsening financial deficits, the Treasury had stepped in to constrain spending under the Modernisation Plan of 1955–65 and replace the British Transport Commission with the British Railways Board.[195] But there was also another government stance of long vintage—the

[192] RPC, Stakeholder briefing note, 25 November 2004, DfT file R101/1/2 Pt. 6; *Times*, 11 February 2005, p. 35, 12 February 2005, pp. 23, 30.

[193] SRA, *Community Rail Development Strategy* (November 2004), *Cycling Policy* (November 2004), *Railways for All: The Accessibility Strategy for Great Britain's Railways* [consultation document] (March 2005), *Train and Station Services for Disabled Passengers: A Code of Practice* (March 2005), *Gauging Policy* (June 2005). The DfT's accessibility strategy followed in March 2006.

[194] SRA, *Annual Report 2004/5*, pp. 17–19, 22–3, 33–4, *2005/6*, pp. 19, 29, and see papers in SRA 57/01/01 Pts. 58–60.

[195] Gourvish, *British Railways 1948–73*; Charles Loft, *Government, the Railways and the Modernization of Britain. Beeching's last trains* (Abingdon, 2006).

condemnation of decades of 'chronic underinvestment' in the railways while at the same time contemplating drastic cost-cutting exercises during a more limited period of financial control. The two are not mutually exclusive of course, but the SRA could feel more than a little sore at the repetition of this mantra, given that it had tried to think outside this constraint to produce the enhancements that politicians were keen to achieve before the Treasury directed them to look more closely at the public finances. In terms of structure and organization, the SRA was able to argue that many of the powers heralded under the radical new regime already existed: the Government's ultimate strategic responsibility; the broad setting of outputs by government; the role of the regulator in ensuring that these were reasonable; improvements to franchising bid assessments; and Network Rail's responsibility for overall network performance, including the timetable.[196] It was true that the Government had already been accountable for the railways through the SRA, but the Treasury could see that the SRA–DfT relationship had not always produced clarity of intent. However, it could be argued that the detailed interface arrangements under the new regime were unlikely to be simpler or more transparent than under the old. Furthermore, with some of the balance of power shifting from a strategic NDPB to an engineering/infrastructure business, it remained to be seen whether the DfT could respond to the expectations of the post-Gershon reform world, where efficiencies in procurement and transactions were expected, and act as the 'informed, intelligent and experienced public sector client' within a more professional, reforming, and cost-cutting environment.[197] It also remains to be seen whether the Secretary of State could handle his or her unaccustomed position as detailed specifier of railway services, a marked contrast with the situation established by the Transport Act of 1947 and the Railways Act of 1974. The SRA had been accused of 'micromanagement' in its franchising activity: what then were the prospects for the Department being dragged into endless debates on matters of railway detail?

---

[196] Cf. Nicola Shaw, Memo. on 'The Future of Rail—White Paper—An SRA review', n.d. [2004], SRA.

[197] Sir Peter Gershon (for Treasury), *Releasing Resources to the Front Line. Independent Review of Public Sector Efficiency* (July 2004).

8

Conclusion

8.1 Railway policy 1997–2005: the importance of precedent

The precedents set by the Conservatives, in constructing the railway privatization architecture of 1993–7, and by the Labour opposition, in responding to
it, did much to shape the parameters of railway policymaking under the Blair
administrations. The fragmented structure—two regulators and the separation
of infrastructure owner, train operating companies, rolling stock providers, and
infrastructure maintenance and renewal companies—produced very considerable
problems, and some of the new entrants to the industry faced a steep learning
curve. This was certainly the case with the TOCs; as Moir Lockhead later recalled,
'we learned that running trains is different to running buses'.[1] Less visible, but
no less significant, was the learning process for the infrastructure companies.
Many of these were new to the industry, even if the workers they inherited were
not. They had to wrestle with the unfamiliar complexities of railway maintenance
and renewal routines and their impact on the operating of trains, things which
were managed in a more integrated fashion in British Rail days.

A particularly important step was the decision made by John Major and
Kenneth Clarke to accelerate the privatization of Railtrack before the company's
record as guardian of the railway network could be fully assessed. Here the
Conservatives' anxiety to take the entire industry out of the public sector, coupled
with the uncompromising stance of opposition spokesman Clare Short on the
move, not only affected the valuation of the company but also had a pronounced
effect on the attitude of the private sector and capital markets to investment

---

[1] Interview with Lockhead, 2007.

Conclusion

and risk in the industry more generally. The same thing happened with the sale of the ROSCOs, which in the midst of uncertainty about the intentions of a future government were sold off at what proved to be knock-down prices. At the same time, the headlong rush to dispose of the remaining passenger franchises in 1996–7, in preference to leaving some of the more problematic service groups with British Rail, had an enduring impact on the performance of the passenger railway. The anxiety to sell, together with the over-optimism of some of the bidders about the scope for cost reductions, produced more than a few poor deals which were repented at leisure. One of these was the North Western franchise, serving North-west England and North Wales, which was operated by the Great Western MEBO from March 1997. FirstGroup, by acquiring the Great Western company in 1998, added this franchise to its portfolio, but this was a business which it quickly recognized was in 'dire straits'.[2] With hindsight we may identify others which developed more substantial problems, such as Cardiff Valleys and South Wales & West (Prism) and Regional Railways North East (MTL), where delivery of the promised trajectory of lower subsidies rested more upon cost reductions than upon revenue growth, and where the latter was more dependent on the 'discretionary' demand of travellers than on the inelastic demand of commuters.[3] The flotation and subsequent resale of the ROSCOs set another defining precedent. The profits made by the ex-British Rail managers, who bought the initial businesses from their former employer and then made extensive capital gains, were the subject of considerable criticism, not least by the NAO. More significantly, this example of entrepreneurial risk influenced the attitude of politicians such as John Prescott to the involvement of the private sector in the railway industry.

Corporate culture was also an important ingredient in the privatized railway mix, and to a certain extent this was nurtured, if not created, by the way in which privatization was pursued in 1993–7. The fact that so many ex-British Rail managers found a home in the new structure was not itself either surprising or remarkable given the fact that many of the skills within the industry were not easily transferable. However, with the break-up of the highly integrated structure to which the British Railways Board was moving in the early 1990s under the banner 'Organising for Quality', these managers were given the task of dismantling much of what had been erected during the formative, 'shadow' period of privatization. Thus, many of the nascent businesses began with a somewhat negative, even cynical, ethos, and once embedded in the new businesses this proved hard to shift, particularly within middle management.[4] Railtrack was the prime example. The way it behaved in the private sector in its initial years under Bob Horton (Chairman) and John Edmonds (Chief Executive) reflected a determination, at least at the top, to control engineers in an arms-length manner.

---

[2] Interviews with Long and Lockhead, 2007.
[3] Cf. here Nash and Smith, 'Passenger Rail Franchising', 2007.
[4] Gourvish, *British Rail 1974–97*, pp. 374–83; Interview with Adrian Shooter, 31 August 2007.

It is sometimes easy to forget the confident, even arrogant, stance of the company in the second half of the 1990s, fed by healthy operating profits and a rising share price. The self-congratulatory tone in *All Change*, the book by Roger Freeman and Jon Shaw on railway privatization published in 2000, just before the Hatfield accident, was exemplified by the bullish contributions of Edmonds and Prideaux (Angel Trains) about the establishment of Railtrack and the ROSCOs. But the same book also sounded warning noises about the 'parsimony' of Railtrack's initial investment strategies, and any remaining arrogance was quickly dispelled by the Hatfield accident in October 2000 and its aftermath.[5] Both ministers and officials must share some of the blame for Railtrack's subsequent problems in setting up a business without ensuring that it was adequately staffed at a senior level with expertise in what was the 'core' activity—the predictable, routine task of operating, maintaining, and renewing the railway infrastructure.[6] This left the company with power effectively delegated to regional managements, and with insufficient expertise in railway technology and project management at the top. Nowhere were the 'legacy' effects of this omission more evident than in the signing in 1997 of the 'PUG2' contract with Virgin for the upgrade of the West Coast Main Line, which tied Railtrack to an innovative but unproven signalling technology. The contract, negotiated by Bowker and Winsor on Virgin's behalf, left much of the risk with the infrastructure provider, and was quickly recognized to have been a disaster by Edmonds's successor, Corbett, almost before the ink was dry.[7] The deal contained the seeds of problems which would ultimately bring Railtrack down, materially damage Virgin's reputation as a train operator, and provide substantial headaches for Bowker and Winsor when they put on other hats at the SRA and the Rail Regulator's office. On top of this, public interest in, and complaints about, the performance (punctuality and reliability) of passenger services, which became a prime ministerial obsession after Hatfield, owed more than a little to the way the industry's performance penalty regimes had been set up as part of the privatization process. These complex and adversarial instruments encouraged perverse incentives and all the distractions of a legalistic blame culture. And, as Rail Regulator Swift's work in producing the Condition 7 amendment to Railtrack's network licence demonstrated, it was evident that some of the problems arose from the fact that Railtrack's initial licence and the relationships between the TOCs and OPRAF were insufficiently precise to work well.[8] All this clearly affected the subsequent behaviour and regulation of the industry from 1997.

[5] Roger Freeman and Jon Shaw (eds.), *All Change: British Railway Privatisation* (Maidenhead, 2000), pp. 57–82, 95, 97–118. A study by Kennedy and Smith in 2003 claimed that Railtrack delivered substantial improvements in maintenance productivity prior to Hatfield: John Kennedy and Andrew S. J. Smith, 'Assessing the Efficient Cost of Sustaining Britain's Rail Network: Perspectives Based on Zonal Comparisons', *Journal of Transport Economics and Policy*, 38:2 (2004), 157–90, though how this was achieved remains a matter for debate.
[6] Interview with Rowlands, 2007.   [7] Above, p. 49.
[8] Interview with Winsor, 2006.

8.2 How the SRA was lost—the Morton/Prescott years

The Strategic Rail Authority was in hindsight a lost cause before it became a statutory entity in February 2001. The proposal for a strategic non-departmental public body, which would provide a central focus and fill the planning vacuum produced by a fragmented, privatized railway, was almost universally welcomed by politicians, railway commentators, and the media in the mid-1990s. Support for the idea intensified after the Southall and Ladbroke Grove accidents in 1997 and 1999, which were followed by acrimonious meetings with the Transport Secretary, John Prescott, and stressful rail summits called to discuss faltering rail performance over the period 1997–2000.[9] However, the SRA's honeymoon period proved to be as short as that facing most British governments. To a degree this cooling of enthusiasm was the product of Prescott's approach. After Southall and Ladbroke Grove he was fearful of suffering the same fate as Paul Channon, who as Transport Secretary had been damaged politically when required to contend with a plethora of disasters in 1987–8: the London Underground fire at King's Cross, the sinking of the *Herald of Free Enterprise*, and the Clapham rail accident, among others. The Deputy Prime Minister certainly inculcated a sense of crisis. He condemned the railways as a 'national disgrace' at one point and thus contributed substantially to the post-Hatfield 'collective nervous breakdown', in Sir Alastair Morton's words, which did much to put the industry's institutions under pressure.

In contrast, Prescott was able to exploit the position he occupied in holding the ring between the Blair and Brown factions within the Labour leadership to launch something bold in the 10 Year Plan for transport of 2000. This was a real achievement in getting a longer time horizon and a long-term funding guideline into the transport department, which had frequently suffered from the short-termist approach of successive governments. Nevertheless, as so often, aspiration was not to be confused with delivery, and Prescott was clearly distracted by the challenge of managing the unwieldy, sprawling Department of the Environment, Transport and the Regions. Furthermore, neither Blair nor Brown seemed interested in public transport or the railways. Indeed, Prescott once gave Blair a wooden toy train set, telling him: 'There you are, Tony, you play with that and leave me to get on with the railway.'[10] But the immediate impact of the 10 Year Plan was necessarily limited by the long lead-in time required to produce any results, and the manner in which Prescott sought to make an impression was not in retrospect very positive. His rather theatrical denunciations of poor performance, accompanied by threats of tougher monitoring, appeared to motivate neither Railtrack nor the TOCs, while his promise that

---

[9] Above, pp. 28–33, 71–2.   [10] Interview with senior official.

the SRA would rectify the 'curse of a fragmented and incoherent industry' placed a weighty burden on an institution which had yet to be established. And his main contribution, making sweeping changes in personnel at the top, left the railways with an excess supply of fat controllers. Although John Welsby and the British Railways Board had played a significant, and perhaps surprising, role in preparing the ground for the SRA, there was no room for him or indeed the old guard of Swift, the Rail Regulator, and O'Brien, the Franchising Director, in Prescott's vision for the future. In April 1999 Morton replaced Welsby as Chairman of the British Railways Board, and became the SRA's Chairman designate. In July Tom Winsor replaced Chris Bolt as the Rail Regulator.[11] These appointments were applauded as bold. However, it was soon evident that there was not room for both Morton and Winsor at the top, since each of them wished to impose his own authority upon the industry. Energy, creativity, and determination are worthy attributes, but they are not always sufficient. The main problems—the railways' fragmented structure following a long period as a single enterprise, adversarial relations between the New Labour Government and the industry's private sector institutions, and a fair measure of media hype—called for managerial patience, negotiation, and compromise. When it came to treading a delicate path through the conflicting interests in the railway matrix, it was far from certain that Morton and Winsor could call on these qualities.

There was no shortage of vision during Morton's period as Chairman of the SRA. But most of Sir Alastair's time was spent in a 'shadow' hinterland in which his well-known contempt for all things Whitehall came together with Whitehall's increasing nervousness about the beast it had created to dampen enthusiasm for anything radical being introduced. The situation did little to entice a risk-averse private sector to part with investible funds. The 10 Year Plan, Morton's rallying cry of 'investment, investment, investment', and the means to achieve his ambitions—longer franchises, Special Purpose Vehicles (SPVs), and so on—were soon regarded as something of a Holy Grail. And yet it was difficult to see how a government elected on an education ticket and having made bold promises about health could find room to deal with the rail industry, which was distinctly less sexy. Of course, as each year went by, it became clear that, far from declining, demand for rail travel was rising steadily. It may have been 'politically understood' that the railway was growing and would require higher levels of investment,[12] and Prescott may have assured Morton that the 10 Year Plan would give the SRA the resources to 'promote a substantial programme of infrastructure enhancement'.[13] But Hatfield threw the industry into some disarray, and these aspirations were never tested in stable conditions. In any case, once Prescott left Transport in June 2001, the SRA lost its champion.

[11] Bolt had served as Rail Regulator following Swift's departure at the end of 1998. Mike Grant, one of Morton's managers at Eurotunnel, succeeded O'Brien as Franchising Director.
[12] Morton, file note, 3 February 2000, reporting meeting with Rowlands, Morton's papers, SRA.
[13] Prescott–Morton, 17 July 2000, ibid.

Conclusion

If it was intended that the SRA should act to constrain the independence of the Rail Regulator then Prescott's decision to appoint Winsor was ultimately counter-productive. The feisty new regulatory champion regarded the SRA, somewhat contemptuously, as 'OPRAF on steroids', and went to considerable pains to delineate the extent of his jurisdiction.[14] A case could be made, and at times certainly was, for reducing the number of regulators from two to one. In the area of economic regulation the railways are very different from utilities such as electricity, gas, and water, in that service provision requires substantial sums of public money. Competition issues might safely have been entrusted to the Competition Commission, leaving either the ORR, or the SRA, or a merger of the two to hold Railtrack to account, prevent it from exploiting its monopoly position in its dealings with the train operators, and discharge public interest oversight on the Government's behalf.[15] But the SRA was given little more real power than that of OPRAF. Morton was clearly gifted, and perceptive, and in general his diagnoses were sound. For example, he was right to tell Number Ten in September 2000, before Hatfield, that Railtrack had been 'snatched out of the conventional utility mould by the switch from static/declining network to growth network'.[16] But he failed to heed O'Brien's warning that he would have little room to manoeuvre himself since the discretionary resources available to the SSRA/SRA would be extremely limited.[17] People did matter. Bolt, had he continued as Regulator, might have constructed something less adversarial for the ORR, though it is difficult to see how the basic contradictions in the system would have changed. Clearly some problems were caused by the fact that Morton had failed to grasp the essential point that in dealing with Whitehall there is a need to form coalitions with both the politicians and the officials.[18] And someone other than Morton might have realized that before grandiose plans were mounted for creating new infrastructure, it would be important to ensure that the existing network was being utilized as efficiently as possible—something which was corrected later under Richard Bowker and Jim Steer with their route utilization strategies. On the other hand, at the time there did not seem to have been a credible alternative to Morton, and whoever had been at the helm, the SRA's emerging ambitions would have been quickly eaten up by Winsor and Railtrack.[19] Finally, Morton's investment strategy must be deemed a failure. Chiltern aside, there was precious little sign of the SPVs, which proved to be much harder to organize than Morton realized. The assumptions that Railtrack would act as an efficient provider of capital, that the TOCs would commit themselves to large investment schemes, and that an SRA infrastructure fund could be used to lever in large sums from the private sector proved misplaced.

---

[14] Interview with Swift (2006).
[15] See Dieter Helm–Geoffrey Norris, March 2002, cit.; Tony Grayling, *Getting Back on Track* (2001).
[16] Morton–Hackland, 28 September 2000, Cabinet Office file on Rail Transport, R14/6 Pt. 2.
[17] O'Brien–Morton, 26 March 1999, Morton's papers, SRA.
[18] Interviews with Newton and Mayhew (2006).   [19] Interview with Mottram (2007).

Scepticism soon surfaced within both Railtrack and the Treasury. As Rowlands noted, the SPV was a bit like Lewis Carroll's Jabberwock—'an imaginary beast much spoken about but seldom seen'.[20]

8.3 How the SRA was lost: Byers and the Railtrack hiatus

Railtrack's fall from grace after Hatfield in October 2000 and the decision to place the company in administration a year later were key milestones in the short history of Britain's privatized railway. They also had a profound impact on the SRA in the months immediately prior to and following its emergence in full statutory form. In many ways the Hatfield accident was a personal tragedy for Railtrack's Chief Executive, Gerald Corbett. The archives indicate that although he was an outsider to the industry, and was somewhat discomfited by the media attention its activities attracted, he had certainly acquired a clear understanding of what was wrong with the company before the accident. But solutions were more elusive, and Corbett's response to the accident was at best an exaggerated one, at worst an indication of corporate panic.[21] At the same time, the railways were picked up on Tony Blair's antenna. He had shown little interest in the industry in the previous three years. But his more active involvement from November 2000 had the effect of raising the political profile of 'delivery' and 'performance' in passenger transport, even if it did rather less for the identification and resolution of the longer-term problems the industry now faced. And Blair had a more unexpected impact in choosing Stephen Byers to succeed Prescott as Transport Secretary.

The events unleashed by the Hatfield accident are fully considered in Chapters 3 and 4. Railtrack's subsequent actions in embarking on an expensive maintenance programme challenged the agreed funding for railways set out in the Government's 10 Year Plan and the Spending Review of 2000, thereby constraining the ambitions of the SRA. Much has already been written on the personal contribution of Byers as Transport Secretary; his actions have been frequently, if wrongly, interpreted as pushing the company into administration, particularly since he sought to capitalize politically on the Government's actions in replacing it with a not-for-profit alternative.[22] But, as we have seen, the company did much to determine its own fate. As early as January 2001 its advisers were talking freely about its 'precarious' position, prompting the SRA Board to minute

[20] Interview with Rowlands (2007).
[21] Corbett went on to manage Woolworths, another company with a disappointing record.
[22] Cf. Wolmar, *On the Wrong Line*, pp. 189–200. Byers failed to respond to an invitation to be interviewed for this book.

Conclusion

that the company was clearly 'not fit for purpose'.[23] The 'Project Endeavour' arrangements in April provided more support to Railtrack in preference to more draconian solutions, but the debate about the company's requirements continued. And by the time of Byers's appointment in June, the SRA was already being effectively marginalized from much of the serious activity in Whitehall. Here the essentials were: responding to Railtrack's assertions that Winsor's access charges review, published six days after the accident, was patently inadequate; and assessing its continuing viability, driven by its demands for more government support and Blair's evident irritation with the company.

The SRA's hopes of making a difference persisted. After 'Project Endeavour' the arrangements for its network enhancement partnership with Railtrack were agreed, with plans for a public–private, off-balance sheet venture called 'Renewco' and a commitment to progress the existing SPVs. However, the prospects grew gradually dimmer over the course of 2001, and disappeared with the administration order. Historians may well be tempted to conclude that the seeds of the SRA's demise were firmly sown in the winter of 2000–1. Certainly there was much irritation with Morton's performance in the areas of strategy and budgetary control, and the argument that the hiatus caused by Hatfield had done much to interrupt his preparations for full statutory status fell on deaf ears. Treasury officials in particular criticized Morton for presenting a list of investment projects without indicating how they fitted into the strategic whole. Morton, on the other hand, argued that the 10 Year Plan had set the broad parameters, and that it was up to the SRA to embark on detailed planning, a process that had been profoundly disturbed by Hatfield.[24] By the summer of 2001 the Treasury was arguing that the Authority had shown itself 'incapable of creating or communicating a clear strategy' and had 'developed a public line which is not backed by Government'. And on appointment Byers was told that its 'present ambitions are unfocussed and unaffordable'.[25]

The SRA continued the more routine tasks of franchise management and performance monitoring, adding new functions such as consumer protection, PTE-support, and freight in 2001. But financing concerns blocked its broader ambitions for infrastructure enhancement and for franchises such as the East Coast Main Line, South Central, and South West Trains. Within a year of Blair's second election victory and the establishment of the DTLR in June 2001, Morton, Railtrack, and Byers had all departed. Morton left the Transport Secretary with a diatribe on Railtrack's shortcomings and with his franchising plans in tatters. Railtrack had lurched from bail-out to administration in the space of six months. Finally, Byers, having acted to exert closer control of the SRA via new Directions and Guidance, and in particular to restrain its ambitious plans for refranchising,

---

[23] Above, p. 75.   [24] Above, pp. 82–3.
[25] Wheatley–Balls, 20 June 2001, DfT, Weir doc. vol. K5; Linnard–Byers, 11 June 2001, cit.

fell victim to the Jo Moore e-mail,[26] though he had already lost credibility by mismanaging the public relations aspects of Railtrack's plight. And if the SRA's prospects had been damaged by the demise of the infrastructure company, they were undoubtedly affected by the creation of its successor.

8.4 How the SRA was lost: the Bowker/Darling years

The appointment of Richard Bowker in late 2001 was welcomed as heartily as that of Morton had been. He was expected to provide more strategy, drive, and purpose at the SRA while operating more effectively within the parameters of government than Morton had been able to do. Younger than his predecessor, more informal and more experienced in matters rail, his boyish enthusiasm invited comparisons with the 'Milky Bar Kid'.[27] He undoubtedly gave impetus to the SRA's contribution to strategic planning and operations, and he filled the SRA with creative people such as Jim Steer and Nicola Shaw. There was a more engaged board, more centralization, more staff, higher salaries, and more consultants. Bowker introduced yet another franchising model, this time based on fewer TOCs, the concentration of operations at the main London termini, and a more detailed specification for the operators to follow, including performance improvements.[28] He also got to grips with some urgent investment projects, notably the upgrade of the West Coast Main Line, and the replacement of Mark I stock with new trains and a power supply upgrade south of the Thames. Ultimately, however, he suffered the same fate as Morton. Like Morton, Bowker had some radical ideas and wanted to lead the industry. He also insisted on combining the posts of SRA chairman and chief executive. While the impact of this may have been more symbolic than real, it nevertheless was indicative of a confrontational, if engaging, management style that tended to grate on people as much as it inspired them.[29] The TOCs resented his 'micromanagement', Network Rail, Railtrack's successor, resented his insistence on intervening in organizational and managerial affairs as the company's principal underwriter. Bowker's relations with Ian McAllister, Network Rail's chairman, and with his former colleague, Winsor, were every bit as acrimonious as Morton's had been with Winsor and the Treasury. He began his job by pronouncing that the railways had suffered from a 'fundamental failure of process and people', but did not succeed in addressing these essentials. A widely reported comment came to haunt him: his apparent insistence that the Authority's staff should 'fit in or fuck

[26] 9/11—'a very good day to get out anything we want to bury'.
[27] Joanna Walters, *Observer*, 28 October 2001, p. 16.   [28] Above, pp. 118, 136 ff.
[29] Interviews with SRA board members, 2007.

275

Conclusion

off'.[30] Not all were able to do this, notably Julia Clarke, his freight director, while his communications director, Ceri Evans, ruffled feathers on a number of occasions.

Bowker had six months with Byers, then spent the rest of his $2^3/_4$ years at the SRA reporting to Alistair Darling, who was appointed to head a further reorganized (and slimmed down) Department for Transport in May 2002. Byers's enforced resignation did more than raise a question mark about the New Labour Government's internal workings and its use of 'spin'. It resulted in a Blairite Secretary of State being replaced by someone with clear Brownite credentials. Perhaps the shift of emphasis was inevitable given the fact that concern about rising railway costs had already begun to dominate the policy agenda. The SRA's strategic plan of January 2003 showed more realism, but there was still much aspiration (disturbing to Whitehall doubters) in the SRA's efforts, and this was further demonstrated in the *Everyone's Railway* document of September 2003, which was widely interpreted (in fact, misinterpreted) in government circles as a case of begging bowl tactics.

The process of refranchising was complicated by the mess into which many of the regional franchises had fallen before Bowker's appearance. Existing plans to improve both the West Coast and East Coast main lines were fragile, to say the least. Bowker and his team introduced more prescriptive arrangements, essentially service contracts which put an end to the tendency of some operators to introduce extra trains in order to gain a higher revenue share on jointly operated services, a process known as 'ORCATS raiding'. Several new franchises were put firmly on the drawing board. A strong message was sent to franchise managers when Connex South Eastern was taken back into public ownership by the SRA in November 2003, albeit on a temporary basis. However, in Bowker's time only three new franchises were established (Arriva Wales, TransPennine, and Greater Anglia); the efforts to place Virgin's problematic franchises onto a firmer footing were protracted; and, under pressure from the Department and the Treasury, the SRA began to lead the industry towards a round of rationalization measures in an attempt to exert a stronger grip on creeping franchising costs. There was a relative absence of new entrants in passenger services, while the apparently healthy competition for franchises tended to involve the 'usual suspects' in a process which resembled the shuffling of a pack of cards and where decisions often seemed divorced from past performance. Some of these defects were put right before the SRA was wound up, but they remained the subject of critical comment. Questions also began to be asked about the ability of the SRA to control its franchise budget. Increases in access charge payments had by far

---

[30] As reported by Barrie Clement in *Independent*, 15 April 2002, p. 17. It is difficult to find a provenance for this. When Bowker presented the SRA's 2002 strategic plan, he was reported in Rail magazine to have warned critics in the industry that they should 'shape up or ship out': *Rail*, 6–19 February 2002, cover and pp. 4–7.

the greatest impact on the total subsidy bill, and here the TOCs were fully compensated by the SRA for any changes. But as observed in Chapter 5, the apportionment of responsibility is a challenging task, and it is evident that both the TOCs and the SRA must bear some share of the blame for rising costs. It is also clear that the SRA's anxiety to avoid a hiatus or breakdown in the provision of passenger services was a strong driver of policy, despite the risks of moral hazard.[31]

The SRA was also much involved in the extensive—and expensive—work required to establish Railtrack's successor, the company limited by guarantee called Network Rail, which finally assumed responsibility for the infrastructure in October 2002. But the impact of this work, and the subsequent emergence of Network Rail as a credible, quasi-public alternative to Railtrack, served to constrain the status of the SRA and eventually contributed to its demise. During the early period of administration there was a prospect that the SRA might absorb the ORR, but this possibility soon faded. Winsor's determination to remain in post, the Government's anxiety to obtain his cooperation in getting Railtrack out of administration, and the train operators' insistence that independent economic regulation be retained combined to ensure that the existing structure was retained. In addition, relations between the SRA, the Regulator, and Network Rail began to crystallize. While the SRA thought that it should specify the necessary requirements for the railways, the Regulator would price them, and Network Rail would deliver them, this view was not shared by the latter (led by McAllister, John Armitt, and Iain Coucher), which tended to look to Winsor as the major influence in its planning. Bowker and the SRA were increasingly seen as an irritating complication in the management process.[32] In this way it soon became evident that the new infrastructure company, rather than the SRA, would be favoured as the vehicle for government transactions, particularly after the complexities of administration and with the financial requirements produced by Winsor's access charges review of December 2003. Whatever the proponents of private sector status might aver, Network Rail was, to all intents and purposes, in the public sector.[33] And this meant that there were two such bodies for the Department for Transport to transact with in the railway arena. It soon became apparent that there was room for only one of them.

With the Regulator's access charges review of 2003, an emerging financial crisis in the industry created pressures which invited comparison with the Beeching and Serpell reports of 1963 and 1983. Via the 2004 Rail Review this prompted the Government to dispense with the SRA. Problems had already begun to surface before Winsor's determination of infrastructure expenditure requirements for 2004/5–2008/9 plunged the industry into further crisis. The DfT had taken the decision to cut the SRA's budget by some £300 million for 2003/4–2005/6; the

---

[31] Above, pp. 186–7.   [32] Above, pp. 188–9.   [33] Nash and Smith, cit.

Conclusion

Potters Bar accident in May 2002 had removed any complacency there may have been about post-Hatfield safety. And anxieties had been expressed about the cost of refranchising deals and 'rescue' operations, notably the letter agreement with Virgin Rail in July 2002. In the process the Treasury had been drawn more closely into railway policymaking, and its involvement intensified in 2003/4. Earlier, it had been bruised by the attack on its rail privatization model and, influenced by the Blair–Brown hiatus, had adopted something of the traditional, 'arms-length' position in relation to rail issues. But the problem of rising rail costs, drawn to the attention of a wider audience through Roger Ford's references to 'boiling frogs' in his articles for *Modern Railways*, demanded a more 'hands-on' approach. Alarm bells began to ring when the fledging Network Rail revealed, in March 2003, that its core functions would require funding of over £6 billion a year in the three years to March 2006, almost double the provision agreed by Winsor in his earlier review in 2000. The Regulator's final determination, which envisaged a net revenue requirement of £21.4 billion for 2004–9, was accompanied by some tough efficiency and performance targets for Network Rail. However, he had also made a large hole in the Government's existing provision for railway spending. His decision was followed by a rather hectic scramble to alter the balance between access charges (which passed through to government) and capital grants and to persuade Network Rail to increase its borrowing in the early years of the award. In the process, more radical ideas, including a draconian cut in rail services and the writing-off of Network Rail's legacy debt, were rejected.[34]

Did economics, organizational structure, politics, or personality clashes do for the SRA? The Authority began with high hopes but its friends quickly evaporated, and personal relations did play a part here. The fact that Bowker had been told by Blair, in much the same way as Prescott had briefed Morton, that he was expected to create significant change in the industry only heightened his sense of frustration with the realization that he lacked command powers. Winsor may have irritated civil servants, but Bowker's public arguments with the Regulator did little to enhance his reputation, and in his desire to swallow up Network Rail into an expanded SRA he appeared to overreach himself. But if personalities had an influence, so too did organizational structure and financial reality. The 2004 Rail Review, which chose the SRA as the sacrificial victim of 'fragmentation' and organizational complexity in the industry, was very much the product of an anxiety about cost control. The SRA's dealings with the DfT and Treasury prior to the Review had produced numerous warnings about its running costs, the use of consultants, and the 'affordability' of its enhancement programme. The writing was surely on the wall when the SRA was required to axe the publication of its strategic plan for 2004.[35] The broader aspects of the Rail Review were something of a charade; pragmatism clearly dominated blue skies thinking. Although the SRA's National Rail prescription for structural reform attracted more interest

---

[34] Above, pp. 196–8.   [35] Above, p. 200.

9. The end of the SRA, 2005. The two surviving chairmen, David Quarmby (centre) and Richard Bowker (right, wearing tie!), with Janet Lewis-Jones (Board Member), at a dinner for past and present board members on 21 November.

than might have been supposed, for key civil servants and advisers in the DfT and Treasury the Review's outcome was a foregone conclusion. The only practical organizational change was to dispense with the SRA.[36]

8.5 The SRA's legacy (i): 1999–2005

We have noted that the Authority added value in areas where there had been a conspicuous absence of value-adding for much of the 1990s. It sought to identify the optimum use of the existing network with the development of a network utilization strategy, the specification of maintenance and renewals requirements, and the formulation of individual route utilization strategies. Detailed work was undertaken on passenger franchise specification, together with a major contribution to cost–benefit analysis.[37] The SRA also developed a strategy for both freight and rolling stock. Freight offered a real challenge. There were undoubted opportunities for rail with the rise in container traffic, but in the UK trans-shipment

[36] Above, pp. 236–7.
[37] Cf. Steer Davies Gleave (for SRA), 'Revised Estimates of the Economic and Social Benefits of GB Rail Services', September 2003, SRA.

Conclusion

costs and modest smaller lengths of haul produced clear constraints. The SRA devised policies designed to attract freight to rail, notably with the refinement of the sensitive lorry-miles analysis, which indicated the wider benefits of transferring freight flows from road to rail, and the establishment of new types of freight grant, such as CNRS (Company Neutral Revenue Support). However, its plans for infrastructure improvements and intermodal interchanges were largely frustrated.[38] With rolling stock, the SRA did much to supply a risk-mitigating 'visible hand', providing guarantees when orders were affected by changes of franchisee. It made progress in developing risk-sharing arrangements with the private sector in passenger franchises, notably with the 'cap-and-collar' principle. It also produced a developmental policy for local and rural railways under the banner of 'community rail', and contributed substantially to policymaking for rail users with disabilities. These and other contributions provided ample evidence that the SRA did contribute to the formulation of strategy. More controversially, after a fares review, published in June 2003, it reversed the RPI − X approach to regulated fares, replacing it with RPI + X. Britain's railway services may be comparatively expensive in European terms, but given rising demand, capacity constraints, and the persistence of overcrowding at peak times, this was a nettle that had to be grasped.

The SRA also exposed opportunities that were being missed elsewhere in the rail industry when it provided a more determined lead in project development and project management. Bowker and his team gave badly needed impetus to the faltering WCML upgrade, led the rolling stock/power supply upgrade south of the Thames, and contributed substantially to policy in new technologies such as ERTMS and GSM-R and to smaller schemes. All this revealed what some critics had realized when the crisis-ridden Channel Tunnel project had been rescued by Morton from 1987, and when Britain's privatization structure had been put in place in 1993–7: that for large, complex infrastructure projects to succeed there needed to be a strong and committed project champion to provide the central, 'directing mind'. Other players were involved, of course, and the part played by Network Rail, the ROSCOs, TOCs, and train manufacturers must not be underestimated. But earlier Railtrack had revealed serious shortcomings in project management, particularly in relation to the WCML upgrade, and the industry's fragmentation made this worse. The history of major rail projects is in general a history of centralized decision-making, and Bowker revived this tradition in the short time he wielded authority.

Reviled for much of its life, the SRA has attracted a modicum of respect since its demise in 2005, and there have been calls to create something like it again.[39]

---

[38] Above, pp. 163–8.
[39] Cf. Nigel Harris and Christian Wolmar, *Rail*, 31 January–13 February 2007, pp. 3, 27.

After a slow start it began to fulfil the expectations of its progenitors in the broad field of strategy.[40] And it clearly achieved much in areas where structural fragmentation had produced gaps, for example, standard-setting, research, and technological development. Ironically, the appointment of David Waboso as a technical director was just beginning to bear fruit when the decision to wind up the Authority was announced.

8.6 The SRA's legacy (ii): after 2005

The changes introduced after the DfT assumed responsibility for most of the SRA's responsibilities in mid-2005 were not hatched in a vacuum. After all, as we have seen, the DfT took on over a third of its staff, and major executives found a home in the other important areas of the industry: Network Rail, the ORR, and the TOCs. Furthermore, there was a fairly lengthy period of transition before all of its functions were transferred.[41] It is scarcely surprising that there was a continuity in franchising, with the Department echoing aspects of the SRA's approach—more concentration, clearer specifications, performance requirements, for example—in its White Paper on *The Future of Rail* in July 2004. It also completed the SRA's work in establishing the Greater Western, Capital Connect (Thameslink/Great Northern), and Southeastern (Integrated Kent) franchises, and, more recently, has re-let the ECML franchise to National Express, who have undertaken to pay the Government premia totalling £1.4 billion (£100m. more than GNER promised), and re-let Cross Country to Arriva. It has also announced the winners of the new East Midlands and West Midlands franchises. Created by merging parts of the old Central franchise with MML and Silverlink, these were secured by Stagecoach and Govia, respectively.[42]

Of course, the new world, presided over by the DfT, also claims to be very different from the old. Network Rail has assumed overall responsibility for the network including planning, route utilization, timetabling, and performance. The remit of the Office of Rail Regulation is to price the rail outputs—there is after all some truth in Ceri Evans's remark that the Regulator is essentially a price

---

[40] Cf. R. Haywood, 'Britain's National Railway Network: Fit for Purpose in the 21st Century?', *Journal of Transport Geography*, 15 (2007), 208–15, who suggests that since the demise of the SRA there are risks of a policy vacuum in regional and freight planning.

[41] Above, pp. 251–7.

[42] Above, pp. 259–64; *Guardian*, 22 June 2007, p. 30, 23 June 2007, p. 36; *Financial Times*, 11 July 2007, p. 22, 15 August 2007, p. 16.

Conclusion

checker—and deal with economic regulation and safety.[43] In franchising, the new London Overground franchise (North and East London lines) establishes a precedent. Won by a new entrant, MTR Corporation of Hong Kong, acting with Laing, it involves the transfer of responsibility to Transport for London. TfL will manage it on the London bus model: it will set fares, retain the revenue, and meet the costs of the franchisee. Elsewhere, some of the recent awards on the rail model have included pronouncements about raising unregulated fares by substantially more than inflation: in the Midlands, for example, by RPI + 3 per cent.[44]

Nevertheless, we may see evidence of the SRA's legacy in the DfT's development of the High Level Output Specification (HLOS), in which the Government specifies what it wants from the railway in terms of capacity, safety, and performance, and the Statement of Funds Available (SoFA), in which the Government sets out the amount of money it is prepared to pay for the realization of these goals. The SRA's Route Map of October 2002, an approach which embraced capacity/route utilization and cost reduction, and emphasized the specification of outputs expected from Network Rail, caused the Regulator to criticize the Authority for asserting powers it did not have,[45] but it may be seen as a precursor of the HLOS methodology. Both the HLOS and SoFA for England and Wales were elaborated in the Department's recent White Paper, *Delivering a Sustainable Railway*, of July 2007.[46] They require a marked improvement in punctuality and reliability, to levels not seen since privatization; and for the first time estimates of the demand to be accommodated are given (for England & Wales). At the same time funds of £3 billion per annum are committed, with a shift from revenue or resource payments (franchise support) to Network Rail capital grants over Control Period 4, 2009–14 (Table 8.1). The farebox is expected to provide £9.0 billion in 2013/14, 80 per cent more than the £5.0 billion in 2006/7. The ORR is now required to set charges compatible with the funding specified in the SoFA when determining the next access charges round for CP4. Another product of the SRA's experience has been the belated recognition that a more cooperative approach is required by the major railway players for both planning and delivery mechanisms.[47]

[43] See Chris Bolt, 'Developing the Framework of Rail regulation', in Colin Robinson (ed.), *Utility Regulation in Competitive Markets: Problems and Progress* (Cheltenham, 2007), pp. 175–6.

[44] *Guardian*, 20 June 2007, p. 30, 22–3 June 2007, cit.; *Financial Times*, 20 June 2007, p. 2.

[45] SRA, *Route Map to 2004* (2002), and cf. Winsor–Mengel, 19 November 2003, SRA.

[46] DfT, *Delivering a Sustainable Railway*, July 2007, Cm7176.

[47] Cf. presentations to the Waterfront conference on 'HLOS, SOFA and the Future of Rail', 26–7 November 2007, and in particular Andrew McNaughton's statement that the design and procurement of new trains should be aligned with the lifetime impact on railway infrastructure costs in a systems approach.

Table 8.1 Government output specification and statement of funds available for CP4, 2007

	Specifications by end CP4, i.e. 2013/14			
Safety	Reliability		Capacity	Supplementary specifications (major projects, &c.)
3% risk reduction	PPM:	Reduction in significant lateness:	England & Wales demand to be accommodated (bn passenger-km): 2008/9: 46.1 2013/14: 52.7 +Specified peak load factors	Thameslink upgrade by 2011–15 Reading (£421m.) Birmingham New Street (£128m.) Reading (£425m.) ERTMS/GSM-R New express trains Station improvements (£150m.) Freight support (up to £200m.)
	Inter-urban 92%	−36%		
	London & SE 93%	−21%		
	Regional 92%	−27%		
	Total 92.6%	−25%		

Funds available (£m., CP4)				
2009/10	2010/11	2011/12	2012/13	2013/14
Funds				
3,156	3,031	3,122	3,043	2,977
Suggested split				
Franchise support 1,612	1,386	1,105	856	535
Network grant 1,544	1,645	2,017	2,186	2,442

Source: DfT, Delivering a Sustainable Railway, July 2007, Cm7176, Appendix A.

8.7 The same old railway?

Is the SRA story part of the creation of a new railway industry in Britain, or are we merely seeing evidence of the 'same old railway'? There are certainly signs that we have moved on from the old railway of British Rail days. First, there is the new structure. After 160 years of vertical integration and hierarchical management systems in the railway industry,[48] this well-understood framework was dismantled in favour of a multiplicity of institutions, contracts, and trans-action costs.[49] And, in spite of some important modifications, notably taking the infrastructure back into quasi-public ownership in 2002, it has endured thus far.[50] Moreover, with the 2004 Rail Review and the 2007 White Paper, the DfT has introduced a new organization, following the appointment of Robert Devereux as Permanent Secretary in succession to Sir David Rowlands. There is now more than an echo of the way in which the SRA organization developed in the clear distinction between 'strategy' and 'delivery'. Mike Mitchell now leads a Rail and National Networks Group, which in response to the 2006 Eddington Study (see below) and unusually in the transport department's history encourages a bimodal approach (road and rail) to strategic thinking. The Division includes the 'delivery' functions of rail projects, rail service delivery, rail strategy, rail technical, finance and planning, procurement, together with a new post for 'strategic roads, plan-ning and national networks'.[51] In addition, there has been a new shift towards devolved power, particularly in Scotland, where the Scottish Executive is now responsible for the country's network.

Another new element is the fact that the privatized railway has not been confronted with a period of recession, which is important for an industry histor-ically vulnerable to the economic cycle, notably, in recent memory, with the long downturn in the early 1990s. Indeed, there has been an unprecedented period of sustained growth since 1997. While it remains to be seen whether this rise in demand will endure—and current prognostications are more gloomy—the growth phase has seen passenger traffic increase by 44 per cent in the period 1996/7–2006/7 (or by 61% since the trough of 1994/5) (Table 8.2), the highest growth rate in Europe.[52] This period is longer than that enjoyed by British Rail chairman Bob Reid I in 1982–8, and longer than both the upswing of 1932–7 and the increase in rail travel during the Second World War, when road transport was substantially disrupted. Furthermore, the 46 billion passenger-kilometres

---

[48] Vertical integration was endorsed by the *Select Committee on Railways*, 1839.

[49] On the organization change/transaction cost issue cf. Anne Yvrande–Billon and Claude Ménard, 'Institutional Constraints and Organizational Changes: The Case of the British Rail Reform', *Journal of Economic Behaviour & Organization*, 56 (2005), 675–99.

[50] It may be argued that the current framework is similar to that which would have obtained if there had been no SRA, and Railtrack had remained in the public sector.

[51] www.dft.gov.uk.

[52] Cf. ATOC, *Ten-year European Rail Growth Trends* (September 2007). Here, we ignore the mini, Hatfield-induced, 'blip' in demand in 2000/1.

Table 8.2 The pre- and post-privatization railway: key indicators

Year	Traffic National rail passenger bn km	freight bn tonne-km	Performance PPM (%)	Safety Significant train incidents per m. train-km	Investment (£bn 2006/7 prices)	Government support (£bn 2006/7 prices)	Pass support/ pass support + fare-box (%)	Total support/ total support + fare-box (%)
1982	27.2	15.9	/	0.43	0.9	2.2	49e	49e
1986/7	30.9	16.6	86.0e	0.43	1.1	1.7	36	37
1988/9	34.3	18.1	88.0e	0.45	1.3	0.8	26	20
1994/5	28.6	13.3	90.0e	0.26	1.6	2.3	50	44
1996/7	32.1	15.1	90.0e	0.17	1.5	1.4	45	29
1997/8	34.7	16.9	89.7	0.12	1.9	2.3	39	40
2000/1	38.2	18.1	79.1	0.14	3.3	1.5	25	27
2003/4	40.9	18.9	81.2	0.08	5.7	3.9	31	48
2006/7	46.1	22.6	88.1	0.06	4.1	6.3	26	56
Improvement (%)								
1982–88/9	+26	+14	/	–5	+44	+64	+47	+59
1994/5–2006/7	+61	+70	–2	+77	+156	–174	+44e	–32
1996/7–2006/7	+44	+50	–2	+65	+173	–350	+38e	–50

Source: Tables 1.1, 1.2, 3.1, 3.2, 5.9, 6.4, 7.1; Treasury, GDP deflator; Mike Anson, 'Appendix', in Gourvish, *British Rail 1974–97*, pp. 455–6, 461, 504–5.
e: estimate (no PPM before 2000: very approximate estimates derived from disaggregated performance for British Rail).
The DfT's calculations of the Government's share of passenger railway funding, 1991/2–2005/6 appear in DfT, *Delivering a Sustainable Railway*, 2007, p. 127.

Conclusion

recorded for 2006/7 is Britain's highest figure since 1946. Growth on this scale would surely have stretched the capabilities of British Rail.[53] And, contrary to the impression left by the Ladbroke Grove, Hatfield, and Potters Bar accidents and the critical reactions of commentators such as Christian Wolmar, the railways' safety record has continued to improve, with the number of significant train accidents per million train-kilometres currently (2007) at an historically low level (Table 8.2).[54]

It might also be argued that the industry has emerged from the financial crisis of 2003/4 produced by the failure of Railtrack and the large number of faltering franchises with a stronger, and more realistic, partnership between the public and the private sectors. Although the partnership has taken a severe knock with the recent collapse (in July 2007) of the Metronet PPP for London Underground's infrastructure, the establishment of Network Rail, its expanded role after 2005, and the improvement of relations with the TOCs have led some in the industry to speak of a renewed faith in the private sector. The sector still expects to deliver more efficiency than its public counterpart has done, and there is some confidence that risk has been allocated to the parties best able to manage and mitigate it.[55] The extent to which privatization has brought with it more evidence of entrepreneurial flair should also be considered. In freight, for example, there have been some signs of this in new entrants and new traffics, though some of these have been rather fragile. New entrants have also come forward in the passenger market under the open access banner. Hull Trains, now 80 per cent owned by FirstGroup, has enjoyed a fair measure of success since starting train services in September 2000. We are also promised similar things from Grand Central (Sunderland–London), which intends to begin operations in the autumn of 2007, and the Wrexham & Shropshire Railway (Wrexham–London), promoted by Renaissance Trains, which has just been granted a licence.[56]

On the other hand, in many ways we are still left with the same old railway. Train performance has not improved, whether one takes 1994/5 or 1996/7 as the benchmark (Table 8.2). Overcrowding continues to give concern in commuter areas during peak times, and the level of some unregulated fares is frequently criticized. Comparisons with continental railway systems are often unflattering, though we should be careful to compare like with like. Britain provides a denser passenger service than most countries, but visitors to the UK from say, Italy, would scarcely be impressed on arrival at Stansted Airport to pay £15.50

---

[53] Cf. data in B. R. Mitchell, *British Historical Statistics* (Cambridge, 1988), pp. 545–9.

[54] This is not to say that there should be complacency about the railways' safety regimes. Cf. Shelly Jeffcott, Nick Pidgeon, Andrew Weyman, and John Walls, 'Risk, Trust and Safety Culture in U.K. Train Operating Companies', *Risk Analysis*, 26:5 (2006), 1105–21, and the same authors' report for the HSE: *Organisational Dynamics and Safety Culture in UK Train Operating Companies* (2006).

[55] Cf. Ned Railways, 'Private Sector Participation in the Railway', *Best Practice* (Summer 2006), pp. 4–7.

[56] *Guardian*, 8 February 2006, p. 27; *Times*, 4 September 2007, p. 43, *Modern Railways*, October 2007, p. 13.

(June 2007 price) to reach London Liverpool Street, 3–5 times the charge for a comparable journey in their own country, in vehicles which frequently leave a great deal to be desired. Indeed, although the average age of the passenger stock has fallen since privatization, the persistence of difficulties surrounding train procurement may be seen in the current arguments over the idea of lengthening the Pendolino trains, the Government undertaking to buy 1,300 more carriages, and the recommissioning of mothballed stock.[57] Clearly, there is much to be done to satisfy customers when the RPC continues to criticize the design of new trains, and some passengers prefer the comfort of refurbished HSTs designed 30 years ago to being squashed in a Pendolino with a restricted view.[58] Investment, while difficult to measure consistently over the long run, has fluctuated considerably. Levels that were not much higher than in British Rail's time before the Hatfield accident have increased substantially afterwards. However, some of the increase has been definitional, a matter of allocating expenditure that would earlier have been classed as revenue to capital account (Table 8.2). And the aspirations of the privatizers about reducing the railways' call on the public purse have certainly not been realized. The situation is quite the reverse in fact. Total support, having fallen in the early years of privatization, soon returned to British Rail levels, and then rose sharply after 2001/2, reaching £6.3 billion in 2006/7. It is envisaged that support will fall back to £3 billion a year from 2009/10, but this is a much higher figure than those in the last decade of British Rail. Government assistance is also greater (although direct comparisons are problematic) than that provided to the loss-making British Railways Board from its inception in 1963, when there were annual deficits, in 2006/7 prices, of around £2 billion.[59] And if there are some unexpected 'boiling frogs' simmering in the pot, this figure may rise still higher.

There are other areas of *plus ça change*. While there has been a revolution in structural terms in the industry, it is difficult to argue that this has produced efficiency gains in areas such as operating costs, renewals, and maintenance. The notion accompanying privatization that railway costs under nationalized British Rail were too high and could be reduced substantially by a private sector approach has proved to be erroneous. Nor were infrastructure costs a soft target, as Railtrack's arms-length approach to track maintenance revealed. No one should assume that maintenance is an easy area to manage, as is evidenced by the engineering companies' distinct preference for renewals work, and British

[57] See Ford, *Modern Railways*, March 2007, pp. 16–19; DfT, *Delivering a Sustainable Railway*, 2007, p. 43; *Parl. Deb. (Commons)*, 6th ser. (Session 2006–7), Vol. 459, 26 April 2007, Gwyneth Dunwoody, c. 359WH; *Rail*, 26 September–9 October 2007, p. 68.
[58] RPC, *Annual Report 2001/2*, p. 18; Andrew Smithers, letter in *Rail*, 31 January–13 February 2007, p. 37, and see also *Modern Railways*, October 2007, pp. 38–44. New trains have generally produced a positive response from passengers: cf. Passenger Focus, *The Pennine Class 185 Experience: What do Passengers Think?* (May 2007), p. 10.
[59] BRB losses were £166m. p.a. 1963–8 (Gourvish, *British Railways 1948–73*, p. 585), or £2.3bn p.a. in 2006/7 prices.

Conclusion

Rail would have encountered difficulties in recruiting labour for track work as much as the private sector has done. In addition, a more densely worked network has brought further pressures. However, the investigations into the major train accidents of the period all revealed aspects of unsatisfactory infrastructure management, and one must be drawn to the conclusion that Railtrack was unable to distinguish between efficiency and cost-driven economies which were a threat to safety. In this regard, Hatfield was a cathartic but necessary experience. Network Rail may have turned some things round since then, but the Grayrigg accident has indicated an enduring truth in the industry. As Dr Beeching used to say of British Rail, 'our face is our bottom'. Intent may be strong at the top, but this has to be replicated lower down in the organization. There remains considerable room for improvement in project management too. The unfortunate experience of the Metronet consortium suggests that the lessons of 'PUG2' have not been learned. Complexity, the participation of several players, over-optimism about the capacity of the private sector to deliver, variations to contract, and the absence of competitive tendering and a clearly delineated work programme—these have all contributed to the failure, and they were present in Railtrack also. Had he turned his attention to it, Gordon Brown might have learned much from the experience of the WCML upgrade before embarking on such a risky PPP.[60]

The same old railway attracts the same old debates. There are those who continue to attack privatization as 'botched', 'flawed', even 'a mistake', a raid on the public sector with little to show for it in terms of public benefit. Others defend the move equally vigorously, seeing benefits flowing from the separation of train from track, franchising, and private sector disciplines.[61] These arguments persist because of the unique and enduring challenges presented by the railways. Furthermore, radical changes to basic services cannot be made overnight. As Morton noted in 1999: 'Neither oil tankers nor capital-intensive rail industries are turned around quickly.'[62] The Conservatives' privatization strategy *was* flawed, and few would defend it now. There has been much to criticize in the behaviour of Railtrack, and in the risk aversion and bail-out requests of some of the TOCs. On the other hand, Labour's attempts to remedy the botch were slow, half-hearted, and to a certain extent, misconceived. It might be argued that the DETR was short of railway expertise when the post-1997 assumption was that it could leave monitoring to the Rail Regulator, OPRAF, and then the SRA. At the same

[60] See Rob Ball et al., 'Private Finance Initiative—a Good Deal for the Public Purse or a Drain on Future Generations?', *Policy and Politics*, 29:1 (2001), 95–108; Jay H. Walder and Thomas L. Armenta, 'Financing New Infrastructures: Public/Private Partnerships and Private Finance Initiatives', in Richard E. Hanley (ed.), *Moving People, Goods, and Information in the 21st Century* (New York, 2003), pp. 86–96, *Observer*, 22 July 2007, business p. 5; *Private Eye*, 3–16 August 2007, p. 26.

[61] Cf. the debate in *Public Money and Management*, 26:5 (November 2006), where Adrian Lyons (DG, Railway Forum) and George Muir (ATOC) defend railway privatization from academic critics such as Jean Shaoul and Robert Jupe.

[62] SSRA News Release, 19 May 1999.

time the Treasury's position on the railways was overly negative. This stance was perhaps inevitable given its traditional role as an arms-length controller of departments, and no one was expecting the Treasury to keep a dog and bark itself. Yet all too often it kept the SRA as a dog but growled loudly in the background. Here was another hardy perennial of BR days which the SRA perpetuated: the demands for adequate funding combined with a difficulty in spending what was obtained within the budgetary period. Unsurprisingly, this attracted negative sniping, for example, the following complaint in 2001: 'it is a sad reflection on the SRA's incompetence that they were telling us that our meanness would mean the end of civilisation as we know it and then three weeks later they say they can't spend even the reduced amount they ended up with.'[63] But the on–off turn of the funding tap, which inhibited British Rail planning, had not been rectified in the post-privatization period. And the Treasury's faith in private sector solutions for the railway included more than a little wishful thinking, not least in relation to the sector's capacity to undertake risk and transform railway economics.[64]

The SRA's experience provided an important element in the Blair governments' railway learning curve. History customarily provides both similarities and dissimilarities. There were clear similarities between the SRA and the British Transport Commission of 1948–62, for example. Both presided somewhat uneasily over the whole, both did lots of useful diagnostic work without being able to drive policies home, and both failed to get a grip on costs. Finally both moved from being regarded by government as the answer to the railway problem to being seen as part of the problem.[65] Of course, the responsibilities of the two bodies were very different, and we must not push the analogy too far. If the SRA was necessary to the development of an 'intelligent' and 'informed' public sector client' for an industry where many of the players were private companies, then Labour's experiment may be judged a success.[66]

8.8 Looking ahead

There is of course much to do. Labour's record with railways, as with health and education, has been full of mixed fortunes and mixed messages, producing the perennial trade-offs between choice, competition, and public service for

[63] Wheatley–Ian Kemsley e-mail, 20 July 2001, Treasury redacted fileTRA4/2 Pt. 1.

[64] Cf. Treasury, paper on 'privatisation assessment', 4 Feb. 2004 (redacted).

[65] Gourvish, *British Railways 1948–73*, pp. 307–22; Loft, *Government, the Railways and the Modernization of Britain*, p. 53 ff.

[66] Cf. Winsor's recent remark that 'we have now got it right but we went through the fires of hell to get there': Tom Winsor, 'British Rail Franchising: An Experience in Choppy Seas', in ECMT, *Competitive Tendering of Rail Services* (Paris, 2007), p. 37.

all, between investment and budgetary constraints, between public interest and private profit, and between the fare-payer and the taxpayer, all inevitable in an industry which has received government support since the Second World War. According to the journalist Nick Cohen, Labour 'has managed to combine the insulation from competition that characterises the worst of the public sector with the greed, audit culture and unaccountability that characterises the worst of the private'.[67] This is uncompromising stuff, but we have certainly identified areas of competitive insulation and private sector unaccountability, and it is clear that the railway industry remains one of the public–private battlegrounds, along with health and education.[68]

There are many uncertainties ahead. What will happen to the railways' elaborate contractual arrangements if there is a recession? How will the new structure cope with a serious challenge? Bowker's anxieties about the position of Network Rail as 'both client and contractor' may have been overdone, but it remains to be seen whether the warnings he made about 'production-led planning, lack of customer focus and increased costs' will be avoided.[69] In the most recent franchising agreements, the TOCs have nailed their colours to the mast of rising demand, the payment of substantial premia to the government, and regular fares increases: but will these arrangements endure in a recession? The aspirations contained in the DfT's White Papers of 2004 and 2007 are welcome, as is the stimulus provided by the Eddington Transport Study of December 2006, which highlighted the relevance of improving the transport network's capacity and performance for Britain's productivity and competitiveness. Advocating a 'sophisticated', multi-modal approach to the problem, Rod Eddington asserted that there was a strong economic case for targeted new infrastructure.[70] The railways remain a 'minority mode' in the total transport market, but they have received a boost on environmental grounds following the increased concern about global warming.[71] Nevertheless, there remains a distinct possibility that the more ambitious plans for rail will fall by the wayside. The 2007 White Paper presents fairly modest aims, in comparison with the SRA's aspirations in its Strategic Plans of 2002 and 2003, or indeed, with Prescott's 10 Year Plan, and certainly when compared with some of the more radical railway plans of the past, for example, Peter Parker's electrification report of February 1981 or Bob Reid II's lesser known Future Rail report of July 1991.[72] Railway commentators in France and Spain are frequently puzzled why, for example, the Great Western Main Line

---

[67] *Observer*, 1 April 2007, p. 10.

[68] For a more optimistic view, see Julian Le Grand, *The Other Invisible Hand: Delivering Public Services through Choice and Competition* (Princeton and Oxford, 2007).

[69] Above, pp. 240–1; Bowker, in *Rail*, 23 November–23 December 2005, p. 32.

[70] Sir Rod Eddington, *The Eddington Transport Study. Main Report. Transport's Role in Sustaining the UK's Productivity and Competitiveness* (4 vols., December 2006), and see also the summary volume, *The Case for Action*.

[71] See Sir Nicholas Stern, *Stern Review on the Economics of Climate Change* (October 2006).

[72] Gourvish, *British Rail 1974–97*, pp. 154–5, 312–3. On the White Paper's limited ambitions see *Independent*, 25 July 2007, pp. 4, 28; *Private Eye*, 3–16 August 2007, p. 10.

from London to Bristol and Cardiff has not been electrified, and why the £16 billion Crossrail project appears only now (2007) to have been given a green light by Government, nearly two decades after it was enthusiastically endorsed by Cecil Parkinson (in 1990). Many of our planning documents begin with realistic appraisals of the possibilities in the short–medium term, then promise to make more substantial investments in the future. But, with the exception of the Channel Tunnel Rail Link, now renamed High Speed 1, there have been no substantial investments in new railway infrastructure. This certainly distinguishes Britain from developments in continental Europe, where high-speed services to replace short-haul flights have made more headway. What are the real prospects for High Speed 2, 3, and 4? As one leading railway journalist has put it, current policy smacks of 'Dodging the hard decisions and bodging temporary solutions'.[73] Or, as another has remarked, it involves setting 'up reviews and then reviews of reviews to avoid making decisions when responsibility and ownership were unclear'.[74]

The lessons of 50 years of public sector management of the railway were that the Government should confine itself to the issuance of clear instructions and then refrain from capricious intervention. Today's railway sees the Government closely involved again, and even accused of micromanagement, inviting comparisons with the 1950s–1970s, when successive governments intervened in investment, pricing, and industrial relations. There is something in the argument that we should return to the disciplines of the 1980s, where objectives were clearly set, and where Bob Reid (I) was told by his Secretary of State, Nicholas Ridley, to 'run an efficient railway, providing good value for money', with services to be 'reliable, attractive and punctual at acceptable fares and charges'. He was also instructed to reduce the cost to the taxpayer, with this reduction clearly specified.[75] The HLOS and SoFA are welcome moves towards clarity of intent from government, but how well will the system work?[76] When I wrote about the end of BRB I argued that 'the vexing and multifaceted relationship between the government and the railways remains, as does the mix of profit-maximising and welfare-maximising objectives, and much of the "risk" will continue to reside with the State if a given level of services is required by society'. The events of the last decade have done nothing to alter this view.[77]

---

[73] James Abbott, editorial, *Modern Railways*, February 2007, p. 3.
[74] Steve Richards, *Independent*, 19 July 2007, p. 29.
[75] Ridley–Reid, 24 October 1983, cit. in Gourvish, *British Rail 1974–97*, pp. 127–8.
[76] The publication of Network Rail's formal response to the Government's HLOS—*Strategic Business Plan CP4* (October 2007)—suggests that the new regime will not have a smooth ride.
[77] Gourvish, *British Rail 1974–97*, pp. 450–1.

Bibliography

Armstrong, Mark, Cowan, Simon, and Vickers, John, *Regulatory Reform: Economic Analysis and British Experience* (Cambridge, MA, 1998).

ATOC, *Ten-Year European Rail Growth Trends* (September 2007).

Bagwell, Philip, 'The Sad State of British Railways: The Rise and Fall of Railtrack, 1992–2002', *The Journal of Transport History*, 3rd ser. 25:2 (September 2004), 111–24.

Bartle, Ian, 'Britain's Railway Crisis—A Review of the Arguments in Comparative Perspective', *CRI Occasional Paper* 20 (2004).

—— 'The 2004 Rail Review—Towards a New Regulatory Framework', *CRI Occasional Paper* 24 (2005).

Bishop, Matthew, Kay, John, and Mayer, Colin (eds.), *The Regulatory Challenge* (Oxford, 1995).

Bolt, Chris, 'Developing the Framework of Rail Regulation', in C. Robinson (ed.), *Utility Regulation in Competitive Markets: Problems and Progress* (Cheltenham, 2007), pp. 169–85.

Bower, Tom, *Gordon Brown* (2005).

British Railways Board, *Report and Accounts 1996/7–2001/2*.

—— (Residuary), *Report and Accounts, 2001/2–4/5*.

Butler, David and Kavanagh, Dennis, *The British General Election of 1997* (Basingstoke, 1997).

—— *The British General Election of 2001* (Basingstoke, 2002).

Cabinet Office (CO), *Executive Non-Departmental Public Bodies 1998 Report*, December 1998, Cm. 4157.

—— *NDPB Policy: Developing a New Approach* (April 1990).

—— and Treasury, 'Non-Departmental Public Bodies: A Guide for Departments', 1992.

Central Rail Users Consultative Committee (CRUCC), *Report, 1997/8–1999/2000*.

—— *Rail Passenger Franchise Replacement. A Fare Price?* (March 2000).

Chandler, Alfred D. Jr., *The Visible Hand: The Managerial Revolution in American Business* (Cambridge, MA, 1977).

Committee of Public Accounts, *The Flotation of Railtrack*, 14 July 1999, HC256.

Committee on the Financial Aspects of Corporate Governance, *Report* (1992).

Crompton, Gerald, ' "Squeezing the Pulpless Orange": Labour and Capital on the Railways in the Interwar Years', *Business History*, 31:2 (1989), 66–83.

—— and Jupe, Robert, 'Delivering Better Transport? An Evaluation of the Ten-Year Plan for the Railway Industry', *Public Money and Management*, 22:3 (September 2002), 41–7.

Department of the Environment, Transport and the Regions (DETR), *Developing an Integrated Transport Policy* (August 1997).
—— *A New Deal for Transport: Better for Everyone*, July 1998, Cm. 3950.
—— *Transport 2010: The 10 Year Plan* (July 2000).
Department for Transport (DfT), *Delivering a Sustainable Railway* (July 2007), Cm. 7176.
—— *Departmental Minute in Respect of Certain Changes to the Contingent Liabilities Arising From Government Support for Network Rail Borrowing* (August 2005).
—— *Disclosure Documentation for Weir and Others v. the Secretary of State for Transport and Department for Transport* (2005).
—— *The Future of Rail* (July 2004), Cm. 6233.
—— *The Future of Transport: A Network for 2030* (July 2004), Cm. 6234.
—— *Transport Statistics Great Britain, 2005–7.*
—— *West Coast Main Line Progress Report* (May 2006).
Eddington, Sir Rod, *The Eddington Transport Study. Main Report. Transport's Role in Sustaining the UK's Productivity and Competitiveness* (December 2006).
European Community (EC), *State Aid N159/2005—United Kingdom EWSI Channel Tunnel Freight Support Funding* (22 June 2005), C(2005) 1816.
Foster, C. D., *Privatization, Public Ownership and the Regulation of Natural Monopoly* (Oxford, 1992).
Freeman, Roger and Shaw, Jon (eds.), *All Change: British Railway Privatisation* (Maidenhead, 2000).
Gershon, Sir Peter (for Treasury), *Releasing Resources to the Front Line. Independent Review of Public Sector Efficiency* (July 2004).
Glaister, Stephen, 'British Rail Privatisation—Competition Destroyed by Politics', *CRI Occasional Paper* 23 (2004).
Gourvish, T. R., *British Railways 1948–73: A Business History* (Cambridge, 1986).
Gourvish, Terry, 'The Regulation of Britain's Railways: Past, Present and Future', in L. Andersson-Skog and O. Krantz (eds.), *Institutions in the Transport and Communications Industries: State and Private Actors in the Making of Institutional Patterns, 1850–1990* (Canton, MA, 1999).
—— *British Rail 1974–97: From Integration to Privatisation* (Oxford, 2002).
—— *The Official History of Britain and the Channel Tunnel* (Abingdon, 2006).
Grayling, Tony, *Getting Back on Track: Reforming the Ownership and Regulation of Britain's Railways* (IPPR, 2001).
Hall, Rob, Heafey, Marianne, and King, David, 'Private Finance Initiative—A Good Deal for the Public Purse or a Drain on Future Generations?', *Policy and Politics*, 29:1 (2001), 95–108.
Hall, Stanley, *Hidden Dangers: Railway Safety in the Era of Privatisation* (Shepperton, 1999).
Hannah, Leslie, *Engineers, Managers and Politicians. The First Fifteen Years of Nationalised Electricity Supply in Britain* (1983).
Harding, David A., 'Railtrack: The Administration Order of October 2001 in the Context of Government's Regulation of Railways', University of Nottingham MPhil thesis, 2005.
Hare, Sir David, *The Permanent Way* (2003).
Haubrich, Dirk, 'UK Rail Privatisation Five Years Down the Line: An Evaluation of Nine Policy Objectives', *Policy & Politics*, 29:3 (2001), 317–36.

Bibliography

Haywood, R., 'Britain's National Railway Network: Fit for Purpose in the 21st Century?', *Journal of Transport Geography*, 15 (2007), 198–216.

Health and Safety Commission (HSC), *The Southall Rail Accident Inquiry Report. Professor John Uff QC FREng* (2000).

—— *The Ladbroke Grove Rail Inquiry. The Rt Hon Lord Cullen PC*, Parts 1 and 2 (2001).

Health and Safety Executive (HSE), *Railway Safety 1993/4 et seq.*

—— *Organisational Dynamics and Safety Culture in UK Train Operating Companies*, Research Report 421 (2006).

—— *Report of Joint Inquiry into Train Protection Systems* (chaired by Professor John Uff and Lord Cullen) (29 March 2001).

—— *The Management of Safety in Railtrack* (2000).

Helm, Dieter, 'A Critique of Rail Regulation', in C. Robinson (ed.), *Utility Regulation and Competition Policy* (Cheltenham, 2002).

House of Commons Select Committee (HC SC) on Environment, Transport and Regional Affairs, Report on *The Proposed Strategic Rail Authority and Railway Regulation*, March 1998, HC286.

—— Report on *Recent Events on the Railway*, December 2000, HC17.

HC SC on Public Accounts, Report on *The Office of the Rail Regulator: Ensuring That Railtrack Maintain and Renew the Railway Network*, August 2000, HC536.

HC SC on Transport, Local Government and the Regions, Report on *Passenger Rail Franchising and the Future of the Railway Infrastructure*, January 2002, HC239-I; MOE, March 2002, HC239-II.

HC Transport Committee, Report on *Government Response to the Committee's First Report 2001–02 on Passenger Rail Franchising and the Future of Railway Infrastructure*, MOE, May and November 2002, HC756-i.

—— Report on *The Future of the Railway*, April 2004, HC145-I.

—— Report on *How Fair Are the Fares? Train Fares and Ticketing*, May 2006, HC700-I.

—— Report on *Passenger Rail Franchising*, November 2006, HC1354.

Helm, Dieter, 'A Critique of Rail Regulation', in C. Robinson (ed.), *Utility Regulation and Competition Policy* (Cheltenham, 2002), pp. 19–41.

Hoyle, Susan, 'Organising OPRAF: Organisation and Culture in the Early Years of the Office of Passenger Rail Franchising 1993–96', September 1996.

Jack, Ian, *The Crash That Stopped Britain* (2001).

Jeffcott, Shelly, Pidgeon, Nick, Weyman, Andrew, and Walls, John, 'Risk, Trust and Safety Culture in U.K. Train Operating Companies', *Risk Analysis*, 26:5 (2006), 1105–21.

Jones, Ian, 'Railway Franchising: Is It Sufficient? On-Rail Competition in the Privatized Passenger Rail Industry', in C. Robinson (ed.), *Regulating Utilities: New Issues, New Solutions* (Cheltenham, 2001), pp. 120–41.

Jupe, Robert, 'Public (Interest) or Private (Gain)? The Curious Case of Network Rail's Status', *Journal of Law and Society*, 34:2 (June 2007), 244–65.

—— and Crompton, Gerald, ' "A Deficient Performance": The Regulation of the Train Operating Companies in Britain's Privatised Railway System', *Critical Perspectives on Accounting*, 17:8 (2006), 1035–65.

Kennedy, John and Smith, Andrew S. J., 'Assessing the Efficient Cost of Sustaining Britain's Rail Network: Perspectives Based on Zonal Comparisons', *Journal of Transport Economics and Policy*, 38:2 (2004), 157–90.

Kingdon, John W., *Agendas, Alternatives and Public Policies* (2nd edn., New York, 2003).

Labour Party, 'New Labour Because Britain Deserves Better', Manifesto, 1997.

Legal Director, December 2001.

Le Grand, Julian, *The Other Invisible Hand: Delivering Public Services Through Choice and Competition* (Princeton and Oxford, 2007).

Lieberman, Marvin B. and Montgomery, David B., 'First-Mover Advantages', *Strategic Management Journal*, 9 (1988), 41–58.

Lindsay, Justice, Approved Judgment in *Weir and Others*, 14 October 2005.

Loft, Charles, *Government, the Railways and the Modernization of Britain. Beeching's Last Trains* (Abingdon, 2006).

Millward, Robert, *Private and Public Enterprise in Europe. Energy, Telecommunications and Transport 1830–1990* (Cambridge, 2005).

Modern Railways, 1997 et seq.

Murray, Andrew, *Off the Rails. The Crisis on Britain's Railways* (2001).

Nash, Chris and Smith, Andrew, 'Passenger Rail Franchising—British Experience', in ECMT, *Competitive Tendering of Rail Services* (Paris, 2007), pp. 7–34.

National Audit Office (NAO), *The Flotation of Railtrack. Report by the Comptroller and Auditor General*, 16 December 1998, HC25.

—— *Action to Improve Passenger Rail Services*, August 2000, HC842.

—— *Ensuring That Railtrack Maintain and Renew the Railway Network*, April 2000, HC397.

—— *Network Rail—Making a Fresh Start*, May 2004, HC532.

—— *The South Eastern Passenger Rail Franchise*, December 2005, HC457.

—— *The Modernisation of the West Coast Main Line*, November 2006, HC22.

Network Rail, *Business Plan 2003*, 31 March 2003.

—— *Interim Review of Track Access Charges: Cost Submission*, September 2003.

—— *Track Record*, January 2003.

—— Ltd., *Report and Accounts*, 2003 et seq.

—— Infrastructure Ltd, *Report and Accounts*, 2003 et seq.

New Economics Foundation, *A Mutual Trend: How to Run Rail and Water in the Public Interest* (September 2002).

Norris, Pippa (ed.), *Britain Votes 2001* (Oxford, 2001).

Office for National Statistics (ONS), *The National Accounts Classification of Network Rail: Note by the Office for National Statistics* (November 2005).

Office of Passenger Rail Franchising (OPRAF), *Passenger Rail Industry Overview* (June 1996).

OPRAF, *Report, 1996/7–1998/9*.

Office of the Rail Regulator (ORR), *Developing Better Contracts—A Statement by the Rail Regulator* (December 2002).

—— *Interim Review of Track Access Charges: Draft Conclusions* (October 2003).

—— *Interim Review of Track Access Charges: Final Conclusions* (December 2003).

—— *Interim Review of Track Access Charges: Third Consultation Paper* (July 2003).

—— *Interim Review of Track Access Charges: West Coast Route Modernisation: A Consultation Document* (July 2003).

—— *Network Rail's Long Term Debt Issuance Programme. A Statement by the Office of Rail Regulation, and a Proposed Network Licence Modification* (October 2004).

Bibliography

Office of the Rail Regulator (ORR), *Notice of Proposed Modification to Railtrack's Network Licence: Asset Register* (March 2001).

——*Railtrack's Investment Programme: Implementation of New Licence Condition* (September 1997).

——*Report, 1997/8 et seq.*

——*The Periodic Review of Railtrack's Access Charges: Final Conclusions* (2 vols., October 2000).

——*The Proposed Acquisition of Railtrack plc by Network Rail Ltd: A Statement by the Rail Regulator and Proposed Licence Modifications* (June 2002).

——*The Regulator's Conclusions on the Proposed Tenth Supplemental Agreement to the Track Access Agreement Between Railtrack plc and West Coast Trains Ltd (The 'PUG2' Agreement)* (June 1998).

Passenger Focus, *National Passenger Survey Spring 2006 and 2007* (2006–7).

——*The Pennine Class 185 Experience: What do Passengers Think?* (May 2007).

Pollitt, Michael G. and Smith, Andrew S. J., 'The Restructuring and Privatisation of British Rail: Was It Really That Bad?', *Fiscal Studies*, 23:4 (2002).

Private Eye, 1997 *et seq.*

Public Money and Management, 26:5 (November 2006), debates, 267–70.

Rail, 1997 *et seq.*

Rail Passenger Council (Passenger Focus), *Report, 2000/1 et seq.*

Rail Politic, 2000–5.

Rail Professional, 2004.

Railnews, 2000 *et seq.*

Railtrack, *Network Management Statements, 1998–2000.*

——Group plc, *Report and Accounts, 1996/7–2000/1.*

——plc, *Report and Accounts, 1996/7–2000/1.*

R. v Railtrack plc, Balfour Beatty and Others, 6 September 2005.

Sawley, Kevin and Rieff, Richard (Transportation Technology Center Inc.), *Rail Failure Assessment for the Office of the Rail Regulator* (October 2000).

SBC Warburg, *Railtrack Share Offer Prospectus*, 1 May 1996.

Scott, Derek, *Off Whitehall* (2004).

Seldon, Anthony, *Blair* (New York, 2004).

Shadow Strategic Rail Authority (SSRA), *Report 1999/2000.*

Shaoul, Jean, '*Railpolitik:* The Financial Realities of Operating Britain's National Railways', *Public Money and Management*, 24:1 (January 2004), 27–36.

——'The Performance of the Privatised Train Operators', *Catalyst Working Paper*, September 2005.

Shaw, Jon, *Competition, Regulation and the Privatisation of British Rail* (Aldershot, 2000).

Smith, Andrew J. S., 'Are Britain's Railways Costing Too Much? Perspectives Based on TFP Comparisons with British Rail 1963–2002', *Journal of Transport Economics and Policy*, 40:1 (January 2006), 1–44.

Spectator, 13 August 2001.

Steer Davies Gleave, 'Revised Estimates of the Economic and Social Benefits of GB Rail Services' (September 2003).

Stern, Sir Nicholas, *Stern Review on the Economics of Climate Change* (October 2006).

Strategic Rail Authority (SRA), *Report 2000/1–2007.*

—— *Capacity Utilisation Policy: Statement of Principles* (December 2002).

—— *Community Rail Development Strategy* (November 2004).

—— *Company Neutral Revenue Support* (February 2004).

—— *Corporate Plan 2003–4* and *2004–5*.

—— *Cycling Policy* (November 2004).

—— *Everyone's Railway: The Wider Case for Rail* (September 2003).

—— *Fares Review Conclusions 2003* (June 2003).

—— *Franchising Policy Statement* (November 2002).

—— *Freight Strategy* (July 2001).

—— *Gauging Policy* (June 2005).

—— *Network Utilisation Strategy* (June 2003).

—— *Railways for All: The Accessibility Strategy for Great Britain's Railways* (March 2005).

—— *Rolling Stock Strategy* (December 2003).

—— *Sensitive Lorry Miles: Results of Analysis* (May 2003).

—— *SRA Freight Quarterly*, 1–8 (Winter 2001–Summer 2005).

—— *The SRA's Strategy: Specification of Network Outputs* (September 2003).

—— *The Strategic Plan* (January 2002).

—— *The Strategic Plan 2003: Platform for Progress* and *Route Descriptions* (January 2003).

—— *Train and Station Services for Disabled Passengers: A Code of Practice* (March 2005).

—— *The Value of Rail: Route Map to 2004* (September 2002).

—— *West Coast Main Line Strategy: Refreshing a Prime National Asset* (June 2003).

—— and ORR, *National Rail Trends Yearbook, 2003–4 et seq.*

Terry, Francis, 'The Nemesis of Privatization: Railway Policy in Retrospect', *Public Money and Management*, 21:1 (Jan.–Mar. 2001), 4–6.

Transport Act, 2000.

Treasury, *Implementing Privatisation: The UK Experience* (1997).

—— *Opportunity and Security for All: Investing in an Enterprising, Fairer Britain. New Public Spending Plans 2003–2006*, July 2002, Cm. 5570.

—— *Public Services for the Future: Modernisation, Reform, Accountability. Comprehensive Spending Review: Public Service Agreements, 1999–2002*, December 1998, Cm. 4181.

—— *2004 Spending Review. New Public Spending Plans 2005–2008. Stability, Security and Opportunity for All: Investing for Britain's Long-Term Future*, July 2004, Cm. 6237.

Walder, Jay H. and Armenta, Thomas L., 'Financing New Infrastructures: Public/Private Partnerships and Private Finance Initiatives', in R. E. Hanley (ed.), *Moving People, Goods, and Information in the 21st Century: The Cutting-Edge Infrastructures of Networked Cities* (New York, 2003).

Winsor, Tom, 'The Future of the Railways in the Light of the Government's Rail Review 2004', in C. Robinson (ed.), *Regulating Utilities and Promoting Competition: Lessons for the Future* (Cheltenham, 2006), pp. 7–24.

—— 'British Rail Franchising: An Experience in Choppy Seas', in ECMT, *Competitive Tendering of Rail Services* (Paris, 2007), pp. 35–42.

Wolmar, Christian, *The Great British Railway Disaster* (Shepperton, 1996).

—— *Broken Rails: How Privatisation Wrecked Britain's Railways* (2001).

Bibliography

Wolmar, Christian, *On the Wrong Line: How Ideology and Incompetence Wrecked Britain's Railways* (2005).

www.dft.gov.uk.

www.ft.com.

www.information.wales.gov.uk.

www.rail-reg.gov.uk.

www.red-star-research.org.uk.

www.rtgroup.co.uk.

www.sra.gov.uk.

Yvrande-Billon, Anne and Ménard, Claude, 'Institutional Constraints and Organizational Changes: The Case of the British Rail Reform', *Journal of Economic Behaviour & Organization*, 56 (2005), 675–99.

Index

Index

Index

Index

McCarthy, Tom 206
Macdonald, Lord (Gus) 21, 43, 58, 71, 75, 79
McGann, Martin 55 n. 104, 120
McGreal, Kevin 90
Macgregor, John 92 n. 43
McKie, Paul 39
McNaughton, Andrew 73
Macpherson, Nick 226
Major, John 267
Mark I slam door trains 20, 54, 209–12, 214
Marshall, Steven 72, 102, 107, 174–5
May, Theresa 222–3
Mayhew, Jeremy *38*, 39, 110, 184, 256
Mellit, Brian 2 n. 3
Mendip Rail 50, 167
Mercers (consultants) 173, 226
Merseyrail 8, 46
Merseyside franchise 136, 143
M40 Trains 44
Middleton, Richard 50, 70, 73
Midland Main Line 48, 94, 154
Milburn, Alan 43, 44
Minimodal 50, 168
Minimum Support for the Current Railway, *see* MSCR
Mitchell, Dr Mike 252, 284
Montague, Adrian 112, 113, 116, 178, 185, *186*, 187
Moore, Jo 107, 108
Morgan, Piers 56
Morton, Sir Alastair 52, 57, 58, 87, 91, 118
  and Byers 92–3, 95, 99, 100, 110–11
  and Government, post-Hatfield 82–4
  leaves office 92–7, 109
  and Railtrack 53, 72, 75 & n. 63, 93
  and SRA 32–4, 79, 270–3, 274
  and SSRA 39–41, 42
  and TOCs 43–4
  and WCML upgrade 49, 203–4
Mottram, Sir Richard 21, 50, 75, 109, 110, 181
  as accounting officer for SRA 58, 85
Mouchel Parkman 207
moving block signalling 49

MSCR (Minimum Support for the Current Railway) 142, 146, 197, 200, 247–9, 250
MTL Trust Holdings 8, 46
MTR Corporation, Hong Kong 282
Murray, Simon 77
Muttukamaru, Chris 226

NAO (National Audit Office) 62, 152 & n. 113, 181–2, 209
Nash, Chris 157
National Express 47, 48, 148, 153, 262
  franchises 136, 145, 146, 147
National Passenger Survey 30, 55
National Rail Co. concept 229, *233*, *234*, 235, 236, 239, 323
national rail summit (1999) 29–32
national rail summit (2000) 55
NedRail 143–5, 219
Nelson, John 45
NERA 173
net franchise payments *150*, *151*
Network Grant Company Ltd (NGCL) 98–9
Network Rail 130, 235, 237, 276–9
  Bowker's complaints about 241
  creation of 179–89
  debts/borrowing 184–5, *192*, 245–6
  network grants 149
  new role 243–4
  Project Elephant 197
  Project Violet 198
  and punctuality 189, 191, 193–4
  rail infrastructure costs, escalation in 189–90
  Railtrack plc, bid for 177, 183–4
  and SRA 188–9
  structure/governance of 185–8
Network Rail Infrastructure Ltd 185
Network Rail Ltd 185
New Deal for Transport: Better for Everyone 15, 19, 20, 21
New Economics Foundation 187
New Opportunities for the Railways 3
Newco/Newtrack (CLG) 171
Newton, Nick 39, 41, 88, 89, 251, 256
  and SRA 120, 122, 124, 253, 254

Index

Index